RITUAL AND WORLD CHANGE IN A BALINESE PRINCEDOM

Carolina Academic Press
Ritual Studies Monographs

Pamela J. Stewart
and
Andrew Strathern
Series Editors

Ritual and World Change in a Balinese Princedom

Lene Pedersen
Central Washington University

Carolina Academic Press
Durham, North Carolina

Library of Congress Cataloging-in-Publication Data

Pedersen, Lene.
  Ritual and world change in a Balinese princedom / by Lene Pedersen.
     p. cm. — (Ritual studies monograph series)
  Includes bibliographical references and index.
  ISBN 1-59460-022-8
  1. Political customs and rites—Indonesia—Bali. 2. Rites and ceremonies—Indonesia—Bali. 3. Daggers, Malay—Indonesia—Bali. 4. Bali (Indonesia)—Kings and rulers. 5. Bali (Indonesia)—Courts and courtiers. 6. Bali (Indonesia)—Politics and government. 7. Bali (Indonesia)—Social life and customs. I. Title. II. Series: Carolina Academic Press ritual studies monographs.

  GN635.I65P43 2005
  306.4'09598'6—dc22

2005007638

CAROLINA ACADEMIC PRESS
700 Kent Street
Durham, NC 27701
Telephone (919) 489-7486
Fax (919) 493-5668
www.cap-press.com

Printed in the United States of America

For Nicolas

CONTENTS

List of Figures   XI
Acknowledgments   XIII
Series Editors' Preface   XVII

Chapter One   Introduction   3

Prelude: An Heirloom Dagger and Two Ancestral Ceremonies   3
The Jero Gede Sidemen, Balinese Kingship and Princedoms   12
Precolonial Kingship Debated   16
   Colonial and Postcolonial Kingship   22
Maligya Ritual: Symbolism, Sociogenesis, and Social Action   25
   An Integrated Approach to Ritual   27
   Emotion and Reflection   28
   History and Current Events: Mediating Connections   30
   Ritual, Risk and Resistance   33
   Not Just a "Showcase" Response   38
The Perspective from the Sidemen Maligya   40
Positioning of the Anthropologist   43
Balinese Caste and its Terminology   46
Plan of the Book   48

PART ONE   THE PERFORMANCE OF A PRINCEDOM   53

Chapter Two   A Ritual Unfolds in Historical Context:
               The Sidemen Maligya   55

The Maligya Ritual and Deification of the Ancestors   57
   The Maligya Ritual and Worldly Status   60
The Sidemen Maligya from Inception
   to Creation of Ritual Spaces   65
The Progression of the Maligya Ritual:
   Ancestral Time and National Politics   73
Climax in Ritual, a Princedom, and the World   90

Photo Plates: The Sidemen Maligya   95

Chapter Three   Mobilizing the Structures of a Princedom   119

Mobilizing Invisible Relationships:
    Setting in Motion Mandalas of Prayer and Holy Water   120
The Raja-Bagawanta Priest Relationship   128
Mobilizing Connections to Followers   133
Historical Connections   138
Discussion of the Categories of Historical Follower Connections   143
Villages with Historical Connections   145
Conclusion   157

PART TWO   RECASTING BALINESE HIERARCHY   161

**Chapter Four   Land Matters: Obligations to the Source
                   and the Ancestors**   163

Princes, Pacatu, and People   165
Pacatu in the Sidemen Princedom   167
Dutch Colonial Policy to Dismantle Pacatu   170
Postindependence Land Reform   171
The Jero Gede Sidemen's Relations in this Period of the 1960s   177
The Role of Population Expansion and Bartering with the Lord   181
The Land Embodies a History: Ongoing Material Proof   185
Ancestral Oaths and the Risks of "Forgetting"   186

**Chapter Five   Populist Princes: The Hard Work of
                   Hierarchical Privilege**   193

Divine Kingship Revisited   193
Characteristics of the Ruler: Leadership of the Sidemen House   197
Working the People: Populism and Philanthropy   202
The Everyday Work of Maintaining Hierarchical Privilege   207
Roles of Other Men of the House   218
Women of the House   222
The Role of the Jero Gede Sidemen in
    Village Temples and Agriculture   225
Conclusion   229

Chapter Six   Circumscribed Royal Power   233

Divinely Imbued Powers of the People   234
Contemporary Examples of People Power:
    The Rise of Megawati and the Threat of Mob Actions   244
Historical Shifts and Conscious Strategy   252

Part Three   World Change   259

Chapter Seven   The Keris, The Princedom, and the Nation State   261

Megawati in Sidemen: Not Politics; A Ritual Coup   262
The Sidemen Heirloom: A Remarkable Claim   267
Assessing the Claim to Ownership of Keris Bangawan Canggu   271
Endorsement of President and Princes   273
Reestablished Connection between Sidemen and Klungkung   278
Counter-Government Strategy: For the Common Good   280
Ritual and World Change   289

Chapter Eight   Conclusion   295

Accommodations and Appropriated Discourses   296
A History Object and Displaced Agency   301
Ritual and Status Elevation through a Power Vacuum   304
Revival and Escalation versus Reformist Trends in Ritual   306
Indigenous Political Form in the Twenty-first Century   310
World Renewal   316

Glossary   319
References   325
Index   341

List of Figures

Chapter 1
  1. Map of Bali
  2. Map of Bali and the Court of Majapahit within Indonesia
  3. Genealogy: Core Family Members of the Jero Gede Sidemen

Chapter 2
  4. Payadnyan Layout—Sidemen, Bali 1998
  5. Map of The Sidemen Princedom with Global Connections

Chapter 3
  6. Map of Prayer Trip
  7. Map of Holy Water Trip
  8. Map of Villages in the Local Princedom of Sidemen

Chapter 7
  9. Genealogy: Rulers of Gelgel according to Klungkung Babad Dalem
  10. Genealogy: Rulers of Gelgel according to Sidemen Babad Dalem

Acknowledgments

The course toward this book has been long and rewarding, allowing me the privilege of accumulating many debts of gratitude along the way. The research for the book, with stays in Bali in 1995, 1997-8, 2000, and 2003, was assisted by two grants from the Social Science Research Council, an International Pre-Dissertation Fellowship and an International Dissertation Field Research Fellowship, with funds provided by the Andrew W. Mellon Foundation. I was supported also with a dissertation grant from the University of Southern California Graduate School, a travel grant from Australian National University, and by LIPI, the Indonesian Institute of Sciences. In 2003, an Australian National University post-doctoral fellowship in Southeast Asian Studies provided me with the time and milieu to bring the manuscript to near completion. The Faculty Research Fund of Central Washington University granted support that allowed me to carry out revisions to the book during the summer of 2004.

In Bali, I am ever grateful to Cokorda Raka, Jero Wisma, Cok Sawitri, and Cok Lilush. In Sidemen, I am deeply indebted to the entire family of the Jero Gede Sidemen who encouraged me to participate in and write about their "ritual work" and at all times, then and since, have welcomed my family and I. For their extraordinary hospitality and generosity of spirit, I sincerely thank all of them. A special thank you to Tjokorda Gede Dangin as head of the noble house, and to Cokorda Pemangku, Dewa Ayu Alit, Cokorda Mayun, Jero Mekele Wite, and Dayu Mas, and to all of the historical followers of the noble house and others who shared with me their time and their thoughts. I am very grateful also to Richard Berg, who contributed valuable insights, as well as to his wife Madé and to Hugues de Montalembert and Lin Utzon.

I Wayan Alit Artha Wiguna and Tatik Inggriati, Danker Schaareman, I Nengah Mangga, Memek Tusti, Ming, Ngurah, and their surrounding family, as well as Made Citra, Ibu Liz, and Nyoman Sudarsana, Jero Mekele Suratmi, Mirah, Gipper, I Dewa Gede Catra, and I Nyoman Darma Putra all provided assistance, both practically and intellectually. Anak Agung Ketut Agung, who is since deceased, generously discussed his knowledge and perspectives (see also Agung 1991). Thanks are due also to the members of the banjar and subak associations that I frequented, and to all of the other people who so kindly welcomed me and shared their experiences.

In Janet Hoskins and Steve Lansing I have had the most gifted and dedicated teachers, mentors, and friends one could hope for. Janet Hoskins, who chaired my dissertation committee and so much more, has given me unwavering intellectual guidance, friendship, and support. Steve Lansing first inspired and encouraged me to work on Bali and has continued to do so since. Both of them have read, critiqued, and helped shape several versions of the manuscript for this book. I extend heartfelt thanks also to Nancy Lutkehaus, Geoff Robinson, Gelya Frank, and Sylvia Bryant, each of whom made many and valuable comments to my dissertation, with suggestions that helped guide my development of the book. I am grateful as well to Kaja McGowan for her early enthusiasm for the approach that I was developing to the maligya ritual, which gave me the courage in the first place to pursue this topic in depth, and to Carol Greenhouse, whose supportive advise on an initial interpretation of the ritual events was influential in helping me clarify my emphasis. I am grateful as ever to Lydia Black, my first anthropology professor, and to Mette V. Madsen, my first colleague.

In Australia, I enjoyed a stimulating and collegial environment. I am grateful to Ben Kerkvliet and Philip Taylor of the Research School of Pacific and Asian Studies, who ran the fellowship program, to Francesca Merlan, chair of the Department of Archaeology and Anthropology that hosted me, and to Margo Lyon, Jennifer Badstuebner, and Stephan Lorenzen, who graciously helped my family and I in many ways. Thank you also to the members of the writing group I was invited to join, which in addition to Francesca Merlan and Philip Taylor, included Chris Barnard, Tamara Jacka, Andy Kipnis, Kathy Robinson, and Alan Rumsey. I am appreciative as well of Laura Bellows, Helen Creese, Robert Cribb, Patrick Guinness, Melinda Hinkley, Margaret Jolly, Mark Mosko, Thomas Reuter, and Jaap Timmer. Each of all of the above either read and critiqued individual chapters of the book or listened and responded to its ideas in other fora. All provided generous inspiration and friendship for which I am most grateful.

Pamela Stewart and Andrew Strathern have offered helpful comments on the entire manuscript and I have greatly appreciated their professionalism and encouragement. I would like also to acknowledge my colleagues at Central Washington University for their support and collegiality and the administrative assistance of Penelope Anderson. Kathleen Barlow has been a valued sounding board as the final stages toward publication drew nearer, as has my long-time friend Audrey Eyler.

The longest standing debt and appreciation are owed to my family. My parents, Ingeborg Christensen and Holger Pedersen, instilled in me confidence and curiosity, and started me out early toward a life of anthropology when they moved our family to Tanzania. Thank you also to Valentina Pedersen for her support since joining our family. I have the deepest gratitude for my husband Kent Swanson, who shared in portions of the fieldwork, made friends and provided perspectives that I would not have enjoyed without him, helped take pictures, generate figures, and provided insightful input to the manuscript. Above all, his love and support have seen me through the years of research and writing that have gone into this work. Finally it is to my son, Nicolas Crosby, a wonderful person to whom I am grateful for everything, that I dedicate this book.

With all of the assistance and guidance that I have received, responsibility for the shortcomings of this book lies with me alone. I present it to the Jero Gede Sidemen and their followers as my humble offering, with apologies for all of its imperfections.

Series Editors' Preface

— Pamela J. Stewart and Andrew Strathern

We are very pleased to include Lene Pedersen's *Ritual and World Change in a Balinese Princedom* in the Ritual Studies Monograph Series. The work presents a lively ethnographic account of a Balinese princedom, informed by the historical positionality of a range of actors, e.g. the Balinese themselves and the Dutch colonial personages. Through an exploration of ritual performativity the contemporary political context of the study arena is detailed in relation to the agency and motives of the persons involved. Also, important questions of how local constructions of identity and power relations are sustained in conjunction with the nation-state are examined.

Pedersen's work is written in an accessible and lively manner while addressing topics of interest to researchers in a range of disciplines (e.g. Anthropology, Religious and Ritual Studies, History, and Southeast Asian Studies). This study exemplifies the ways that people cope with structuring their political and ritual lives at the local level while balancing influences from the nation-state and other outside forces. This approach is of particular interest in terms of the study of globalization, transnational flows of ideas and practices, and glocalization (the local appropriation and transformation of globalizing influences and their incorporation into local sets of practices).

The processes by which people create a place with identities of a particular sort are numerous. In our research work in Scotland (see Strathern and Stewart 2001) and Ireland since the mid-1990s we have seen that a proliferation of local and regional festivals that celebrate traditions, crafts, food, dancing, recitations, and re-enactments have been taking place. These activities are all centered on specific places where particular local identities are being emphasized. The Ulster-Scots movement in Ireland that we have described in our writings is an excellent example of the local re-imagining of identities which are both transnational and local in character (see Stewart and Strathern 2003, 2004a, 2004b, 20004c; and Strathern and Stewart 2003, 2004a, 2005a, 2005b). History is a vital component of these studies.

The relationship between history and anthropology is clearly represented in Pedersen's work. Her research fits neatly with the growing trend in which anthropological work has become much more historical in character as researchers have become more aware that what they observe and discuss as customs or structures are in fact elements in history. Everything has a history, and everywhere customs, practices, and structures are in processes of change; sometimes these changes are large but sometimes they are small and gradual. A concern with the dynamics of these changes is fundamental in research work nowadays. Anthropologists at one time argued that one could not take history into account where it was not known. But ethnohistory, the history of a people as they themselves recount it, is always available, since universally people do have their own accounts of history. And when we are working in the midst of peoples with long written histories and traditions of scholarship it is obvious that history must be a large part of our knowledge basis. Every anthropologist, then, must be to some extent a historian. We have found this true in our fieldwork in Scotland and Ireland. But it is equally true for our work in the Highlands of Papua New Guinea, where much can be learned from studying the people's own ethnohistory and from taking to heart the fact that they do not make the distinction between history and myth in the same way that anthropologists have tended to do.

For example, in the Duna area of the Southern Highlands Province of Papua New Guinea, stories of the founding of groups among these people are important for understanding their patterns of social structure today, since they define the structure of authorized leadership in local groups (see Stewart and Strathern 2002; and Strathern and Stewart 2004b). But these same stories have gained a renewed importance in dealing with mining companies in the late nineteen nineties, since the people have used the geographical basis of their stories to make claims for compensation for environmental pollution on the companies. The Duna also mix pre-colonial ritual practices with introduced Christian ones to recreate and emphasize relationships with the local environment, its fertility, and the cosmos at large.

The use of ritual practices to balance the emplaced relations of persons within their cosmological worlds is aptly demonstrated by Pedersen's study. She encapsulates this by stating that "through these chapters [of the book], a combined theme of fertility and power has wound, like the snake of the *keris* [a long dagger], the cosmic object that embodies both male and female characteristics, the symbol that binds together the realm. The ritual of *maligya* [a post cremation ceremony to purify and deify deceased ancestors] is about the recycling of souls and regeneration at all levels of existence."

Pedersen's study tackles and provides new solutions to some fundamental problems in the analysis of early state forms in South-East Asia, particularly those arising from Clifford Geertz's work on the 'theater state' in Bali. While stressing the effective roles of ritual and ceremony, she also notes the importance of charisma and violence in maintaining the ruler's powers, and the significance attributed to magic in the spheres of both ritual and charisma: a significance well exemplified in the symbol of the *keris*, dagger and snake, male and female. The *keris* can be seen as a transform of the python symbol, which carries potent associations throughout Eastern Indonesia (Strathern and Stewart 2000).

Pedersen's work is also a valuable contribution to the theory of ritual generally. She reviews the ideas of Valerio Valeri on Huaulu rituals, and of Maurice Bloch on the Merina circumcision rituals, and concludes that Balinese rituals are complex and multi-centered, that ritual meanings change because of flexibilities in their symbolism, and that over time they become the object of contests over power and resistance to power: all conclusions that are paralleled by investigations we have made into Taiwanese ritual practices centered on Mazu, a powerful female figure who is thought to protect those who fish for a living from shipwrecks at sea (Stewart and Strathern 2005). Pedersen's argument thus not only illuminates her own ethnographic materials but also provides suggestive pointers in the direction of cross-cultural comparative studies in the wider Asia-Pacific context.

References

Stewart, Pamela J. and Andrew Strathern 2002. *Remaking the World. Myth, Mining, and Ritual change among the Duna of Papua New Guinea.* For the Smithsonian Series in Ethnographic Inquiry. Washington, D.C. and London: Smithsonian Institution Press.

Stewart, Pamela J. and Andrew Strathern. 2003. Crossing Borders, Dividing States: Donegal, Ireland. *The European Union Center and Center for West European Studies Newsletter*, University Center for International Studies, University of Pittsburgh, April, pp. 1,7.

Stewart, Pamela J. and Andrew Strathern 2004a. Ulster-Scots: Memory, History, and Imagination in the Construction of Irish Identity in the Border areas of Ireland. Paper presented at the Institute of Ethnology, Academia Sinica, Taipei, Taiwan for the "History, Memory, and Cultural Construction" Research Group on 5th Jan. 2004.

Stewart, Pamela J. and Andrew Strathern 2004b. The Ulster-Scotch Movement in Ireland: The Reassertion of a Minority Identity in the Context of the European Union. Paper presented at the 14th Biennial Conference of Europeanists, Council for European Studies, "Europe and the World: Integration, Interdependence, Exceptoinalsim?" in the panel "History, Memory, and the Path to European Integration", at the Palmer House Hilton, Chicago, March 11-13, 2004.

Stewart, Pamela J. and Andrew Strathern 2004c. Narratives of Violence and Perils of Peace-making in Irish Border Contexts: European Union Recognition of Diverse Identities. Paper presented at the Colloquium on Europe, Dept. of Anthropology, University of Pittsburgh, April 2, 2004.

Stewart, Pamela J. and Andrew Strathern 2005. Introduction to Asian Ritual Systems: Syncretisms and Ruptures. *Journal of Ritual Studies* 19.1: i–xiv.

Strathern, Andrew and Pamela J. Stewart 2000. *The Python's Back: Pathways of Comparison between Indonesia and Melanesia.* Westport, CT. and London: Bergin and Garvey.

Strathern, Andrew and Pamela J. Stewart 2001. *Minorities and Memories: Survivals and Extinctions in Scotland and Western Europe.* Durham, N.C.: Carolina Academic Press.

Strathern, Andrew and Pamela J. Stewart 2003. Epilogue. In Pamela J. Stewart and Andrew Strathern eds. *Landscape, Memory, and History: Anthropological Perspectives.* For the Anthropology, Culture, and Society Series. Sterling, Virginia and London: Pluto Press.

Strathern, Andrew and Pamela J. Stewart 2004a. Scotland and Ireland: Identity, Diaspora, and Dislocation. Paper presented to the Center for West European Studies / European Union Center, University of Pittsburgh, on March 30th, 2004.

Strathern, Andrew and Pamela J. Stewart 2004b. *Empowering the Past, Confronting the Future. The Duna People of Papua New Guinea.* For the Contemporary Anthropology of Religion Series. New York and London: Palgrave Macmillan.

Strathern, Andrew and Pamela J. Stewart 2005a. "The Ulster-Scots": A Cross-Border and Trans-national Concept. *Journal of Ritual Studies* 19.2: 1-24.

Strathern, Andrew and Pamela J. Stewart 2005b. Narratives of Violence and Perils of Peace-Making in North-South Cross-Border Contexts, Ireland. In Andrew Strathern, Pamela J. Stewart and Neil L. Whitehead eds. *Ter-*

ror and Violence: the Imagination and the Unimaginable. Sterling, Virginia and London: Pluto Press.

4 November 2004

RITUAL AND WORLD CHANGE IN A BALINESE PRINCEDOM

CHAPTER ONE

INTRODUCTION

Prelude: An Heirloom Dagger and Two Ancestral Ceremonies

In 1998, a minor noble house in the eastern Balinese village of Sidemen (figure 1) prepared and performed a *maligya*, an ancient and elaborate postcremation ceremony to deify the souls of its royal ancestors. Situated in its modern foil, this traditional ceremony turned out to be remarkable in many ways. The months of its preparation overlapped with events surrounding the fall of former Indonesian President Suharto, and in the course of this coinciding, thousands of people came from villages near and far to contribute to the royal endeavor. Here decades after the official dismantling of lord-follower ties and obligations, people nevertheless participated in a labor of royal implication. They helped create elaborate ritual sites and structures. They assembled a splendid array of offerings and prepared meals to sustain the crowds assisting. People defined their participation in the ritual as carrying out their ritual duty to the princes.[1] For the August climax of the ritual, moreover, the princes invited many dignitaries, among them the "monarchs" of the age of presidents: the new president of Indonesia, former Vice President B. J. Habibie, and his strongest political opponent, Megawati Sukarnoputri, head of the Democratic Struggle Party and a presidential candidate herself. While Habibie did not attend the event in the small highland valley, Megawati did. In the course of the ritual, this granddaughter of a Balinese and daughter of Sukarno, Indonesia's first president, who three years later was herself to become Indonesia's fifth president, interacted with the *keris*—the ancestral heirloom dagger of the noble house, the Jero Gede Sidemen.[2]

---

1. I use the term "princes" to refer to all members, male and female, of princely rank in the noble house, much as Balinese may refer to them as "raja people."

2. Megawati was in Bali also in connection with a meeting of her faction of the Indonesian Democratic Party, the Indonesian Democratic Party of Struggle.

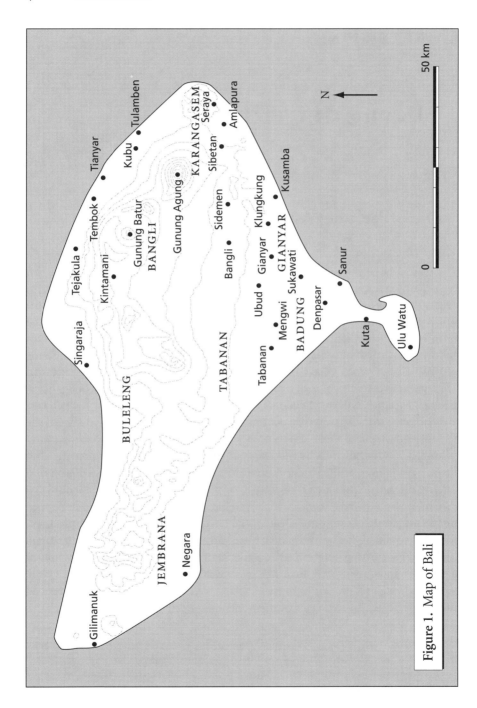

Figure 1. Map of Bali

August 18, I was part of an expectant crowd waiting in the outer courtyard and surrounding streets of the Jero Gede Sidemen for Megawati to arrive from the nearby bungalow where she was staying. A member of the noble house standing next to me mentioned that earlier in the day, women who had been preparing offerings in the inner family temple, near the place where the heirloom keris lies stored, had come running out with reports that a strong light was emanating from its shrine. The wait for Megawati, meanwhile, extended to hours, and word started circulating that she had been delayed by a force indicating to her that it was not yet the right time, that the ancestors were not yet ready for her arrival. By the time she did arrive at the noble house, it was dark. She came quietly and was led to the inner courtyard of the high caste family temple. After prayer, the head of the house and his younger brother, a non-Brahmana priest, carried out the family heirloom keris for Megawati to see. Megawati took the keris and looked at it closely. She is said to have pronounced that she had had a dream of precisely this keris.

Originating from Java, but found throughout much of the archipelago, keris are double-edged daggers considered to have mystical powers. Much symbolism is linked to their creation in fire, in a process that may be likened to the kind of volcanic eruption which according to some legends has produced deities, or to death rites of fire performed to release the souls of the deceased, as in the Balinese cremation and postcremation ancestral deification ceremonies:

> Through transmutation by fire, [the smiths] achieved objects of un-
> questioned power. The forge was a holy place.... possibly a place that
> relates to the spirits of the ancestors, whose traditional abode is the
> mountains, the fire being the medium through which the souls of the
> ancestors could be released or an ancestral spirit could enter the blade.
> [Solyom 1978:7; see also O'Connor 1985]

Although usually considered male objects, keris may be seen to embody double-gendered symbolism, for keris blades—sometimes undulating, sometimes not—are likened to serpents, sometimes in motion, sometimes at rest, which are considered female. Although contrary to standard Freudian theory, this symbolism is found across much of Southeast Asia and the Indonesian archipelago, where the snake is associated with the earth and with fertility.[3] "The snake," explains Janet Hoskins, "is a female ancestress, a powerful giver of fertility and rain, but also a sometimes dangerous and capricious woman"

---

3. Van Duuren explains that, "because of its physique, the serpent has strong connections with the earth; it writhes along on its belly, and lives in holes and caves, guarding— so say the Indian myths—the luxurious earthly treasures" (1998:35).

(1998:108; regarding the power of gender duality and complementarity, see also Hoskins 1998; Strathern and Stewart 1999). In the case of keris, there is sometimes a literal depiction or relief of a snake writhing along the undulations of the blade. David Van Duuren notes that there may be "inlaid gold foliage surrounding the serpent," representing its role in Hindu mythology as a guardian of treasures with fertility-giving power, for "when, at the beginning of the rainy season, the serpents emerge from their subterranean hide-outs, the floral world too springs to life" and "the serpent itself renews itself periodically by casting off its skin" (1998:36). The serpent, then, is the keris, itself forged from earthly iron, but also sometimes achieved from heavenly *pamor*, striations in the blade from forged layers of meteorite nickelous iron (Solyom 1978:64). Through its combined symbolism and powers of heaven and earth, the serpent/keris became associated with Southeast Asian kingship.[4] The snake links the ruler to the earth, connecting him with fertility and the basic life force, while the process of fire links him to divine and ancestral powers—all of which may be symbolized in the keris.

The stories of keris and their owners are told in terms of each other, and keris may be considered what Hoskins has termed "biographical objects," that is, "a reflection on the self deflected through the medium of the object" (1998:112). It is critical that a keris and its owner be well matched and often much care is put into selection or forging of keris to suit particular individuals. As Garrett Solyom notes in his study of Javanese keris, "[A man's] keris served not simply as a weapon but more as an affirmation of his identity as a mature man and a responsible member of his family and community"

---

4. Heine-Geldern reports dynastic legends which he believes existed in most parts of Southeast Asia, around the theme of kings descended from the daughter of the Indian Naga King. "The meaning is clear," says Heine-Geldern: "The Nagas, the serpent demons, are the original masters of the soil. By his descent from the daughter of the Naga king the monarch had a legitimate claim to the soil of his kingdom which, in theory at least, thereby became his personal property" (1956:9). Heine-Geldern also mentions a Chinese report "that in the 13th century the people of Cambodia believed that the king nightly cohabited with the serpent goddess of the soil who visited him in his palace in human form," by which he was thought "to renew the connection between himself and the soil of his kingdom" (1956:9). Both Southeast Asian inscriptions and Indian literature reveal the theme of conjugal union between kings and the earth (Wolters 1999:85; Coedes 1937-1966; Hara 1973). Strathern and Stewart cite an interesting example from Papua New Guinea where "the giving of bodily substances to the soil [female menstrual blood and a sacrificed fertile male, respectively] generated fertility and heralded a new earth" (1999:78). Regarding serpent symbolism, see also their book, *The Python's Back: Pathways of Comparison between Indonesia and Melanesia* (2000).

(1978:5), and, indeed, keris may be stand-ins for their owners. Royal keris, meanwhile, not only symbolize "the power of the ruler and the mandate to rule" (1978:5), but both oral and textual sources, in Bali as elsewhere, suggest that it may be the keris rather than the raja that was "the divinely 'true' (*wyakti*) source of power" (Schulte Nordholt 1996a:152). Conversely it is a prevailing theme that the loss of a powerful keris also entails the loss of kingship (cf. Worsley 1972; Wiener 1995). An heirloom keris, as it is passed on through generations and centuries, also can become what Hoskins calls a "history object," an object that embodies and generates collective history and identity (1993).[5]

It is more common for men than for women to wear keris and, although there are special female keris, usually smaller but also potentially powerful (Jessup 1990:64–65), women generally must not handle male keris until they are menopausal. Yet Megawati was permitted to handle the heirloom without any attempt at verifying whether she was gynocologically qualified. Although at fifty-one, she probably was beyond menses, the reason given for the permission focused on her being a powerful woman with an important cause for the benefit of the whole country, who could receive power from this keris.[6]

Later, as he reminisced about the events of the ritual, the head of the noble house, Tjokorda Gede Dangin[7], referring to ancient manuscripts and oral tales, began to tell about the conferral of one of Bali's historically most emi-

---

5. Even an heirloom keris, a history object such as the keris of the Jero Gede Sidemen, can be conceived of as biographical in that it brings together all of the notions of kingship, with which the Sidemen noble house identifies. It expresses their sense of selves, as rulers, the sense of the realm, and its place in the nation and the world. In the end, it may even be said to represent "Balineseness," which (as with all of the emphasis on Majapahit connections in establishing the identity of many Balinese) holds some irony, as the keris came from Java. Since the ruler of the house to which the keris belongs (in this case, Tjokorda Gede Dangin) is the foremost human embodiment of the characteristics for which the lineage and the keris stand, the heirloom keris may be especially associated with this individual person. The conflation of "biographical" and "history" objects is perhaps reflected linguistically in a first person pronoun conflation of historical ancestors with ego, typical in Bali.

6. This situation where a female politician receives power from what is usually considered a male gendered object compares interestingly to the cults in the New Guinea Highlands where male political careers were forwarded by female spirits in a situation where Strathern and Stewart emphasize gender complementarity (1999:77).

7. Cokorda or Tjokorda is a noble title. The most widely used spelling is "Cokorda," as used in this book except, in accordance with his wishes, for Tjokorda Gede Dangin, who has resumed used of the older spelling.

nent keris upon a Balinese raja, king or lord, whom he called his forefather.[8]
His story links not only heirloom keris and ancestral ritual but also the fourteenth-century Javanese Empire of Majapahit (1292–ca. 1520), royal legitimacy, and this very noble house, the Jero Gede Sidemen. Tjokorda Gede Dangin explained that what he referred to as "the first maligya ritual ever attended
by Balinese" took place under Emperor Hayam Wuruk at the court of Majapahit.[9] This was at a time when Bali, following its conquest by Majapahit in
1365, stood in a tributary relationship to the Javanese empire (see figure 2 for
the location of the court in relationship to Bali).[10] Tjokorda Gede Dangin continued:

> When the Balinese delegation was about to return home, the Emperor
> asked the ruler of Bali, Dalem Ketut Ngulesir, if they in Bali lacked any-
> thing. "What is missing," was the reply, "is something to purify the earth,
> the realm of Bali. That we do not yet have." "If that is so," responded the
> Emperor, "I will give to you this purificatory suda mala keris. With its
> suda mala qualities it cleanses both the micro and the macro cosmos."[11]

> On the way back to Bali, at the crossing of the river Canggu, the Keris
> Suda Mala fell in the water and sank to the bottom.[12] But through

---

8. The manuscripts are *Buku Kayu Manis* and *Babad Dalem*, in particular the *Babad
Dalem* in the noble house's possession, which chronicles their family's history. For the story
from the *Babad Dalem* of the priestly house of the larger royal center of Klungkung, see
the translation/paraphrase in Wiener 1995. See also Creese 1991 and 2000.
9. The ceremony to which Dangin refers is dated to 1362 (Pigeaud 1960, volume 4).
Others place Ketut Ngulesir's visit to Majapahit at the great council called by Hayam Wuruk
(cf Creese 1991:244).
10. Majapahit was an in-land rice-based kingdom that also engaged in trade, with connections to Burma, Siam, Cambodia, and Vietnam, as well as China.
11. Sudamala, lit. good-bad, or cleansed from stain and impurity, "connotes the destruction of bodily blemishes or deformities" (Hobart et al. 1996:146; Hooykaas 1973:160).
Suda Mala is the title of a Javanese myth from between the fourteenth and sixteenth centuries, of the youngest Pandawa brother, "a powerful healer who neutralizes evil" when he
restores Durga to her benevolent form of Uma, Siwa's consort (Hobart et al. 1996:180)
(after she has requested him as an offering in return for her help in fending off monsters
threatening the Pandawas). The story features on the eastern Javanese reliefs of Candi
Tigawangi. It may still be told in Balinese shadow puppet performances held for purificatory and exorcistic purposes, and there are also sudamala fabrics used for ceremonies, just
as there is the sudamala keris. These objects are held to possess purificatory and exorcistic
qualities.
12. The court of Majapahit was located in the foothills, west of the river Brantas.
Canggu was a river port on the Brantas (another important port was Bubat, with colonies

Figure 2. Map of Bali and the Court of Majapahit within Indonesia

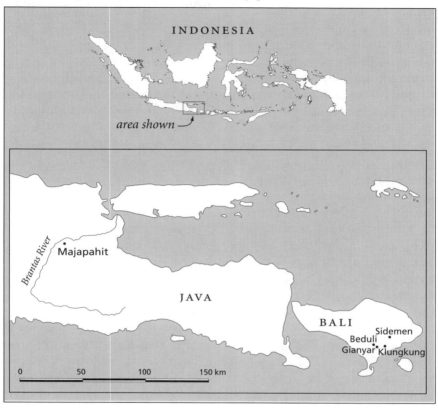

meditation it came back out, as the water opened for the keris to reemerge and reenter its covering. From then on, it acquired the additional name of Bangawan Canggu, River Canggu. Whenever there was a big ceremony in Bali, holy water prepared from the keris was used to purify the realm.

It is none other than the fourteenth-century Keris Bangawan Canggu given to the Balinese *raja* (king) by the Majapahit Emperor that is in the Jero Gede Sidemen's possession, explained Tjokorda Gede Dangin. As outlined in the noble house's dynastic chronicle, several generations after the death of the recipient of the keris, dissension grew among his descendants in the once-unified Bali-

---

of Indian and Chinese merchants). According to one myth, Gilimanuk, the less than two mile wide strait between Bali and Java was created by a keris.

nese kingdom of Gelgel. Foreseeing the fractioning of the court, one of the contending brothers, the forefather of the noble house, left with a share of the named regalia (*pajenengan*), including this keris. It was one of his sons who later was called to rule in Sidemen and whose heirs to this day continue the line of the Jero Gede Sidemen.

In concluding his story of the Majapahit keris passed on through his line of ancestry, Tjokorda Gede Dangin underscored the preeminence of Keris Bangawan Canggu over all others: "The Keris Bangawan is a gift directly from Majapahit, from the Emperor himself. It is the only such keris in Bali. The keris of Bali's foremost kingdom, Klungkung, was given not by the Emperor, but by his minister, Gajah Mada, and therefore ranks lower; it is not as powerful as Bangawan Canggu." The occasion for the original gift of the keris had been the death ceremony, usually referred to as a *shraddha*, held by the Majapahit Emperor for the soul of his grandmother, a ceremony which Tjokorda Gede Dangin compared to the maligya ritual, the Balinese high-caste postcremation ceremony for deceased ancestors. By 1998, it was more than half a millennium since the keris had been presented to the raja of Bali when it featured again in the maligya ritual performed by Tjokorda Gede Dangin and his family of the Jero Gede Sidemen.

In the interaction between Megawati and the heirloom, the presidential contender and the historical keris symbolizing the utmost in Balinese kingship entered into what was culturally understood to be mutual recognition of one another's powers. It should be said that Megawati's father, President Sukarno himself, had a keris collection and that he, too, made use of their association to kingship by letting word out that his holdings included powerful heirloom keris from some of Indonesia's most notable kingdoms (Vickers 1989:180). Adrian Vickers observes that Sukarno's survival of a number of assassination attempts confirmed the public's imagination of keris' magical powers, and that, conversely, his loss of power in 1965 was associated with their magical disappearance (1989:180). The meaning and power of keris thus are part of Megawati's own experience, as they are of other Indonesians.[13] Some

---

13. See also Tambiah for a description of ongoing royal ritual in Thailand involving the Emerald Buddha, which he discusses in connection with the role of sacra, such as Balinese keris to Southeast Asian kingship (1985:333). To give but one other recent example from Indonesia of continued mystical belief—In January of 2004, the nation's main newspaper, the Jakarta Post, reported that a group of treasure hunters was arrested in the well-known Bogor Botanical Gardens. One of them told the police that she had "received a *wangsit* (divine inspiration) from a Dutch woman in a dream…in which she was told to make a devotional visit to the graves of Dutch people the woman said were buried inside the garden compound." On that first visit she had uncovered a pouch containing two stones and a note in Dutch indicating that there was a treasure in the garden. The note was dated 1802. Again

readers might nonetheless be thinking that the above sounds rather too fantastical and could, as was the case with another visiting scholar upon hearing the stories surrounding the keris and Megawati, shrug it off as mere "make believe." Yet there is something much more interesting behind these events than just make-believe, a more complex story perhaps of "complicity and belief" (cf. Dirks 1994:498), and, along with that, a story of lived experience and desire for efficacy in the contemporary world.

Rather than with Megawati's use of the idiom of the keris, the focus of this book lies with the claims to status and power being forwarded by the Balinese noble house, the Jero Gede Sidemen, and with the power of the maligya ritual to provide a framework for events to be set in motion and the claims to be realized. The ritual becomes the lens through which we can observe the deliberate reconstitution of the princedom's old forms of hierarchy at a time of historical upheaval. Looking into what lies behind everything that came together in the context of the ritual from the perspectives of both princes and their followers, it is striking the extent to which they are replicating the classic dynamics and relationships of Balinese *negara*, a term often used to refer to precolonial kingdoms or princedoms.[14] As I continue to probe the meaning of the maligya ritual to the present-day participants, moreover, I return to issues long debated about the *negara*, concerning the roles of ritual and of land to kingship, and the source and character of royal power. In this realm, it becomes clear the princes must work hard outside the arena of ritual to maintain their hierarchical privilege and to make the ritual possible in the first place. Not only the head of the house but a whole family system orients itself toward maintaining their connections with the people so these will recognize their histori-

---

she was visited in her dreams, and it was to act on that message that she had returned with six others to locate gold and platinum, which, she argued, "would be enough to pay the state debts." The paper goes on to report that this is not an isolated incident, that in fact a couple of years ago, the Minister of Religious Affairs, on a tip from a "wise man" had "ordered an excavation on a site near a stone inscription from the 16th century Pajajaran Kingdom," also for a treasure that "if discovered, could repay the country's ballooning foreign debt." The article states, "The government is burdened with domestic and foreign debts of US$130 billion."

14. *Negara*, a Sanskrit term, glosses as town, court, or realm (Zoetmulder 1982). Following Geertz's book *Negara* (1980) it has become the common term by which to refer to the Balinese royal realms. Today it may also be used to refer to the nation-state (*Negeri* is also used to refer to a country). In Karangasem and Sidemen people are more likely to use *kerajaan*, but to avoid confusion, I will follow the practice of using negara or, for the small realm, the English term "princedom." The *negara dynamics*, however, apply to both small and larger scale realms.

cal ties and perform ritual duties to the princes. At the same time it also becomes evident that participants, through their princedom and joint ritual action, continue to position themselves in and try to influence a continuously changing world. The maligya ritual becomes a site where we can look at both scholarly and indigenous claims about kingship, ritual, and politics, and at the role of traditional sociopolitical forms in the era of globalization.

The Jero Gede Sidemen, Balinese Kingship and Princedoms

Sidemen sits along one of Bali's most spectacular mountain-to-ocean spurs, located at roughly 500 meters above sea level between the island's highest mountain and its highest ranking court, Klungkung, with which the Jero Gede Sidemen, although just a noble house on the subregional level, claims shared descent from Bali's foremost line of rajas, the *Ksatria Dalem* (royal Ksatria), descendants of the first Javanese Majapahit-appointed ruler of Bali, Sri Kresna Kapakisan. While Mount Agung rises majestically and immediately to the north, the view south spreads down slope to Klungkung and the coast in the distance. To the east, Sidemen is positioned at the foot of smaller mountains with side valleys that are home to remote villages and temples. On the other side of the mountains and farther east lies the kingdom of Karangasem, by which Sidemen was conquered in the mid-eighteenth century and under which it since has belonged politically. In the valley on Sidemen's western side flows the Unda River, lined by a small range of hilltops and a string of villages, bordered farther west by the deep ravine of the Telaga Waja River. The whole area is one of terraced irrigated rice fields and upland crops such as vanilla, cloves, and coffee. It is a valley fairly contained by topography. As do the rivers, so do road and most human traffic move along the north-south axis, whereas east-west communications are limited by borders of relief (cf. Geertz 1980). The Jero Gede Sidemen lies almost cradled in this upland mountain valley, with side-spurs revealing smaller irrigation systems and villages from which this smaller palace draws its followers.[15]

---

15. Such positioning conferred advantages also, including the protection from potential invaders provided by the very communications-inhibiting geography itself. Another significant advantage was strategic location in watershed irrigation systems, as farmers upstream can control and interfere with water flow to those further downstream (Geertz 1980:22-23; cf. Lansing 1991, 1993, in press; Schulte Nordholt 1996a).

The Jero Gede Sidemen exemplifies how even small-scale Balinese prince-doms developed as instances of what have come to be known as *negara*, South-east Asian cosmic kingdoms modeled on Hindu-Buddhist images of Indic king-ship. Such kingdoms arose throughout Southeast Asia from the fifth century on and had appeared in Bali, as in Java, by the ninth century.[16] By the first mil-lennium AD, the Balinese, descendants of Austronesian colonizers from around 4000–5000 years ago, already had developed irrigated agriculture and social stratification, and, being on the path of a spice-islands trade route to the north, Bali was exposed to many influences from beyond. In terms of the process that is referred to as Indianization, whereby aspects of Indian culture were incor-porated into Balinese culture, Bali at first most likely was interacting with Indic ideas through its own direct contact to Indian traders and holy men (Ardika and Bellwood 1991, 1997; Creese 2000:17; Lansing et al. 2004; Karafet et al. in press). It is generally held that the new ideas were spread through Indian epics, the notions of Hindu-Buddhist cosmology and divine kingship seized upon by emerging kings and disseminated to villages through performances by court-sponsored troupes (Lansing 1983b). In the process, the foreign notions were not merely adopted but transformed into local ones (Wolters, 1999:55–57, refers to this as "localization," comparable to what sociolinguists, regarding lan-guage, called "nativization," Kachru 1982, 1983; Smith 1987).

In Bali, what is usually emphasized in terms of kingship is the connection to the Indianized Javanese Empire of Majapahit, by which Bali was conquered in the fourteenth century and from which envoys and heirlooms were dis-patched to tame and govern the island. When Cokorda Sawitri, Tjokorda Gede Dangin's niece, who is emerging within her family as someone with a serious interest in its history, first told me about her family's heirloom, Keris Ban-gawan Canggu, she highlighted what it signifies to her by relating its powers of attraction and unification at a time when many areas of Bali still were re-sisting Majapahit rule. When the initial Majapahit-appointed ruler to Bali, Sri Kresna Kapakisan, first got here, explains Sawitri, Bali still fought: "So Gajah Mada [Bali's conqueror, the Majapahit chief minister] conferred the first keris weapon [upon a Balinese raja,] to convince the people of Bali that this is your raja." But, she continues, "It was still not possible to win them over. Not with the second keris either. It did not make Bali peaceful; it did not make Bali har-monious." The situation improved only when Ketut Ngulesir, who had suc-ceeded Kapakisan as ruler of Bali, received from the Emperor the keris to

---

16. The oldest known Balinese inscription dated 882 AD already indicates a Hindu-Ba-linese king (cf. Goris 1954).

which Jero Gede Sidemen now claims ownership. "When this keris was given," explains Sawitri, "only then did Bali become peaceful." Dalem Ketut Ngulesir, the holder of the keris, came to exemplify good kingship, and the Majapahit-modeled Balinese court of Gelgel, which existed from the fourteenth to the mid-seventeenth century, was to become the seat of Bali's "Golden Age."

No precise succession of Balinese rajas has been recorded. As the story usually is told in local chronicles, fourteenth-century Dalem Ketut Ngulesir was succeeded by sixteenth-century Watu Renggong, for Watu Renggong stands out as another successful raja whose reign became associated with the flourishing of Gelgel (see Creese 1991 regarding this "telescoping" of generations to highlight the most notorious rajas). A further marker in Balinese historiography is the Flight of Majapahit in the late fifteenth century, when, with Islamic rule prevailing on Java, nobles and priests, accompanied by sacred objects, artists, and scholars of the crumbling court, are said to have fled Java for Bali. Hence, from standing in a tributary relationship to Majapahit, Bali is considered to have become its refuge. The historicity of the mass exodus is in question, but not so the very prominent role that connection to this event continues to play in forming local identities and status claims (see e.g. Creese 2000). The next most significant event that was to shape kingship in Bali and that was to result also in the establishment of the Jero Gede Sidemen was the disintegration of another court, this one a couple of centuries later, the court of Gelgel.

Not even during the height of Gelgel, considered Bali's one most unified kingdom, did Balinese kingship consolidate into an authoritative imperial state,[17] and when Gelgel disintegrated, following a mid-seventeenth-century succession dispute and a coup that placed an unpopular contender on the throne, a multitude of smaller kingdoms were established that came to characterize Balinese kingship until colonization in the late nineteenth and early twentieth centuries.[18] In the new kingdoms, heirs of nobles and ministers from Gelgel set themselves up as sovereigns in their own domains and with their

---

17. Scholars have tended to agree that there is little evidence of political fragmentation during the centuries of Gelgel's rule: "On the contrary," says historian van der Kraan, "the royal edicts issued from the tenth to the fifteenth century as well as the European accounts of the sixteenth and early seventeenth centuries indicate that Bali was a unified realm" (1983:338), its influence extending to eastern Java, Lombok and western Sumbawa. Creese, however, points to the fact that considerable strife already characterized the court prior to its eventual disintegration (1997).

18. Note that there is not consensus concerning the chronology of the Gelgel period (see for example Hägerdal 1995a, 1995b, Creese 1995).

own claims to royal power based on descent from Majapahit. Here began the political processes of continuous state formation and dissolution for which Bali is so notorious and which increasingly included competition also at the symbolic level, through dynastic chronicling and ritual. The Gelgel dynasty, the line of Kapakisan rajas of the royal Ksatria Dalem kingroup, meanwhile, was re-established in Klungkung, just north of Gelgel (ca. 1687), by one of the formerly ousted heirs, who is said to have received safe haven in Sidemen and assistance in defeating the usurper at Gelgel. But though Klungkung did take on a special position in relation to the newly established kingdoms and generally was acknowledged to rank above them, it never was to subsume the others (however, see Wiener 1995 for an argument of Klungkung's power as hegemonic). Within the nine kingdoms that had taken shape by the end of the eighteenth century, moreover, were numerous even smaller principalities, such as the Sidemen Princedom, with lords and princes who became rajas in their local realms, laying claim to some of the highest levels of legitimacy, even as they continued to pay homage to and sort under rajas larger than themselves. At this level, too, there was competition for followers who would give allegiance to a lord or prince in return for rights to use and harvest lands. In the end, while a few Balinese villages resisted court culture, those known today as *Bali Aga* villages, most became connected to different courts to various degrees.

As Tjokorda Gede Dangin related when he told the story of Keris Ki Bangawan Canggu, his forefather had fled Gelgel in connection with the political dissension that was to lead to its breakup. It was one of this forefather's sons, I Déwa Anom Pemahyun Di Madé, who was summoned by the lord of Sidemen, I Gusti Ngurah Sidemen, to marry his daughter and take up reign in that realm. According to descendants both of the former lord and of the princes of the noble house, this happened because the lord at the time did not have a successor and specifically wanted to bring in someone with the legitimacy of the Ksatria Dalem line. In the Gelgel period, the lord of Sidemen had stood in a special relationship to Bali's ruler in regard to certain ritual responsibilities at Besakih (Bali's paramount Hindu temple, often referred to as its "mother temple," located to the northwest on the slope of Mount Agung) and was seated with him in the "pavilion for dignitaries" (see Stuart-Fox 2002:284–286). The honored position of the lord of Sidemen also is indicated by the location of the descent group's shrines within Besakih's central temple. And to this day the ritual procession of the gods of Besakih stops in Sidemen on its journey to the coast for the *malasti* ceremony of ritual bathing, spending the night at the old *Pura Puseh* (village origin temple) at the village of Desa

Tabola within Sidemen.[19] Although never one of the main regional kingdoms or palaces in the Balinese landscape, the realm of Sidemen thrived at its height in the late seventeenth and early eighteenth centuries, extending across much of western Karangasem. The descendants both of the former lord and of the princes talk of this as a time when their forefathers collaborated and Sidemen "had not yet declined," a time when things went well—until they were conquered by the expansionist kingdom of Karangasem and, locally, the Arya Dauh descent group gained in favor.

The conquest left the Jero Gede Sidemen situated between the palaces of Karangasem and Klungkung, between the rajas by whom the area was conquered and those with whom they share genealogical descent, but in relation to whom the princes of Sidemen have fallen in worldly rank. Yet, as we shall see, they never entirely relinquished their claims to higher status.

Precolonial Kingship Debated

Since the earliest Western writings on Bali, including the works of Dutch colonial administrators and scholars, observers have struggled to understand the unconsolidated nature of Balinese kingship. Although there was some commentary of Balinese being "ruled in a tyrannical manner" (Dubois 1837) and this kind of image was exploited to justify the colonial project as an "ethical" project of liberating Balinese from their rulers, Balinese kingship typically has been considered lacking in effective government (cf. Korn 1932). Also, given that Bali was an island with a well-developed system of irrigated terrace agriculture, many have applied the ideas of Marx and Wittvogel regarding states and their relation to modes of production and irrigation systems, in particular, to what they saw in Bali. "Oriental despotism" and "hydraulic bureaucracy"—these, it generally has been agreed, Bali was not.[20] Along with absence of strong government, there was not the expected explicit connection between central rajas and ownership of land

---

19. Stuart-Fox surmises, "Political authority of the region where the temple lay and where its supporting rice fields were located, important as this undoubtedly was, would not, I think, be alone sufficient to give Anglurah Sidemen such a exceptional and exalted status at Besakih equal to Ida Dalem's. It seems that his special status derives in part from his legendary ancestor Ida Manik Angkeran's position as priestly caretaker of Besakih" (2002:286; see 2002:286–88 for this story).

20. Hauser-Schaublin argues that Marx's views have been conflated with those of Wittvogel and, given his distinction between common property and private property in the Asiatic versus feudal modes of production, respectively, encourages a reconsideration of Marx in relation to Bali (2003:153).

or control of irrigation. In Bali, moreover, as we see in the case of Sidemen, lords or princes at very small scales within the larger *negara* (kingdoms) were able to create local versions of negara with themselves at the center, while villagers, even when they were connected to courts, did not have to depend entirely on these, but also could hold land freehold, and continued to work within semiautonomous local irrigation associations.[21] The negara of Bali, in short, were not integrated, territory- based, bureaucratically governed "states," but at each level, from the largest to the smallest realms, consisted of shifting alliances of lords, lesser lords, and various groupings of people. Elsewhere in Southeast Asia, classical negara, such as Pagan (in present day Myanmar), Angkor (Cambodia), Ayudhya (Thailand), and the Javanese Majapahit, did develop larger scales of kingship with relatively more elaborate centralization than ever occurred in Bali,[22] yet scholarship continues to reveal how much kingship in Bali had in common with early Southeast Asian negara in terms of what we may call negara dynamics: Negara, involving local adaptations of Hindu-Buddhist ideas of Divine Kingship and of parallelism between the universe and the human world, were characterized by multi-centricity and fluidity,[23] by nonterritorially defined amorphous relationships of variable personal linkages, in which people rather than land were the resource base of royal power. From their human resources, kings and lords extracted taxes and labor, as followers were mobilized for what Stanley Tambiah has referred to as "spasmodic and short-lived public activities," such as palace construction, wars, and rituals (1985:322) (for developments of thought on this issue, see especially Tambiah 1985; Wolters 1999; see also Van Leur 1955; Coedés 1968; Adas 1981; Gesick 1983; Reid 1983, 1988; Hall 1984).

---

21. While many scholars accept that there was some degree of autonomy, which is not to claim full autonomy, Hauser-Schaublin recently (2003) has published an adamant critique against such notion, arguing instead that royal control extended to the farmer (she prefers "peasant") and irrigation association levels as well; but see also the responses to her article in its adjacent comment section.

22. The state in Bali did not develop dimensions of kingship as powerful even as those of neighboring Java although the two islands shared centuries of cultural exchange. See Creese (2000) for a succinct historical overview of Bali's outside relations.

23. Generally the Indian notion of *mandala*, designs of satellites arranged around a center, is used to image the multi-centric Southeast Asian polity as consisting of not just one royal center but multiple centers. To better reflect the polyvalence and integration of ideology and practice of the indigenous concept, Stanley Tambiah proposes the related term "galactic polity," which codes "in a composite way cosmological, topographical, and politico-economic features" of traditional Southeast Asian kingdoms (1985). Compare this to Geertz's argument that the ideal cultural models were contradicted by the actual social structures. (See also Christie 1986; Kulke 1986. Hagesteijn 1989 reviews studies on mandalas.)

Recognizing the inadequacy of Western models for understanding the Balinese and indeed the Southeast Asian "state," in the face of the question of unconsolidated kingship and the pervasive concern for competing claims between
a multitude of rajas and princes, Clifford Geertz, in his classic *Negara* (1980),
developed a model of the nineteenth-century Balinese polity as something different from existing Western notions of state and governance. He suggested that
here was a "theatre state" that rather than emphasize government, land relations, and control over irrigation, emphasized the symbolism of royal rituals.[24]
According to Geertz, rajas, in "complementary pairing" with their court priests
who were "parts of the king's regalia" and "effectors of his sanctity" (1980:125),
claimed godlike status with universal powers, but remained passive rajas, emanating rather than exercising power (1980:130). Their middlemen (*perbekel*)
did the governing and tax collecting, while the rajas, instead of focusing their
attention "toward government," did so "toward spectacle, ceremony, public
dramatization of the ruling obsessions of Balinese culture: social inequality and
status pride" (1980:13). In this view, Balinese rajas were theatrical performers
who were statesmen through ritual (1980:133) and the negara "a complex hierarchy of ritually expressed and managed status" (2003:171).[25]

---

24. Geertz specifically sought to get away from the term "state," as he says in a later commentary, to "free us from the tyranny of those terms," in this case a term which "names a
modern (i.e. post-sixteenth century) European concept which indeed applies poorly to
Bali" (2003, 1980:121ff, nn. p. 235). Wolters, too, rejects the term "state" "as implying
monolithic and uniform characteristics which the Southeast Asian political systems never
exhibited" (1999:49).

25. Conversely, there have been studies of spheres of life in Bali that remained relatively
independent of royal control. Recently, for example, Steve Lansing's work has focused on
how rice terrace and watershed management happened without overarching planning by
royal engineers and administrators, through a nested hierarchy of farmer organizations and
their associated water temples (1991, in press). Having outlined the socio-religious system
of management, Lansing next sought to understand the ecological workings of the system
and, further, through computer modeling to explore hypothetical scenarios for how such
a complex system of watershed coordination might have come about. His work at the very
least shows that such a system conceivably could have emerged over time from the ground
level up as farmers grew rice and coordinated with one another, that it conceivable could
have come about without state-level masterminding (Lansing and Kremer 1993; Lansing
in press). From yet a different perspective of an area not under royal dominance, Thomas
Reuter (2002a) has presented an argument about the Bali Aga of the highlands of central
Bali, the largest grouping of villages which remained unconnected to Balinese court culture, that they through old networks of ritual alliance have maintained a common identity
as founders of early Balinese civilization and as ongoing custodians of important mountain sanctuaries. In other words, Lansing and Reuter both emphasize that there are realms,
the irrigation associations and Bali Aga networks, respectively, whose regular operation or

Geertz brilliantly fulfilled his purpose of presenting an alternative to received ways of thinking about states, power, and politics. *Negara* received enthusiastic recommendation in the *New York Review of Books* by political scientist, Quentin Skinner, who found both its challenge to Western political theory and propositions regarding the role of public ceremony to states to be of broad relevance (1981:35–37, though see also Walters 1980). At the same time, Geertz's book sparked immediate critical response from Bali and Southeast Asia experts, among whom it continues to inspire debate (Schulte Nordholt 1981, 1993; Howe 1991; Hauser-Schäublin 2003; see also Tambiah 1985 for a sustained engagement with Geertz's model in larger Southeast Asian perspective, proposing modifications which Tambiah suggests might apply to Bali also). Most widely seized upon have been some of his catchier claims, especially his proposition that state rituals were "not means to political ends: they were the ends themselves, they were what the state was for," an argument that Geertz concludes with flair by pronouncing that "power served pomp, not pomp power" (1980:13). Although Geertz's whole point was that ritual in the theatre state was inherently political, he also created an untenable dichotomy between the expressive, which happened through royal ritual at the center, and the instrumental, which happened through others than rajas at local levels. Although Geertz saw ritual as integral to the competition between centers, critics have felt that his notion of exemplary center as a model for the relationship between centers and peripheries did not sufficiently emphasize the tensions and instability in these relationships. As exemplary center, the court was seen to be at once reflective of supernatural order and paradigmatic of social order. Supposedly "by the mere act of providing a model, a paragon, a faultless image of civilized existence, the court shapes the world around it into at least a rough approximation of its own excellence" (1980:13). As Tambiah points out, it is difficult to reconcile "that status/power be seen as a gradation of excellence scattering down from a divine unity as a radiation of it dispersing from a divine core to the king, his kinsmen, his lords, their henchmen, and finally the peasantry—with the cutthroat politics of these same segments" (1985:320). It is also difficult to reconcile, as we shall see from the perspective of the princedom, with the need to be both expressive and instrumental and with the level of claims that could be made by lords as rajas of their own smaller realms, where they were at once a center and on the periphery.

Critics of Geertz's model of the Southeast Asian polity as a theatre state, as well as the work of Oliver Wolters (1982, 1999), although he does not specifi-

---

existence have been relatively independent of interference from kings. Interestingly, in both of these cases, too, ritual plays a central role.

cally address Geertz, converge on issues concerning the character of governance. Tambiah questions Geertz's depiction of "kings at the summits of exemplary centers as still points, immobilized into passivity and reflective trances…reduced to 'mere signs among signs'" (1985:321), arguing instead that "divinity, or claims to universal and righteous kingship, was based on personal charisma as much as or even more than on institutionalized rules pertaining to the tenure of office" (1985:325). Wolters (1999), too, emphasizes personal qualities and the necessity for sustained activity on behalf of a ruler. His arguments that "strong government was, literally, on the move all the time" and that "the sinews of government were the ruler's personal energy and surveillance" (1999:31) stand in marked contrast to Geertz's image of the ruler's "divine immobility."

The ruler's active role also involved establishing auspicious connection to otherworldly realms, connection that he must display to legitimate his rule and to be in a position to mediate relations, not just between people, but also between people and the supernatural (Wolters 1999; Onghokham 1978), or, as it is termed in Bali, between *sekala* and *niskala*, the visible and invisible worlds. Significantly, the ruler did not just passively possess and exude this connection; he had to activate and exercise it through various pursuits, including rituals. Tambiah draws attention as well to the significance of sacred objects. He emphasizes that they take on a special role in the unstable environment of "dynastic shallowness" and perennial rebellion that characterized Southeast Asian states: "Recognized as permanent embodiments of virtue and power, [sacred objects] helped provide their temporary possessors with legitimation, and at the same time embodied a genealogy of kingship by serving as the common thread" (1985:329). In her study of the Balinese realm of Klungkung, Margaret Wiener demonstrates the centrality precisely of supernatural powers and of keris to constituting and exercising Balinese kingship (1995; see also Schulte Nordholt 1996a).

As did Geertz, Wiener challenges common assumptions pertaining to governance, in this case addressing the colonial conception of ineffective and largely powerless rajas by arguing, in particular, that the rajas of Klungkung had a more powerful role than is usually acknowledged. Wiener draws on the understandings of power that we gain from the works of Gramsci (e.g. 1971) and Foucault (e.g. 1979, 1980), "that power at its most effective operates less through obedience to the wishes of others than through internalized constraint and the domination of social convention" (1995:72). Comparable to Geertz's argument, she makes the case that "there are other ways to recognize power than through the terms deployed by nineteenth-century administrators" (1995:151), who expected to see evidence of contractual relations and surveillance or of "command and obedience" (1995: 13, 151). Where Geertz emphasized ritual over governance, Wiener emphasizes the role of those who set the terms for discourses of claims to authority and also the role of actions, including actions in war, which demonstrated supernatural powers. While Wiener's ultimate claim—that, based on this broader understanding of power, Klungkung in fact did have a hegemonic place in Bali—is not necessarily accepted by scholars working from the perspectives of other realms (see Schulte Nordholt 1996b; Reuter 2001), she has presented a persuasive case that, to Balinese, Balinese rulers were powerful.

We may view the role of ritual, of powerful objects, and of the supernatural in establishing status and attracting followers as forms of displacing agency away from individual actors. These are important expressions in Southeast Asian understandings of power, and, as such—again applying Gramscian and Foucauldian notions—they are effective. Or, in the language of French sociologist, Pierre Bourdieu, they are forms of "symbolic power," transformed forms of power, which have "magical" effect, allowing those in power to demonstrate and exercise it indirectly (1991:165, 170). Recognizing culturally significant signs of power surrounding rulers and associated with rituals plays into participants' decisions to align themselves with such rulers. To this day, participants perform their duties as subjects, even without external controls, because they thereby fulfill obligations to their ancestors, fulfill their *dharma* (duty to behave according to religious and social codes), and obtain religious merit. But they also gain the feeling of being a part of something significant and establish or maintain connection to the benefits that may derive from association with people of power. On one level, displaced agency is about seeing things through a mystical framework (cf. Bloch 1986:168) or, as Geertz phrased it, about making inequality enchanted. Yet, as we shall see through the example from Sidemen and as supported by broader understandings of Southeast Asian precolonial polities, the various forms of the rulers' displaced agency are effective also because they do not stand alone, but are linked to and backed by direct forms of agency. Indeed, in Balinese conception this must be so; the invisible and visible worlds interrelate. A ruler can surround himself with signs of power, but if he does not realize power in practical terms in the manifest world—if he does not win the war or draw together great numbers of followers to produce momentous rituals in which all can participate—he will have revealed himself to not be powerful after all.

Most, if not all, of the above insights into Southeast Asian and Balinese kingship come together in Henk Schulte Nordholt's rich historical ethnography of the Kingdom of Mengwi from its rise in 1650 to its demise in 1940 (1996a). Schulte Nordholt combines Geertz's "theatre state" model (1980) with

Michael Adas' notion of the "contest state" (1981)[26] to examine an aspect of Southeast Asian *negara* also emphasized by Tambiah (1985) and Wolters (1999): the role of conflict and war in the kingdom (Schulte Nordholt 1996a:7–8). Large public rituals were important indeed, says Schulte Nordholt, but not so much, as Geertz had emphasized, for the expression of status differences of the ruling nobility; instead, "much more was at stake: life itself" (1996a:8). Schulte Nordholt finds that "What has generally been neglected, or at least underestimated, in studies of pre-colonial political systems is the imminence of death and, hence, the necessity to seek protection" from dangers of both visible and invisible worlds; it was this protection that rulers, in part through their rituals, brought to their followers (1996a:11; see also Reid 1983). In Schulte Nordholt's account from Mengwi, we see the role of rituals, keris, and supernatural powers at work, while he also shows that "the more successful of the Balinese rulers were anything but anonymous objects of ritual; they were clearly leaders who survived by person- ally commanding the respect of those around them" (1996a:7). What Schulte Nordholt presents, in short, of a specific Balinese *negara* through the centuries, is anything but the "flat, static, immobile, and 'ritualized' view of the Balinese ruler and his court" that Geertz's rendition of the theatre state has been criticized for being (Tambiah 1985:336). However, it ends in the mid-twentieth century and, as a historical account, cannot present the kind of texture that comes from observing lived experience, spells of power and Balinese politics in the making.

Colonial and Postcolonial Kingship

Following two centuries of trading and eventual colonizing in the Indies, the Dutch completed conquest of Bali between the mid-nineteenth and early twen- tieth centuries. It took them three substantial military expeditions to conquer even one Balinese kingdom, the northern kingdom of Buleleng, by 1848. Sub- sequently, they signed treaties with other rulers, but eventually set about to fully conquer these too. Some rulers aligned themselves with the colonial powers while the raja of Tabanan killed himself in captivity and the kingdoms of Badung and Klungkung, in 1906 and 1908, respectively, fought to the finish with *puputan*, "finishings," mass sacrifices or massacres at the hands of the Dutch.[27] It was

---

26. The "contest state" was a state in which "there was a constant struggle between the ruler and nobility, between factions of the elite at various levels and between supravillage elite groups and village notables and peasants for the control of labor and the agricultural production which formed the basis of these predominantly agrarian states" (Adas 1981:218).

roughly the kingdoms that had formed by the beginning of the nineteenth century that the colonial government took over and upon the otherwise ever-changing configurations of which they imposed an unprecedented rigid administrative structure and bureaucratic rule. The existing negara (approximately) were designated as subdivisions, within each of which a Dutch administrator was stationed. Each subdivision was divided into districts under authority of a Balinese *punggawa* (lord), a term taken from northern Bali, from then on to be applied throughout the island (Schulte Nordholt 1996a:219). For this post the Dutch generally selected the most influential local lord, who usually was able to retain or even expand his domain, while other lords were left with no or lesser appointments and with loss of domains (Schulte Nordholt 1996a:219).

During their rule, the Dutch effected a number of administrative reforms. For example, in 1921, the colonial administration changed the status of lords (*punggawa*) to district heads (*perbekel*), while also in 1929 appointing an indigenous administrator for each negara. In 1938, meanwhile, in the late years of the colonial state, the Dutch administrators, as part of broader colonial policy to restore self-rule (and forestall the spread of nationalism), reinstated eight of the negara administrators as "self-rulers" or rajas for each of the kingdoms, often referred to as "puppet-princes" of the colonial government. The raja of Karangasem was all along one of the foremost collaborators with the Dutch (the opposing faction of the palace having been exiled), and as a result enjoyed relatively boosted powers under colonial rule. In the periphery of the realm, meanwhile, through the decades of Dutch administration, the Jero Gede Sidemen, which already had seen its stature diminished, experienced further demotion when commonly lesser lords lost power, as their realms were incorporated into the larger regional districts of the colonial administration. According to Tjokorda Gede Dangin, his grandfather, who was a *punggawa* (lord), "was still very strong," as was his grandmother, also still a punggawa. It was his father and uncle who became *perbekel* (district heads). (Later, when the Indonesian nation-state inherited and further transformed the colonial bureaucratic structures [see Warren 1993a], they became mere village heads, *kepala desa*.) At the same time, the princes also enjoyed benefits of association with the palace of Karangasem, a number of them living for extended periods with the raja in Amlapura, who took as his eleventh wife a woman from the Jero Gede Sidemen.

---

27. Wiener takes issue with the common interpretation of puputan as some form of mass suicide or suicide ritual, pointing out that "for Balinese, puputan and suicide could not be less alike," for where the latter is about giving up and is "the worst kind of 'bad death,'" the former is about persevering and is an honorable death (1995:325). Wiener herself glosses puputan as "a fight to the finish" (1995:375).

The view of Western scholars generally has been that Dutch colonization brought to an end the social form that characterized the Balinese kingdoms, the negara. Although Geertz analyzed the nineteenth-century Balinese polity as relatively continuous with that of the fourteenth century,[28] he concluded that for all the diverse social forms that exist in contemporary Indonesia, the negara, "perhaps the most important" of them all, and of which there were possibly thousands in Indonesia, "vanished with…completeness" and is "gone" (1980:3–4). With the 1908 puputan ("finishing") in Klungkung, said Geertz, "it was quite literally the death of the old order. It expired as it had lived: absorbed in a pageant" (1980:13). Given the brutal nature of Bali's conquest and the impact of colonial rule and, later, the formation and transformations of the nation-state of Indonesia, it is generally recognized that the traditional polity, the negara, is no more. Furthermore, while Wiener advances understanding of the import to Balinese kingship of supernatural powers and magical objects, in particular heirloom keris, she finds that this, too, ended with colonial conquest (1995:329).

It is all the more surprising then, at the cusp of the twenty-first century, in the smaller realm in eastern Bali, to find the extent to which the contemporary princes of the Jero Gede Sidemen continue to present themselves through many of the same means as did the rajas of precolonial Balinese negara— through the performance of powerful heirlooms and dynastic genealogy, through relationships to court priests and activation of auspicious connection to the supernatural world, and through the ability to attract followers and witnesses from near and far, drawing in an ever expanding world—all of which may be brought to bear in royal ritual. Through conquest by the easternmost kingdom of Karangasem and Dutch colonization, through the nationalist fight for independence and the establishment of the Indonesian nation-state, the noble house has continued to exist in some form. Through modernization, touristification, and globalization, which one might expect to have flattened the landscape of local politico-religious diversity, the Jero Gede Sidemen, with its ritual underpinnings, in 1998 again asserted its prominence.

Today the history and dynastic chronicle of the noble house combine with its heirloom keris to effect a claim that the princes of the Jero Gede Sidemen in fact are some of the most direct heirs to kingship in Bali, for they trace themselves to a line senior to that of the rajas of Klungkung. The story related by Tjokorda Gede Dangin, the story of the conferral of the keris by the Emperor of Majapahit upon the Raja of Bali, exists not only in oral version but

---

28. There were a number of reasons for this: Bali remained marginal to the international trade economy, to Islamization, and to intense Dutch domination (Geertz 1980:9).

also in the *Babad Dalem* of the Ksatria Dalem, the written genealogy of Bali's most recognized line of rajas, the Kapakisan rajas of Gelgel and Klungkung from which the princes of Sidemen, too, trace descent. It is the Jero Gede Sidemen's own additional genealogy linking them to the *Babad Dalem* that goes on to separate the keris from the rest of the Kapakisan lineage as it chronicles the fate of the more immediate forefather of the princes in connection with the seventeenth-century dispersal of the dynasty in Gelgel. The genealogy tells of how his son and the heirloom ended up in Sidemen, so in 1998—more than half a millennium after the keris Ki Bangawan Canggu had been presented to the raja of Bali at the Majapahit ritual, and three centuries after its claimed dispersal from the central seat at Gelgel—it could feature again in a maligya ritual, this one performed by the princes of Sidemen as part of their bid to reconsolidate their legitimacy, past and present.

Maligya Ritual: Symbolism, Sociogenesis, and Social Action

To Geertz, the role of royal ritual—what the lords, "from the most petty to the most high...each at his own level," were "trying to effect with their great ceremonial tableaux" (1980:18)—primarily was a "public dramatization" of "social inequality and status pride" (1980:13). He viewed it as a symbolic construction or, as he put it, an "almost aesthetic correction of the present to conform to a vision of what the past had once been," to create "a more truly exemplary center, an authentic negara, which...could at least seek to imitate [Gelgel] and so recreate, to some degree, the radiant image of civilization that the classic state had embodied and the postclassic degeneration had obscured" (1980:18). Although, with this, the purpose of ritual also was competitively to indicate status differences between nobility, it remained to Geertz symbolic and cosmological rather than functional or pragmatic, "to project local status onto a universal plane, not to define the boundaries of popular solidarity" (2003:171). A few scholars, on the other hand, have emphasized the sociogenic role of ritual in bringing people together to constitute a realm.[29] Steve Lansing (1983a) and Brigitta Hauser-Schäublin (1997) present intriguing examples of social networks surrounding temples and of the role of contemporary temple cer-

---

29. For the role of ritual for agricultural associations at different scales of organization see Lansing (1991), and for maintaining ancient realms of the mountain Balinese, separate from Bali's kingdoms, see Reuter (2002a). Most other studies of Balinese ritual have focused on symbolic exegesis or have been largely descriptive (e.g. Goris [1939] 1960; Belo

emonies in temporarily resurrecting former kingdoms. Based on such examples, Hauser-Schäublin describes the precolonial negara as "a state in which the raja, in cooperation with the priests, organized mass mobilization by means of rituals and brought people—as pilgrims—to the 'center,' the state temples" (2003:170). Graeme MacRae, meanwhile, shows that in the former kingdom of Ubud—as in Sidemen—it is not just a vanished realm that is reenacted in ritual but a realm that continues to recraft for itself a role in contemporary life (1997, 1999). In the case of the Sidemen Maligya, as in Geertz's study which emphasized royal cremations, it is a local life-cycle rite, the noble house's postcremation ceremony, that is at the center of a rite of kingship constituting the local realm and that also connects to the role the local lord plays outside of ritual. As a rite of ancestral deification and world renewal and as a vehicle for a social system that provides local identity and agency in a complex nation and globalizing world, the maligya ritual is multifaceted, operating on both symbolic and functional levels.

The maligya ritual is, first, the final Balinese rite-of-passage, a symbolic second cremation to complete the purification and deification of the deceased that they may attain ancestorhood, and, as such, a maligya ritual is sated with symbolism. With an array of priests presiding, carefully constructed representations of the souls of the deceased are elaborately hosted and processed in enclosures and structures replicating the Balinese universe. Comparable to hierarchies of social order built into the architecture and shrines of temples, in the maligya ritual hierarchical symbolism is embedded in temporary structures assembled in a ritual enclosure specifically for the ceremony. In addition, because a maligya ritual not only is the last in the sequence of Balinese life and death rites but also is the highest level at which these rites can be performed, living descendants strive to honor their ancestors with as large of a ceremony as they can—bringing in priests and performers, summoning all the followers possible to prepare as extensive an assortment of offerings as possible, and inviting as many people for the climaxing days of the ceremony as they can find ways to feed. The royal maligya ritual, moreover, may be viewed as a rite of kingship in the sense that, in the past, a raja would perform these final rites for his forefathers before assuming his full set of titles. Overall, the ritual makes a splendid show of taking the ancestral souls through their final rites, serves status by providing an arena through which those holding the work can demonstrate what they can bring about, both materially and symbolically, mobilizes the forces that (re)generate the assemblage that is termed the princedom, and is finally perceived as a rite of world renewal and, as

---

1953; Hooykaas 1977; and, with a chapter focusing on maligya rituals, Mershon 1971; Brinkgreve 1981). Also, Connor (1979) and Warren (1993a, 1993b) have analyzed cremations as rites of rebellion (see chapter 6).

we shall see, even of resistance. Other than presenting initial symbolic exegesis in setting up for the ritual and outlining the progression of ritual events (chapter 2), this book, rather than focus on the details of offerings and symbolism, analyses mainly the ritual's course as a part of wider social, cultural, and political process.

An Integrated Approach to Ritual

In what I learned from the Sidemen Maligya, I recognize the enduring value of Victor Turner's analyses of rituals and his insightful consideration of both their symbolic and functional facets—how every ritual has a purpose with its symbolic action but also has varied collective and functional purposes or effects.[30] Analysts often set up such diverse aspects as different even conflicting perspectives on rituals, as symbolic versus functionalist approaches, sometimes also distinguishing them as actors' versus observers' points of view. Alternatively, we may analyze a ritual event in terms of the points of view of differently positioned actors. Yet in the Sidemen Maligya it became clear that a ritual may operate on several levels for any given actor or group of actors as well: Actors may at once be aware of and dedicated to the symbolic action on behalf of ancestral souls (even if the non-ritual-specialist actor deciphers only a fraction of the ritual's surfeit of symbolism) and at the same time have awareness of how, through their participation in the symbolic action of the ritual, they are also situating themselves in the differential positions of the princedom's hierarchy, and at the same time be thoughtful of engaging in joint action not just for the ancestors or princes, but also vis-à-vis the wider world. For participants in the maligya ritual made connections between what was happening in the context of the ritual and what was happening in the world around them. All of the ritual activity, participants agree, amounts to action in the world—it makes a difference to the ancestral souls, to the participants' own lives, but also can help bring change, even global change, under control. In all of this, as with the keris, there are prevalent themes of fertility and regeneration, themes which surface throughout in the relationships between the noble house and their followers:[31] The noble house bestows rituals, blessings, land, and leadership, and the followers, too, contribute to the fertile enterprise; they cultivate the uncultivated,

---

30. Turner realized regarding a West African fertility ritual, for example, that it is at once about the ritual symbolism activated on behalf of a couple's fertility problem and about the social gathering to smooth out the rift threatening the relationships between the matri- and patri-kin thought to be behind the problem (1969).

give wives, and provide labor and loyalty. Together they make possible the rituals and the realm.

The maligya ritual is "holy work," and it is about fulfilling obligations to ancestors and to those with whom you have historical relationships. This is sincerely what people are doing. But that does not mean that they do not also recognize social effects and purposes of giving temporary form to the local hierarchy in relation to the rest of the world. The ritual generates a sense of being a part of something both cosmologically and sociologically. Ritual and war were the two main areas in which followers in precolonial times owed service to their lords. "Today," people say, "we come together for ritual," but they remind each other and the observer, that they could also do so again for war. We do not need to confuse cause and effect, presuming that observed effects explain why the ritual came about in the first place, to recognize that over time people might nonetheless become aware of multiple sociological effects of ritual.

Emotion and Reflection

In taking an integrated approach to ritual, Turner's analysis was important as well for its emphasis on the emotional aspect of rituals, what Emile Durkheim (1893) termed communitas or "effervescence," the idea that people feel connected to the social group through the enjoyment and even elation of joint ritual activity. Working toward a similar point, Valerio Valeri describes a boys' initiation ritual among the Huaulu of Seram island, a small, relatively egalitarian, mixed hunter-gatherer and horticultural society that in many ways is very different from the Balinese princedom, yet that also remains dispersed during most of the year and is brought together mainly in this ritual, which "constitutes the most encompassing, and at the same time most intense state of social relations" (Valeri 2001:299). Valeri continues about the Huaulu ritual:

> It realizes as pure action the image of global society which is normally realized only statically in material objects, such as the heirlooms and the community house. The feast animates these symbols...and in the process appropriates them: signification, moving from the usually empty house to the dancing crowd that fills it, ceases to be purely transcendent...to return into the pulsating, self-signifying body of the community. In terms of belief, this sudden collapse of the cleavage between signifier and signified is interpreted as the coming to-

---

31. Adas, too, highlighted the importance in regard to Southeast Asian "contest states" of the power of rulers to provide protection and fertility (1981).

gether of the living and of the dead, who are supposed to participate invisibly in the feast and to add their strength to that of their descendants. Sensuously, the provisional—and always precarious—coincidence of signifier and signified is experienced in the body, as pleasure. It is precisely this element of pleasure...which gives [the ritual] much of its power to create sociability." [2001:299–300]

This is an interesting case for comparison, for despite the similarities—the role of ritual in bringing together an otherwise dispersed group of people, the significance of heirlooms, the union of the living and the dead—the emotional experience of communitas with contemporaries or, as Valeri puts it, the element of pleasure, is not what best explains what happened in the Sidemen Maligya, where it was at once a hierarchy and a unified group that were reinforced. Whereas among the Huaulu the group comes together to dance in a community space—a night dance with "orgiastic implications"—Balinese group ritual is almost bewilderingly multi-centered: other than in moments of joint prayer, there are so many things going on simultaneously at any given time that attentions, rather than toward a focused shared activity, inevitably are diversely directed. In the maligya ritual the most emotional connectedness was expressed as happening with the ancestors at the climax of the ritual. The connection between contemporaries had emotional component in the joint activities within specific work groups and, as people milled together, there was emotional experience of being a part of something larger. At the same time, much of this recognition was characterized also by reflection, reflection upon who could come together, through their link in a hierarchical system to the noble house, for the purpose of joint endeavor at this particular historical moment.[32] For while it is true that there is considerable symbolism in ritual to which participants usually do not pay much attention, and there is faith or "ideology interred in habit" (Bourdieu 1977:188), there may also be reflection surrounding ritual action, and thoughtful participation on the basis of conscious positioning in temporal predicaments. At the Sidemen Maligya, engrossed though people were in the "holy work" and connection to ancestors, they also made sense of the power of the ritual to draw in an unexpectedly large number of people and to attract the participation of Megawati in relation to circumstances external to the ritual.

---

32. This is thus a little different from what Hauser-Schäublin describes regarding precolonial royal rituals at regional temples: "There localities emerged in which people experienced a sense of community and of belonging to a principality by participating in the same rituals. There they were able to witness not only the basis of the king's divine power but also how the many different and competing segments of the state—the contest state—were temporarily, integrated into a single overarching hierarchy" (2003:170).

History and Current Events: Mediating Connections

Rather than look at how history or events might have affected one genre of ritual over time (cf. Bloch 1986), this book takes an approach inspired by the Sidemen Maligya, by how events or the broader context in which the ritual happened affected this particular performance and proved crucial to participants' actions and understandings, as the ritual became a means for individual and collective positioning in particular historical and political circumstances. Indeed ritual can be, and in Bali for centuries has been (cf. Schulte Nordholt 1996a), one means for such positioning. Peoples throughout the world, as Pamela Stewart and Andrew Strathern have put it in an earlier introduction to this series and also show in much of their own work, "try to come to grips with dramatic changes and bring them into a realm that they can understand and feel they can partly control" (2002c:x).

Maurice Bloch, who considers ritual as it relates to state power as part of its ideological apparatus, traces a genre of ritual, the Merina circumcision ritual, over the course of two centuries to examine how events have changed (or not changed) it (1986).[33] In his interpretation Bloch makes much of how static the symbolic, as opposed to the functionalist, aspects of ritual are, to the point

---

33. Bloch has tracked one genre of ritual, the Merina circumcision ritual, over almost two centuries, 1800-1970, to see how a particular genre of ritual has changed over time. Bloch is also interested in the link between the ritual and the broader political context, but his purpose is to "look at what happens to rituals in the course of history" and see how the ritual has changed in the context of changing political situation (1986:46). In the Merina case, Bloch finds that the ritual has ranged from being a private to a royal/state ritual and back to private. Balinese rituals, too, have undergone changes of intensifying and decreasing in scale over the past centuries, depending on times and resources available to people—and on political situation. There were times during the colonial era when kings did not have the resources to produce the grand state rituals, a situation that, following independence, caused people to urge the nation-state to sponsor them, as they are seen to be essential to the well being of the island and the world. Overall, rather than private rituals being taken up as state rituals, there appears in Bali to have been a proliferation of ritual, whereby royal rituals are being adopted also by non-royal kin groups and thus are being performed more and more. Urs Ramseyer noted, for example, that it was only during Watu Renggong's reign—in other words, ca. sixteenth century—that lower castes started holding cremation ceremonies at all (1977:59). Up until then it was the privilege of princes and lesser nobility, but it began to be practiced by ever-increasing strata of the population. In the twentieth century, including in connection with the maligya, lower castes were beginning to also hold grander postcremation ceremonies (regarding inflation in performance and expenditure on rituals, see also Howe 2001:99). There continues to be, if anything, an increase in ritual in Bali, and in the tourist hubs of Bali there are now entrepreneurs who organize bus-loads of paying tourists to attend some rituals.

even of viewing rituals' symbolic aspects as therefore not being "adaptable." Yet it is precisely the polyvalency of symbolism that makes it adaptable without the symbols themselves necessarily having to change over time, even as they may play a far from static role in rituals.[34] Bloch's history also reveals some cases that compare intriguingly to Balinese royal ritual, such as the example of a Queen who used the Merina circumcision ritual to boost her own position and legitimize her heir (1986:127–132): "This particular ritual had all the appearance of a stage-managed performance for short-term political ends," says Bloch, begging the question of intentionality (1986:161). Bloch cites evidence, which, although not conclusive, does indicate that Merina rulers were aware of the political effects of their rituals (1986:161–162). To Bloch, however, most participants remain "mystified" as to the social effects of the ritual.[35] In the Sidemen Maligya, by contrast, with the benefit of being able to consider contemporary participation, we can access a more complex awareness, not only of the princes but also of the people concerning their participation in a status confirming ritual.

As we delve deeper into the event of the 1998 maligya ritual and into an examination of the historical relationships reenacted in the ritual, looking at the explanations that people give of their participation as well as at what they say about the role of the noble house within the princedom, both a long-range his-

---

34. The same goes for language, for example, without us being perplexed as to why the symbols do not change as much as do the uses and contexts to which they are put. See also chapter 2 for an argument that the kinds of symbolic variations and changes that Bloch finds to be negligible in fact can be considerable. Goody, meanwhile, in an earlier volume of the Ritual Studies Monograph Series, presents a fascinating example and argument of the importance of variation in recitations: "these are not simply verbal variants around a permanent core but include radical changes of philosophical attitude, for example as between creationist and evolutionary perspectives on the origin of the world" (2002:xiv). See also Keane's study of ritual speech on Sumba, Eastern Indonesia: "Although ritual speech strives to have the effect of pure repetition of ancestral words, it would not work if it were no more than that. Even in the most restricted of forms, certain prayers, ritual speech is not merely a fixed or liturgical text, for it must speak in the name of particular identities and have context-specific effects" (1997:120).

35. Bloch suggests that "the ritual of circumcision, when used as a royal ritual, is the very opposite of what the theory of ideology would lead us to expect: that it was a mystification carried out by superiors on inferiors. Rather it was a case of collusion between inferiors and superiors, with the inferiors accepting the implications of their own submission because their submission as Merina implied their ultimate domination and conquest of others;" but he concludes that "for nearly everyone…this promise of conquest was equally illusory…" (1986:193). In the case of Sidemen we shall see that there are a range of more tangible results from submission to the hierarchy.

torical perspective and the immediate historical moment prove significant. Explanations why people performed ritual duties to the princes, when solicited from both people and princes, bring out the structural categories and relationships significant to the princedom, such as slaves and various kinds of subjects. Linked to these "historical relationships," another reason given involves recognition of centuries-old gifts of land and ancestral decrees that continue to obligate people to ritual labor and thanksgiving over time. The ability to activate these ancestral ties to draw followers to the ritual performance, meanwhile, has much to do with the ongoing basis the princes build for themselves with the people, a governance related reason whereby the princes, in the present, work hard to earn the privilege of having followers. This includes the prince who assumes the leadership position. Although genealogy is important in Bali, he too has to earn his position (and genealogies, after all, can be manipulated or interpreted to back up achievement). Not only does the prince in a sense have to create himself through his actions, he has to do so in a context wherein his followers and, increasingly, extra-local state actors wield considerable powers to circumscribe his local royal power. The long-term history and ancient connections are taken into reflective and sometimes creative consideration in relation to this, and also in relation to current events. Contemporary circumstances play into the working of historical memory and may combine to cause people to rally around their princes at particular historical moments. For in addition to conceiving of the ritual effort as acting upon the world, in their assessment of how and why the ritual came together as it did, participants pointed to the particular historical context in which it was happening.

In the case of the Sidemen Maligya, the situation surrounding the resignation of President Suharto and a perceived need for local positioning in relation to forces outside of the princedom proved important to how people made sense of the way the ritual came together. The local ritual and national politics do not play out in separate domains of experience, in other words; in fact, the larger historical context turns out to be central to how participants engage with and think about the ancestral ritual. At the outset it was by chance that the Sidemen Maligya coincided with the national economic and political developments that led to the resignation of President Suharto and brought to an end his New Order regime of more than thirty years. Less coincidental was that the ritual events, stretching over several months, became intertwined with these developments, and that at this time of historical upheaval great numbers of people who identified themselves as subjects of the noble house presented to serve at its ancestral ritual. That the ritual should draw as well a prominent candidate from the land of the former Majapahit, Megawati Sukarnoputri, who engaged in mystical interaction with the noble house's heirloom, all contributes to a Balinese process of causation whereby, as Vickers has argued, "things do not just 'happen'" (1990:173). In Bali things "happen according to a convergence of divine and demonic influences that we would call 'fate'" (Vickers 1990:173), or a convergence of the visible and invisible worlds (cf. Wiener 1995). Similarly we might also say that things happen in convergences of time frames and of events (cf. Balinese calendrical notions; see Lansing 1995 for an introduction). In the case of the Sidemen Maligya, there was a convergence, then, of ancestral ritual and national political events. Focused as participants of the maligya ritual were on processing souls and doing their part as subjects or princes, they were also mediating a connection between the ritual and the wider world, and ongoing "evaluation" of this was fundamental to the way the ritual developed as practice. It is not just analysts that process events and generate "totalizing representations;" they are a crucial aspect of social action (cf. Keane 1997).

Ritual, Risk and Resistance

In addition to ritual having multiple aspects to any given group of actors and to the importance of reflection and connection to broader events, uncertainty is another key theme in regard to ritual that emerged from the Sidemen Maligya. This was not an automatic ritual congregation that assembled to reassure and confirm local hierarchy at a time of risk. An atmosphere of unpredictability characterized each step of the way toward what was, in the end, to turn out to be a remarkable enterprise. Listening to participants and observers alike reflect on the progression of the ritual, it became clear that it was not a given who would contribute to this effort, let alone that it would all come together as it did. People, not least the princes themselves, registered surprise at just how many subjects turned out to help with the ancestral ritual, a ritual that also served to confirm the status of the Jero Gede Sidemen. Of course there were also groups that chose not to participate, and although these happened to be groups that were not expected to do so, the situation served to underscore that nonparticipation may occur as well. Similarly, there were people who chose to participate only in limited capacities, people whose participation fell somewhere in between the range from complete absence to all-out enthusiastic and devoted service. There were even a few people who appeared to participate a bit grudgingly or with some skepticism, and they, too, served as reminders that support could not be taken for granted. It should also be noted that eager support of the princes in their ritual does not necessarily reflect submission to them in any universal way. For many it means mainly that, given the overall situation and options, they are at this time identifying themselves among the princes' subjects and supporters. One person from outside the area who did not stand in any subject relationship to the noble house but participated in the capacity of witness—the least demanding role in terms of time and resources, yet one that indicates acknowledgement of the princes' ritual—expressed a precautionary principle. As he said, maybe some day his contribution to the noble house's endeavor will be repaid in ways that he could not now anticipate. This particular person happens to be a person of commoner caste who otherwise has an apparently growing resistance to caste-based hierarchy and works in other ways to counter or overcome his own lack of caste privilege, for instance by taking up scholarly activities associated with Brahmana, such as reading *lontar* (palm leaf manuscripts). In recent years he also has supported the leadership candidate in his neighborhood organization who most exhibits courage to stand up to members of the palace of Karangasem, who progressively are being pressured to expand their participation as nonprivileged members in the activities of this egalitarian-principled association.

In the Sidemen Maligya, finally, there was an element of gamble involved on the part of the noble house in extending invitations to as many high-ranking witnesses as was the case, only the highest of which was Megawati Sukarnoputri—The princes also invited regional heads, other people in important positions, and foreign guests. Holders of rituals cannot entirely recklessly send out such invitations in the hope that someone might take them up on them. The gesture could seem presumptuous if reaching too high, and if no one were to accept ambitious invitations, this would entail loss of face. Note that Wiener, too, indicates how taking risks and, in this case, literally gambling may have positive value for rajas: "Given Balinese ideas about the invisible world, gambling becomes particularly exciting, as a test of the strength of one's intent," while "unusual success…would indicate an especially strong connection to the invisible world" (1995:114).

The elements of unpredictability and uncertainty that became evident in the course of the maligya ritual accord with other recent work on ritual with a focus on practice, highlighting themes of risk, conflict and resistance. In tandem with a shift away from viewing "culture" as a shared consistent whole, scholars have looked beyond the coherence of ritual and the community generated by ritual by also linking ritual to resistance studies (which, in turn, are criticized for not paying enough attention to ritual). Because of ritual's long-established role as being constitutive of community (Durkheim 1893; Robertson Smith 1972), ritual typically has been seen as incompatible with resistance, as an ideological tool not only legitimating and reinforcing social hierarchy, but also disguising rather than subverting domination (cf. e.g. Bloch 1986). Even rites of reversal have been interpreted almost exclusivley as release valves of tension, moments of anti-structure, all the better to allow a return to reinforced social hierarchy following the ritual (cf. Gluckman 1954, 1955, 1965; Marriot 1968), although Turner allows for greater potential for change through the notion of liminality (see also Alexander 1991). Advancing the relevance of ritual to resistance studies, Jean Comaroff's book on the Tshidi during the oppressiveness of Apartheid South Africa (1985), has been an inspiration to many. Working under circumstances that do not allow open expression of dissent, argued Comaroff, "we must look beyond the conventionally explicit domains of 'political action' and 'consciousness,'" including to the domain of ritual (1985:196). From there, others have gone on to consider resistance in and through ritual under any circumstances (Dirks 1994, Holmberg 2000).

Nicholas Dirks, with a stress on resistance within ritual in India, makes a particularly strong argument for viewing ritual as a core arena of resistance. He gives a number of examples to illustrate that ritual often is disputed and points out that people could resist simply by withholding their services, and that in fact it was not unheard of for rituals to end up not happening at all (1994:492–494). Dirks relates how difficult it was for him to recognize contentiousness beneath the surface veneer of ritual (1994:489–490). He emphasizes that "We need not make... [the] case that ritual is a fount of outright resistance in order to find struggle, disorder, and appropriations from below taking place through, and within, ritual practice" (1994:501). He finds that "because of the open and disorderly character of the ritual process, ritual is one of the primary arenas in which politics takes place:" In the Indian cases of his focus, "not only are caste identities and relations deeply politicized, they are contested throughout the field of ritual practice; all symbolic correlations within the ritual domain and between it and the social are opened to doubt, question, contest, and appropriation" (1994:501). Dirks concludes that struggle and disorder exist everywhere, but that social scientists have not been able to see this because of our bias to seek order and assume that this is the "universal human need" and "the basis of the social" (1994:501).

On Bali it has long been recognized that precolonial Balinese states "fought" by trying to out-compete each other through claims made in ritual, but, until recently, other than with regard to the customary practice of rushing, twirling and tilting cremation towers as they are carried to the burning grounds for cremation ceremonies (see chapter 6, cf. Warren 1993a, 1993b; Connor 1979), there generally has not been a focus on the uncertainty and tension within rituals— although the theme pervades a Balinese commemorative text about a mid-nineteenth century maligya ritual in Klungkung (cf. Vickers 1991). The recent exception is Leo Howe's article on "Risk, Ritual and Performance," where he, too, argues that ritual is "inherently risky" (2000:67). He points out that there is always something at stake in ritual, that unpredictable forces are released, inviting as well the very real risk of failure. Howe identifies extrinsic risks in rituals, including the risk of incorrect performance, of gambling one's status, and of attracting disruptive witches, as well as intrinsic risks, as when rituals deliberately include the presence of unpredictable, even dangerous, forces (2000:69–71). These elements are also employed in a rhetoric of risk surrounding rituals, shows Howe, serving to enhance their significance. It is precisely this riskiness that also imbues rituals with power and makes success all the more meaningful.

In the Sidemen Maligya, the uncertainty inherent to such a grand ritual was overcome as this particular ritual succeeded, as people joined in with thought to ancestral connections and gifts of land, with thought to the qualities of the noble house and its work, as well as with thought to current local and national events, with the end results meeting or perhaps exceeding even the most ambitious expectations of the princes. When this happens, once a ritual like the maligya ritual does come together, certainly there emerge also the sociological effects of generating order, confirmation and actualization of the potential for a larger social grouping of people linked through the noble house. Yet this does not become permanent. The maligya ritual did constitute the social hierarchy of a small-scale local negara, an example of what Schulte Nordholt terms "micro kingdoms" (1996a:61), but it is important to recognize that in Bali these hierarchies were and are fluid and unstable. That grouping, meanwhile, could allow the princes, on the one hand, and their subjects, on the other, to be capable of larger positioning in relation to, and indeed resistance to, developments, forms of domination, and threats from without the realm, revealing the connection between in-group cohesion, in this case within a hierarchical system, and external opposition, even as there was also a cooptation of external forces into the local project.

In Sidemen there exists a society still where, although there are class differences, there also are pre-capitalist-based hierarchical asymmetries that bear out Sherry Ortner's point of being "inseparable from complementarities and reciprocities that are equally real and equally strongly felt" (1994:399). Regarding "the centrality of domination within the contemporary practice framework," Ortner argues, "I am as persuaded as many…that to penetrate into the workings of asymmetrical social relations is to penetrate to the heart of much of what is going on in any given social system. I am equally convinced, however, that such an enterprise, taken by itself, is one-sided. Patterns of cooperation, reciprocity,

and solidarity constitute the other side of the coin of social being" (1994:401).
As also Ortner says, such patterns have been treated largely as ideology, based
on false consciousness (1994:401); yet—even in Bali, where caste is increasingly
contested (Picard 1999, Pitana 1997, 1999)—there may be more to it than that,
as, for example, when there is cooperation in relation to broader issues, including against wider domination. To the participants, the maligya ritual became a response to the "power vacuum" experienced following Suharto's resignation, a vacuum they sought to fill through ritual efforts to reconstitute
hierarchy. The Sidemen Maligya involved at once establishing the locally based
hierarchy (while drawing on extra local powers) and influencing the state hierarchy in flux (which those at the top of the local hierarchy also may become a
part of). The power of ritual to serve status usually has been conflated with serving the status quo, but that is not necessarily so. The Sidemen Maligya demonstrates that the effort through ritual to regenerate souls and keep the world steady
is not necessarily conservative of the status quo. As we shall see, for example,
the governmental regional head was right to worry that the gathering of people
for the princes' ritual could be boosting the power of the head of the noble house
and thus threatening his own position, and Megawati was, as subsequent developments have borne out, a realistic contender for national presidency.

It has been important for scholars to consider ways in which rituals are not
just about creating community and cohesion, nor are they necessarily just
temporary release valves, but they also are about conflict and resistance with
a real potential for disruption and change. They can be part of a process of
challenging the existing state of affairs as well as part of generating something
new. The present study draws attention to all of these aspects of ritual: it reiterates the aspect of rituals that is sociogenic, but also recognizes elements of
conflict and components of resistance without reducing one to the other.[36] A
ritual like the maligya can be part of an effort to work together on something
larger that can be not just cosmological, but also this-worldly, which may in-

---

36. For Holmberg, too, Chhechu is about "the regeneration of the local collectivity" in
relation to the extra-local: "I attempt to demonstrate how local Tamang communities created themselves historically and continue to create themselves as power-infused collectivi-
ties in opposition to the dominant representatives of state society" (2000:930); and: "Rivalry was an integral aspect of the performances I attended in the mid-1970s; however,
these rivalries played out in ritual processes that at another level placed the community in
opposition to the dominant political forces in Nepal" (2000:932). Interestingly, in this case
"the ludic plays expose the arbitrariness of orders of domination, and the exorcisms of an-
tisocial beings linked to that political order constitute the symbolic first steps of a
metaprocess to produce collective oppositional power represented as wang" (2000:933).

clude joining as a form of community at one level to respond to other groups and forces at other levels. For, as the ritual operates on both symbolic and functional levels, so it operates on several levels in regard to local and extra-local hierarchies and circumstances. In the different levels of authority and dominance, to the participants the local hierarchy represents something quite different than the state, and indeed may, depending on circumstances, be seen as less exploitative. And although it means having to agree to the local hierarchy whereby they define themselves as subjects of the princes,[37] participants may thereby gain a stronger position in relation to the extra-local than would be the case otherwise. We should not ignore that people might have false consciousness and unknowingly be complicit in their own oppression, but what stands out nonetheless is that they reflect critically on this, on their relationship to old hierarchies and to new ones, and balance their options. For even when they are acting to fulfill obligations in accordance with faith, there is room for interpretation and for slippage (to borrow from Keane 1997) between "remembering" and "forgetting" their connections to the princes.

Not Just a "Showcase" Response

Anyone familiar with the role of traditional culture to the Indonesian nation-state may wonder if it might not be because of Bali's position as a "showcase" of such culture (Pemberton 1994; Picard 1997, 1999) that the participants in the maligya ritual are responding to the nation-state through ritual. Inevitably both princes and people in Sidemen are affected by how "the admiration of foreigners for the culture," as Picard says, "has reinforced pride in being Balinese" (1999:16), and the role as a national showcase would have played a role in the extension of invitations to nation-state dignitaries. Yet, we should keep in mind that similar invitations were precolonial practice too.[38] It cannot be concluded that the local participants in the Sidemen Maligya are positioning themselves *through ritual* because an identification of Bali with ritual features prominently in nation-state discourse or because this is how

---

37. Bloch gives a more extreme example of willingness to subjugation in ritual: In Merina circumcision ritual he emphasizes violence, struggle, and ambiguity in rites that women must undergo, wondering why they participate in this. He concludes, "Women are willing to participate because if as women they are humiliated, as *deme* [group] members they are blessed" (1986:93). Submitting in the present day to the princedom hierarchy through ritual participation does not involve suffering violence and humiliation in the ritual, nor is it easily explained in terms of false consciousness.

38. Note also that during the colonial era the king of Siam is said to have participated in the 1937 maligya of the last raja of Karangasem (Schulte Nordholt 1996a:310).

they have been taught "how to keep on being authentically Balinese" (see Picard 1999:22)—for this is the role ritual has long fulfilled.

Protecting Bali and "the Balinese way" and responding to perceived threats do turn out to be important concerns to the princes and participants in the ritual, and the whole performance is in some ways an affirmation of self—as a prince or participant in the princedom and as Balinese (see chapter 7). What constitutes "Balineseness," including the emphasis placed on religion, along with what constitutes a threat to this, have invariably been coproduced over time in engagement with colonial and later national as well as tourism related discourses (cf. Picard 1997, 1999; Schulte Nordholt 1999). Picard's work is important to understanding the construction of a self-conscious Balinese identity, yet the concern with *authenticity* in being Balinese is, as Picard also recognizes, an intelligentsia debate, and was not integral to making sense of the maligya ritual. The participants are not here searching for their "Balineseness" in the mirror held up for them by the Dutch, the Indonesians, or by tourists, nor are their efforts about trying to express a "primordial essence." This is not why their response to perceived threats is done in part through ritual. There was much going on in the Sidemen Maligya beyond the issues central to intelligentsia debates, all of that which lies in the both religious and social roles of ritual and is about striving for efficacy in the world. We should note also that the Sidemen Maligya is not an example of a Balinese performance that has been co-opted as spectacle by the official promotion of "cultural arts" (*seni budaya*) (Picard 1997:201).[39]

Not all parts of Bali are equally saturated with tourism. Although Sidemen is a stop-over on tourist excursions and the area does have a scattering of bungalows and home-stays, not so much as one tourist showed up in connection with most of the preparations and rites of the Sidemen Maligya. Tourists were brought in only for the few days of the major and climaxing ceremonies of the ritual. The sheer proliferation of ritual, the extent to which Balinese continue to perform rituals—if anything more than ever—even with no tourist in sight, cannot be explained by the role of cultural activities in national and touristified discourses, other than that tourist related income plays a role in making possible the elaboration of ritual performances. Rather, what we see in the present example of royal ritual resonates still with the conclusion drawn by Schulte Nordholt regarding the role of ritual in the precolonial kingdom of Mengwi, which, as he points out, was not a static world either. Schulte Nordholt agrees with Geertz's emphasis on the role of

---

39. Brett Hough looks at how even "institutions such as STSI [The Bali Arts Center] are significant sites for the assertion, mediation, and contestation of local and national demands" (1999:256).

ritual, but adds the importance of "the ever-present threat of death and destruction and the need to seek protection from it" (1996a:13). This role of ritual and kingship transfers easily into other contexts of varying threats of various ages.

The Sidemen Maligya was an extraordinary event, richly demonstrating symbolic as well as functional facets of ritual, and giving rise to questions concerning kingship in Bali long after it is supposed no longer to exist. In the present, the Sidemen Maligya revealed that this ritual of ancestral deification still may constitute one of the most prominent displays and reinforcements of living royal status.[40] The power that surrounded the keris in the context of the ancestral ritual and presidential presence indicated an ancient sphere of royal power that also at that moment was established as a modern sphere. Although participants generally agree that this event should not be termed politics (see chapter 7), it did not pass unremarked locally that three months after the events at the ancestral ritual, Megawati's party received the largest number of votes in Indonesia's first open elections, including the vast majority of votes in Bali. Megawati served first for nineteen months as vice-president in a compromise government headed by Abdurrahman Wahid, and then became president in July 2001. More significantly for our purposes, the Jero Gede Sidemen was confirmed as an important locus of traditional power and charisma (*kesaktian*). Through performance of the maligya ritual, featuring its dynastic heirloom and an impressive show of followers and spectacular witnesses, the Jero Gede Sidemen reconstituted itself as a princedom, and assumed a prominent role at a time of wider political uncertainty.

The Perspective from the Sidemen Maligya

The perspective from Sidemen differs from that of existing major studies of Balinese kingship in a number of ways. Rather than the perspective of rajas at larger centers (Geertz 1980, Schulte Nordholt 1996a, MacRae 1997, 1999) or the royal or Brahmana perspective from Klungkung, Bali's foremost kingdom (Wiener 1995), based primarily on historical texts and contemporary memories, this study is situated at the peripheral and smallest scale of negara dynamics, in the princedom surrounding a minor noble house, presenting the perspectives of princes and subject participants in the context of ongoing experience

---

40. The maligya may thus be framed as a mortuary ceremony that has political aspects to it of which there is also a broader Austronesian literature; cf. e.g., Weiner regarding the Trobriand Islands, 1976, 1988, 1992; cf. also the literature on how political ritual may be in general: e g. Mauss 1967, Dirks 1994, Ortner 1994, Holmberg 2000.

in a postcolonial world. The present princedom to a remarkable extent replicates the classic negara dynamics of the larger precolonial kingdoms and speaks
to the main issues raised in trying to understand Southeast Asian kingship and
the role of ritual and governance in an amorphous realm. Geertz specifically
said in connection with his arguments regarding kingship that they applied from
the biggest to the smallest of rajas (1980:33), but questions concerning kingship
have not been pursued from the intermediary level where the lord is indeed raja
in the local context of his own realm, but also is subordinate to larger shifting
powers—as we see in Sidemen. Interestingly, my perspectival critique of Geertz,
meanwhile, turns out to correspond to the main findings concerning negara dynamics in other Southeast Asian polities regarding the active role of the local
ruler in relationships of some mutual benefit with followers.

From the perspective of the peripheral realm, the typical imaging of negara
as multicentric *mandala*, patterns of concentric circles, wherein the smaller circles are encompassed by ever-larger circles, is not the most fitting. Sidemen was
not oriented toward one exemplary center, but was situated in overlapping
spheres, influenced from and looking toward both Klungkung and Karangasem.
Also, according to the above model—and on this Tambiah accords with
Geertz—there was progressive dimming as you moved outward: A "replication
of the center on a progressively reduced scale by the satellites" (Tambiah
1985:276), often illustrated by the Javanese analogy of the diminishing intensity
of a torch's radius of light (Moertono 1968:112). The princedom does, as a center in its own realm, replicate the larger centers, but in this case the claims being
made are striking, not much dimmer than those of larger centers.[41] The princes
perform one of the highest forms of ritual possible, lay claims to one of the
grandest keris and the associated foremost kingship in Balinese history, bring in
one of the most impressive political figures in contemporary nation-state politics, and, in that small realm, they are sometimes accorded the most eminent of
royal titles even by modern followers. This may always have been a feature of
peripheral realms as centers in their own right. On the other hand, although the
history on which the princes draw to justify their claims dates to the seventeenth,
indeed to the fourteenth century, there may not have been many historical-political contexts in which to make their claims quite as grandly as was the case in
1998. The end of the twentieth century, at a time when larger kingdoms of Bali
have in many ways themselves diminished, made for one such context.

---

41. The Jero Gede Sidemen thus does not fit Geertz's pattern of sinking status, where
regional kings are secondary and tertiary kings who are not Dalem (see 1980:16-18).

Notably, the princes' claims were not made in the form of grand authoritative proclamations, but through the very idioms of power we saw to be significant to precolonial negara as well: It was by displacing agency away from individual actors—to ancestors, to the keris, and to the ritual—that the princes revealed their connection to various sources of legitimating power. This practice of displacing agency on some level supports Geertz's notion of immobility at the center, but at the same time, it also becomes eminent from the perspective of the princedom in the contemporary era—and indeed is held to be integral to Balinese conception—that the forms of displaced agency, however important to local notions of power, do not stand alone; they must correlate with direct agency. Looking at divine kingship from this viewpoint, movement and ongoing work to manifest leadership qualities and maintain connection with followers are more important than any apparent immobility at the center.

Aside from being positioned at the smallest scale of kingship, at a time when what remains of precolonial negara dynamics result from interaction with, among other changes, colonial and nation-state administrative structures, this study is also the first to approach negara dynamics with a specific ritual as the starting point for analysis, in this case as it unfolds in the current of major historical change, bringing out the significance of both received historical categories and ongoing historical events. In recent years, there has been a tendency for anthropologists, inspired by the work of Bourdieu, to follow the theoretical turn toward an increased concern with practice—which, as Ortner has pointed out, most basically is "anything people do" or "the study of all forms of human action," though, "given the centrality of domination in the model," it tends to be so "from a particular—political—angle" (1994:393). The move toward practice has tended also to lead to a turn of attention away from ritual (cf. Ortner 1994), considered exotic behavior, extraordinary rather than everyday experience, a turn that matches earlier Marxist views of ritual as action that hides the world rather than reveals it (cf. Bloch 1986, 1989). Yet precisely a practice approach to a contemporary "traditional" ritual interfacing with "modern" historical change and national political upheaval, which the observer and analyst can follow as it unfolds, proves very rewarding in bringing to the fore what the ritual means to the participants beyond an immediate focus on the symbolism and symbolic action. It allows us to query, in context, why people participate in the hierarchical realm. Connections to human resources, which emerge as central issues in regard to larger precolonial centers, are brought into more relief, perhaps, at the princedom level where the link between lords and followers can be expected to be more immediate; and they certainly are so in the present day. At a time when lord-fol-

lower relationships are presumed largely to exist no longer, one has to wonder more than ever, what is the basis of the links between princes and people?

In all, the Sidemen Maligya presents an intriguing case, which allows a perspective on the tension between symbolic and material aspects, and between the
proclamations that an all-encompassing ritual can create a universe and the question of why people actually participate. Though colonization obviously entailed
drastic changes for the Balinese—and the puputan or court sacrifices/massacres
were devastating—the processes that constituted the negara did not "die," nor
have they entirely disappeared during the subsequent decades of nation-state governance. First colonial and then nation-state administrations have penetrated into
the most local levels of life in Bali, and, in this process, there is no question but
that they in many ways have marginalized palaces and noble houses. In each instance, however, there have also been nobles who have been able to benefit from
the situation to enhance their positions, to gain local prominence as either representatives of or mediators to the new power structures. In the case of Sidemen,
the head of the noble house has at different times, even as the house experienced
declines in power, done both. Relationships of Balinese negara were always fluid,
and, aside from the period of colonial rule where they were restructured and upheld with more fixity, what remains of such relationships are now more fluid
than ever. Although the princedom is reproducing the classic features of negara
dynamics, it is doing so in the context of being highly engaged with the present
world, and, in this regard, the circumstances are very different from those of precolonial Bali; yet the negara dynamics of a modern princedom characterized by
more fluid conditions than ever may offer a worthwhile perspective nonetheless
on the role of ritual in a form of polity always characterized by fluidity.

Positioning of the Anthropologist

When I became involved in the maligya ritual in early 1998, I at first began
traveling to Sidemen to participate in the ritual preparations on weekends,
as did family members of the noble house who live and work away from the
village. My previous trips to Bali (1993, 1995) had been related to projects
involving mainly the farmer and temple systems of irrigation and rice terrace
management, and when I initiated my doctoral research in late 1997, I was
focused on studying the relationship between hierarchy and egalitarianism in
Bali. Knowing that I wanted to look both at areas wherein hierarchy is accentuated, such as in priestly and princely households and in ritual, as well
as areas in which it is suppressed, such as in irrigation and neighborhood associations, I had been concerned to position myself multiply for a variety of

perspectives, and had ended up settling in Amlapura, the regional capital of Karangasem, as the central location from which I could connect to surrounding villages. In Amlapura, rather than be tied to the palace perspective, I had opted to live in a nearby commoner neighborhood, from which I still could make visits to the palace. In Sidemen, today about an hour's drive from Amlapura, however, my study of the ritual and the princedom is situated, first, within the noble house of a Balinese Ksatria (princely) family, the Jero Gede Sidemen. Some of the main voices from this family are heard throughout the book (figure 3 diagrams the core members of the contemporary Jero Gede Sidemen). Tjokorda Gede Dangin is the head of the noble house and Cokorda Raka, his older brother, is an active member who chose a teaching career and residence away from Sidemen and now resides in Amlapura. The youngest of the house's three most active brothers is Cokorda Pemangku, who has become a non-Brahmana priest and is in charge of the family temple and its rituals. One of the most powerful female voices of the house is their older sister, Dewa Ayu Alit, who was never married. In the younger generation, Cokorda Raka's daughter Cokorda Sawitri—a journalist, writer, activist, government accountant, and, following the maligya ritual, a graduate student in Human Resources—stands out. In her thirties and also unmarried, she is recognized for her charisma and maintains a strong interest in her family history. It should be noted that I had access also to a number of the more marginal members of the family, including commoner wives.

Maintaining my residence in Amlapura even as I commenced involvement in Sidemen allowed me to retain access to perspectives from the outside. Here I had ongoing contact with the Amlapura palace of Karangasem, under which Sidemen historically sorted and in contrast to which it today sometimes defines itself, while I continued to live amongst Sudra and their perspectives on both the Amlapura palace and the Jero Gede Sidemen. In the Sidemen area, I sought over time, including during follow-up fieldwork, to speak with as many of the historical followers of the Jero Gede Sidemen as possible—both in Sidemen and in outlying villages—recognizing that they undoubtedly would see me as connected to the noble house. Also, I recognize that contacts to followers often were through people in leadership positions—village heads, lineage heads, and so forth, and I have not actively sought out dissenting voices. There is no question that a study from the perspective primarily of followers would look different, as would one situated among non-followers. It is also worth noting, though, that what I heard from different participants in the princedom rang true to the range of opinions and beliefs that I heard from people outside of it. Even what I heard

Figure 3. Genealogy: Core Family Members of the Jero Gede Sidemen Featured in This Study

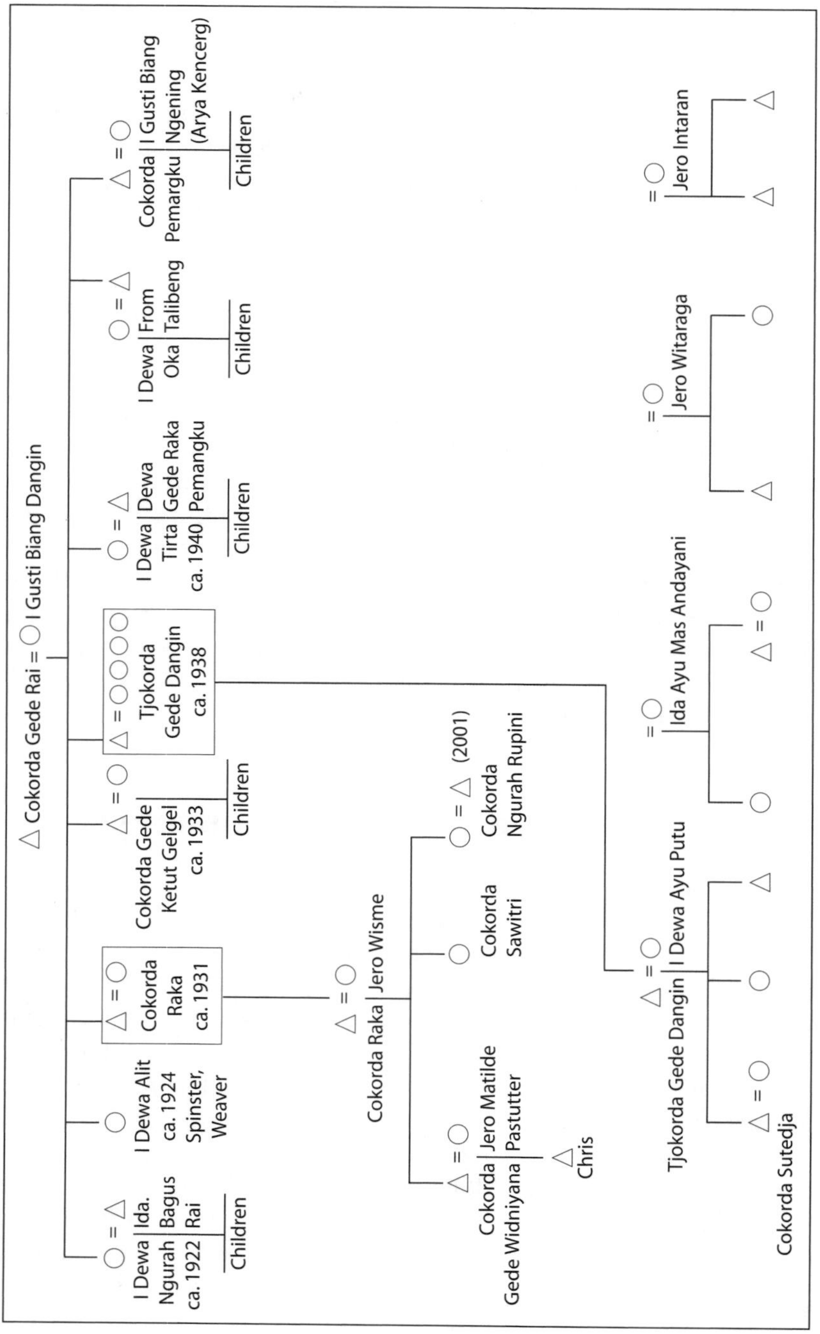

from the followers of the noble house, in the presence of what would be construed as agents of this house, was by no means glamorizing nor without admissions of tension.

Although I strove to access a variety of perspectives, the study remains inevitably biased and I make no claims to completeness on its behalf (cf. Appadurai 1986:759). I am confident that this is also the case for the people who have contributed perspectives to this book, as people in all positions themselves were concerned that it be understood that they could speak only from their own experience and, in the case of leaders, on behalf of the specific group that they represent and with which they identify. At the same time, the very partiality resulting from looking at the 1998 maligya ritual in its situatedness is key to the understanding gained—the situatedness of the ritual in a particular historical moment as well as in longer historical perspective, and how it relates to the situatedness of the noble house between two larger palaces and its long range strategy of recovering its perceived proper position as well as establishing a contemporary position, and, finally, how the followers situate their ritual obligations to the princes between ancestral responsibilities and present needs for representation and efficacy in the world.

Before proceeding further, to the reader not familiar with Bali, an introduction to some of the issues and terminology of caste might be helpful to understanding more about the context for the relationships already being talked about and to be presented in the chapters to follow.

Balinese Caste and its Terminology

There has been some debate as to whether Bali even has caste. Hildred and Clifford Geertz have argued, and in many ways rightly so, that "the Hindu concept of 'caste' is inappropriate and confusing when applied to Balinese status distinctions," encompassing all of it instead by the gloss of "title groups" (1975:6, 61; see also Howe 1987). Within Bali, as well, you will find the viewpoint that the notion of caste does not apply—for example on an occasionally encountered t-shirt proclaiming, "In Bali there is no caste." Most Balinese, however, appear to think otherwise. I have been in situations where people who did not know I was an anthropologist with an interest in these issues, embarked on a self-initiated "explanation of Bali" by stating something along the lines that "the most important thing to know is that in Bali we have caste." Its presence is reflected also in the need at the outset of this book to explain caste related terminology.

The categories (or *varna*) of Brahmana, Ksatria, Wesia, and Sudra pervade Balinese society; that is, the structural positions of the realm, respectively, of priests, rajas and princes, merchants or lesser nobility and "ordinary" people. The four varna are further classified into *Triwangsa* (the twice born, those "who have caste;" in other words, high caste: Brahmana, Ksatria, or Wesia) and *Jaba* (outsiders, those who "do not have caste;" i.e. Sudra). In this scheme, ironically, the *Triwangsa* are those who trace descent outside of Bali from Majapahit, while *Jaba*, the outsiders, are those descended from the pre-Majapahit population of Bali. It is the Majapahit connection that forms the main focus of Balinese historiography. Interestingly, since independence, more and more *jaba* groups, even some *Bali Aga* (members of the villages who originally resisted Indianized court culture), have been "discovering" their own Majapahit connections, to the point that there are few groups left in Bali who do not in some way claim Majapahit descent (cf. Pitana 1997; Reuter 2002b).

The titles already encountered and to be encountered in the following chapters reflect the above caste standings, though readers should be aware that especially the titles of nobility, in part reflecting histories of contestation, vary regionally within Bali.[42] Titles appearing in this work include *Anak Agung* and *Cokorda* for high-ranking Ksatria (rajas or paramount lords) and can be male or female. *Dewa Gede* and *Dewa Ayu* indicate a male and female Ksatria, respectively, while *Jero* refers to a Sudra woman married into a high caste household. *Ida Bagus* and *Dayu* (or *Ida Ayu*) are male and female Brahmana titles; *Pedanda* and *Pedanda Istri*, the titles for consecrated Brahmana priests and priestesses. *Gusti* are lesser Ksatria or Wesia. Sudra (or *jaba*) usually go by birthorder names, such as *Wayan, Made, Nyoman,* and *Ketut* (for first, second, third, and fourth born, respectively, be they male or female), or omit titles altogether, using the caste-neutral Indonesian polite forms of address, *Pak* or *Ibu*. Caste standing is also indicated by designations for residences: Brahmana live in *Griya*, priestly or Brahmana compounds, rajas in *Puri*, palaces or courts, and paramount lords or princes in *Jero Gede*, noble house compounds. These terms may be relative. Locally, for example, the Jero Gede Sidemen is usually referred to as the *puri* (palace), though it is a smaller noble house in relation to the bigger palaces. In either case, Jero Gede or Puri, the term designates both an institution and the configuration of its members, individuals and families, past and present.

Although Louis Dumont—who denied the existence of caste outside of India—did not mention Bali, the constitutive principles beyond the nomenclature of caste, as defined by him ([1966] 1980) and problematized by sub-

---

42. Some of the people featuring in this book may also be referred to differently outside of the Sidemen area. It was in the time period of the maligya ritual that I heard Raka referred to as Cokorda. In Amlapura he usually goes by I Dewa Gede Raka. Cokorda Sawitri usually goes by Cok Sawitri.

sequent scholars (e.g. Dirks 1987, 1995, 2001; Sharma and Searle-Chatterjee 1995), do in fact exist here in some form. In Bali, as in India, caste is instantiated by a series of practices. There is ranking of hereditary groups, preferred endogamous marriage and hypergamy, elaborate rules of commensality, rules concerning spatial proximity and relationship, and ordering according to principles of purity and pollution. Though there is also some correlation between caste and occupation—for example the occupations of smith, craftsman, or high priest—this is a much less salient caste marker in Bali than in India. There is no *jati* or *jajmani* system of occupational groups; nor is there any caste of "untouchables." In Bali, on the other hand, language takes on added significance, for here language firmly embeds hierarchy. Balinese, unlike Hindi, has obligatory language registers. While many words remain the same in high, medium, and low Balinese, there are a thousand or so words of core vocabulary, which differ altogether, often etymologically. Respect forms in many cases oblige a person of low caste to express ideas of subservience and dependence in relation to persons of higher caste. In fact, it is impossible to speak Balinese without indicating the relative caste position of the speaker, listeners, and subjects referred to in speech. As Howe has observed, "when children are born in Bali, they grow up in a world drenched in hierarchy" (1991:452).

In Bali, however, there exists also a strong countervailing egalitarian ethos, as explicit as is the hierarchical ethos—a belief that in some contexts all should sit at the same level and give shape to a shared voice. These coexist in daily life in Balinese villages and the egalitarian and counter-hierarchical ethos, too, find expression surrounding caste-based hierarchical practices, as indeed we shall see in the princedom. Historically, there has been incessant contest among Balinese concerning the employment of caste principles—as Clifford and Hildred Geertz once phrased it, "*Homo hierarchicus* and *Homo aequalis* are engaged in Bali in war without end" (1975:167). They also, however, have been and are—as through the maligya ritual—engaged in collaboration. Caste related behaviors in Bali, as is the case with kingdoms and kingship, and princedoms and lordships, in the end may be most felicitously characterized in terms allowing for fluidity and flexibility.

Plan of the Book

Part 1, the Performance of a Princedom, describes the maligya ritual of 1998 and looks at what kinds of relationships the Jero Gede Sidemen mobilized to make this event happen. Chapter 2 contextualizes the maligya ritual in the Balinese ritual cycle, discusses related issues of status and deification, and presents a narrative of the Sidemen Maligya. As the story progresses, from the inception to the completion of the maligya ritual, the narrative highlights how extra-local developments became a counterpoint to the local ancestral ritual. Chapter 3 overviews themes related to the sources of power of the negara and details these relationships as mobilized and manifested in this particular ritual of the Jero Gede Sidemen. Again, the small princedom in Sidemen confirms several of the points made regarding negara dynamics—the activation of powerful connections, the importance of the priest-raja relationship, and the mobilization of human resources. It is revealed that the ritual both reflects and generates the structures of the princedom. What emerges is perhaps even more "mystefying"—to refer to Marxist critiques of the Geertzian approach—than Geertz's claim of "state ceremonials" as "metaphysical theatre" (1980:104), for here we find the voluntary performance in the contemporary era of old follower-to-lord obligations expressed in ritual service.

In the modern era, where the princes lack obvious forms of power to coerce, the question that rises to the fore is "why"—Why do their subjects still voluntarily perform labor as followers of the noble house? This is the question that leads us through the remainder of the book, which looks more closely at the maligya ritual's political dimensions and at the ways in which the various participants became involved and why they did so. The answers are revealing of how both long-term history and short-term historical-political issues are negotiated in this more-fluid-than-ever realm of the princedom. Two discourses join in a surprising way, for questions about modern motivations and the broader meaning of the maligya ritual—what people articulate about their participation—lead back to the issues debated at the level of the nature of the Balinese state. In an interesting way we are faced with the same kind of question as the first observers to Bali were, although under very different circumstances—There is no strong governance in this realm, so what holds it together?

Following the view in Part 1 at how the ritual succeeds in constituting a symbolic universe and princedom hierarchy, Part 2 shows that royal power does not just happen in and emanate from grand ritual. This section, "Recasting Balinese Hierarchy," examines some of the elements that, given the tendency to focus on larger rajas, may not have been sufficiently pursued in relation to Balinese negara. Specifically, the significance to the princedom of land relations emerges as the topic of chapter 4, for a form of land relationship called *pacatu* and obligations to the subjects' ancestors lay at the heart of their contemporary ritual participation. While kingship as completely tied to the material base of the realm did not develop; that is, where the raja had complete control of the land, its production and its produce, then kingship as Geertz proposed it, as virtually detached from its material base, in this realm did not do so either. Also, the model of the raja presented here is clearly no icon of passivity. Chapters 5 and 6 look at the ongoing interrelations of status elevation and subjectification between Balinese subjects and princes. Here we see at the level of the princedom, and in the present day, the kinds of effort and consideration that go into maintaining hierarchical privilege and connection to followers. Chapter 5 focuses on the everyday practice of the princes, when they are acting not through ritual, bringing to light values of populism and forwarding the argument that the princes actively must work the people and work for the people to gain and retain hierarchical privilege. Chapter 6 goes on to examine the powers of the people and the significance of shifting historical contexts. This kind of kingship does of course entail as well the possibility of abusing power: In the process of ongoing accommodations between people and princes, the Balinese lords could also be autocratic figures. But what we see in Sidemen in the new millennium—that lords have to be attentive to what their people would think and conceivably do—is likely a very old pattern that becomes especially accentuated during certain structural moments in history. It could be as old as Southeast Asian kingship itself.

In Part 3, "Ritual and World Change," chapter 7 returns us to the ritual, the Sidemen Maligya, taking a closer look at the events surrounding Megawati and the heirloom keris, at how this foremost symbol of Balinese kingship is mobilized at the level of the modern princedom and what this means. The chapter presents how the participants in the modern princedom are not just enactors of ancient rituals, but are actors in the complex world of nation-state politics who seek empowerment on their own terms, which includes action through ritual. The princedom is seen as a system wherein the Jero Gede Sidemen facilitates fertility for the realm, and its ritual is also a ritual of world renewal, a ritual for the regeneration not just of ancestral souls, but also of the living, of the nation, and of the world.

Thus, at the turn to the third millennium, in a smaller realm in eastern Bali, we find a contemporary princedom according with many of the established dynamics and principles of the negara, while also, given its decentralized and contemporary situation, bringing to the fore some new dimensions. This is not an ancient survival, but a princedom fully in the modern and postmodern context, constituted by knowing subjects acting with and within national and global forces. The negara is transformed, but it lives—and it does so *also* in the pageant of grand ritual featuring powerful people and ancestral objects.

The Sidemen Princedom, the area within which people still refer to the Jero Gede Sidemen as their raja, is not a clearly bounded territory, nor does it consist of a measured amount of people. Estimates of the numbers who follow the noble house range from twenty-five to thirty thousand; but when asked to give a figure, the immediate response of the head of the house was that "it cannot be counted." "It depends on our deeds," he said, "on our performance with the people." Indeed, their great maligya ritual said much about the Jero Gede Sidemen's performance with the people, as descendants of former feudal subjects voluntarily dedicated months of labor toward a ceremony that effectively recreated the ancient structures of the realm and revealed the extent to which Sidemen is still a functioning princedom.

PART ONE

THE PERFORMANCE OF A PRINCEDOM

CHAPTER TWO

A RITUAL UNFOLDS IN HISTORICAL CONTEXT: THE SIDEMEN MALIGYA

In Eastern Bali people still talk of notable maligya rituals held by the region's major royal palace of Amlapura, Karangasem. A particularly magnificent one was conducted by the last raja in 1937,[1] while another faction of the palace highlights a more recent and also very large maligya ritual it held in 1985. People in the area date events in relation to the respective royal maligya rituals, as they do in relation to other markers, such as the eruption of Mount Agung in 1963 and what they call the "era of communists," referring to the events in the years of 1965–67 surrounding the coup against President Sukarno that brought Suharto to power and led to extensive killings of alleged communists throughout both Java and Bali (see e.g. Cribb 1990; Robinson 1995; Dwyer and Santikarma 2003).[2] By the outset of 1998, there was talk in some circles of the upcoming maligya ritual in the periphery of the region, the maligya ritual of the royal family of the smaller noble house, the Jero Gede

---

1. The 1937 maligya ritual of the Amlapura raja is described in detailed observational style by dancer and writer Katharane Mershon (1971), who had traveled to attend this, as had Gregory Bateson and Margaret Mead. Dr. Djelantik, a son of the raja, devotes a chapter to it in his autobiography (1997). Francine Brinkgreve (1981) describes some of the symbolism and presents a chronology of a week of the events of a 1980 maligya ritual by the royal family of Cokorda Gde Agung Sukawati, Ubud, a maligya ritual that included the soul of the Dutch painter Rudolf Bonnet. The most interesting treatments in relation to the kinds of issues pursued in regard to the Sidemen Maligya are a poem (*geguritan*) by a Klungkung prince to commemorate a maligya ritual held in 1842 in Klungkung, just west of Karangasem, and Adrian Vickers' analysis of this poem (1991). Beyond these treatments, there are no analyses of maligya rituals, nor are there other accounts of how a Balinese ritual like this unfolds in broader context.

2. Precolonial commemorative texts (*pangeling-eling*) concerned with recollecting and connecting important events also tended to focus on rituals along with war (Vickers 1990).

Sidemen. The event was already years in the making and its preparations were about to intensify. This chapter traces that event from inception to completion and provides a narrative of how it unfolded in its final months, which coincided with former President Suharto's fall from power. Revealed is not just that two kinds of markers, notable rituals and political events, may overlap in time, but also (since we are looking at this from the perspective of the ritual) that the ritual both marked time and dynamically shaped and was shaped by it too. Local ritual may be generated from the imperatives to perform ancestral and ritual duties, but also is formed in interaction with ongoing extralocal events. As becomes clear when we follow it in practice, the Sidemen Maligya set people and things in motion, and as ancestral deification became wound up with worldly developments, the relationships that constitute the princedom materialized in not entirely predictable ways.

By presenting a narrative of the Sidemen Maligya—and I must emphasize that this is but one possible account, a construction compiled from observations and conversations with people on my particular path through the complex of events that make up the ritual—I hope to convey some of the experience of it to the reader, as a background to pursue the questions of the chapters to follow. I also want to make a couple of immediate points. In keeping with the idea that rituals entail uncertainty, it should become clear that this ritual came together only bit by bit and that not much was a given at the outset. Even how to carry out the symbolic rites for the ancestors was not an automatic reenactment but had to be worked out. And the configuration of the princedom came together only as the ritual progressed, and the interrelation with the historical/political situation was played out only in that process. It is also interesting to note that participants in the ancestral ritual did experience internal climax of the event, given that scholars once wrote of Balinese life as being characterized by absence of climax. Following Gregory Bateson (1970b), for example, Geertz expressed in a famous article on Balinese personhood that "Balinese social life lacks climax because it takes place in a motionless present, a vectorless now. Or, equally true, Balinese time lacks motion because Balinese social life lacks climax" (1973a:404). While such interpretations have long been contested they also have been resurrected: Hauser-Schäublin cites Geertz's line to argue that "there *is* 'movement' in Balinese genealogies and histories," but she says as well that Geertz's characterization "may be true especially in the context of rituals" (1997:16). There is undeniably something of the perception of timelessness and invariability that lingers and resonates with how visitors often experience Balinese rituals; for it is true, as Geertz also noted regarding temple celebrations, that, although spectacular, they often seem to "consist largely of getting ready and cleaning up" (1973a:404). One point that should emerge from the narrative of the Sidemen Maligya is that participants themselves may experience ritual differently than so, including, in fact, experiences that we would call climactic. Finally, although ritual is often viewed as stereotypical reproduction associated with action that reveals lack of historical consciousness, the ritual did constitute thoughtful and active engagement with the world, and participation can be viewed as a response to conflict and uncertainty within that world. The ritual in the end did legitimate a hierarchy (and what lies behind that we shall see in chapters 3 through 6), but it also asserted the local vis-à-vis the national, as participants, through the ritual, were positioning themselves within and in relation to a particular historical moment (topics to be pursued further in chapter 7).

By considering the Sidemen Maligya in the larger context of months of preparation leading to climaxes on various levels, in other words, we shall experience this ritual differently than the typical visitor. By considering it in broader historical context, moreover, we shall see that in the end the maligya ritual may be viewed also as a state ritual and indeed as a ritual of world renewal, since from the perspective of the princedom's participants, through the ritual of ancestral deification and status elevation, they were also acting upon the larger world at a time perceived as one of particular historical need. But before following how the specific ritual of the Jero Gede Sidemen in 1998 was conceived and came about and how it gained momentum and came to interface with national events, let us consider first what a maligya ritual is in the cycle of Balinese life and death rites, what it achieves for the deceased as well as for the living.

The Maligya Ritual and Deification of the Ancestors

Hindu Balinese categorize their life-cycle ceremonies according to whether these are focused on the newborn in the process of exiting the realm of the divine or on the deceased reentering it. As they believe in reincarnation (*numetis*), they believe that the newborn arrives on earth from the realm of the divine, and the life-cycle rites are concerned with this passage and with the process of becoming a complete human and social being. The early ceremonies facilitate the transition of the child who is still godlike into the human world, while also purifying her or him of any accompanying vices and evil influences, as well as boosting beneficial influences and connection to the divine. It is generally accepted that you cannot eliminate all bad elements but through ritual you can, as several Balinese put it, minimize the bad and maximize the good. These life-cycle rites include the various rites surrounding birth, followed by three-month and six-month rituals, and around puberty or in connection with marriage, tooth filing. There can be additional purification rites interspersed with these if the personality or well being of the child indicates the necessity for this; otherwise, the next major ceremony is marriage. With marriage, the process of becoming a full adult, firmly rooted in this world with all of the attendant rights and duties, is completed. The newly married couple gains membership of the local neighborhood organization, and soon, between their own procreation and their own deaths, they start performing the ceremonies for their children and, when such time comes, the death rites for their parents. This second set of rites, the rites that transition the soul back out of this world, may include burial for those who cannot immediately afford a cremation; otherwise cremation occurs, followed by a series of final purification or postcremation rites to complete the soul's journey "home to the gods," to await reincarnation and the commencement once more of the life rites. With the death rites, in other words, there is a reentrance of the soul into the realm of the divine that must be effected by ceremony, much as is the case at birth with the soul's exit from the divine.

In differentiating the cremation and postcremation rites, people say that where the purpose of the cremation ceremony is separation of the soul from the body, that of the postcremation ceremony is its separation from the earthly realm, so the ancestors may be finally deified. A distinction is thus made between the deceased who have not yet had the series of purification ceremonies for them completed (*pirata*) and the deities (*pitara* or *betara*). Accordingly, explains Cokorda Raka, the oldest brother of the Jero Gede Sidemen,

> Balinese consider heaven to be layered....There is a special place for the souls that have not yet made it all the way to heaven....If they have only had the cremation, they still are subject to the consequences of their deeds [*karma phala*]. If they have made it to heaven, only then have they become one with God [and with the substance of the universe].

Similarly, there are special places in the household shrine for the souls, depending on where they are in this process (cf. McGowan 1995:80; 1996). Only after completion of the last rites of death do the now deified ancestors get their place in the different shrines of the family temple (*ngelinggihan*). Dewa Ayu Alit, the elderly spinster sister at the Jero Gede Sidemen, explains that this is the ultimate goal for the maligya ritual. As she puts it, it is done "so the deities ascend to the leaves of the banyan tree [a kind of fig tree with aerial roots that develop into new trunks] in the family temple," following which they are addressed as *Ida*: "It means that their place is already good, that they already have become deities" (are *Betara Ida*). This change of appellation happens only upon the completion of each of a long series of rites that are part of the post-cremation ceremony, the final one of which takes the name of the deceased, inscribed on a palm leaf, "on an excursion" (*melelancaran adane*), on a trip from sea to mountain (*metirta yatra*). Only then is the ritual work finished, explains Dewa Ayu Alit, and her niece, Cokorda Sawitri, continues, "Only then are they called deities, our ancestors." At this point people no longer can refer to their deceased relatives as they used to, but must add the title of a deity, even when addressing their own parents.

On one level, these ceremonies are about doing all within the power of the living descendants to help their ancestors on their way. Cokorda Sawitri explains that there is even hope that through the maligya ritual they will break out of the cycle of reincarnation, that they will enter the orbit of God. She tells the story of the *astawa* tree:

> This tree is backwards, because the roots extend up and the leaves are in the ground...; that is, the deeper you go, the thicker the leaves. That thickness represents humans with all of their desire, all of their ambition. Now, this can only be felled with this ceremony, this maligya ritual. This tree, you must ax it with a death ceremony, so that it is broken off, so that there is not impurity, so that it no longer has a tie to the earth.

The belief that you never really reach full rank until you are dead and that ancestors can become deified through the performance of the proper funerary rites is an ancient Austronesian idea, recently described by Denis Monnerie in regard to Mono-Alu in the Solomon Islands (1998). Monnerie, who welcomes perspectives from broader Austronesian context, argues for a need in comparative studies of Oceania to better recognize the significance of considering status, rank, and indeed the whole social system beyond the life-span of the individual, "from the vantage point of funeral rites" (1998:93). It is an idea that has been elaborated to an extraordinary degree in Bali. As we see in the maligya ritual, through ceremonies your descendants can keep furthering your rank after you are dead, whereas, conversely, if they do not do this, you can in a sense posthumously lose rank in the Balinese political system. To the Balinese who participate in these rituals, deification of a person of course does not entail rendering that person an omniscient, omnipotent kind of God (cf. the argument concerning deification between Obeyesekere 1997 and Sahlins 1995). As should be becoming clear from the description of the ritual cycle, where souls cycle in and out of the realm of the divine, there is more continuity here between person and god than in Western tradition. Another aspect of the idea of deification in Bali is indicated when Cokorda Sawitri remarks, concerning the deification of her ancestors, "That is, they become deities for our relatives, not for other people." At issue, in other words, is also the difference between particularistic ancestor worship and universalist religion.[3]

When asked how it can be that his high caste Ksatria ancestors must wait for a rare maligya ritual before they are fully deified, while the ancestors of commoner Sudra may become so almost immediately, usually at a minor rite (the *ngeroras*) soon after the cremation, Cokorda Raka explains that Ksatria believe that the souls of their ancestors already "are in a good place" compared to Sudra, even if these might have had the deifying ceremony. But once they have had their ceremony, the ngeroras, are the Sudra ancestors not already "one with God?" ["bersatu sama tuhan," the phrase Raka has been using]. He responds, "Yes, according to them, that is." And your ancestors only just became one with God with this maligya ritual? He laughs, "yes." All of this makes more sense when we consider that there is a secular purpose, too, with postponing the final deification until a large ceremony can be held.

The Maligya Ritual and Worldly Status

As a symbolic second cremation, the postcremation ritual strives to heighten the purity of the soul of the deceased and thus attain for it a more sublime place in heaven. The well-being of the ancestral souls is considered not a matter of significance unto the souls alone, however, but unto the entire family. It has been expressed aptly that "the Balinese community must be understood as a partnership of the living and the dead" (Guermonprez 1990:57). Almost invariably, if someone becomes ill or suffers financial or other difficulties, it is determined through consultation with a spirit medium that some deceased family member is displeased due to a ceremonial shortcoming, be it an outright failure to carry out a ceremony or merely failure to carry it out properly. Since the deceased continue to influence the lives of the

---

3. In other parts of the archipelago that have been Christianized it has therefore been difficult to maintain ancestral rites. From the far reach of the Austronesian expansion, though, Bloch describes an interesting case of a Christianized society in Madagascar that has retained an ancestor-based tradition (1986). See Ramstedt (2004) for discussion of the pressures for Balinese religion to become more universalist.

living in this way, the death rites are deemed of utmost importance also for the healthy, peaceful, and successful lives of those left behind.

Performances of the death rites are important to the living in another way as well. All Balinese ceremonies can happen at one of three levels of elaboration, low, medium, or high (*nista, madia,* or *utama*), all of which, theoretically, serve the same religious purpose of purifying and transitioning the living and the dead through the requisite phases of the life-cycle. In practice, however, much import is associated with the performance of the highest-level ceremonies, which remain closely linked to assertions of caste status. Cokorda Raka conveyed the most typical assumption when he explained, "My family chooses the highest of them; Sudra families choose the low one." These status asserting variations in the levels of ceremony are particularly conspicuous in the death ceremonies. Much mention has been made in the literature of elaborate cremation ceremonies, but the extravagance even of the cremation may be exceeded by the postcremation ceremony. At the lower level, this is called *ngeroras,* at the medium level, *mukur,* and finally, at the highest level, *maligya.* The name *maligya* derives from "Bali," which means "first" or "the absolute highest" and *gia,* meaning "manner and behavior;" in other words, the highest form of conduct or behavior.[4] Many Balinese refer to this ceremony as the highest level possible in Balinese ceremony altogether.[5] Balinese will say that they are obliged only to spend within their means on rituals; yet in reality considerable pressure usually is felt to push one's limits, through ritual, to give to one's ancestors—and, when of high status or desiring thereof, to assert this within the community. Bloch (1986), who struggles to find a link between the symbolic and functionalist aspects of ritual, sees differences in scale of symbolic elements and numbers of people and time involved, along with a few innovations, as insufficient to account for much of significance; but in Bali precisely such variations—scale and extravagance along with variations that range from the number of tiers on a cremation tower to the number of leaves on an effigy—can account for the difference between a king and a commoner. What may seem like negligible variations can be differences full of significance.

Aside from more extensive and expensive offerings, what most fundamentally distinguishes a maligya ritual from the lower levels of postcremation cer-

---

4. In Sidemen, the members of the noble house chose to use the spelling "Baligya."

5. Though the maligya ritual is one of the death ceremonies, it may in some cases also include other life-cycle ceremonies, especially tooth filing. A "lesser" ceremony can accompany a larger ceremony such as the maligya ritual as "a follower." The term used is that the toothfiling, for example, "ngiring," follows, the maligya ritual. They also refer to such a ceremony as "nunas banten," requesting the offerings already used by the ancestors, even if they also add new offerings.

emony is the pair of *betara lingga*, the "suns" or souls of deceased Brahmana priests that act as guides for the souls in transition. As it is only Brahmana and "those of raja ["kingly"] descent" (in other words, not all Ksatria) that can procure this service of a priestly house, it is technically only those who can call their ceremonies maligya rituals. Others, by contrast, simply use their own ancestors' souls for guides. Even wealthy Sudra cannot pay their way to this right or otherwise somehow earn it. Low caste souls can be guided by priestly betara lingga only if they come along in the ceremony as "followers," as subjects of a priestly or princely house. Members of the Jero Gede Sidemen explain that it is the priests who do not want it otherwise. They are willing to serve in this way only for someone of raja descent; they will not do it for just any high caste people either. "Yes, it reeks a bit of feudalism," offers Cokorda Raka, for he is ever conscious of defining himself and his house around and against this term.

While it remains that even well-to-do people of lower caste cannot secure the priestly participation of betara lingga to put on a true maligya ritual, some Balinese do push the categories.[6] The very year of the Sidemen Maligya, alone, at least two other ceremonies in the Karangasem region were billed as maligya rituals. One of them was executed by a group of the Wesia caste, the head of which is a wealthy contractor: Indeed, explained one man, "it is said that in 1963, when Mount Agung erupted, he started out with no more than a trunk of a coconut tree. Now he is an outright developer. He owns three gas stations and has two wives" (Nyoman). At this ceremony a consecrated Brahmana priest officiated, but, significantly, the guiding souls were from the sponsors' own kin group rather than from a priestly household. The second maligya ritual, on the other hand, was put on by a *Pande* group, traditionally the caste of blacksmiths and sometimes referred to as elevated Sudra. This ritual was officiated by the group's own Pande priest (an *mpu* or *sulingga*) and also was led by its own ancestors' souls.

That such occurrences can nonetheless be construed as a form of challenge to hierarchy was evident when it emerged that a man with genealogical connection to the Jero Gede Sidemen, whose family at times in the past has stood in some opposition to the noble house, was involved in encouraging and supporting these "maligya rituals." Interestingly, he also was drawn in to fulfill his duties to the Sidemen house by playing a part in their ritual. His support of the non-royal maligya rituals could be interpreted as a way of countering the

---

6. Ramseyer notes that it was only during Watu Renggong's reign, approximately the sixteenth century, that lower castes started holding cremation ceremonies at all. Up to then it was a privilege of princes and lesser nobility, but it began to be practiced by ever-increasing strata of the population (1977:59).

Jero Gede Sidemen's claims to uniqueness. He explained that in terms of the prescriptions of Bali-Hindu religion "there should not be a difference between dynastic groups [*wangsa*]," yet, he admitted, "There obviously is. But this is only because of historical power intervention [*intervensi kekuasaan*]," he continued.[7] "It is not [religiously] forbidden to hold the ceremonies above your caste standing." The very examples of the two 1998 lower caste "maligya rituals" that he had helped engineer already serve as evidence for his position, for as he said, "We already have the proof here; anyone can have a maligya ritual." Another man, a commoner and loyal follower of the Jero Gede Sidemen, put it this way: "the question as to whether people have a right or do not have a right to do this, this is difficult nowadays."

There is a risk involved, however, in holding a ceremony beyond your standing. This is illustrated through the story of an *ngeluwer* (also meaning "high"), another postcremation purification ceremony, which is actually even higher than the maligya ritual. Most people agree that in Bali nobody has ever attempted to carry one out.[8] The requirements are so stringent, it is said, as to be next to impossible. For example, no fly or insect may alight on any offering, which means that everything must be placed at highly elevated levels and that the ceremony must be completed in one day. Tjokorda Gede Dangin relates that such a ceremony was performed once on the neighboring island of Lombok, but it was not a success, as indicated by how civil war and colonization followed in its wake. "They had the *ngeluwer*, and then the Dutch came to Lombok—and everything was over. So the ceremony maybe was not fitting," explains Dangin:

> If you hold a high ceremony but are not able to make it absolutely complete, you are eaten up [i.e., you suffer bad consequences—illness, misfortune, etc.]....Often people now have material wealth and so they hold big ceremonies. Do not do that. It is not fitting. It is dangerous....Now people often are arrogant....They have money....That will not get you to heaven, no. Achieving heaven depends on your deeds, not your material possessions.

---

7. He is not referring to the Dutch, for he disagrees strongly with the suggestion that the Dutch tightened caste related practices and rules, arguing that they in fact eased them by taking away the raja's powers to punish infractions by force. There is not disagreement so much regarding the content of specific policies of the Dutch administration as there is regarding interpretations as to whether these constituted overall tightening or slackening of caste practices.

8. Cokorda Raka, though, thinks there might have been one in Gianyar and possibly a pretense to one by a Gusti (i.e. Wesia) in Sibetan, and Schulte Nordholt reports one as actually having been conducted in Mengwi in the nineteenth century (1996a:113–114).

Similarly, one of hell's punishments, as related in a shadow puppet perform-ance of the story of the Pandawa brother, Bima's, journey to hell to retrieve the souls of his stepparents and take them to heaven—a story also performed at the Sidemen Maligya—deals with this issue by making a man suffer under a heavy crown. In one recorded performance Bima explains to his servant, Twalen:

> "He is suffering. The crown is too heavy for him. He was given the wrong cremation."
> "Oh yes, I get it now....He had a more elaborate send-off than his caste entitled him to....He should have made sure that his family would follow the custom," Mredah [Twalen's son] interrupted....
> "Precisely," said Bhima. "A peasant should not have a prince's tower built for himself, not even if he can afford it. This is the punishment dealt to all those who are social climbers. One should not trespass the boundaries imposed by one's birthright and, by so doing, play an-other man's role." [Pucci 1985:106]

These kinds of stories, of course, serve well to maintain hierarchy. In prac-tice, people balance their status assertions with the likelihood of having them accepted by their community, and some may prefer to err in favor of the lat-ter. Leo Howe tells of people who uncovered that they supposedly were of higher ancestry than they had thought, but nonetheless opted to not try to forward any claims lest they risk their neighborly relations (2001). That de-termining the right level can be an issue also within the maligya ritual was re-flected in how one of Dangin's commoner wives was visited in a dream by her deceased mother, who brought reassurances that she was not dissatisfied to have her soul processed as a follower rather than as a family member. That this was the decision regarding her mother's soul had obviously weighed on the daughter's mind, but she appeared content after the dream.

As it turned out in the case of the Jero Gede Sidemen, their ritual was to provide remarkable affirmation of their hierarchical position. In 1998, the Sidemen Maligya was performed for fifty-some high caste forefathers of the noble house and more than thirty of the lowest ranking of their subjects. Es-timates are that, in all, thirteen thousand people attended.[9] At the apex of the

---

9. This figure includes those who came to help, with any person being counted only once, no matter how many times they participated over the months. According to the poem written for the Klungkung Maligya in 1842, that ritual included three hundred effigies and was attended by one hundred thousand people. For the raja's maligya ritual in Karangasem in 1937 the figure for number of attendees is given at fifty thousand (Schulte Nordholt 1996a:310).

ceremony, five thousand people participated. One hundred vehicles, many of them trucks, and two thousand five hundred people traveled to the beach for one of the final rites in the ceremony. The course of ritual events bore every sign that their maligya ritual confirmed the suitability of this level of ritual to the princes.

The Sidemen Maligya from Inception to Creation of Ritual Spaces[10]

The idea of carrying out a maligya ritual emerged at the Jero Gede Sidemen already in 1992, six years prior to its final performance. Members of the noble house explain that it began as an abstract idea, with discussions among the family elders as to how important indeed it would be for them to carry out such a ceremony. Not surprisingly, differently positioned family members have different perceptions of how it all came about. As Dewa Ayu Alit, the older spinster sister, recalls, it was she who initiated the process. Her niece, Cokorda Sawitri, talks to her about this. (Dewa Ayu Ngurah, Dewa Ayu Alit's older, but married sister—and therefore not one with as prominent of a role in the family—is also present).

> Sawitri: So in 1992 when you first talked with Bapak [father, i.e. Cokorda Raka], with Aji Dade [King Dade, referring to her uncle, Tjokorda Gede Dangin], you already had been making preparations?
> Aunt: Yes.
> Sawitri: What exactly were the preparations then?
> Aunt: I made thread. I prepared the fabrics that I had. Whatever was fitting. I started assembling the *muka* [the small gold faces or masks for the representations of the ancestors to be used in the ritual]. Already with Ayu Tu [Dangin's first wife], I, along with Tu Mas [Dangin's second wife], we each got some, two each, five each....I urged on Tu Mas and all of these; I urged Wite [Dangin's third wife], and my Intaran [Dangin's fourth wife]. I just urged them like that. I just urged my in-laws. And also Tu Rah [Queen Rah, the older married sister at her side] and Tu Mas [another spinster of the noble house].

---

10. For another example of a ritual presented from inception to performance, in this case interspersing photographic and textual materials, see Strathern and Stewart's *The Spirit is Coming: A Photographic-Textual exposition of the Female Spirit Cult Performancin Mount Hagen, Papua New Guinea* (1999).

Married aunt: Not the rest.

Aunt: Not the rest. I did not dare urge just anyone.

And so the spinster sister championed the women of the house around her cause, after which she brought it to her brothers, whom, as she put it, had the resources to dedicate the whole family and beyond. For these brothers different memories emerge surrounding the beginning of it all. Among them, the perspective is generally that it was Tjokorda Gede Dangin who first got the idea for the ceremony, and "then was urged on by his wives." Cokorda Raka adds that he, himself, was instrumental too, "because, in the course of my lifetime, I wanted to have carried this out....I wanted this from the heart, from deep inside, because of love for our ancestors. [We wanted this] because we believe. If we did not hold such a ceremony, their souls would be in limbo."

Tjokorda Gede Dangin tells how the idea to hold a maligya ritual took root in him: "I was sitting in our family temple; it was like a dream. Someone, an old person [not a specific ancestor], came to me and said: You must put on an ancestral ceremony." It was to be a while yet before he notified everyone in the family: "I thought about it a long time. Then I invited them and they all agreed." He also relates that an earlier vision had bid him plant a banyan tree in the family temple: "So I waited for the banyan tree to grow. I said, 'Do not cut it.' I let the children know not to cut it: 'Until I die, do not cut it.'" It was the leaves of this tree, he explained, that were used to symbolize the bodies of the deceased in their representations in the maligya ritual, and it was of the leaves of this tree that Dewa Ayu Alit spoke when she said that the deified ancestors would descend into the leaves. Tjokorda Gede Dangin continues, "Soon arose the concerns of where to find the money for this endeavor." He realized that people would come to pitch in, he explains: "It will happen. That is what I thought. The old person [in his vision] said, it will happen at the wink of an eye. This banyan tree has to be there; then people will help from all over. I believed and it was true. People came to help. That is from my dream."

Cokorda Raka reiterates, "As long as we had not had a maligya ritual, all of my family felt that we were indebted to our ancestors, but it was a difficult thing to attain because we did not have large funds, we did not have money." A commitment to material support on behalf of the nearest family had to be ensured before the family approached the priests on whom they would rely for spiritual support, for ancestral effigies, and to preside at the ritual. Only then did the family make their commitment to their ancestors. As Raka describes it,

We all gathered our money, bit by bit; the entire family wanted to contribute to finance it. The greatest outlay of money was by my younger brother, Dangin. Then we had a meeting. Was the family in agreement about carrying out this ritual work? After declaring our agreement, we talked about how much money we would need.

When we were in agreement about all of this, we went to the place of the priests, at Griya Ulah [the priests' compound], from whom we have to ask permission because they are my *surya* [literally: my sun] my *purowita* [also *bagawanta*, Brahmana priest in ritual service to him as lord]....The whole family went there, including women; more or less thirty people went. This was about one year prior to the ritual. We conveyed our request and asked that the already deceased priests there, those that already long since passed away, would become our *lingga* [priestly effigies, who lead the way to heaven], become the most important figures in that ritual work [*karya*], maligya ritual. They agreed.

Later Raka and the priests at Griya Ulah point out that, unlike the case for Christian priests, Balinese priests cannot carry books to the scene that tell them their mantras—especially not in Sidemen, they say. This reflects a ritual as opposed to a text-focused religion, the latter remark emphasizing that they, in Sidemen, are not following the rationalization of Balinese religion by religious reformers. Raka adds: "Without books, your concentration is better. If you read your prayer, your concentration is less. You would weaken the mantras for God. That is why the priests had to be notified a year in advance of the maligya ritual that we would ask them to preside with mantras at the ritual work, so that they could study for it."

Following this, says Raka, "our entire family went to our family temple on an auspicious day to promise that we were going to perform the ritual....This was a year prior to the ritual work." He goes on to indicate that they also relied on the promise of human resources:

After that we asked for help from people from the village; we summoned the heads of the neighborhood organizations, the elders of the kin groups, and the like: "This is my intention; I hope that you will help." Nobody refused. At this point it was about six months prior to the ceremony. They gave their word. After that, because they gave their promise, we went ahead.

One might wonder how people go about orchestrating a ceremony held only once in several generations. The women of the house, in particular, explain that experiences from other maligya rituals were drawn on to inform their own preparations. Also, all of them helped make offerings for other ceremonies at priestly compounds or palaces. They went there to assist, but also to "study" and "learn." As the niece explains, "They also learned how to organize that work, learned where we had to ask, what we needed, how to respond to difficulties.... All of that had to be studied carefully. We did that for the ligya [i.e. maligya ritual], to be inspired."

And thus the stage is set—or ready to be set. As the apex of the ceremony nears, two ritual spaces, referred to as the *suci* and the *payadnyan*, are prepared and purified. Through this there is also a transition into "ritual time," defined locally as apart and aside from everyday life, as indeed it has been by scholars of ritual (cf. e.g. Turner 1969; Bloch 1986; recall also Ortner 1994 on the assumption behind the turn away from ritual when analysts became influenced by practice theory). Yet, as we shall see, what goes on in the ritual space in the end cannot be completely set apart from, but in fact takes place in interrelation with political life.

The "suci."

The first ritual space is constituted by the noble house's high caste family temple *(pemerajaan)*, which has to undergo a special purification after which it changes name for the duration of the maligya ritual. It is now the *suci*, the area in which offerings are made for the ancestors, deities, and demons (*bhuta kala*, the negative supernatural forces).[11] Following the existing subdivisions of the family temple, the suci is divided into three, of which the innermost courtyard containing the family shrines remains the most restricted. Here Brahmana women alongside women of the house construct the most sacred ritual paraphernalia. Much of this category of work spills over into the central yard, which also remains quite restricted. In the outer courtyard, meanwhile, women from village associations as well as from outlying villages and lineages work on other ritual preparations and offerings.

Early in the process, a sign is prepared for the entrance to the suci, reminding people that there are certain requirements, liminal restrictions if you will, to which anyone wishing to help in this area must adhere. You may not be disabled of body, behave basely or be in a "polluted" state, such as from association with death or menstruation. The sign further outlines that, once in the purified area, no one may spit, scratch, talk at random, or criticize anything they see. They may not joke nor debate. All should come and carry out the holy work with purity of "thought, word, and deed" (*kayika*, *wacika* and

---

11. This genre of ritual work is done almost entirely by women.

manacika). Forbidden behaviors include speech impeded by stinginess. You have to distance yourself from the dispositions of *sadripu*, the "six enemies," such as jealousy and other negative traits. People are fond of making the point that nothing negative should take place in the suci, and that this, technically, means that one could ask anything of anyone in there, and the request would have to be granted. To deny someone would constitute a negative act. They stress also another principle of this highest ceremony of all: There may not be so much as one person in the vicinity that goes hungry. "We have already used about seventeen years' worth of rice," remarks Tjokorda Gede Dangin's third wife at one point. "We had eight tons of rice, and it was not two months before it was used up....We have to give food!" Embraced in this spirit, the work of various preparations is carried out in the suci every day from sunrise to sundown. Anything to be used in the maligya ritual has to pass through here to be purified.

"Payadnyan."

As must be for death rites, the second ritual space is constructed at a separate location, specifically and exclusively for this ceremony. Where the suci is the area in which all items for the ceremonies of the maligya ritual are prepared and purified, the *payadnyan* is the center at which all of the ceremonial activities are performed, the site where the ancestors, hierarchically arranged, will undergo the major processes toward deification.

The best selection for this is an open space, in the irrigated rice or other fields, for example, as is done for the Sidemen Maligya. Such agricultural land is considered purer than ground used for and defiled by human habitation, more fertile for the regeneration of ancestral souls. To select a good site is considered to "bring more honor to those for whom the ceremony is being undertaken; the ancestors will feel more comfortable" (Dewa Ayu Alit).[12] In return, it is considered desirable for the ground, too, to be used for this kind of a ceremony, not only for the benefits of a fallow, but it is said also to absorb special power in the process. It is said that it is good for it to be trampled by all the people who will attend and that it will be rendered more fertile. In the case of the Sidemen Maligya, furthermore, the site selected was located north of the village, toward Mount Agung and in the opposite direction from the noble house of the burial and cremation

---

12. The spinster sister tells various stories about the consequences of inappropriate site selections and stresses that it just is not prudent to initiate a ritual work with everyone already angry and "ready to take up the keris."

grounds.[13] Generally, once an appropriate site has been selected, an offering has to be made to ask permission before the ground can be laid fallow and construction can begin according to the maligya *lontar* (palm leaf manuscript).

The ritual site for the Sidemen Maligya is an impressive configuration of bamboo structures, rising with the speed of some of the bungalow complexes that continue to mushroom up on Bali, not unlike the one it looks down upon in the valley below, the one from which international high society guests later will ascend for one of the final phases of the maligya ritual. The payadnyan, of course, is not really modeled on bungalows, but rather replicates the open enclosures of Balinese temple structures.

Symbolic Explication of the Payadnyan (figure 4)

It is said that the payadnyan as a whole represents Mount Kalaisa, the place of Siwa's meditation or where he at unoccupied times rides about on his mount, the white bull Nandini. It is also a symbolic representation of the tripartite Balinese universe, with upper, middle, and lower worlds, for Deities, humans, and demons, respectively. The tallest structure of the compound is a tower (*Sanggar Tawang*) in its northeastern kaja corner, where it sits like a peak in the skyline company of Mounts Agung and a couple of smaller peaks to the east. This tower extending toward the sky is described as a "lotus seat" (*padmasana* or *padma linggah*), or place of worship of Siwa. Aside from the imposing height of the tower, the most prominent presence on the payadnyan site is the *Balai Bukur*. On it are five cremation towers (*bade*) where the ancestors referred to as deities (*betara*) will rest: Toward the north is one for the priests' souls (*surya bagawanta*), the effigies from Griya Ulah (*betara lingga*). This, as is the tower for Siwa, is a "lotus seat" (padma, the form of cremation tower used for Brahmana). To the south of this are two tiered towers for the ancestral souls (*betara dewata*), each of nine steps, a number which indicates that in this regard the noble house is not making the highest claim to royal status, which would have meant venturing a tower of eleven steps. Immediately to the south of the cremation tower platform is an adjacent lower platform with a tower for the souls of the followers of the Jero Gede Sidemen (*pengiring*). There are two more towers, one for male and one for female deities that may arrive in the course of the ceremony.

---

13. See Hobart (1978) for an analysis of "the movement between sites in rites of passage." Adding the postcremation site adds a northern triangle to Hobart's diagram (1978:17).

Figure 4. Payadnyan Layout—Sidemen, Bali 1998

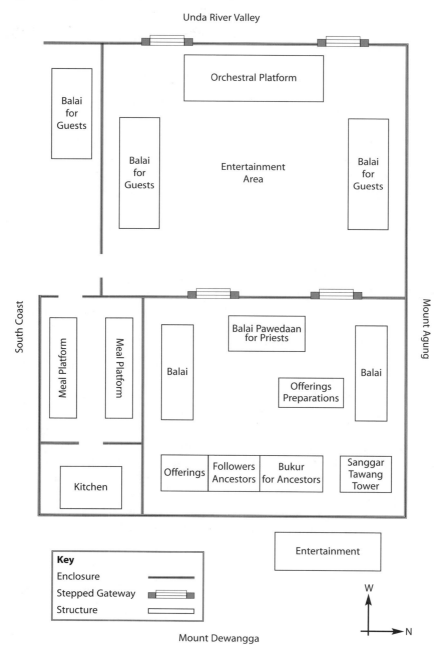

Unda River Valley

Orchestral Platform

Balai for Guests

Balai for Guests

Entertainment Area

Balai for Guests

South Coast

Mount Agung

Meal Platform

Meal Platform

Balai

Balai Pawedaan for Priests

Offerings Preparations

Balai

Kitchen

Offerings

Followers Ancestors

Bukur for Ancestors

Sanggar Tawang Tower

Entertainment

Key

Enclosure

Stepped Gateway

Structure

W

N

Mount Dewangga

Each of the towers is supported by two swans (or geese) and a turtle. Under the entire structure of the cremation tower platform, beneath its floor, are the *Badawang Nala* (turtle that holds up the world), the *Naga Basuki* and *Naga Anantaboga* (serpents that hold together the world), and the *Naga Banda* (the serpent for rajas and pedanda). The back and side walls flanking the cremation tower platform are lined with hangers loaded down with fine fabrics (*sangsongan*). Along the sidewalls, fish structures with small cups of drinks for the deities are suspended from the ceiling. In front there are several large offerings called *bayuan*. There is a *bayuan sanganan* with rice sweets and a *bayuan buah-buahan* with fruits. Finally, there is a *bayuan kue goreng*, a tall offering of fried rice cakes decorated with a white fabric and a pen drawing depicting Semara Ratih, the bisexual symbol of sexual union.[14] Presiding at the top of the two flights of stairs ascending to the cremation tower platform are a couple of puppets called the *piring*, a beautifully dressed man and woman.

Immediately across from the cremation tower platform, with ground in between to seat people for prayer and to lay out offerings on the ground for the demons, is the *Balai Pawedaan*, an also elevated and very large platform from where the priests pronounce their prayers facing the cremation tower platform. To the side of the cremation tower platform, on the ground toward the *Sanggar Tawang* tower, are two *barong* (mythical lion or dragonlike creatures) called *salaran*, also translatable as tax. These are constructed from products of harvest, one consisting of mainly fruits and the other of rices. Cokorda Raka describes the history of the *salaran*, which he also refers to as *barong sajen* (barong offerings), as having been a form of tribute paid by one's subjects (*upeti pajak*); but here it is the princes, on behalf of their ancestors for whom the maligya ritual is performed, who offer a "tax of the land" to God. "Now, since Balinese truly are artists," says Raka, "they do not just simply set out those items, but they create something from them, what we call *salaran*." Reminiscent of ancient Austronesian first fruits offerings by chiefs on behalf of the realm, all of the produce of the earth is shaped into a *barong* to be offered. On the *payadnyan* site are *penjor* too, a part of every major Balinese ceremony. These long bamboo poles are mounted to reach to the sky, their tips arching from the weight of the earthly fruits attached to them.[15]

---

14. Semara-Ratih is also the symbol of beauty and is able to guarantee success in all ventures, cure sickness and chase away evil (Eiseman 1990). And Semara is the term for the man's seminal fluid, named after the god of love (Covarrubias 1946:123). Semara-Ratih is highlighted in puberty ceremonies.

15. Brinkgreve writes that "the penjor is often said to be the symbol of the Gunung Agung.... The offerings on its little altar are directed to the gods of the holy mountain who

The progression of the maligya ritual picks up as the ritual spaces are filled with the months of activity and ceremony that constitute the ritual and bear witness to the status and power of the Jero Gede Sidemen to mobilize human, natural, and supernatural resources, and also to how ritual takes place in historical context.

The Progression of the Maligya Ritual: Ancestral Time and National Politics

When the pulse of work for this maligya ritual intensified in March 1998, preparations already had been underway for six years. By March, though the main series of ceremonies were not until late August, members of the family were returning home every weekend to join in, sometimes from as far away as the neighboring island of Lombok. On the day of the ground breaking of the ceremonial site, all the royalty of the house, men and women, young and old, had themselves been in the field moving boulders and hoeing up ground. The physical labor was followed by a communal meal (*magibung*) specific to eastern Bali, where people in groups eat from the same platter. Later there was a several-hour-long family meeting to assess the progress on everyone's assigned duties and to outline a list of materials still to be procured.

Acquisition and inventory lists included items such as eighteen thousand bamboo poles for the ceremonial enclosure, thirteen tons of rice for offerings and ordinary consumption, hundreds of pigs, approaching two thousand large ducks, thousands of smaller ducks, three thousand duck eggs, a sea turtle, wild boar meat from Lombok, buffalo and antelope, porcupine, a cooing dove, a bird of paradise, and thousands each of ten different kinds of coconut, fine fabrics, rubies and gold, and much, much more. In addition to such "produce lists," count also was taken as to which foreign countries would be represented—Japan, Germany, Denmark, France, the United States, Italy—for such exotic witnesses, too, serve a role in demonstrating the draw of the princes and ensuring the success of a ceremony (figure 5). Beyond this, there was a seemingly curious requirement for parts of a rhinoceros, a requirement that appears to date to a maligya ritual held in Klungkung in 1842. As interpreted by contemporary residents of Klungkung, "so beloved were [the rulers] by the gods, that a spirit had provided a rhinoceros, an animal only known

---

bestow life and prosperity. The fruits and jaja symbolize the natural products that sustain human existence. But other interpretations exist as well" (1996 [1992]:81–82).

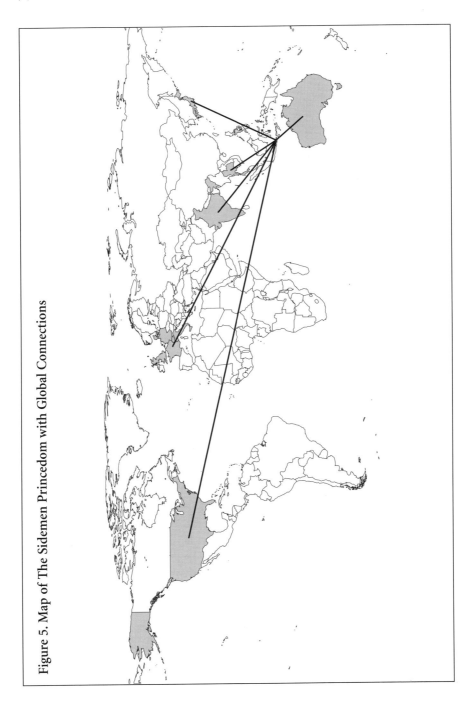

Figure 5. Map of The Sidemen Princedom with Global Connections

through legends, to be sacrificed for the occasion" (Wiener 1995:70–71). It is an interesting illustration of the cumulative innovation in ritual that by the time of the Raja's maligya ritual in Karangasem in 1937, rhinoceros meat had come to be considered a necessary ritual ingredient, such that it was pointed out regarding a particular offering that "no other meat is holy enough" (Mershon 1971:314). It is now recorded in lontars along with lists of other animals and birds that must be used in a maligya ritual. According to Cokorda Raka, four components are needed from the rhinoceros: some dried blood, some tusk, some tooth, and some dried meat. Apparently you just need scrapings from which to make an oil and a drink for the ancestors. "With the rhino," explains Raka, "you achieve heaven (sorga) forever after. It means that nothing is lacking." The tale also draws in anthropologists—for at the Karangasem maligya ritual, as a token of appreciation for the royal invitation, Gregory Bateson and Margaret Mead, who were working in Bali at the time and attended the ritual, contributed a tooth, a tusk, and some skin of a rhinoceros (see Mead and Bateson 1972 [1942] for some images from this maligya). Having heard this, I could not help but wonder if this was a precedent I should seek to follow and I asked in Sidemen if such items would be needed. The answer was affirmative, but in fact the items had already been secured. Thankfully the burden of acquiring them did not fall on me!

At this point, the family is informed, grandchildren included, that there henceforth will be ongoing work in the suci and at the payadnyan as well as regular family meetings. Anyone who lives away from Sidemen is to try to make it home at least on the weekends.

The rhythmic pounding of a wooden trough in the family temple marks the beginning and end every day of the "holy work." This is referred to as "sounding the trough" (menyuarakan ketungan, from ketung, "resonant sound") or, onomatopoeically as producing the oncang-oncangan sound of the ketungan asti—tung tang tung ting tang—"so that people will know that there is a maligya ritual in the makings here." The sounding of the trough accompanies the sound of wind whistling in long bamboo poles (sunari), which further is believed to summon fairies to descend from the abode of the gods to help in the preparation of offerings. A bamboo "seesaw" (kletug) tipping to measures of water, marks passage of time in the innermost holy area now alive with ritual preparations. Talking, smoking, eating, must happen outside the suci (the purified family temple). We gradually, in time and space set aside, move into "ancestral time."

Dreams abound, indicating that the ancestors have arrived.[16] Robed in white, they are mingling at the payadnyan, observing the preparations. Small offerings are always put out for them, but not until later will the ancestors be extravagantly banqueted. People also are contacting spirit mediums to ask the reactions of their ancestors to the ritual preparations. In all, the reports back are of pleasure and approval, and of encouragement for all, young and old, to continue the work, and to do so with honesty and integrity.

At the same time, the relationships of the living are becoming manifest, too, as people are mobilized for the work: the family, the priests, the people of surrounding neighborhood and irrigation associations (*banjar* and *subak*), and eventually village/lineage delegations from far and wide. Cokorda Raka explains:

> Now the issue settled in meetings is who to invite, how many pigs we will need, how much rice, how much money, and so forth. We calculate it together. Then we ask people from the villages for help. Who will receive guests, which guests, and so forth....We form a committee. Those that we involve are not just our family at the house, but also villagers, so it is a big committee. Because everyone has their duties, we can control the issues of feeding the guests and arranging the offerings. As the owners of this work, it is left to us to seek the materials, for example according to the requests of the priestess in charge of offerings. "I ask for so and so many tons of rice," she might say. "I ask so and so many coconuts." "I need lontar leaves." And we will find them.

A couple of months after the groundbreaking, May 11 brings the big purification for the family temple area. A woman of the house, whose menstrual period coincides with this ceremony, is out of ritual commission that day. Instead she is asked by her elderly aunt to undergo a special purification ceremony on a big garbage heap outside the gates of the noble house, by the street and under the eyes of the villagers (Pedersen 2002). Family members arriving from "overseas," that is, from outside of Bali including just across the strait from Java, where bad influences and demons abound and might have tagged along, also will have to undergo a rite to cleanse them and in this sense reaffirm their identity as Balinese.

In the period since the ground-opening ceremonies in early March, enormous changes have been taking place on the national political scene and it becomes evident that ancestral ritual time, for all of the prioritizing of it as such, also is very potent time and is not in practice so categorically kept separate and apart from national political time as it is in theory. People discuss the po-

---

16. As the Balinese were not christianized, they were not faced with the kind of dilemma that for example Hoskins reports in Sumba and McWilliam in West Timor, of not being able to summon their ancestors (cf Hoskins 1998:28, 94; McWilliam 2002).

litical events and are responding to them also in their dedication to the ritual, and players in the political events, too, are responding to the ritual.

In what follows, as the narrative of the maligya ritual progresses, to indicate the inter-relation of ritual and political events, a change in indent and font will designate where national, political occurrences interface with the ancestral ritual.

May 12, four students are shot to death at the Trisakti university campus in Java following a demonstration to protest Suharto's New Order regime. Their deaths trigger riots across the country, as do rising petrol prices and general economic crisis. May 21, in the context of the Asian financial crisis and growing political and economic discontent in Indonesia, President Suharto resigns and his vice-president, Habibie, takes his place in an interim government. Indonesia is in turmoil. The elaborate ancestral ceremony in Sidemen, about which people say that it comes only once a century, but also that every generation of rulers would strive to perform one, has come to embrace temporally the collapse of President Suharto's more than thirty-year regime and Indonesia's beginning transition from his New Order to *Era Reformasi* (the age of reform) and, ultimately, *Demokrasi* (democracy). As bodies stream through the Jero Gede Sidemen, it becomes increasingly obvious that people also participate in and contribute to the ceremony in exchange for leadership.

Tjokorda Gede Dangin, the head of the noble house, has been considered a successful liaison between the nation and his people, providing supporters for Golkar (the government party during Suharto's reign, of which all civil servants were required to be members) and, in return, resources for the area. He has, for example, helped complete an impressive restoration of an important regional temple, the kind of action which traditionally, as David Stuart-Fox points out, "was part of the ruler's dharma necessary to the maintenance and prosperity of the realm," and which, as with rulers past, "would have added to the respect and honour in which he was held by the populace at large" (1991:25). Dangin is seen as a natural leader, as someone who never met adversity, someone with ancestral and divine endorsement. He has followed an explicit policy of at once collaborating with the state and resisting domination (see chapter 5 for more on his role). After Suharto's fall, the lineage leaders who pass through to deal with ceremonial preparations also explicitly ask for guidance regarding the current situation. Dangin tells them to hold off, to not follow anybody or anything, including Golkar. Now he recommends instead that people concentrate on bringing in food and taking care of their families—while they wait to see how things turn out.

In the course of June, trips are made to various villages to procure supplies for the maligya ritual, such as a certain kind of cane from a village on the north coast, holy water from temples in nearby villages, and to check on the progress of towers under construction for the maligya ritual.

> At the noble house the flow of visitors continues. People bring baskets of uncooked rice (*beras*) and sweets for, it is said, "they do not want to come alone"—that is, empty handed—but have to come carrying something. It is called an *alat atur*, an excuse to talk. They do not go home empty handed, either, but with cooked rice (*nasi*) or skewered meat (*sate*), as a response (*sebagai balas aseh*). As they sit for coffee and sweets, the talk goes often to politics, to the situation in the country, the happenings, and to the lack of democracy and freedom of speech.

As the wheels have been set in motion and people have been streaming to the noble house in support of its ritual endeavor, the members of the Jero Gede Sidemen themselves express astonishment at the immense show of followers. By the end of June, people are coming from all over, including some from villages with whom the members of the family were not even aware they had connections, bringing to their attention supposed connections, and informing them that they wish to work on this ritual. [17] When concern is voiced about not being able to feed them all on the days of the major ceremonies, they insist that they will bring their own food. And so it is coordinated with surrounding neighborhood organizations that their facilities will be used to prepare the food. June 21, there is a big meeting at the Jero Gede Sidemen to update various leaders from the village on the ritual plans and to outline their respective roles.

Work is by now in full progress, both at payadnyan where the towers are being decorated as well as in the family temple, the suci, where offerings are made and purified. Preparations are underway for a *matur piuning* ceremony for June 25, a phase of the ceremony which involves setting out from Sidemen in convoys of vehicles to visit temples throughout the island, to give "notification" and ask for holy water and the blessings of all the constituent gods towards a smooth execution of the maligya ritual.

---

17. Note also Bateson's 1937 article (Bateson 1970b) on how interlocal ties can be created opportunistically. In the process of a temple restoration project, new connections between villages are given community expression through trance performances and new myth making.

Another political issue emerges. It turns out that a rumor has spread that the Jero Gede Sidemen is becoming the base for demonstrators against the Karangasem *Bupati*, the government head of the regency; in other words, a base for the Karangasem revolution. Since the May student demonstrations in Jakarta, there have been further demonstrations, calling to account New Order government officials for their corruption, collusion, and nepotism (KKN). Now a call comes in to the noble house from the Bupati himself. "He is afraid," reports Tjokorda Gede Dangin. "He is imagining truck loads of demonstrators descending upon the regional capital from Sidemen." Dangin, meanwhile, assures him that nothing of the sort is happening, and stresses as always that, in fact, it would be ritually impure to engage in this kind of activity in connection with the current state of holy work. At the same time, however, he talks intensely about the need for reformation and for a legislative assembly (*Dewan Perwakilan Rakyat*) that is not nepotistic, a legislative assembly of and for the people. He also acknowledges that he does support and urge on the young, "his children," who are students and activists.

Two days later, in the June 23 *Bali Post*, an article appears stating that the Bupati is offering to submit his administration to an investigation.

And another two days after that, June 25, people do indeed set out by the trucks-full, but rather than on revolutionary errand, they are on an island-wide mission for holy water. Delegations go to all of the major temples on the mountain-to-ocean axis, the *Sad Kahyangan* or six temples of the world: Ulu Watu, BatuKaru, Besakih, Goa Lawah, Lempuyang, and Ulun Danu Batur (see chapter 3). At the end of the day, when all have recongregated in Sidemen, bamboo containers of the procured water are brought into the family temple of the noble house via a ceremony at the Pura Dalem (village temple associated with the cremation grounds and dedicated to appeasing chthonic forces) followed by a procession to the noble house. Here another ceremony is held in the outer courtyard before the water is carried into the inner most area of the suci ritual space.

The regional capital remains safe, but thus already the local ritual calendar and nation-state politics are coming into play with one another. People are responding to the developments in the larger world as they approach the ritual, and they approach the ritual in terms of the political world.

July 4, a procession is held in pouring rain to a tree a couple of miles up the road from the Jero Gede Sidemen. It is one of the three kinds of palm trees from which palm wine (*tuak*) is made, but this tree is referred to as a virgin, a tree that has not yet been tapped. People muse, as they sit waiting under the towering tree protected from the rain by the thick foliage of the forest: "I wonder what this tree dreamt last night. I wonder if she has the slightest inkling that she is the chosen one," for it is believed that such a tree will be reincarnated as a human. July 9, there is a large ceremony to purify the now virtually completed payadnyan, just as formerly the suci has been purified. Here it also involves purification of the cremation tower platform and of the earth, including an extensive array of offerings for the demons. July 14 brings a ceremony to collect leaves from the banyan tree in the suci, as well as to milk a white cow, a *lembu*, on hire for ceremonial occasions from a place farther up Mount Agung. The lembu does not comply easily at this ceremony, which after the milking requires that it urinate and defecate. Crowds surround it, waiting with an energy people later describe as having been enormous. The eventual results are strained and diluted one hundred and eighteen times to be ritually ingested along with the milk by each member of the family. "It was good," people explain later, with the sense of having consumed something purifying.[18]

We have finally neared the culminating sequences of rituals. August 16 brings more procession, now to and around the payadnyan. This is the first of a series of ceremonial "spinnings" linked to the way ritual, as described in Balinese texts, " 'spins' the world by setting events and forces in motion" in order to change the state of things (Vickers 1991:103). Cokorda Sawitri explains:

> We go around three times.... The lembu is at the very front, followed by someone wielding a whip bound with three types of material, copper, gold, and silver. That is *seridatu*, a symbol of *trimurti* (the oneness of the three Hindu gods, Brahma, Vishnu, and Siwa)....It is followed by farming equipment, a smith's equipment, tools produced by a smith, such as a knife, weaving equipment, and so forth. Every kind of work has to be represented, including modern technological equipment...because this is when Siwa begins to work. After going around three times, Siwa meditates....Later there is a mantra for Siwa to wake up all of my ancestors, so that they are awakened.

---

18. Both the bull and the cow are associated with Siwa and there is sometimes an association between semen and milk, and between all of it and fertility. Cf. also Dumont regarding purification and the five products of the cow (1980:51).

As reflected in dreams and overall awareness, the presence of the ancestors has intensified as time has progressed. As the culminating series of rites of the maligya ritual approaches, they are materialized in *puspa*, symbolic representations that are assembled in the elevated Balai Pawedaan. Though women are not prohibited from doing it, this activity is usually carried out by male descendants, including in this case a number of royalty from Klungkung, Bali's foremost kingdom, who acknowledge kinship with the Sidemen noble house. These are descendants of the members of the palace who survived the 1908 puputan at Klungkung. Rather than having lost face because they escaped, their survival, however it came about, may be taken to indicate their superiority over the line that died out (cf. Wiener 1995:337). To construct the representations of the ancestors, also priests are on hand to help. Meanwhile, the same process is going on in a lower pavilion for the production of effigies for the low caste "follower" souls.

The effigies consist of a skeleton of bamboo decorated with banyan leaves, sandalwood, flowers, white cloth, gems, and gold, and they bear a nametag of an inscribed palm leaf. They reflect caste standing, not only in their place of construction, but also in some respects of their construction. Although they appear the same, there is, for instance, a difference in the number of leaves used. For the leading souls of the priests (*Betara Lingga*), there are 108 pieces, while those of the noble house must use fewer, sixty-six, and the followers (*pengiring*) only may use thirty-three leaves. Furthermore, the *Betara Lingga* can use gold, as can those of the noble house, while the followers may not. They use tin coating (*perada*) or gold leaf. Also, the priests and princes may use good quality jewels, while others may use gems of lesser grades only. This is the case if they *ngiring* (follow) at a high caste ceremony. If, on the other hand, they hold their own (lower caste) postcremation, they can do what they want, except with regard to the banyan leaves, of which they must adhere to the prescribed quantities.[19]

A follower of the house explains the hierarchical marking:

> Each *puspa lingga* represents one person undergoing the ceremony. Those made in the *balai* up above and those made here all represent persons undergoing the ceremony. However, those being made here

---

19. One more detail is mentioned regarding the leaves: for men they are reversed, back side up. Pedanda Istri, the priestess, adds that if the leaf falls, they determine whether they are constructing a puspa lingga for a woman or a man, according to the side on which it falls. See McGowan for a detailed description of puspa lingga, emphasizing the symbolic union herein of male and female (1996:158–161).

are the followers (*pengiring*). These lower ones are those that earlier were palace servants or slaves (*parkan*). And those up there are those that are of highest standing…those that are from the extended family of the Cokorda, his ancestors who have passed away, some of them hundreds of years ago, but who have not yet had the ceremony performed for them [Nyoman]

He concludes that, "Now, of course, in this ceremony the ancestors of Tjokorda Gede Dangin and his family have to be accompanied by their life's entourage." That same evening, after all of the puspa lingga have been personalized with name tags, they are carried by their descendants in the rituals. First they are carried out of the payadnyan, up the road to the family temple of the Jero Gede Sidemen, where they are to be lodged until the culminating series of ceremonies. Late into the night people sit around talking of their feelings when they were handed the symbolic representations of their ancestors. They talk of having felt overwhelmed with emotion, of having teared up.

One woman relates that she had felt as though she might trance, but had called herself to her senses, helped by her sister-in-law who had put her hand on her to calm her. This woman had been carrying the representation of her grandfather's grandfather, Kompiang Gelgel. He constructed some of the first roads in this valley, she pointed out, participating in the work himself, amidst the slaves and subjects. One of the daughters of the head of the house, a modern woman married to a banker and living in Denpasar, also talks about the ancestor she carried, this one even older. And we hear that the wife of a prince of the royal house of Amlapura, Karangasem, went into trance on the priestly platform (the *Balai Pawedaan* where the *puspa lingga* were being made). She was entered by a woman from Sidemen, who, like herself, had married into the palace in Amlapura. In Bali, unless a woman's marriage follows the preferred practice of descent group endogamy, she must leave her own descent group to join that of her husband, which is why her subsequent ceremonies take place with her husband's family. This woman complained, through the living woman, that no one prayed for her or brought her offerings any more, that her family had left her. Someone asks if she had not been included in the 1985 maligya ritual of one of the factions of the palace in Amlapura. Apparently not, people concur. Cokorda Raka explains that the woman in question was the mother-in-law of the trancing woman and that she originally was from Raka's family:

She also wanted to be included in having the maligya ritual performed for her, but because she became a wife of the raja of Amlapura, the people at my house would not dare do that. Because she is already a person of the palace, we cannot do the maligya ritual for her. But she wished for it anyway. We are really sorry that we cannot do it.

The woman who had tranced is, as said, married out of the family and therefore did not carry any of the ancestral representations herself. Yet after the puspa lingga were brought into the family temple in the evening, she explained—her eyes tearing—how all of this is with such deep feeling. Many people stayed up until around three in the morning in order, as they expressed, to continue "evaluation" of all of the day's events.

At this point of intensified ancestral time, ancestral and national time deliberately are brought to intersect. Into what in response to prior intersections has explicitly been treated as a vacuum in politics, is summoned presidential candidate, Megawati Sukarnoputri. Maligya ritual invitations were sent to President Habibie as well as to Megawati, the daughter of Indonesia's first President, Sukarno. As it turns out, Megawati, whose paternal grandmother was Balinese, but who has no specific kinship ties to the Sidemen house, has taken them up on their invitation.

There is by now a constant flow of visitors, bringing presents, sitting for coffee and sweets, and being shown around. In context of the fact that Megawati's daughter-in-law already has arrived to prepare for Megawati's visit, there is much talk of the current political situation.

August 17. This morning women start streaming into the suci, past the pavilion where members and visitors of the noble house are having morning coffee and porridge. Members of the family observe how overwhelming it is for them to see this, the outpouring of help. They come from local kin-groups, neighborhood and irrigation associations, and from kin-groups in thirteen different villages, as counted by one young member of the house as they go by. Even he, a son who has married a foreign woman and lives abroad, recognizes these groups. As a flow of men arrive, he points out, "Oh, these are followers" from such and such a village.

August 18. The pair of priestly effigies, Betara Lingga, is constructed by the Brahmana in the family temple of the priestly compound of Griya Ulah, uphill from the *payadnyan*. The ceremonial ground meanwhile is filled with animals and fowl of every sort, bound and panting in the heat, as preparations are completed for another circumambulation of the compound, this one counter clockwise (*mepepadan*) to purify the beasts before their sacrifice.

The evening of August 18, people wait hours for Megawati to arrive from her bungalow just up the road. She apparently had been on her way out the door when something had grabbed her, to let her know that it was not yet the right time for her to go, that the ancestors of the Jero Gede Sidemen were not yet ready for her arrival. So she waited, put on hold by the ancestors.

By the time she shows up, it is dark. A villager-guard who followed her entourage to the noble house later describes that "when they got there, outside of the gate [candi] to the noble house, many were still lined up waiting for her." "Wah," he exclaims, it was a very gay time when her arrival was announced. There were many people there when Mega came."

She comes quietly into the noble house's courtyard, and is taken to the family temple's inner-most purified area. The suci has been opened for this occasion with special mantras. All is quiet and very peaceful. Everyone prays together.

After prayer, the head of the house and the priestly brother (a non-Brahmana priest) of the Sidemen house carry the family keris from its shrine. The keris is extended to Megawati who takes it and examines it—whereupon she declares that she in fact has had a dream of precisely this keris!

Later Tjokorda Gede Dangin elaborates what happened when he brought out the keris for Megawati to see: "I brought it out. 'Oh, this is the keris I saw,' [said Megawati]. She had already seen this keris, before she ever came here, before she came to Sidemen, when she was still in Jakarta. She said, 'I have seen this before,' like that. She had seen that keris." Dangin clarifies further that her vision was not a dream: "She saw it like that, as in a void, in the sky, [he says gesturing in the space above his face]. It was the sculptured handle that she saw, of gold with inlaid jewels.... 'Oh, this is what I saw;' that is what she said."

A family heirloom, the keris is symbolic of the house and its connection to powerful ancestors, but, more than that, it is the hierarchical superior of the house, and is perceived as an agent in its own right. It is power incarnate and the vehicle also for transmitting power. The story of this particular keris, as already introduced, is that it was handed down directly from Majapahit, the fourteenth-century Javanese Empire, a gift from the Emperor himself. During the 1908 "finishing,"

mass sacrifice or massacre (puputan) at the hand of the Dutch, the Ka-
pakisan line in Klungkung lost the keris of kingship that had stayed
with their forefather, so that apparently this is the only keris remain-
ing in Bali providing a link of legitimation directly to Majapahit.

Into the night, after Megawati has departed, people sit around watching video footage from the event. Tjokorda Gede Dangin talks about
how strong Megawati is, about how she is not afraid of anything. He
specifies how impressed she had been with the showing of people at
the maligya ritual and how, on the whole, she wants to be close to
the people. She has expressed a desire to go to the local market in
the morning. Cokorda Raka tells that she was here, with her father,
for the 1963 Eka Dasa Rudra ceremony at Besakih, probably "the
largest ceremony known in Balinese Hinduism" (Stuart-Fox 1991:12).
He also talks of how important it is for Bali that she is attending this
maligya ritual, a purification ceremony so big that it may help bring
a strong balance in her and in the country, in Indonesia.

Megawati is staying in Sidemen in the days leading up to a meeting
of her splinter group from the Indonesian Democratic Party, scheduled
to be held in Bali the upcoming week. In 1996, a government and
military backed faction of the Democratic Party (PDI) ousted her from
its leadership, a manipulation that she responded to by forming the
PDI-P, the Indonesian Democratic Party of Struggle, but also challenged through court battle. The next day, while she participates in
the maligya ritual in Sidemen, the Indonesian Supreme Court is scheduled to determine the outcome of her case.

August 19 is considered the peak of the ceremony *(puncak)*. Compared to the
course of the preceding series of ceremonies, it is only now that any "bu-
reacratization" of ceremonies, as has been remarked upon especially by scholars in Java, becomes evident (cf. Brenner 1998). Particularly striking is the hip
M.C. at the microphone, a personality from Denpasar, who has come to the
Jero Gede Sidemen to offer his services. At the noble house they insist that no
one knew him previously. He has come with grand ideas that Megawati should
have to go through a series of purification ceremonies to cleanse her of the
bad luck of her family. The suggested purifications do not happen; but though
he is considered a little odd, his offer to contribute is embraced. And so he
presides on the day of the peak of the maligya ritual, single-handedly changing the tenor of the ceremonies by his showmanship.

During all of this, various videographers are busy—a follower of the family at the priestly platform and the cremation tower platform getting footage of the holiest elements of this day, the anthropologist trying to do her assigned duty of taping for the house as well, and a French cameraman with plans of a more poetic film trying to avoid images of foreigners, including an anthropologist in the frame. Meanwhile, quite spectacular foreigners are popping up everywhere. At a new age bungalow-style hotel or retreat in the valley below, a high society international wedding has been held, bringing guests from around the world. On this day, it is part of the wedding festivities to attend the maligya ritual, and so they mingle in. Some are clad in flowing white, a sikh wears a turban, a member of Indian nobility is in a sari, and yet others feature tailored summer dresses with sarongs tied around their waists.

Throughout these days of the main series of rites, there has been ongoing entertainment of every sort at the payadnyan, directed at both the visible and invisible audiences, such as spirits and deities. According to religious prescripts, certain sacred dances and puppetry, as well as masked and musical performances, must be included to complete a ceremony like the maligya ritual. Other performances are simply for worldly entertainment. There has been shadow puppetry, dancing, masked dance-theatre, gamelan playing, and lontar reading. By now all of these are going on together, separately, somewhere in or around the ceremonial enclosure.

It becomes time for all of the ancestors to join the festivities, later to be delivered. The pair of effigies constructed at the priestly house descends to the payadnyan site. It is they who will lead and pave the way to heaven for the other souls. Cokorda Sawitri describes vividly how "they will take off together and fly in orbit around the universe, looking for a path." In front of them is a white lembu, symbolizing Siwa, which also indicates that they are aiming for heaven. At the payadnyan they are joined by the rest of the effigies, and now everyone, led by the white lembu, walks in procession around the enclosure.

The procession ends as all of these symbolic representations are carried along the spread-out hide of the sacrificed buffalo that walked in procession just yesterday. The path along its body from tail to head, between its horns tipped with gold, leads the ancestors to the steps of the cremation tower platform. The buffalo is symbolic of the bridge to heaven, the participants explain, the *titi mahmah*, where *titi* means bridge, and *mahmah* "a kind of power, something like lava" (McGowan 1995). The ancestors must pass over it as part of the efforts to cleanse any bad karma they might have.

Once on the big cremation tower platform, the effigies are placed in the towers according to hierarchy. While all others sit below waiting to pray,

Megawati, her husband, and her daughter-in-law come to *payadnyan* and ascend the cremation tower platform, to which the keris also has been brought. Up here the ancestors are surrounded by the finest of fabrics and decorative offerings. Art Historian Kaja McGowan proposes a wonderful image of deities alighting in Balinese temples, "relaxing and refreshing themselves, pondering their reflections in pocket-sized mirrors, combing their hair with miniature combs, chewing on specially wrapped betel nut, and absorbing the essence of the offerings of food and flowers—all provided for their enjoyment" (1995:79–80). Such is now the ancestral activity at the cremation tower platform. The payadnyan area is teeming with energy.

On this day, the climaxing day of the maligya ritual, Megawati, after praying in front of the tall tower and talking with a number of the priests, goes to follow from her Sidemen bungalow as the Indonesian Supreme Court throws out her legal challenge to her ouster as head of the Democratic Party. Word circulates that she watched the verdict with composure, offering no reaction. At this point, she was planning a separate congress for her own faction of the party to be held in Bali in October and continued to urge the government to recognize her as the legitimate leader of the party.

Immediately following their conversation with Megawati and her departure, the priests are feasted through a *Resi Bojana* ceremony of thanksgiving. Priests from throughout the region have been invited for this peak day of the ceremony to include the ceremony in their honor and, not insignificantly, an encounter with Megawati. Lines of platters are prepared to be presented to them ceremoniously by the women of the noble house, who enter in gracious procession, some dancing, with the trays on their heads. Each woman stands behind a seated priest, each of whom already has received a pedestalled tray of food. Tjokorda Gede Dangin speaks, asking the forgiveness of the priests should anything be lacking, should there be any faults in the ceremony, should anyone in the family have any faults, and so forth. The priests say mantras over their food to ensure its purity and begin to eat, the women holding the gift trays on their heads still standing behind them.

The food provides a sampling from every category of food habitat, from the sea, the land, and the air. Tjokorda Gede Dangin and his older sisters sit watching, getting up to assist as needed, and the rest of us, mingling around, watch too. The scene bears some contrast to how the caste sensitivity that pertains to eating is ordinarily portrayed. Mark Hobart, for example, writes regarding the high caste prince, what usually also pertains to priests, that he "should not ideally be observed eating by persons of lower status," and that "there is commonly a high pavilion raised such that the food and participants are placed above the heads of all others, so that they may not only remain superior, but effectively invisible" (1979:426). The standard that priests eat with separate utensils on separate dishes and in separate locations is still maintained here, but there is nothing invisible about this meal, with priests and food on display.

Next the priests are presented with trays of gifts (*punia*). The idea is symbolically to give them a bit of everything they might need, to give them food and drink as well as items required "for getting around," such as an umbrella should it rain, a flashlight and batteries for the dark, a pair of sandals, cigarettes, matches, white cloth, fabrics, rice, and money. After all of the food and gifts have been presented, the priests respond with worshipping mantras "directed toward world harmony and toward the sources that provide us with food and drink, as well as thirst and hunger" (Cokorda Sawitri). This is similar to what the visiting deities are said to do when they have savored the offerings provided for their enjoyment—"these deities may then show their gratitude by unleashing cosmic energy (*sakti*) over the remaining offerings, as if into a bowl, the contents of which are brought home again to be consumed by the community of worshipers" (McGowan 1995:79–80). Some people sleep in the *payadnyan* at night, for there must always be someone there with the ancestors.

> Back at the Jero Gede Sidemen, there is continued talk late into the night of how fantastic it is to have accomplished this ceremony and how important it will be to write about it, so that grandchildren and their descendants can know. There still is much talk about Megawati and the steady stream of calls from journalists and the tactics to ward them off. And there is talk of the significance of this ceremony in a time with such "crisis of mind and faith." "This will give strength," the members of the noble house say: "The people need something and someone to believe in; they need a strong anchor."

August 21. The Jero Gede Sidemen is awake early with people drinking coffee and talking sleepily. Tjokorda Gede Dangin's third wife returns from the market with porridges and sweets for the morning coffee and for the visitors to come. She starts in on the food preparation for the day. Cokorda Raka's wife is sweeping the courtyard. Some people are asleep still on the household platforms. Dangin's eldest daughter walks by to go bathe. Those who spent the night at payadnyan return.

Down at payadnyan the area has been swept. One man lights incense. Now, at around eight o'clock in the morning, the place is nearly empty. The tall penjor poles with rice hanging along their whole length attract birds and birdsong. There is a noticeable peace over the cremation tower platform hosting the ancestral effigies, where the pair of puppets presides. Today a smaller ceremony is to be carried out, and there will be prayer as well as preparation for the night when the nametags of the effigies are to be burned. But this will not happen until midnight, after a night of entertainment. Tomorrow there will be a procession of trucks to take them to the ocean.

There has been an increasingly strong odor of rotting meat and rice in the payadnyan area. It is especially strong in the cremation tower platform. But fresh offerings are brought down for today's prayer. Afterwards, the women from the house eat ritual leftovers (*layuban*), the food components of the offerings, with great relish. Cokorda Sawitri turns to me:

> We may just eat a morsel, but this is for a kind of feeling of respect.... We also believe that this is to purify flaws and misfortunes (*malah*) and to make them disappear. It helps reestablish introspection. Now those who have put on this ritual work must be introspective. [And the ancestors] have to burn together; they begin from zero. The anticlimax is now. They are going to start to live like us [*hidup wajar*], all day long. This day is the beginning of a new introspection, to think about being reborn. They have already awakened. Now the burning will dissolve them, and then they begin; as if they are pregnant, they get food cravings [*nidam dia makan*], to be born again.

In the middle of the night, there is a rite, again attended by members of the Klungkung palace, of preparing and sharing a kind of porridge to feed the ancestors before they head off for reincarnation: "The ancestors are given porridge. We also participate in eating that porridge. There is a mantra to wake them up; wake up! We are ready to depart before entering that orbit of rays... and then we eat the porridge" (Sawitri). The nametags are burned and the ashes are prepared in coconuts, along with the gold faces from the effigies, all to be thrown in the ocean on the morrow.

August 22. On this day the ashes of the effigies are taken to the North Coast in as many coconut shells as there are souls and burned effigies. The Jero Gede has chartered local boats to carry the coconuts out to sea, an occasion also for the living to enjoy boat rides. And thus, as with the cremation, a ritual of reanimation and redisintegration has been performed. The souls are off to the heavens to await reincarnation.

From this day, everything seems spent; it feels as if the ceremony is over. But by August 25 there is lively activity once again. Outside the kitchen, women are making trays of food for the various local priests who have participated these past months. The trays will be carried to the griya, the priestly compound. It is startling, after all of these months, to see the suci open again.

And the payadnyan is looking ramshackle. People are crowding around on the cremation tower platform, which is almost empty of ceremonial paraphernalia, though the puppets, symbolically deactivated on the night of August 21, and towers are still there. People continue to sleep there. There have not been ceremonies or presiding priests since the day of going to the ocean, but today there is a ceremony to officially close the ceremonial enclosure. In September a delegation will go to temples on an ocean-to-mountain axis, to perform rites of thanks for the maligya ritual. More rites follow as the maligya ritual itself is ceremonialized as a human, with a three-month and a six-month ceremony. There is also to be an *ngenteg lingga*, wherein the shrines of the family temple, the *pelinggih-pelinggih*, are opened at their base to be filled with an offering called *pedagingan*. This is done "so the ancestors or the deities will be stable there, for they can only reside there with that *pedagingan*" (Raka; see McGowan 1996:153ff. for related details). As for another maligya ritual, this may not happen again for several generations. The spinster sister expresses that it may be one hundred years before there is another maligya ritual, for "this work, this is the biggest," she says. Cokorda Raka, on the other hand admits that it is the wish of any generation to be able to perform such a grand ritual. As Cokorda Sawitri sees it, "the responsibility for that is maybe that of my nephew, niece, or my grandchild. They will feel they need [a maligya ritual] again, so that the level is raised again. That is how it happens." The cycles keep moving, the world keeps turning, and to keep your level up, you must keep effecting the necessary rituals and transitions.

Climax in Ritual, a Princedom, and the World

In advocating a practice over a systems approach to social analysis, Bourdieu has argued that "for the analyst, time no longer counts: not only because…arriving post festum, he cannot be in any uncertainty as to what may happen, but also because he has the time to totalize, i.e., to overcome the effects of time" (1977:9). Of course, even the totalizing analyst does not necessarily "arrive after the fact," and participants totalize too; in fact, it is an inherent aspect of the practice of the ritual to take stock and "evaluate" as events progress. Just as separate ritual spaces were created, so people consciously entered into ritual time about which they stressed repeatedly that it is time set apart from "ordinary" and "political time." This time, just as is the case with the *suci* space, is sacred, and it would not be *suci* (pure) to engage in political activity while preparing the maligya ritual. At the same time, in their evaluations of the ritual, participants also related the two kinds of time and events to each other. It is in the context of the historical-political developments that the way in which the ritual played out is to be understood. In Bali, as Vickers said, "things do not just 'happen'" (1990:173), but as reflected also in the interlocking cycles of Balinese calendars (Lansing 1995), result from conjunctions of various influences, natural and supernatural. In the course of the ritual, participants interpreted the convergences of ancestral ritual and national time and events, a connection between the ritual and the wider world.

But Bourdieu is also concerned, and rightly so, to restore the element of unpredictability to practice that we otherwise forget in our reification of events that have already transpired. As he points out, "the shift from the highest probability to absolute certainty is a qualitative leap out of proportion" (1977:9). Indeed, by setting out to stage as involved of a ritual as the maligya ritual, there is always, in a sense, a gamble being effected. The performers of the ritual knew that they could not take it for granted that things would turn out in any given way. Even as the preparations for the Sidemen Maligya intensified and entered their final phases, no one knew what would come to pass during the culminating days of the ceremony. Though the ceremony does follow a general structure, no one can be sure exactly what will transpire, let alone when. So many forces are set in motion that it is beyond that kind of control.

Recent scholars of ritual are indeed emphasizing elements of conflict and risk as inherent to much ritual, too easily glossed over by earlier theories of ritual that gave almost exclusive attention to ritual's formulaic reproduction and integrative function. The risks and uncertainty in connection with Balinese ritual appear long since to have been recognized by indigenous observers themselves.[20] In a poem about the 1842 Klungkung maligya ritual, points out Schulte Nordholt, "The writer explicitly compared the ritual with warfare, since on both occasions the risks were high and the outcome insecure. Just like warfare the ritual opened an arena in which chaos might prevail" (1991:10; cf. also Vickers 1991). As it turned out in Sidemen, everything succeeded in grand style and beyond expectation, with every sign that this endeavor was approved of by the deities. The event drew unexpected numbers of followers, visitors from far and wide, including presidential candidate Megawati Sukarnoputri, and it resulted in a remarkable legitimating interaction between her and the heirloom keris. It was a pageant indeed, an elaborate public performance of the princedom in interaction with local and national developments.

20. For a recent analysis of risk as a "prominent feature" of Balinese rituals, see Howe 2000.

Two years after the maligya ritual, everyone contacted—be it at the noble house, at the priestly house, or in the surrounding villages—say that the procession when the ancestors descended, at literally the peak or summit (*puncak*) of the ceremony, stands out to them in a way that can only be glossed as climax, that is, "the point of greatest intensity in any series or progression of events, culmination" (*The American Heritage Dictionary*). About "the heart of the ceremony," however, Geertz, who as we saw at the opening of this chapter once argued that Balinese social life and ritual lack climax, also wrote that this stage,

> [with] the obeisance to the gods come down onto their altars, is deliberately muted to the point where it sometimes seems almost an afterthought, a glancing, hesitant confrontation of anonymous persons brought physically very close and kept socially very distant. It is all welcoming and bidding farewell, foretaste and aftertaste, with but the most ceremonially buffered, ritually insulated sort of actual encounter with the sacred presences themselves. [1973a:403]

"It amounts to the fact," Geertz has explained, "that social activities do not build, or are not permitted to build, toward definitive consummations" (1973a:403). And yet as we have heard, people spoke of very immediate encounters in the form of trance and emotional connections as they carried the symbolic representations of their ancestors. Almost reflecting Geertz's metaphor of "definitive consummation," Cokorda Sawitri spoke of the climax of the ritual as a kind of conception for the ancestors, and, conversely, she referred to it as a kind of "anti-climax" when they, following conception, were awaiting rebirth. To a group of women this latter was expressed in food cravings, in which Sawitri herself partook as she ate the ritual leftovers.

What to outside observers may be just an incredible bustle contains something different to Balinese participants; and a muting—as happens quite literally in some Balinese rituals when the priests' bells stop ringing at the moment when the deities alight—can also be experienced as intensification. The tangibility of the encounter, as when ancestral presence is felt through the shaking of the keris or in trances and dreams, is evident in the reminiscences of a member of the priestly house: "We felt it, the deities.... We could feel that we already were in their presence, the ancestors, those who were being maligya'ed. It was as if they came on that day...at the time of the *puncak karya* (the peak of the ritual work). All of our concentration and thoughts already were there. There was no other goal or focus but that" (Ida Bagus Ketut Dangin). Cokorda Raka adds: "This is also why all of my family cried....Almost my entire family cried, not because of sadness, but because they were overwhelmed with emotion."

Most visitors to rituals arrive only at their very peak, at or near the climax, in which case they will not experience it as such. But not only does the ritual have climax, the very ritual itself is a climax on the scale of lives, both personal and political. The Sidemen Maligya became a historical climax for the power of the princedom in a time full of motion. Through its interface with events related to changes at the level of the nation-state, the maligya ritual boosted the noble house's claims for expanded symbolic and political powers, such that even in the approach to the twenty-first century, ritual was revealed as an important arena for the display and constitution of royal legitimacy.[21]

The postcremation ceremony always has had great significance for the status of living Balinese rulers, for only after finally releasing the soul of their predecessor can they fully assume succession themselves. Thus, Schulte Nordholt points out that Agung Putra of Mengwi,

> bent on restoration of eroded dynastic authority and out to establish his own position as the new king, organized two great royal rituals. The first was the abhiseka ratu, his own inaugural ceremony. The second was related to this: the ngluer [ngeluwer] ritual for the soul of his father, Agung Ngurah Made Agung, who had died in 1829. [1996a:113–114] [Note that the ngeluwer ritual actually is a step up from the maligya ritual; see the beginning of this chapter.]

As Schulte Nordholt continues, "the burning of the body and the freeing of the soul were not only salutary for the deceased, but were of great significance for his successor as well. The heir could legitimate himself as rightful new king only if every vestige of a bond between the dead king and the earth was meticulously severed" (1996a:114). Later, when Agung Putra had been murdered and his wife was preparing to succeed him in dual leadership with his cousin, "much ceremony accompanied the cremation of the murdered king," for "it was only after he had truly left the earth that his successors might truly assume power" (1996a:119). In the case of the last raja of Karangasem, it was in preparation for his installation as raja by the Dutch in 1938, that he staged a maligya ritual in 1937. He needed to complete his ancestral ritual duties and sever the earthly ties of his predecessor in order to clear the way for his own assumption of kingship (Schaareman 1986:33; Schulte Nordholt

---

21. By contrast to a tendency observed in other parts of Bali (cf. Picard's publications), there was no indication in Sidemen that this ritual was shaped for tourism. Based on my observations, I would venture to say that the majority of Balinese rituals still are not conducted with any degree of tourism in mind at all, although the money available nowadays for ritual purposes is linked in various ways to a tourist economy.

1996a:310). So there is precedent in regard to kingship with this category of ceremony, to assert a renewed and elevated status.

In Sidemen it was also as has been described for nineteenth-century Bali:

> One important effect of the rituals was that contact between the royal centre and the...people was re-established. The rituals served as a public announcement of a new leadership, confirmed by the Dewa Agung [paramount lord of Klungkung] and the gods. Presumably thousands of people witnessed them, so that the restoration of the hierarchy was proclaimed to all of Bali. [Schulte Nordholt 1996a:119]

It was ultimately the case in Sidemen, too, as has been pointed out for earlier maligya rituals, that the noble house's maligya ritual was a form of state ritual and that the purification and deification of royal ancestral souls was linked to world harmony (cf. Vickers 1990:174–175).

But, again, the endeavor also was embroiled in risk, for it had not been a given that the maligya ritual would turn out as it did: The princes from the beginning had concern that it might not work, and they registered amazement at just how many followers did come together to fulfill services to them. All of this is in keeping with notions of Balinese kingdoms and princedoms as having been fluid. Of course, in the present day, what remain of negara relationships are if anything more fluid and unpredictable than ever.

The chapters to follow look more closely at the hierarchy that was formed in Sidemen—Of whom does it consist and why do people participate? What are the princedom's sources of power? And what characterizes the relationships between rulers and followers? We shall see in the end that the maligya, indeed, served not only to deify the ancestral souls and as a rite of status intensification for the princes, but that the ritual is about facilitating harmony and ensuring empowerment in the wider world: Through its culminations of events, the Sidemen Maligya of 1998 was considered a ceremony of world renewal for all.

Photo Plates

The Sidemen Maligya

The photographs marked (KS) were taken by Kent Swanson. All other photographs were taken by Lene Pedersen.

1. Dawn view toward Mt. Agung over a part of the Sidemen Princedom.

2. The entrance to the middle courtyard of the Jero Gede Sidemen.

3. View up a side street of the village of Sidemen.

4. Payadnyan ritual site: constructing the serpent that
holds together the world.

5. Payadnyan ritual site: looking up at the ancestral platform, *Balai Bukur*, along which winds the body of the serpent.

6. Payadnyan ritual site: offering with fried rice cakes and Semara Ratih, the bisexual symbol of sexual union.

7. Payadnyan ritual site: a priest on the priestly platform, *Balai Pawedaan*, looking across to the ancestral platform.

8. Pounding of wooden trough to mark the beginning of daily ritual work.

9. People are mobilized to participate in the maligya ritual.

10. Holy water is collected from around Bali and
brought to the Jero Gede Sidemen.

11. Items to be used in the maligya ritual are activated in
processions around the payadnyan ritual site.

12. Ancestral effigies are constructed on the priestly platform, *Balai Pawedaan.*

13. Clipping from Bali Post of truckloads of soldiers:
"Suharto has to step down" (May 1998)

14. Clipping from Bali Post of Suharto:
"I'm done being president" (May 1998)

15. Clipping from Bali Post of Megawati
(with background image of Sukarno) (May 1998)

16. After prayer in the high caste family temple Megawati inspects
the keris (with her husband and daughter-in-law).

17. Priestly effigies are constructed at the priests' compound
north of the ritual site.

18. Procession with effigies of ancestors to transport them to the ancestral platform (Cokorda Raka is in the foreground; Sawitri two positions behind him).

19. Buffalo "bridge to heaven," en route with the effigies to the ancestral platform.

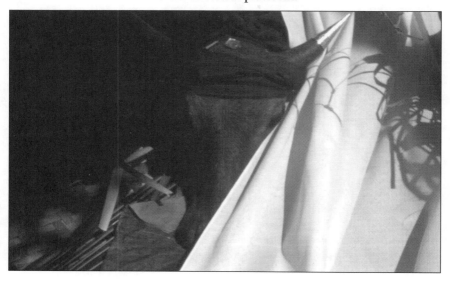

20. Two towers on the ancestral platform, with effigies at their
base and offerings in front.

21. Effigies at base of tower on ancestral platform.

22. Young girls dance at ceremony.

23. A follower of the Jero Gede Sidemen is one of the
videographers of the maligya ritual.

24. Megawati and entourage visit the ancestral platform,
where the keris has been placed too.

25. Tjokorda Gede Dangin on the steps to the ancestral platform.

26. Tjokorda Gede Dangin presides at the thanksgiving for priests.

27. Women of the noble house serve and wait on the priests.

28. Women of the noble house at the end of a day of ceremony.

29. The reassembled effigies are taken to a beach on the
north shore of Bali. (KS)

30. Boats take the effigies to sea. (KS)

31. Within a year after the maligya ritual a gathering platform
on the street above the payadnyan ritual site is painted
with the colors and emblems of Megawati's party.

32. The fields where the payadnyan ritual site was located are brought under the plow again. Some of the remaining structures from the ritual are still visible in the background.

33. Fields in the Sidemen area under preparation for new growth of rice.

CHAPTER THREE

MOBILIZING THE STRUCTURES OF A PRINCEDOM

Even as the maligya ritual was taking shape, prior to any of the events of a more spectacular nature, the family of the Jero Gede Sidemen remarked at how well things were proceeding and at how many people were materializing to help them. It was the not altogether foreseeable practice of the grand-scale ritual at the time of a not very foreseeable future for the Indonesian state that provided an opportunity for the princedom to come into being, for everyone to see, passing through one place, who makes up this realm and what kinds of powers this noble house might summon. In the past, although the head of the Jero Gede Sidemen was lord or prince to the raja ("king") of the larger region of Karangasem, he also, himself, was a raja in his own realm. To this day, many people from the Sidemen area will refer outright to Tjokorda Gede Dangin, or the noble house, as their raja, and also frequently say palace (*puri*) instead of noble house (*Jero Gede*). Indeed, the model according to which the princedom came together is classic, evoking in the smaller realm all of the sources of power long held to be central to Balinese kingship. To this day, the noble house operates by the claims to legitimacy of any raja, including claims to royal descent and to one of the most powerful royal keris in Balinese history, claims to be explored further in chapter 7. The claims to legitimacy include as well the topics of this chapter: the evocation of invisible forces, special relationships to Brahmana priests, and connections to human resources, to followers—all of which had to be mobilized on behalf of the princes and their ritual.

Mobilizing Invisible Relationships: Setting in Motion Mandalas of Prayer and Holy Water

After the family of the noble house had agreed among itself to undertake the maligya ritual, before the priests and then the people of the realm were formally approached, invisible forces were summoned and brought to work propitiously for the anticipated endeavor, for power in the material world (*sekala*) derives from auspicious connection to the immaterial world (*niskala*). People automatically gather around anyone obviously favored by the gods, ancestors, and other invisible beings. Wiener has described this idea of power well: "Power, *kesaktian*, results from the generation or maintenance of connections between a person and the invisible world, especially (though not exclusively) the gods. In the broadest sense, kesaktian is the ability to achieve any goal...; it is synonymous with efficacy" (1995:58). Wiener explains the notion of cultural modesty concerning kesaktian, also related to the role of displacement of agency, that "it is never really the self that accomplishes things but invisible forces working through the self" (1995:58).[1] But as also becomes clear, the actions of the self play a determining role in realizing kesaktian, in generating or maintaining the necessary connection.

In Bali the landscape is imbued with invisible forces with which one must maintain good relations, especially so mountain peaks and sources of water, which are the abodes of ancestors and other deities, and the ocean, which is the home of demons and chthonic spirits. The Balinese example reflects a typical Austronesian pattern (Adelaar 1997), where the direction toward the interior of the island (*kaja*), especially toward Mount Agung, which at 3142 meters is Bali's highest mountain, is auspicious compared to the direction toward the ocean (*kelod*). It also resembles the conception among some Austronesian peoples of their island as a body, with its head inland by mountains or lakes and the feet stretching toward the sea (cf. Fox 1997, Grimes 1997, McWilliam

---

1. It is interesting to compare this to notions of power elsewhere, such as Chinese "ling" (cf. Sangren 1991) and Tamang, Nepal, "wang" (cf. Holmberg 2000). Holmberg explains: "The bounty of grain (hong), prosperity of wealth (yang), and the quintessential power of things (chyut), all ultimately the products of human labor when it intersects with good fortune, are seen by Tamang as originating in transcendental and extrahuman wang" (2000:938).

2002).[2] Royal centers were located along and mediated this axis between mountains and sea via earth and flowing waters. The model of kaja-kelod reverberates throughout Balinese social space, including in the layout of house yards and temples and in the definition of commoners versus nobles.[3]

Bali is further influenced by the Southeast Asian model of *mandala*, the Hindu-Buddhist magical cosmological scheme or geometric composition of satellites surrounding a powerful center, also, as we have seen, an image for the negara as a fluid polity.[4] Balinese surround themselves with and situate themselves within mandala of forces, cosmological maps, with smaller mandala within larger mandala, mandala of offerings, family temples, house compounds, villages, and so forth.[5] The maligya ritual invoked mandala of

---

2. In Bali, in fact, the same terms of kaja and kelod may be used to refer to arrangements of space as well as to the human body itself; kaja for the direction toward the head, kelod for the direction of the feet. In Sumba, the head is the east and the rear end is the west, placing Kodi in Western Sumba as "the world's rear end" (*kere tana*) (Hoskins, personal communication). For a fascinating example of the notion of the island of Papua New Guinea as covered with the body of a giant riddled with holes from mining operations, see Stewart and Strathern 2002a and 2002b (this featured in a newly created myth for negotiating with mining companies).

3. McGowan contests the idea sometimes proposed that the (impure) ocean should be associated with the feminine, the (pure) mountains with the masculine (1996). Also, see Hobart (1978) for an integration of these axes with the Balinese ritual cycle as decribed in chapter 2.

4. Mandala, a term used also in Balinese inscriptions, "according to a common Indo-Tibetan tradition is composed of two elements—a core (manda) and a container or enclosing element (la)" (Tambiah 1985:252). See Tambiah 1985:252–253 for different uses of mandala. Tambiah coined the term "galactic polity" "to represent the design of traditional Southeast Asian kingdoms, a design that coded in a composite way cosmological, topographical, and politico-economic features" (1985:252). See also Wolters (1999) for fascinating application and discussion of mandala. Rather than mandala as geometric diagram, he emphasizes "the secular uses" of mandala, that is "as a metaphor for a territorially ill-defined but nonetheless recognizable sphere of personal influence, exercised by an overlord, knit by personal relationships between the center and beyond, and within which people could gradually become aware of what they had in common" as well as "denot[ing] a specific territory such as...the royal residence and immediate environs of Sriwijaya." He also cites definitions from Charles Higham, such as, "a political apparatus fluid in terms of territory and therefore without fixed frontiers" (1999:108) and Sunait Chutintaranond: "mandalas were 'continuous networks of loyalties between the rulers and the ruled" (1999:114). He finally suggests Southeast Asia has entered a "neo-mandala" age, saying: "I have come to believe that mandala and globalization history in Southeast Asia have something in common. In both cases the scene is multicentered and boundary-less, and the dominating category is immense prowess, a flexible category capable of accommodating religious, political, or economic power" (1999:221).

all scales, from the smallest offerings, to the ritual site of the payadnyan, to the realm, the island, and the world beyond. Particularly prominent as representative of the source of royal power is the mandala of a sacred mountain at the center of the realm, the mythical Mount Meru surrounded by mountain ranges and ocean (cf. Heine-Geldern 1956). Throughout much of Southeast Asia, kings constructed their capitals according to this pattern, striving to achieve "harmony between the empire and the universe...by organizing the former as an image of the latter, as a universe on a smaller scale" (Heine-Geldern 1956:1). Given Bali's physical layout, it is not surprising, perhaps, that the two models have been accommodated in one, whereby the mountain = the head = the center and the ocean = the feet = the peripheral circle. Within this framework, Balinese in general retain the belief that all of human activity is influenced, for good and for bad, by forces originating from the directions of the compass; and much of their ritual endeavor models and channels relationships within this universe. It was reflecting these pre-Hindu animist beliefs, the Austronesian axes of orientation between inland and ocean, as well as Hindu-Buddhist concepts of mandala that members of the noble house made trips into the landscape — first a prayer trip and later a trip to summon holy water—as part of a process of activating its forces and seeking endorsement and assistance for the upcoming ritual endeavor.

Prayer Trip

Robert Heine-Geldern, in the 1950s, described rites of kingship from elsewhere in Southeast Asia that set in motion the symbolic power of the mountain-centered mandala: "The circumambulation of the capital formed, and in Siam and Cambodia still forms, one of the most essential parts of the coronation ritual. By this circumambulation the king takes possession not only of the capital city but of the whole empire..." (1956:2–3). In a not altogether dissimilar way, it is ritual practice in Bali, at the outset of an endeavor such as the maligya ritual, for those "owning the work" to activate and enlist the supernatural powers in their landscape of mandala and mountain-to-ocean axes.[6] Such was the purpose of the first trip embarked upon by family of the Jero Gede Sidemen a full year in advance of the ritual itself (see figure 6).

---

5. See McGowan (1996) for a rich discussion of the concept of "manik" within these.

6. Note that there is also a connection of identity between the ruler and the realm—A blemish on Dalem Ketut's body, for example, is indicative of a problem in Bali (cf. chapter 7). Also natural calamity in the realm could justify murdering a ruler (cf. chapter 6).

Figure 6. Map of Prayer Trip

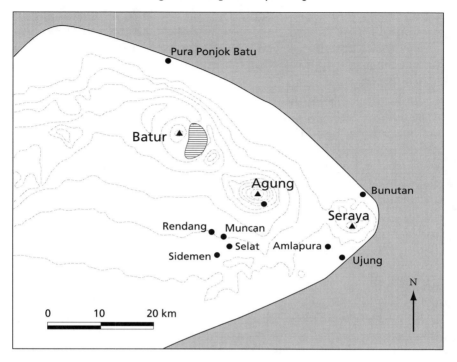

Already in July of 1997, a journey was set forth on the day of the full moon, when several car loads of family members drove a circumference around the eastern part of the island, praying at cosmologically significant locations and in significant directions. Prior to departure everyone assembled in Sidemen and started the tour with prayer in the high caste family temple (*merajaan*). From there, following figure 6, they drove north to Selat, Muncan, and Rendang, praying before Muncan at a river, Tukad Telaga Waja, a tributary of the Unda which flows through the Sidemen valley. This is the river referred to in the *Raja Purana Besakih*, the main textual source for Besakih, Bali's paramount Hindu temple, as a dividing line between groups supporting different shrines at Besakih, and "East of the Telaga Waja" was a way of referring to Sidemen (Vickers 1982a:446). En route to Mount Batur, the group stopped to pray in the forest—"a place with many pine trees," perceived as wilderness. They then prayed at The Temple of the Crater Lake, Pura Ulun Danu Batur, and, farther along, at another temple on the north coast, Pura Ponjok Batu. From here, they went onwards and eastwards to pray at Bunutan, on the coast and on the north eastern flank of Mount Seraya, directing their prayer towards the mountain on which is located the Lempuyang temple. They drove around the eastern tip of the island, stopping again to pray towards the south-eastern ocean. In the dark by now, they drove through Amlapura to return to Sidemen. It was critical that all complete the circle by driving all the way back to the noble house, even if some had to turn right around to backtrack to their homes in Amlapura.

On this trip, prayer thus was offered at a river close to the source of an irrigation system once connected to the noble house and at a defining boundary of its realm. This was worded as praying at the cultivated and irrigated rice fields (*sawah*). Prayer also was offered toward "the forest," to the west, representing the uncultivated. It was offered at the Mount Batur temple to the Goddess of the Crater Lake, Dewi Danu, female counterpart (usually viewed as either consort or sibling) to the male god of Mount Agung.[7] Finally prayer was offered toward both the northern and southern oceans as well as toward Mount Seraya, the easternmost of Bali's string of volcanoes. Through its tour of prayer, the noble house was activating sources of sacred power in an eastern-Bali mandala within which Sidemen defines itself, all the while circumnavigating Bali's highest mountain, Mount Agung, on the slopes of which Besakih is located. The mountain is the domain of the God of Mount Agung and dwelling place as well of the island's prominent ancestors.

Later, it is said, immediately following the ritual, a French filmmaker reported a sighting of the ancestors of the noble house at the summit of Agung. This story has joined the repertoire of stories told of the maligya ritual, again enlisting the power of foreigners as witnesses. People related with great vividness, as if they had observed it themselves though they had even the story only second hand, that the French cameraman, atop Mount Agung, had come upon a gathering of ancestors. Here, as when they were seen at the ceremonial enclosure or in dreams, the ancestors were dressed all in white (for as Cokorda Raka explained, "if people have already died, have already become pure, they have to wear white"). One was described as an old man with a cane and a long white beard, another as having gotten very angry when filmed, while yet others were beautiful women. Tjokorda Gede Dangin later commented on it himself, concluding that he was anxious to see the results, to see if the film turned out.

---

7. Lansing has described The Crater Lake, domain of the Goddess, as defining a mandala of its own (1991). Kaja McGowan tells the story from Batur that the Goddess of the Lake at Batur (*Dewi Danu*) and the God of Mount Agung were born from an erupting volcano, following which the Goddess of the Lake gave birth to Mount Batur (1996:13, 118).

The pre-maligya ritual tour of the landscape reflected the power of natural sites, the significance of the mountain-to-ocean axis, as well as the mandala with the mountain in the middle, all of which are associated with the regenerative potential of the earth. Comparable to how processions in the maligya ritual activated everything from deities to objects, so this was a clockwise circling to set in motion all of these forces. Years after the eastern circumnavigation and the established success of the ceremony, people have eager memories of this trip and remember it as having launched the whole event of the maligya ritual to an auspicious start.

Holy Water Trip

On June 25, 1998, as the main series of ceremonies was approaching rapidly, another activation of powerful sources took place when "notification" was performed and holy water summoned and returned to Sidemen from temples of island-wide importance. These temples, the *Sad Kahyangan* or "six temples of the world," are located not at court centres (cf. Stuart-Fox 1991:20), but at points of power relating to the cardinal directions and mountain to ocean axis: [8]

—Pura Agung Besakih, Bali's foremost Hindu temple, often referred to as Bali's "Mother Temple," lies at about 1000 meters above sea level on the slope of Mount Agung, Bali's highest mountain and abode of the deity Tolangkir. Besakih is a complex of many dozen temples, some of which could be prehistoric; in other words, they could predate the earliest known Balinese inscriptions of 882 AD. Besakih would have been important by virtue of its association with the mountain. Though there is uncertainty regarding origins and antiquity, Stuart-Fox does state confidently that "Pura Besakih has become the unchallenged paramount world temple, the very pinnacle of the hierarchy, at least since Gelgel times," by which time it had connection to the court of Gelgel (2002:65). Besakih includes shrines to prominent forefathers of Bali's rajas and princes. (For a detailed account of Pura Besakih until the mid 1980s, see the 2002 publication of Stuart-Fox's already widely recognized and cited dissertation.)

—Pura Luhur Lempuyang is located toward the summit of Mount Seraya (1174 m), Bali's easternmost mountain. (*Luhur* means "above" or "superior," and is the root of the term *laluhur*, which is glossed as "ancestor.") This, ac-

---

8. There is variation as to which temples are considered the Sad Kahyangan. "The Sadkahyangan," says Stuart-Fox, "poses a number of problems difficult to answer with any certainty. Even the meaning of the term is not absolutely clear, for although *sad* does mean 'six,' it has been suggested that it might mean 'essential' or 'core' (from Sanskrit *sat*, 'being, existing')" (2002:63). There also are mandala of three, four, five, and nine axial temples.

cording to one legend, is the abode of a god related to the gods of Mounts Agung and Batur. In the temple enclosure there are groves of bamboo that yield a liquid used for holy water.

—Pura Goa Lawah, on the south coast near the border between Klungkung and Karangasem, is a temple at a cave thick with fruit bats, regarded as the guardians of the temple. The cave hosts as well a gathering of pythons, which feed on the bats. This, it is said, is home to Naga Basuki, the sacred serpent of Mount Agung and caretaker of the earth's stability. It is believed to have underground passage to the "Cave Temple" at Besakih on Mount Agung, though entrances to the passage collapsed during a past earthquake.

—Pura Luhur Ulu Watu, on Bali's southern peninsula, sits on a limestone promontory of steep cliffs dropping dramatically to the ocean. This is where Danghyang Nirartha, around the middle of the sixteenth century, is said to have merged with the universe, freed from the cycle of reincarnation (*moksa*). Nirartha, also known as Dwijendra, was a Javanese high priest who earlier in the sixteenth century,[9] along with his nephew, Astapaka, entered the court of Watu Renggong, one of the successful successors to Ketut Ngulesir (the recipient of the keris), thus introducing Brahmana tradition to Bali. Bali's various Siwa Brahmana groups (followers of the Saivite as opposed to the Buda branch of Brahmana) trace their genealogies back to Nirartha through his various marriages. (See Rubinstein, 1991a, for a summary of the *babad* or historical writing that tells the story of Dwijendra.)

—Pura Luhur Batukaru, on the slopes of Mount Batu Karu, Bali's westernmost high peak (2276 m.), is considered another of Bali's most ancient sacred sites. The temple complex contains a tall, tiered shrine (*meru*) in honor of the deified rajas of Tabanan and shrines honoring the Goddess of Lake Tamblingan and the God of Mount Batukaru (see Geertz 1980). At the apex of the Tabanan-based irrigation system, this temple is often compared to Pura Ulun Danu Batur (below). More recent research suggests that the principal temple of the Batukaru complex was once "controlled by a small mountain 'kingdom'" ruled by a highland clan (Hauser-Schaüblin 1997, 2003; Ottino 2001).

—Pura Ulun Danu Batur, which also was on the route of the family's prayer trip circumnavigating Mount Agung, lies on the rim of the crater containing Lake and Mount Batur, Bali's northernmost volcano (1750 m). This

---

9. Again dating is uncertain. As to the historicity of Nirartha's existence, Rubinstein notes that she finds no evidence to either confirm or refute this (1991a).

Figure 7. Map of Holy Water Trip

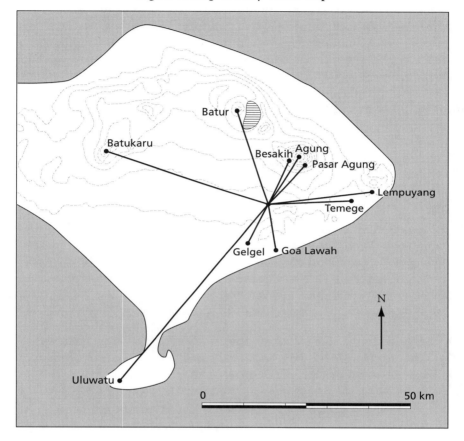

is the temple of the Goddess of the Crater Lake, the female counterpart to the male god of Mount Agung. It is the temple at the apex of the irrigation system of the area referred to as Bali's rice bowl (see Lansing 1991 regarding its role in agriculture).

In addition, holy water was procured from temples at Gelgel, from where the forefather of the Jero Gede Sidemen departed in the mid-seventeenth century; from Temege, where he settled prior to sending his son to Sidemen; and from Pura Pasar Agung, a temple honoring Mount Agung and with relationship to Pura Besakih. Located on the slope of the mountain above Sidemen, it is of special significance to the noble house (see Stuart-Fox 2002:419–420). Holy water was also gathered from near the summit of Mount Agung (figure 7).

On this occasion of the trip to summon holy water, everyone congregated in Sidemen before dawn, as it was important that all delegations set out at the same time and expedite their missions as efficiently as possible. As dawn broke over Mount Agung, participants radiated out from Sidemen (figure 7; see Tambiah 1985:254 regarding radial and concentric mandala). They could not all return simultaneously, but before the sun set everyone was back, had gathered in a village temple, and from there, in one procession, reentered the courtyard of the noble house.[10]

The Raja-Bagawanta Priest Relationship

In addition to auspicious invisible relationships, the maligya ritual manifested the special relationship between rulers and priests. For centuries it has been practice for specific Brahmana priests (*bagawanta or purohita*) to stand in ritual service to specific lords. They were considered part of the lords' regalia, like the keris, among their most important "jewels" or "heirlooms" (cf. Geertz 1980; Worsley 1972). To illustrate the relationship between the noble house and its priests, one follower of the noble house told a story about how, not just objects and places, but also priests have mystical powers with which the princes align themselves:

A priest from Sidemen did not have any *betel*. [Betel leaves and betel nut are chewed with lime for a mild stimulant.] He asked a tree for some, upon which it bent to bring it to him. He also did not have any food. So he went to Klungkung, to the market, where he asked for some on credit. He said he would repay his debt before the sun set. Well, he did not come into any money by then, but he kept his promise nonetheless: The sun did not set. The Cokorda at the Jero Gede wondered at this. Why was the sun not setting?.... When he was in-

---

10. This is a different process from that described by Hauser-Schäublin, whereby royal rituals were held in regional temples as the "actual centers" and bases for the kings' powers, from which centers then people brought home holy water, which "represented the emanation of these divine-royal rituals. The essence of this locality was carried out to the periphery, to the individual neighborhoods," etc. (2003:158). In the Sidemen holy water trips, it is not a question of royal ritual at regional temples. Here the nobility are drawing in powers from the important all-Bali temples to their local center. There is in this case too "an essence of this locality...carried out to the periphery," but for the princedom their "actual center" is local. Sometimes from this local center of royal power, there are other rituals too from which followers receive holy water to take to their households.

formed as to what was going on, he promptly gave money to the priest, who in this way had demonstrated immense powers. The priest paid his debt, and finally, the sun could set. [Pak Komang]

This story presents the priest-raja relationship as one wherein the priest is the purview of supernatural spiritual powers while the raja is so of the world material. The priest relies on the raja, but the raja and the well-being of the realm also rely on the priest. Although non-Brahmana priests from within the royal family itself can produce holy water for everyday needs, they cannot produce the highest forms of holy water, which they must receive from consecrated Brahmana. Priests and rajas have been symbiotically allied in Bali in this way since the priest Nirartha and his nephew joined the sixteenth-century court of Watu Renggong. Nirartha, born in Java at about the time when Majapahit fell and Islamic rulers came to power on the island, had gradually moved east and eventually left Java for Bali.[11] Here, once he had proven his spiritual and magical powers, he became court priest. The flourishing of Gelgel is often attributed to the relationship between raja and priest thus established.

At first, the separation of secular and religious power implied in the story about the Sidemen priest and prince appears similar to the status/power distinction that Dumont makes in his analysis of the Indian caste system (1980), but the idea of dual sovereignty and a separation of spiritual and temporal power is significant in eastern Indonesia as well (see e.g. Fox 1980; Francillon 1980; Hoskins 1998). The Balinese relationship of raja-bagawanta also seems to adhere to Dumont's theory of the *varnas,* the four major endogamous caste groups, a system which, "whilst it subordinates king to priest, power to status, [also] establishes solidarity between them which opposes them conjointly to the other social functions" (Dumont 1980:75).[12] But, it has remained a critique of Dumont, a critique that gained momentum with Foucault's attention

---

11. There is sometimes reference to an exodus of members of the Majapahit court from Java at that time, referred to as the "flight of Majapahit." Whether there really was a mass migration remains in question, but from standing in a tributary relationship to the Majapahit, Bali at this point is considered to have become its refuge. See Creese 2000 for an analysis of the history of how Balinese have defined themselves in relation to Majapahit.

12. Guermonprez points out that although kings are subordinated to priests in Bali, we must note that they are so in a Balinese rather than Dumontian way: In Bali "1) the priest is of a higher status than the king 2) the ruler as such has no sacerdotal functions 3) the priest-king relation results in a form of dual sovereignty. In India, however, the king is opposed to the priest as artha to dharma, namely as power to purity (Dumont 1967). Not only is the king, like in Bali, subordinate to the priest, but he is the opposite. This is congruent with the Indian ideas of purity and dominance which, as far as I can see, do not

to power, that we cannot categorically separate spiritual status and secular power.

In Bali, secular power commingles with spiritual power. For example, the line of Kapakisan rajas—appointed to Bali following the Majapahit conquest and from which much contemporary royalty of Bali, including the Jero Gede Sidemen, trace descent—is said to have derived from the Brahmana Buda priestly caste. And Hobart has pointed out that in the "ceremonies surrounding the enthronement of Balinese monarchs," specifically "in the purification of the king," "purity and power come to be enjoined" through his person (1979:473). Wiener, meanwhile, has argued in depth that Kapakisan royal power is based largely on a magico-religious aspect (1995). Conversely, gods in Bali—and we might add priests—are distinguished "by being both pure (*suci*) and powerful (*sakti*) although they may not manifest this latter because of their purity" (Hobart 1979:473; see also Rubinstein, 1991a for an examination of the multifaceted role of Brahmana as presented through their *babad* or historical texts).

In a different vein, it also should be noted that local legends and performance traditions refer as well to power struggles between priests and rajas. Leo Howe points out that the raja-bagawanta relationship was not always uncomplicated, for "whilst there was often co-operation between them there was also a great deal of rivalry," and, their purity notwithstanding, Brahmana priests could be war-waging rulers with subjects of their own (Howe 1995:49–50; see also Worsley 1972; Vickers 1984:27–28; Guermonprez 1989; Rubinstein 1991a, 1991b). Similarly, while a Dumontian or Austronesian distinction generally pertains to the relationship between raja and bagawanta in Sidemen, it becomes evident as well that a clear demarcation between status and power does not bear out. Tjokorda Gede Dangin explains that those of raja status rely heavily on their bagawanta, Brahmana priests who are their teachers in matters of religion, etiquette, and culture, and who can preside at their ceremonies. But, in keeping with the complication of Dumont's distinction between status versus power, the situation in Sidemen, where there are nine priestly or Brahmana compounds (*griya*), also illustrates ways in which priests have played a more political role than acknowledged in any idealization of priest-raja or status-power distinctions.

Priests and Politics in Sidemen

In the mid-seventeenth century, when the forefather of the Jero Gede Sidemen fled from the disintegrating Balinese kingdom of Gelgel, taking with him

---

avail in Bali. Thus, it is wise to assume that dual sovereignty has an entirely different significance in these two cultures" (1989:203).

the heirloom keris, his entourage included priests that were aligned with him. As the story is told from the perspective of the Jero Gede Sidemen, moreover, the priestly house with the most seniority in Sidemen, Griya Ulah, was instrumental in the maneuvering that brought the forefather's son to power in Sidemen, and to this day, the priests of Griya Ulah remain bagawanta to the noble house. A second priestly house, Griya Pidade, which has been the other most central priestly player in Sidemen—and which provides the bagawanta to the neighboring palaces of Amlapura and Klungkung—arrived after Ulah. Tjokorda Gede Dangin explains that their coming to Sidemen was embroiled in politics, as it was the Raja of Karangasem who, after having conquered Sidemen (ca. mid-eighteenth century), brought them in "for corrosive purposes." He explains that it was "political maneuvering," pointing out that, in fact, most of Sidemen's priestly houses were sent there by the raja of Karangasem and played a role in undermining the legitimacy of the noble house and their relationships with others. Tjokorda Gede Dangin emphasizes that it is not that he dislikes them; in fact, he also has them "among [his] Brahmana," but he talks about a proclivity for politicking as "maybe being their descent" and "their character:" "Every generation, it has always been like that....The education is different now, but their character remains constant." He emphasizes that the priestly house of Ulah, by contrast, always has been more oriented toward knowledge and philosophy, in which respect "they are outstanding." He goes on to say that "I do push them so that they study....I feel sorry for them because they have long been poor, very poor. In terms of material goods they are lacking....But their morals were never ruined, because they study many lontar."

Here, in other words, we encounter a status/power distinction attributed to priestly houses themselves, a distinction between a predilection toward spiritual knowledge versus one toward secular politics. Though both the priestly houses of Ulah and Pidade have played an acknowledged political role—bringing in the heir of the Jero Gede to Sidemen versus aligning with the raja of Karangasem—only the latter is construed as "politicking." To Dangin, the ideal distinction of the special purview of the Brahmana is upheld and, interestingly, his comments indicate that a notable component of the relationship between the priestly house of Ulah and his noble house is the noble house's role in assuring the priestly house's success in this distinction. Tjokorda Gede Dangin, whose power also depends on this priestly house, actively supports its foundation in learned and religious matters. On many an evening, no matter how busy his day, he makes his way to Griya Ulah to read lontar with them.

The Priests at The Maligya Ritual.

It was following the first activation of the Eastern Bali mandala by those who performed the prayer trip circling Mt. Agung that the members of the noble house made their formal request to the priestly house, Griya Ulah, to serve in the maligya ritual. They go to them, they say, because these priests are "our *surya*" (literally: our sun),[13] or "our *purowita*," the same as "*bagawanta*," the lord's closest and highest-ranking Brahmana priest. Cokorda Raka explains: "We conveyed our request and asked that the already deceased priests there, those that already long since passed away, become our guiding souls (*betara lingga*), become the most important figures in that maligya ritual work. And they agreed."

Two years following the maligya ritual, sitting again at the griya with two male members of the priestly house as well as the old unmarried priestess,[14] who had been in charge of coordinating the making of offerings for the maligya ritual and who, herself, had carried the priestly effigies (*betara lingga*) down the hill to the ceremonial enclosure, Cokorda Raka expresses that to Balinese people, matters such as the maligya ritual are like a debt or obligation. To pay that debt, he says, weighs on them heavily and it is a debt that cannot be paid without the priests: "[These] are our *purowita*. To put on this ritual work, we plead from them the figures that become the peak of the ceremony." Only when this kind of priestly participation is secured can anyone have a postcremation ceremony at the level of the maligya ritual, explains Raka. In being able to achieve this, he places the noble house on a par with the larger palaces of Karangasem and Klungkung: "In Karangasem, the Anak Agung [title for the rajas and highest nobility there] uses the *betara lingga* from consecrated Brahmana priests, as does the Raja of Klungkung. And so do we." He goes on to express how tightly aligned his house is with these Brahmana, first presenting the princes' position in relation to the priests as both prompters and followers, then referring to it as "the same," while also acknowledging the reliance of his house on the priests:

> It was our forefathers *that urged* them to come here, *that followed* (*ngiring*) Betara Wayan Buruan [the deified forefather of these priests] here, *so that our position here is the same*; so that if there are big ceremonies at my house, we must use a priest from the line of the deity of Sukaton [i.e. Betara Wayan Buruan, supposedly a great-grandson

---

13. The term is also used to refer to the high caste patrons of a lower caste family, the latter being the *sisya*. Thus some of the Jero Gede followers referred to themselves as sisya, the Jero Gede as Surya.

14. Brahmana women may become consecrated priests either married or unmarried.

of Nirartha]....The deities [in my temple] will not accept a different priest; it has to be a descendant of the deity of Sukaton. [Cokorda Raka, emphasis added]

The special relationship between the priestly house and the noble house comes significantly to light in the context of the maligya ritual. The ceremony could not have come about in the first place had it not been for the noble house's close relationship with a priestly house willing to serve as its *betara lingga*, as the guides for the souls of its ancestors. Only those of higher caste can summon the guidance of the *Betara Lingga*, without which this high and prestigious level of the ceremony cannot be effected, no matter how rich you may be. As noted, the maligya ritual, through this exclusivity, becomes a prominent marker and displayer of status in the worldly realm. Poorer or lower caste people may have just a small ceremony in connection with the cremation to meet the religious requirements of completing the death rites, but for those of high caste, and of means and ambition, it becomes incumbent to put on a large ceremony. As we have seen, the ceremony becomes a vehicle not just for the souls of the ancestors, but also for the status of the raja.

The priests, on their part, through participation in the noble house's maligya ritual, are fulfilling a duty of service too, based on longstanding relationship between their respective houses, but also a service that asserts their own status. Though the priestly house of Ulah played the foremost role in the maligya ritual, numerous other local and extra-local priests also participated, including priests from Griya Pidade and other of the region's most prominent priests. In return, the noble house performed a lavish thanksgiving ceremony for the priests, waiting on them with food and gifts, acknowledging their reliance and gratitude. They acknowledged also their roles of providing for the priests' material needs and of representing secular power through their connection both to people of the realm and to the nation state presidential candidate. More than an expression of gratitude to individual priests or priestly houses, it was a ceremony confirming generalized raja-priest alliances.

With the agreement of the priests, then, it was settled that the ceremony would be undertaken. The invisible powers evoked and the spiritual requirements secured, it became important to ensure the promise of sufficient human resources.

Mobilizing Connections to Followers

Scholarship on Southeast Asian kingship, in general, has emphasized the importance of control of human resources more than that of land resources.

This aspect has been highlighted for Bali, too, that "the struggle was more for men than it was for land" (Geertz 1980:24) and that "control of manpower determined to a large extent the power of noble houses in nineteenth-century Bali" (Schulte Nordholt 1991:7). Even Klungkung's supremacy is seen to have been exhibited in its ability to mobilize human resources from outside of its own realm, which in land area was one of Bali's smallest.[15]

In Sidemen, there was a striking shift in terms of human resources from the first groundbreaking ceremony to the completion of the maligya ritual. At first the immediate family was working manually; even the women of the noble house were out moving dirt. Over the course of time, more and more people from the outside gravitated to do this genre of work. As discussed, it was not a given that the ritual event would succeed as it did. In informal evaluation sessions before, during, and after the ceremony, people at the noble house, themselves, expressed astonishment at the show of supporters and participants, openly remarking on how it is only the ability to mobilize people that makes a ritual work like this possible. Of the groups that materialized it is said that they have obligation to *ngayah*, to perform ritual service, at ceremonies of the noble house.

Ritual Duty: Ngayah

The term *ngayah* already indicates a hierarchical relationship, for it would be only if the priestly house, Griya Ulah, or a regional palace, for example, were to have a maligya ritual that those of the noble house would apply the term to themselves. Ngayah is also the term that may be used for wafting the essence of an offering toward a deity. Although, today, it is sometimes glossed as *gotong royong*, a term connoting the egalitarian neighborhood organization practice of "mutual cooperation," it is quite different from this concept, which also has become an Indonesian buzz-word to ensure free labor for government projects.[16] Hobart explains the term ngayah as "the expression for doing something on the command of a prince or as part of one's duty to a group" (1990:322):

> [It] may range from manual or ritual labour to bearing arms. In Old
> Javanese, on which Balinese draws heavily, aya(h) is glossed as "ef-

---

15. Both van der Kraan (1995) and Wiener (1995) mention the 1849 Kusamba war in this regard, the first war between Klungkung and the Dutch, which forced the Dutch into retreat.

16. Cf. Bowen's 1986 article showing how the government manipulated this "traditional category" to claim that Indonesians should donate their labor freely to government village projects. In 1988, the Head of the Regional Office of Culture listed gotong royong among the "eminent values of the Balinese culture" that were "worthy of inclusion in the Indonesian culture" (Picard 1996:179).

fort, endeavour, the course of action for effecting something," and as a verb connotes "to make an effort, to do one's best" (Zoetmulder 1983:174). (Taking part in such a work is makrama)." [1990:322]

Ayahan kadalem specifically refers to "palace service" which, theoretically, was abolished by the Dutch, who instead instituted *corvée* labor, whereby Balinese commoners had to perform work for the colonial overlords, such as unpaid road construction, for a given number of days a year.[17] Whereas the practice of ngayah at least conceivably was based on—and constitutive of— connections between nobles and commoners, corvée, as Schulte Nordholt has pointed out, "was tangible proof of the rift" between them, for "if a person did not do physical work, he was a noble, and being conscripted showed that a person belonged to the Sudra" (1996a:237). Also the labor involved was more menial, hard physical labor, than was the case with *ngayahan kadalem*, which in most cases ultimately could be construed as acts of devotion to deities. Schulte Nordholt assesses well that "to the people, corvée was a new phenomenon, very different from what they were used to" (1996a:238). He cites the vivid memories of older people in the kingdom of Mengwi, of a system whereby a lord could call upon the labor of his own followers only; that is, "those who worked a *pacatu sawah*" (irrigated rice land), in exchange for which "followers owed their lord loyalty and servitude" (1996a:238). The new policy, he points out, "put an end to this trade-off type of situation:"

> Corvée was mandatory for every single jaba [commoner] household, regardless of their relation to the punggawa [lord] responsible for its implementation. Furthermore, conscripts were made to work not just from six to eleven in the morning, but to the end of the day. The type of work to be performed was new as well. They were used to labour tangibly linked to their lord—repairs to the puri and the like—or of benefit to the workers themselves, as in the case of preparations for large rituals. But now roads had to be built, far from home and for no apparent purpose. [1996a:238][18]

From work that integrated with faith, Balinese subjects were, as Bloch has put it for the Merina of Madagascar in regard to popular revolts against the

---

17. The rajas of the kingdoms under indirect rule received compensation for the loss of such service.

18. Schulte Nordholt adds that "one result of this was that corvée tended to be left to the women. The men experienced conscription as unjust, and were most reluctant to perform useless labour" (1996a:238).

abolition of rituals, "left with the much more stark alternative of pure exploitation" (1986:193). Whereas to Bloch this mainly showed up the ideological power of ritual rather than reflect any substantial difference in the respective hierarchical relationships, there is evidence, in Bali at least, that the difference mattered. There was, as we have seen, a difference in the labor involved when performing it for Balinese versus colonial overlords, and, in Bali as elsewhere in early Southeast Asian negara, there had not precolonially been the basis for an intensively extractive regime (see also Schulte Nordholt 1996a:130). We cannot dismiss either that there was some material reality behind the ideology of mutuality in lord-follower relationships. Corvée, meanwhile, backed by the force of the colonial state, opened new options for still powerful nobles and lords to transfer additional resources into work mainly for their own benefit.

To this day, people adamantly define *ngayah*, voluntary service outside of the bureaucracy, in opposition to service within it, and this is so with people on either side of the relationship between lords and followers. Many also stress, and hold it to be of utmost importance, that ngayah must not involve money. Cash transactions, they say, lead to no relationship, whereas food transactions—referring to how the noble house fed rather than paid those who came to help—lead to relationships "both today and tomorrow." People also frequently mention that those who ngayah would not want to be paid, for it is by giving freely that they gain karmic merit. Pertaining to maligya rituals, specifically, people say that if you participate in such a high level of ceremony eleven times you do not need even to be cremated; you will already have paved your way to heaven. While this, on the one hand, again may underscore the ideological power of belief systems in relationships of inequality, the high value placed on labor and materials without involving money also puts pressure on the noble house, for it is incumbent on the princes to not succumb to renting things or hiring labor. Cokorda Raka, who along with so many others was charged with the procurement of various materials, stressed the importance of having materials given not purchased, so that there would remain a social connection as a result of the transactions: "It would not be right to buy everything; that signifies not having people connections." In keeping again with the notion that it is not a given that everything will work out, this component, too, is a struggle and sometimes a negotiation. For example, you may be given some of the materials but pay for the rest. The sentiment that ngayah should not involve cash was echoed among the followers and was put into perspective by examples of people outside of the princedom, who in some cases would try to take advantage of the situation by asking inflated prices for materials that only they could provide. The spirit of ngayah relates also to the idea that those of the noble house must refrain from doing too much accounting of anything. For example, "you may not think about that which has already been spent on the ceremony. You may not calculate what you have spent, nor may you talk about it. You have to be sincere, to give what you give wholeheartedly. No matter what is asked, you have to offer it, even if you do not yet have it to give." This was applied also to members of the family, who were to make their contributions of the same "free heart," according to what they knew themselves to be capable of.

Just as Cokorda Raka had expressed that his family felt an obligation toward its ancestors to carry out the maligya ritual, so, too, the responsibilities of people toward the noble house were most widely referred to as moral obligation or duty based on ancestral connection. In one village, people joked that, yes, they inherit duty but not any wealth. Today, even in the case of well-to-do descendants of former "slaves" or servants, explains Raka, "if there is a big work or ceremony like this, out of moral duty, they come. They have to.... Even if they hold an important position, they come to help serve. That is their obligation. They would not feel right if they did not get to ngayah."

Tjokorda Gede Dangin, the head of the house, does not feel that "obligation" is the most appropriate way to express the connection, as this implies that they *must* come. He points out that it is not an obligation in that sense, but rather a certain "awareness" or "consciousness." He, as did others including commoners, attributed this awareness to "historical connection:"

> In many cases, their forefathers came here with my forefathers, under my forefathers. Now, this was passed on from generation to generation and is still remembered, and from generation to generation there has continued to be a connection, especially in the case of large ceremonies. If we have a cremation ceremony, they are sure to come also. This is to indicate an earlier social connection, one with the other, before when our forefather...came here.

A Sudra village leader from south of Sidemen explains regarding the connection,

> It is difficult for us to say whether it is an obligation or not. It depends on our own conviction, that we really believe that they raised us and that there is a persistent connection from earlier times, from the times of rajas. Up until now even, we believe that there is this connection.... It is the same as with a husband-wife connection. You could call it an obligation, but because they love each other, you really could say that it is as if it is not an obligation, but is because of faith and belief in the

karma of love. So we consistently "*matur ngayah*" [ask, or literally plead, to ngayah]. And it is the same with them, because they feel that they possess us. Whenever we have any kind of work, also when there is a ritual work such as the big ancestral ritual that we had in 1982, they also continue to come here. It is about awareness and belief. [Sukayasa]

Dangin sums up that his forefathers became the leaders here and that "it really worked well. If there were any difficulties, we helped out. And they also helped us. It was mutual. This is a very good connection..., very much from the heart." Therefore, he concludes, "It is not a question of obligation, but of a historical connection."

Historical Connections

In Sidemen, all of the local neighborhood organizations as well as surrounding villages were represented at the maligya ritual, but it was expressly through the local descent groups (*dadia*) that most of the mobilization of human resources happened, specifically by notifying the head of the group (*klian dadia*), who in turn informed the group members. "Of the dadia in the Sidemen area, there are only a few that do not want to pay homage at my house," explains Cokorda Raka, mentioning Brahmana, due to their special standing, and a particular descent group, the Arya Dauh, due to the rift dating back to the palace of Karangasem's insertion of itself into the region.[19] "The others in Sidemen," he continues, "all pay homage at my house. Our family was highly esteemed." It is also an honor to them, explains Tjokorda Gede Dangin, to be notified and drawn into the ritual preparations; "it means that we still remember those people."

When asked further about these groups that were mobilized for the maligya ritual, Cokorda Raka responds, again exhibiting consciousness of the importance today of not being too feudal:

Besides the fact that it happens through dadia, it is like this—forgive me—but previously at my house, I was a *punggawa* [lord], and my forefather was a raja. That was previously, and most of these were former followers of the raja, when our forefathers came to Sidemen. So if there is a ceremony at our house, all people pray there, at our *merajaan* [high caste family temple].

19. See also Stuart-Fox regarding how the decline of house of Sidemen is linked to the rise of Arya Dauh (2002:288).

This mobilization through descent groups differs from Geertz's assessment for the nineteenth century that "from the peasant's point of view, his obligations to the state were a matter only between him, or more exactly the members of his houseyard, and (via his perbekel) his lord" (1980:65).[20] In Sidemen it is precisely because connections were not so much between individuals as between groups, and who and what these represented in relation to each other, that things happened through dadia, and perhaps this is part of the explanation as to why the connections persist over time. And yet, at the maligya ritual, groups of participants were not referred to by their dadia names. There were the groups of "family" (*keluarga* or *semoton*), which included members of the royal family of Klungkung (see chapter 7 for more on the significance of their participation) and "the gustis," the title group below ksatria, in this case referring especially to the descendants of Arya Ngurah Sidemen, who brought the Dalem line of the noble house to Sidemen. Besides these, participants were referred to by terms that clarify the nature of the relationships that brought them to the noble house in the first place, that is, the different kinds of followers, subjects, and slaves: *pengiring, beraya, kavla* and *parkan*.

Kavla, parkan, beraya.

Kavla is a general term for various forms of servants or vassals, maybe even slaves (some translate the term merely as peasants; cf. Hobart et al. 1996). The term frequently is used to delineate the relationship of followers to the noble house. As explained about the noble house by a member of the Griya Ulah priestly house, "they were rajas, and had many kavla. Formerly the raja controlled the area, and they also became *punggawa* [lords]. The Jero had so many kavla. So because of that...there are these connections [that made the maligya ritual]." Cokorda Raka agreed that "according to the stories of the old people [in the surrounding villages], they really did become... kavla at my house. The olden days were feudal at my home. We had many kavla."

---

20. The difference may in part be due to population expansion; in other words, seventeenth–nineteenth century households in some cases have grown into local kingroups. The principle of mobilization in Sidemen for the local royal ritual differs also from Hauser-Schäublin's characterization of mobilization of neighborhoods in the case of competing regional temple networks (2003:169). Note that she describes this situation as "a process of active recruitment of participants associated with persuasion by all sorts of means" (2003:169).

Those referred to as *parkan* generally were those whose personal freedom was the most restricted; English speaking Balinese usually would translate this category as slaves.[21] They are described as "people who are close to the palace, who eat in our kitchen." They used to live within the noble house, but in the present day they live in its immediate vicinity. They were moved out of the actual palace as their numbers grew and were given a lot on which to construct their own compounds, so that they "would be able better to stand on their own feet." Nowadays they participate in their own neighborhood also; but, as it is put, they "remember their connection to the noble house every day." They "remember to come home" if there is any kind of ceremony or daily work to be done. Raka explained: "Nowadays they are more like what you would call housekeeper." Implicating the anthropologist as a beneficiary of this labor he added: "You have seen that often at home, Lene. If the house is empty, [my brother's wife] calls them so that they can help her cook, can help serve Lene....All of these families were *parkan* before. And," he adds, "these people feel right at home at my home...." Another member of the house explained: "They ask to stay close to the palace. These people always look out

---

21. Raka, for example, glosses them as slaves and also uses the Malay term, *abdi*, explaining that, by contrast, there were those called kavla roban, roban means together (bersama). They were allowed to go out. They got pacatu. They got a distribution of food. Then if there was a ceremony, they would come and ngayah at the puri or the griya." Geertz, too, refers to those living in the palaces as "parkan" (1980:63, 168–169) but adds: "He was not precisely a slave; for parkans were not, so far as I can tell, bought and sold..., nor were they legally forbidden from leaving the lord's employ if they could manage some way to do so and continue to clothe, feed, and house themselves. But he was certainly the next thing to it: a totally resourceless servant" (1980:63). Van der Kraan, however, says that the term parkan "properly describes male slaves performing close personal services for their masters, such as looking after the sirih-box, delivering messages, keeping keys and the like" (1983:338). He continues: "While I agree with Geertz about the fine line dividing slave from servant or retainer in Balinese society, I put parkan just on the slave side of this line, whereas he puts it just on the other side. It is important to note, however, that parkan describes one type of servile occupation, and sepangan (slaves used in agriculture) another — neither refers specifically to slave status" (1983:338).

Other Bali scholars state that this term can refer to any kind of loyal servant to the king, cf. Wiener and Schulte Nordholt. Wiener: "parekan may refer to anyone who served the king, from a lowly sweeper to his chief minister" (1995:294). Schulte Nordholt glosses parekan as "trusted servant," a category which could include minor nobles (1986:102): "In separate yards in this section [the lower half of the puri] lived the puri's parekan, mostly sons of nearby lords staying temporarily at the royal centre to become acquainted with courtly culture. They were the king's retinue whenever he went out, and occasionally they would carry out confidential tasks for him" (1996a:83).

for the house; they can be asked to do anything, like a 'boy.'" It is also said that "they remain loyal and devoted [*setia*]."[22]

In tracing the histories of those connected to the Jero Gede Sidemen who still place in the parkan category, it appears that they did not come to this status as result of capture in warfare, but mainly are illegitimate offspring of the raja or of other unions—outcasts. One woman thus explained that her husband's ancestress was "prostituted" and "unlucky" here and was poor. And so today, she said, "like the hands, we are the feet; if there is work there, we participate. If there is an activity, we follow [*ngiring*]." What she remembers from the ritual is this: "I was just busy. Take this, take that." She did not see Megawati, for, she said, she is not "brave" when it comes to really big matters (i.e., she did not attempt to see her). But, she did add, "Mega's husband is handsome!" (Made Tantri).

Conversely, it is pointed out, these were also the people toward whom the noble house had most responsibilities: they got food on a daily basis, a place to stay, and the house was responsible for their cremations and marriages—and still is. Any extent to which these were slaves, they do not adhere to stereotypes of slaves; yet they were people of no independent means and continue to be people without origin group belonging, people who consider themselves to belong to the princes, and people who can be asked to do anything. As it was put, "they remember their connection to Jero Gede every day."

When asked how many people still are parkan to the Jero Gede, members of the noble house estimated that there are approximately fifteen families, or twenty, that are "close to home;" approximately one hundred people. Nowadays, other than those in the immediate vicinity of the Jero Gede, many former kavla are referred to as *beraya*, the explicit purpose being to use a "softer," less "lowering" term: "Now we just call them *beraya*. But for those who are still close, close to our house, those we call kavla, *kavla roban*" (Raka). Those from the various neighborhood organizations (banjar) within Sidemen mostly are *beraya*.[23]

The term *beraya* denotes affinals, relatives through marriage, but specifically through marriage to a woman of lower caste than that of the Jero Gede; in other words, as Raka specifies, beraya always denotes Sudra status. He continues:

---

22. Leeman notes that "even though serfdom is no longer tolerated in the constitution of the Republic of Indonesia, reminders of it can still be encountered today. When the author asked a servant at the palace of a nobleman his name, he explained that he was nameless because he 'belonged' to the Cokorda (punya cokorda)" (Hobart et al 1996:230).

23. There are also three local Muslim settlements and members of these, too, in some way participated in the maligya ritual. There is in particular talk and enthusiasm for the dance that they "offered" one night.

With the beraya there is still a connection that is very tightly bound, in the sense that we still follow specific regulations. For example, if I have a work at my home, so that they feel that I respect them, I must inform them and ask for their help…to help in the construction, for materials, etc.

Those that live in surrounding villages, meanwhile, now usually are called *pengiring* (followers).[24] When asked how many beraya and pengiring there are, all the princes can say is that there are very many, too many to count.

Pengiring

Those referred to as *pengiring* make up the largest number of participants in the maligya ritual and this is in itself a very diverse subject group. Pengiring, literally meaning followers, mostly are those whose forefathers followed the forefathers of the noble house from Gelgel and eventually to Sidemen, where they were positioned in various surrounding villages. As wife-givers, they are also affinals (beraya) and they are also a variant on the lower category of kavla. But, interestingly, nowadays the head of the noble house is quite adamant to point out that "pengiring" are different from just beraya and kavla, in that the followers are highly honored people, people that came here as military; "these are people held in very high regard." So members of the noble house were generally not heard to refer to them as kavla. It might be salient to note in this context that the people in this category in many cases are *Pasek*, among the clans of an important Sudra group sometimes referred to as "elevated Sudra," who have been quite successful in organizing to counter high-caste privileges and to identify and assert their own joint origins. These they trace back to the same Brahmana priest as do the Kapakisan rajas their origins, the rajas by whom the Pasek were appointed village leaders. Pasek may also be an honorific, a title accorded Sudra village leaders. Yet it remains that in the villages, followers often still refer to themselves as kavla. Thus, one village leader from a village just south of the noble house explained that they had been "the kavla of the prince:"

---

24. But note that these pengiring in terms of their historical relationship to the Jero Gede are not those whose own ancestral souls "followed" at the maligya ritual. Nowadays the former for the most part choose to perform their own ceremonies; only those still called kavla roban *ngiring* or follow at the ceremonies of the Jero Gede. In other words, it was the forefathers of those who still accept the lowest ranking that were followers of the royal souls at the ceremony.

He[25] had many kavla, including [he gives some descent group names that] remained kavla, parkan, there with the Dalem, as His secretary, as Dalem's scribe...such that to this day even, we acknowledge the Dalem at Puri Sidemen. You know it is called Dalem, who formerly was raja....And that Dalem, Cokorda, continuously remembers us here....And we still remember and pay homage and do service to Him [*bakti,* also the term for rites of worship to deities], from our ancestors and up to this day. Because we remember that He urged us so that we came here. It is called *ngiring* [follow], from Gelgel to here.....We followed because we felt close to that Dalem..., because as secretary of the state, no matter where He went, we were sure to follow. So because there is a connection from our forefathers on... now, no matter what happens at the palace, at that Jero at Sidemen and, likewise, no matter what happens with my family,...He automatically must know, and we also must know. If for example there is a ritual work there, all of our family from here ngayah,...that is about seventy-five households, or five hundred people. [Sukayasa]

Sukayasa insists that it does not feel bad to be called kavla or parkan. "No, it does not matter," he responds, "because of the connection;" though, he says, it is more appropriate now to use the term kavla also for what formerly were parkan. But does the connection remain even in these modern times? It remains, he responds.

Discussion of the Categories of Historical Follower Connections

It should be clear by now that the terms—*parkan, kavla, pengiring, beraya*—often are used interchangeably. This is similar to what Geertz noted, that "as always, there was a multiplicity of names for these various states of political condition, some of them denoting slightly different forms or subtypes...[while] also, as always, the terms were rather flexibly used, even though the underlying categories were themselves quite sharply demarcated" (1980:168). Michael Aung Thwin makes the point for Burma, too, that a range of terms, expressing total obligation and loyalty in any relationship, all could mean what we differentiate as subject, vassal or slave, and that rather than abstract legalities, the salient issue was to whom you were bonded (1983). The degree to which the

---

25. I capitalize the pronoun to indicate the respectful form.

various Balinese followers were bound to their lord and whether any of them were actually slaves depends on your definitions. Geertz doubts that any of them really were, while Van der Kraan asserts that they were—but only just to the other side of the dividing line from Geertz (see n. 21). Anthony Reid, in his introduction to his edited volume on *Slavery, Bondage and Dependency in Southeast Asia*, points out that "slave" is "a word frequently misused, even by Southeast Asians themselves." He argues, "for slavery to exist, it must be possible for the slave to be sold or otherwise expropriated to another party" (1983:18). [26]

Linguistically, certainly those referred to as *parkan* and *kavla* were—and sometimes still are—considered possessions of the noble house. Those to whom it pertains outright will say that they were or are "the property of" or "belong to" the Jero Gede (*milik, kepunyaan*). The members of the noble house, likewise, still will use the phrase about many of these categories of people that "these are ours" or "these belong to us" ["kita/saya punya orang" or "ini milik saya"]. Schulte Nordholt observes regarding the concept of ownership (*druwe*), in fact, that it used to indicate "the scope of power the lord had over his followers," and only later was "given the narrower meaning of landownership" (1996a:252).[27]

The commentary of the subjects themselves belies any neat division of people into categories of *pengiring, kavla, parkan*. But also transcending discussions of abstract ideas of ownership and as if to underscore Reid's defining point concerning slavery, people on several different occasions, people from within any of the above categories, volunteered that they could in the past be sold by the noble house if there were a need. In response to subsequent direct inquiry—Had this ever happened?—the answer invariably was "not that we know of." Though there is no trace in the precolonial legal texts of the right to sell people (Helen Creese, personal communication), this of course does not necessarily mean that it did not happen, and by the seventeenth century, the time when the Sidemen Princedom was established, many Balinese certainly were sold as slaves. It seems significant that sale was a theoretical pos-

---

26. Reid makes another point that applies to Bali: "Because this slavery [a form of bondage that arose from within the broader basic pattern] was never sharply demarcated from other forms of bondage, sometimes equally oppressive, it remained a 'mild' variant of the universal genus slave. This does not mean that slaves were not cruelly treated, but that the maintenance of a permanently inferior slave class was not of particular importance to the state, so that manumission or functional absorption into the master's household was frequent" (1983:36).

27. Interestingly, Helen Creese notes that in inscriptions *druwe* has similar overlapping meanings with *ngayah* (personal communication).

sibility underscoring at least the perception of the relationship—which may
be read as well as a critique of the princes—while it also seems significant that
there do not appear to be stories circulating of the loss of family and friends
to slavery. In all of the lord-follower relationships, moreover, corresponding
to findings from Southeast Asia in general (Reid 1983; Gullick 1958), there
are themes of mutuality.

Villages with Historical Connections

Although the mobilization of *pengiring* (followers) occurred through kin
groups, people also would say that certain villages, those in which members
of the kin groups reside, were represented at the maligya ritual. What follows
is a tour of some of the major villages of followers that came from the east,
west, and north, respectively, to assist at the Sidemen Maligya in 1998, and
their stories of how they followed the forefathers of the Jero Gede to Sidemen,
subsequently to be positioned in the surrounding area. (See figure 8.)

Kebung

Kebung is located east and up-slope of Sidemen, though one first must
travel south on the winding road toward Klungkung before turning east along
a road that, at the time of the maligya ritual, turned to dirt, to mud, and finally became a mere soggy path through a beautiful amphitheater of rugged
hills. There is a source of water above Kebung that feeds the irrigation of the
terraced side valley at the head of which this village is located. Eighty percent
of the village lives from tapping the palm trees that proliferate in the area, rendering the sap into the popular alcoholic brew, *tuak*. Voices call down to
passers-by from the treetops, as they do across them through the valley when
the collectors communicate with each other. Every day, the children of Kebung walk this path, an hour each way, to and from school.

Kebung consists of about two hundred fifty households, over a thousand
people of various Pasek kin groups. All the adults, they say, participated in
the maligya ritual in one way or another, with an estimated 300 of them working there from beginning to end. Pak Komang was head of Kebung for many
years. Though he is technically retired now and others have stepped in, his
standing remains. If there is any kind of important matter, he explains, people still come to him: "Until there is guidance from here, they do not dare take
any actions." He is animated and well articulated as he explains that his forefathers had a connection with the family of the Jero Gede, with Cokorda,
which means that whenever there is an *adat* ceremony (ceremony according

Figure 8. Map of Villages in the Princedom of Sidemen

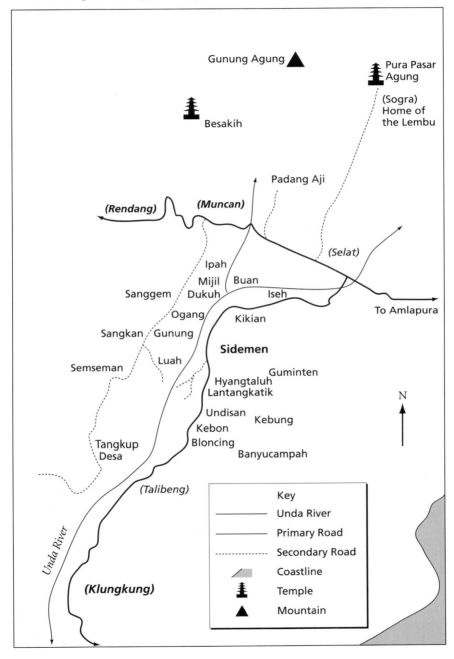

to customary law and religion) at the noble house "I do not remain idle." To explain the connection, he tells the story of the flight from Gelgel and eventual entry into Sidemen of the prince who established the Jero Gede Sidemen, but he highlights the role of his own forefathers, the Pasek, in safeguarding this Dalem line and, with it, the integrity of Bali:[28]

> Previously, during the reign of Dalem Pamahyun at Gelgel [the forefather of the Jero Gede]...the raja's right hand got too bold with him, the one who was called I Gusti Agung Maruti. He went amuck at the Jero there, at Gelgel, he went amuck. He wanted to take over the rajadom. What is the term now? He was ambitious. I Gusti Agung Maruti. Ambitious. He wanted to sit in the palace of the raja. So, for the sake of peace, They [the forefathers of the Jero Gede][29] were rendered safe by the Pasek family. They had to escape.
>
> They escaped to Perasi. They were followed there by the Pasek family. There were many that followed them. Then, after that, their forefather wanted to go to Temege. Again there were many that followed. From there, They arranged matters [delegating people to different areas]: "Oh, you Pasek, stay there. You Pasek, stay there." Then They were asked to come here by Arya Ngurah Sidemen [i.e. Gusti Ngurah or Anglurah Sidemen]; it was requested that Cokorda come stay in Sidemen. And They agreed. I followed; the Pasek families followed.[30]

---

28. MacRae finds that there is an "intellectual patronage," a "control of local knowledge...being centralized in Ubud" (1999:140), including a rewriting of tradition to conform to the grand narrative of Puri Ubud. Although various dadias in Sidemen have their own narratives with hints of challenge to any imagined monopoly on the story and the glory of the Jero Gede, there also must have been a historical process of conformation to the narrative of the Jero Gede Sidemen and of followers asserting their own space within that. That this kind of process is ongoing is evidenced in everything surrounding the maligya ritual; yet what I am presenting here is that there is at least an element of mutual constitution. But see also chapter 7 for how the events surrounding the keris at the 1998 maligya ritual came to be taken as proof—at least by some—of the Jero Gede's claims, in other words, of their "grand narrative." Tjokorda Gede Dangin's role in the local community and as a mediator and sometimes judge, also puts him in the position often of defining tradition and local practice (cf. chapter 5).

29. The respectful form "beliau" is used, which can be translated as both singular or plural. I translate it in the plural to indicate that this refers more to the "collective" house and the "authority" of the Jero Gede (past and present) than to these specific individuals. I capitalize "They" to indicate the respectful form.

30. Note that Balinese often conflate ego with the collective.

Some were placed here at Kebung, some at Sanggem, some at Sidemen..., like that....So, I have a strong connection with Cokorda.

Desa Kebung, he says, turned formerly dry land into irrigated rice for the Jero Gede Sidemen, including the land on which the maligya ritual was held. In return they got repayment from the Jero Gede. That is the story of their connection, Pak Komang concludes. He explains more of the nature of the relationship when it came to war, showing that while Sidemen followed Karangasem, Kebung followed Sidemen:

> As I said before, in the time of the Dutch, there were forefathers of mine here. Now, the Dutch clashed with Singaraja and Karangasem. There was a war. Then Their forefather hit the ketungan [the trough, as in the maligya ritual, rhythmically pounded to summon followers]. "Kebung come give a hand, you must come along to Singaraja." And this, moreover, was by foot. And what were they to use for weapons? Where were they to find any? Bamboo spikes was all they had.[31] And we ran to Singaraja. Following Their forefathers. To the point that my forefather died there, was killed...following the raja god [*ngiring raja dewata*]; in Balinese, the term is raja. They were rajas.[32]

> After that, Karangasem went to war with Klungkung. But nobody lost, nobody won....And then again, to Denpasar. Karangasem also went to war there. And we, we *ngiring*, we followed Them. But there [I came face to face with my extended family]; we met there, Pasek with Pasek.... Previously nobody was bold with the Pasek [i.e. dared mess with them]. But under Their leadership;...if the order was to "kill!," well, we'd kill. In the end it did not happen [laughs]. That is my history with Them.

Now, points out Komang, they go to ceremonies as they formerly went to war.

---

31. Regarding early kingdoms in Burma and Thailand, too, Tambiah writes that "the soldiers were primarily the peasantry mobilized ad hoc from the immediate area" and that they "brought their own [primitive] weapons" (1985:267).

32. It would thus appear that they were not on the frontlines of the uniform troops that surprised the Dutch in 1848, as described by the Dutch Lieutenant-Colonel: "The thousands of Balinese at the approaches to Bungkulan presented a beautiful spectacle, red masses, interpersed with white, glistening in the sun. They were armed with lances as well as rifles and they were dressed in red while some of them, their champions, wore white.... Their lances, too, were uniform....It was obvious that this was not just a bunch of people hastily drummed up" (J. van Swieten 1849:56–57; van der Kraan1995:51).

We remember, he says, the good of the forefathers of Cokorda at the Jero to the people here, so that whatever activity there is at the Jero, the people here ngayah at the Jero. Also when the people here have activities, They descend to lend a hand [lit. descend with their hands], whether it be [he lists every kind of ceremony].

He also mentions a connection that persists through a temple that the Jero Gede Sidemen has at Kebung, maintained for them by people of Kebung:

They have a temple here that the people here maintain and at which They pray. It was constructed by Their forefathers. It is called Pura Gangga Ya. Their forefathers built it, and so They gave the people here the task of overseeing it and performing the ceremonies for it, a ceremony every six months....But They already gave proof, a guarantee in the form of land, five hectares of dry fields, and approximately one hectare of irrigated rice, for taking care of the temple there. And we get the harvest from that.

Pak Komang on a different occasion relates a story of how the Jero Gede Sidemen ensured the very continuity of Kebung. Things had not been going well in Kebung, nobody was having any children, and eventually there was just one old man left, with no descendants. At that point, the Jero Gede Sidemen sent him a very young wife whom he impregnated, although he by now was bent-over and ancient. She bore him descendants aplenty and, since then, whenever there is a wedding at Kebung, they must come to the Jero Gede Sidemen first, to the high caste family temple, to notify them and get holy water (*matur piuning*, as when the Jero Gede Sidemen gave notification at the "Six Temples of the World" that they were going to perform the maligya ritual). This is an interesting twist in the usual wife-giver/wife-taker relationship, for ordinarily it is villages that give wives to the Jero Gede. By contrast to more egalitarian societies where the wife-givers tend to have higher standing, including in much of Eastern Indonesia, in Bali you acknowledge an inferior position in the relationship by giving a wife. Although the telling of the story regarding Kebung emphasized that it was a woman from the noble house that was given, there is also the possibility that the woman in question was a woman of low status linked to the court.[33]

---

33. Boon also refers to "the habit of some rajas to give women from a select noble house to commoners who performed an outstanding service" (1977:233, n.8). As he points out, "This move could be interpreted either as the raja nullifying the ordinary rules of hyper-

So, says Pak Komang, "remembering the good service of Their forefathers, all of the people here ngayah'ed at the maligya ritual, be it to build this or that, the structures, all of them. We ngayah'ed until it was completed." He emphasizes that when you ngayah "there is nothing given in return, there is none of this at all, because there is a connection."

When asked what stood out most to him at the maligya ritual, Pak Komang responds that "this was when Their ancestors descended, at the *Mepurwa Daksina* ceremony. Beh, it was very peaceful then. That is what stands out first. And, second, when Mbak Mega [Megawati] came. Ooy, the people and crowds were extraordinary at the place of the ritual." Later Pak Komang talks quite dramatically about the time Megawati prayed in the Jero Gede's family temple. With flourish, he tells also of how she pulled a small keris of her own out of her purse, holding it up to Bangawan Canggu as she confirmed how powerful, indeed, was the heirloom keris of Sidemen. (This was not a part of the story that was generally emphasized.) Continuing without prompting his account of what stood out, Pak Komang adds, "Third was when the betara lingga descended [the symbolic representations of the priestly ancestor 'guides']. And fourth, finally, when they went to the beach at Amed. That was at the end. Oos, how many cars there were....We went, and I am not disparaging Them, but we did so without food."

This latter comment presents an interesting parallel to the above tale of how loyally his forefathers followed the Jero Gede, to the point of going to war without weapons. Now they worked until the end of the maligya ritual, and even went on the excursion to the ocean, without so much as a bite to eat. While this could be a veiled critique of the noble house, it also underscores the dedication of the people of Kebung, and it is interesting to note the emphasis placed on mutuality throughout Pak Komang's stories. There was a mutual safeguarding of the Dalem line, mutual rendering of fertile land and life, mutual assistance with ceremonies, and mutual respect (no-one messed with Pasek either).

Sangkan Gunung

Although Sangkan Gunung is straight across the river from Sidemen, to get there by car at the time of the maligya ritual, people had to drive north out of the Sidemen valley, turn west to cross the river, and then go back south along a rapidly deteriorating road on the other side of the valley, passing other villages with connections to Sidemen.

---

gamy or as proof of the commoners' rights to a higher rank. The commoners would like to adopt the latter view" (1977:233, n.8).

There are two Pasek dadia in Sangkan Gunung, the largest one of which is the Pasek Gelgel, but both, numbering up to five thousand people, stand in relationship to the Jero Gede Sidemen. These people were also original followers from Gelgel to Sidemen, after which they were assigned to this area.[34] The same goes for the inhabitants in the other villages along this stretch, including some villages of another elevated Sudra group, the Pande or blacksmith clan. Dangin has explained that they all followed his forefather here:

> So they placed some here, some there. In the beginning in Ogang, they lived just in the fields, taking care of the rice fields. They became many and became a village. The same happened at Semseman, and everywhere else. In the beginning those people lived in the gardens... [but they eventually became villages].

The entire area used to be one customary village (*desa adat*) of which a relative of the noble house was made lord. His descendant is still based here and was very active in the maligya ritual. (Five years later his son is married to Tjokorda Gede Dangin's daughter by his third wife, one of the few alliances approved of for her.)

Wayan Poleh, the head of the local *dadia* of Pasek Gelgel, explains that the connection between the Pasek and the Jero Gede Sidemen has been strong since the time of their forefathers, that it is "historical," and that it cannot be severed: "Seven generations of our elders (*pengelisir*) here, and their elders before these, ngayah'ed at the jero. Whatever the ritual performance, they ngiring at the Jero.... Also the Jero Gede asks for girls [in marriage] from the dadia here." Today the head of the main kin group in Sangkan Gunung also explains that virtually the whole subdistrict (*camat*) is controlled (*dipegang*) by the Jero Gede. He confirms that they pray at the temple of the Jero Gede Sidemen every tenth full moon (*purnama kedasa*) and that it is a form of obligation for them to ngayah at the noble house if there is a big ritual work. Concerning the maligya ritual, he recollects that initially Cokorda sent them a letter, and they went there directly. Then the family of Tjokorda Gede Dangin came here to request coconut leaves to use at the ceremony. Once the process was underway, says Poleh, "I went there, to the Jero, to help build the structures. After that, in another seven days, I went there again, to clean the structures. I made it there four times. Finally, during the maligya ritual, I ngayah'ed; I was given the duty of cooking."

---

34. In the case of Sangkan Gunung, the presence of a particular kind of shrine (*kehen*) in their pura pusuh indicates that there was a village predating the entry of the Jero Gede and their followers into the area. Stuart-Fox states that villages with such shrines "are either definitely or very likely old villages (pre-fourteenth century)" (2002:25).

They consider the Jero their *surya* (sun)—the same term that is used by clients of Brahmana households to refer to the priests to whom they stand in relationship[35]—and, again, they cannot forget that. The way you express it, they say, is that "the kavla here cannot forget the surya;" they would suffer a curse. The family of the Jero Gede Sidemen has explained, conversely, that they pray (*ikut nyungsung*, literally "carry on their head") at the temple at Sangkan Gunung, to the deity at the hill (*bukit*) on top of which the temple is located, "because it has been so from long ago." In Sangkan Gunung they confirm that if there is a ceremony at their temple, too, the people from the Jero Gede Sidemen come: "They come and they give assistance." This includes material assistance. For example, they gave the cement for a temple gate (*kori*), providing assistance for the reconstruction of the temple, which burned down after being hit by lightning. So, explains a member of the noble house, "the connection continues also because we from the Jero Gede still remember that there are *beraya* here, in the sense of summoning them to our rituals as well as in the sense of helping them complete their own rituals and assisting them when in need" (Cokorda Mayun).

Leaders of Sangkan Gunung seek the assistance of the noble house on issues concerning local land, water, and leadership problems. They ask for help, for example, in finding clients for some attractively situated land that they are interested in leasing out to foreigners. Moreover, there are problems with an upstream village that is refusing to pass on drinking water. And, finally, there are problems with the new village head selected by the string of villages along this road. The descendant of the Cokorda that originally was sent out from the Jero Gede Sidemen to govern the area is a banker in a nearby village. His father was village head, but currently there is no cokorda to fill this position. The problem with the newly elected village head, a Sudra who was elected over a Brahmana candidate precisely because they thought he would be more inclined than a Brahmana to reach out to and work with the people (*memasyarakat*), turns out not to be working well enough with the people after all. They seek the advice of the noble house in all of these matters.

Sanggem

Near Sangkan Gunung is the village of Sanggem, also of about 250 households. Nyoman Maue, an elder of Sanggem, who was village leader for almost 50 years, from 1937 until 1986, is joined by, among others, his nephew and

---

35. See Rubinstein (1991a) for more parallel terms for priests and rulers.

his daughter, to talk about why the people from here participated or ngayah'ed at the maligya ritual as extensively as they did. Here, too, the point is made that they have a "historical connection," a connection based on being pengiring. And also here it is added that there are those from Sanggem that have married to the Jero Gede, which creates further connection. As in Sangkan Gunung, in addition to calling themselves pengiring they also call themselves beraya; but in this case, despite the use of the term pengiring, this group did not actually follow the forefathers of the Jero Gede Sidemen from Gelgel, but sought refuge at the Jero Gede after invaders had forced them off their own land near Tulamben on Bali's northern coast: "They were attacked...by Muslims from Makassar, by Bugis. They descended upon them and their villages were destroyed by people of the sea" (Dangin). Then, explains Dangin, "people came from Tulamben, 75 households; they came to Sidemen and asked my forefathers for a place to live." The land they were allotted "was not yet a village, but a place of meditation of a person called Sang Caplokan." This land was given for a village, now called Sanggem. It was like that with all of the villages. Take Kebung, Luah, they were all given land in that way" (Dangin).[36]

From the side of the noble house, they explain that if there is a ritual work at the Jero Gede, they notify their followers at Sanggem, and certainly all of them will help, "with heart and soul," and, they add, "there is no repayment." The nephew of the old leader in Sanggem, a young soft-spoken man, who lives in the tourist hot spot of Kuta and works at the duty free shops in Bali's international airport, says that most of the people here participated in the maligya ritual. "It has become an obligation," he explains; "It is called ngayah, to help. There is no profit or reward." Almost all of the people of Sanggem know of this connection to the Jero Gede, he confirms. It may be that not all of them know the dates and details of the historical connection, but "what is clear is that the connection is passed on from generation to generation. This generation will inform its children that we have a connection of *pangayah* (standing in ritual service to), of *pengiring* (followers) to the Jero Gede. And later those children will let their children know." He characterizes their relationship with the Jero Gede Sidemen as "just normal; like me with my older brother...There was always that kind of a family connection." He stresses that "it is as if the people of Sanggem cannot be separated from the Jero Gede," reiterating that "it is like me with my older brother, that is how strong the connection is."

---

36. The people from Tulamben that were settled in Sanggem came to sort under the control of Gusti Bagus Sangkan Gunung, as he did under Sidemen. Today Sanggem and Sangkan Gunung are one desa dinas and have intermarriage.

The old man, himself, participated in the maligya ritual, with the duty of construction. His daughter, who has had to return to Sanggem from her own foray to the city in order to live with and take care of her father, laughs that people liked working at the maligya ritual, that it was a bustle. To travel to Sidemen by car was, as we have seen, circuitous and took a long time; so instead, people walked in a lively group into the valley and across the river. To her what stood out most was making the sweets and offerings in the purified family temple. She also participated in prayer there and was present for some of the processions.

The nephew points out that the noble house also makes contributions to Sanggem's temple: "From the side of the palace, the Jero, they give much help to the temple here, in the form of money, cloth, cement. They help every time there is any kind of construction or ceremonial at our temple. Even the small people here recognize those of the Jero, he says, because those from the Jero reach out to the people (*memasyarakat*) here." Thus, reiterates the nephew, "the connection between the people of Sanggem and the Jero is difficult to sever; it has to be very strong."

Padang Aji

Padang Aji lies northwest of Sidemen, toward Mount Agung. The group of followers at Padang Aji, originally from Aan, Klungkung, also are Pasek who were pengiring from Gelgel. You enter the settlement along a foot path through *salak* trees, which in season bulge with snake-skinned fruit. Wayan Undis and the elder Wayan Dana refer to members of the Jero Gede as *I Dewa Agung*, literally Great God, the title traditionally reserved for the paramount lord of Klungkung. They explain that when their people were first sent to Padang Aji, there were just two of them, a husband and a wife. Now there are 60 households, with a total of over 300 people. This land was wilderness when they first settled it, they point out; now it is fertile with *sawah* and *salak*.

At Padang Aji the Jero Gede Sidemen has nine hectares of land in the name of its family temple (merajaan). The noble house also, in the past, had "ownership" of a major source of water located just up from the settlement, from where it feeds an entire irrigation system. It flows out of the ground with crisp drinking water and refreshing bathing water. People talk about it as being the next best thing to the cleansed feeling of receiving holy water, so fresh and pure, they say, is this water. From the bathing spot, the spring enters an irrigation canal, marked by a master irrigation temple located at the point where the water starts to be dispersed south. (See Lansing 1991, 1993, and in press for analysis of Balinese water temple systems.) It flows on down-valley, ultimately to the irrigated rice fields in the Sanggem and Sangkan Gunung area.

But in between there is also Desa Muncan, which, at the time that the palace of Karangasem was asserting itself in the area, lost its connection to Sidemen. The Raja of Karangasem inserted his own lord (punggawa) in Muncan as he increased his control of the area, such that now, at the maligya ritual for example, they do not automatically ngayah from Muncan, though some do come as invited guests.

Wayan Dana and Wayan Undis emphasize the issue of this water source and its complications. They explain that they at one point lost their control of the source when they refused to pass on water to the farmers downstream. The Raja of Karangarem seized it from them. As was later elaborated from the side of the noble house:

> During the time of rajas, the water was at Padang Aji, but…the Raja of Karangasem had a lot of sawah near Muncan, at Mijil. Consequently, at Padang Aji, they dammed the waterway, they did not want to give it to Muncan, or to any other sawah that did not have a connection with Padang Aji. So they were accused by the Karangasem Kingdom. It was the raja that took action against this, and because of that the water could flow downstream again to the places of those other people, including Muncan and Ipah....After that, Padang Aji was not given that water by the raja.
>
> Now, after this, because it was our forefathers who owned the land that is at Padang Aji, our forefather asked it back of the raja. In the end he conceded it to them, the water....The raja did not dare not honor this…because the land at Padang Aji, afterall, was owned by us. He gave us so and so much,…to irrigate the sawah at Padang Aji that is owned by Ida I Dewa Gede Dangin, the family temple here [merajaan]. [Cokorda Mayun]

Since the land of the water source was actually, by historical and divine right, owned by the deity of the family temple of the Jero Gede, even the raja "did not dare" but to honor their claim ("since it was after all our possession"). Supposedly, now all the subaks downstream get water from it: "the many subaks at Muncan, the subak at Bodog, the subaks get it. And Sangkan Gunung.....They get it all the way to the end of system" (Cokorda Mayun). Dangin explains that "all that got water from there, paid taxes to me, to this place. They paid rice, *soewinih* it was called" (i.e. the tax placed on the use of irrigation water). "Because of that we became rich," laughs Cokorda Raka. All of this, it is said, came to an end by the time of the Dutch. The Dutch are said to have bought the water source: "They paid compensation (*bayar kerugian*)," says Raka, and "after that it was not ours any longer, just the land was ours. And now it belongs to the government.... After Independence, ... the water became the possession of the nation."[37]

Regarding the land, meanwhile, there is talk of the Jero Gede Sidemen at various times having been "forced to sell the land of that water source." For example, explains Dangin, "there was a younger brother of my grandmother's that was in debt, who liked to smoke opium.... Maybe my family did not really understand the significance of the land. So it was sold to get money." In 1971 (or 1978; stories vary) there was again an issue with the Padang Aji land, this time on the occasion of an ancestral ceremony at the noble house. The way the story is presented from the perspective of Padang Aji, the noble house sold them the land for money that they were in need of for their ceremony. From the perspective of the Jero Gede Sidemen, however, they say:

> No, we did not sell. It was only what would be termed "seeking money," it was not what would be termed a sale. The people there were asked for money for ceremonial expenses, and then they would not have to bring the harvest to us.... So it was a different agreement.... So now, although they continue to bring produce every year to the noble house, they are not forced to do so. We do not go by any kind of determination as to what share of rice, for example, they must bring; just however much they are able to. On paper, the land is still the possession of the pemerajaan, under the name of Pemerajaan Jero Ida I Dewa Gede Dangin. [Cokorda Pemangku]

About this situation surrounding the noble house's ceremony and the issue as to whether Padang Aji actually purchased the land, Raka explains:

> It was like this: The people of Padang Aji gave money, but that land cannot be sold, because it is temple land (*tanah laba pura*), and they still have the obligation to go to the merajaan [i.e. to the family temple of the Jero Gede Sidemen]. Because there are already so many of them and they have to reside on that land, they asked for it. And I do not know how much money changed hands.... [It was not Dangin] but my uncle who has already passed away that did this.

---

37. I ask if the raja of Karangasem ever owned it, to which he answers, no. Dangin: "Before the Dutch came, they continued to pay to us at Sidemen. After that it was taken by the Dutch. After the Dutch came independence, and the source of water came to be worried about by the government..."

And so it is still that to this day the land of the source is titled to the family temple of the noble house, Ida I Dewa Gede Dangin. As expressed by I Dewa Gede Catra, a local manuscript specialist, "the deity at the Merajaan owns a lot of land at Padang Aji, and, moreover, it includes the source of water there." It appears, in short, that the history of land ownership is not always clear and is not uncontested—it appears, more specifically, that members of the noble house at times of financial need either (depending on perspective) sold or pawned off the land. Yet, in the end, it also appears that the argument continues to hold sway that, ultimately, the land and the water source are not alienable from the ancestral god. At the same time it is acknowledged that the numbers of people living on and off the land have grown and the Jero Gede has, for all practical purposes, conceded it to them, while the followers of Padang Aji, in return, continue to "owe" an undetermined amount of contributions to rituals of the noble house. Nowadays the irrigation associations of farmers that get water from this source, though they do not pay water tax (*soewinih*), also continue to do ritual duties at the noble house. As for the people of Padang Aji, themselves, says the priestly brother of the noble house,

> their obligation never was called *soewinih*, because that land was owned by my forefathers. It was they who placed them there; it was they who gave them a certain obligation. The obligation was to cultivate that land and to occupy it. And then the harvest had to go to the merajaan every year to be used for expenses or means for a *pujawali* ceremony....Previously, when I was still small, whenever there was a ceremony at the merajaan, they had to bring the agricultural produce there, such as rice and bananas, and also some money....This was just annually [i.e semiannually according to the Gregorian calendar]; the daily produce they ate themselves....[Cokorda Pemangku]

He reiterates: "Now it is just however much they can spare."

Conclusion

In the Sidemen Maligya many components of royal power were manifested, and, in the end, there was a materialization of powers and people that constituted what might be called a princedom. Locally the noble house, the Jero Gede Sidemen, to at least some extent has retained its role and numerous kin groups and outlying villages remain connected to it. The maligya ritual came into being only through the exchange relations between the noble house and other participants, to many of whom they remain rajas. These relationships and their constituent exchanges may not before have been fully activated in current generations, but were brought into play at this particular time, in part also because of the conjunction of the ancestral ritual with a period of crisis in Indonesian history.

There is always an element of unpredictability to large rituals; it is never a given how they will turn out. In the context of historical upheaval in Indonesia and what might be termed a state of power vacuum, there was an added element of risk. But in the end, a hierarchy was completed in Sidemen, a hierarchy which became manifest only in the practice of the ritual, and which will never be more concrete than it was in the months of the maligya ritual preparations—yet which continues to exist to be referred to or drawn on as needed by both princes and people, a memory of what powers can be mobilized should the need arise. The picture completed is one of the caste system in action, a hierarchy with Sidemen and, in the end, Megawati at its apex: The system relies on connections with priests and a base of followers and with the invisible world of ancestors and deities—as well as with the Majapahit heirloom. The point is made that Suharto's vice president Habibie, who by the time of the maligya ritual was interim president, had been invited too, but no connection with him materialized. The configuration with Megawati did and was sanctioned by the keris.

Remarkable as it is to find classic negara dynamics at play in a small contemporary princedom, the noble house's great maligya ritual was far from a timeless, automatic reenactment of ancient ritual. Rather, in a sociogenic way, it was able "to bring forth, define, and empower social relationships" (cf. Lansing 1991:15) in the context of historical process. Social structural allegiances were not just reflected or projected, but indeed took shape in the practice of the ritual. This, in itself, may have been a characteristic as well of earlier negara. As Schulte Nordholt has pointed out about the nineteenth-century negara, it "was not a permanent body, but had to be re-created over and over again" (1996a). Such was borne out in Sidemen in 1998, where, as were the invisible forces at the very outset of the endeavor, sometimes temporarily dormant relationships between people were reactivated.

Having outlined the Sidemen Maligya and the princedom behind it, the remainder of this book takes as its point of departure the question as to how the princedom system continues to have relevance to its participants. All of these people came together at one time and place, in the context of ritual, and this ritual has been the starting point for analysis of the present princedom, all of which concords interestingly with the analyses of Geertz and other negara scholars emphasizing the precolonial role of ritual. But this study also looks more closely at the ritual's political dimensions and the ways in which the various participants became involved and why in their minds they did so. In addition to reflecting the classic dynamics of Balinese kingship, closer inspection of the relationships manifested between people and princes, also reveals some surprises. The typical model for the Balinese kingdom placed the to varying degrees divinely imbued raja at its center, in some form of dual relationship with his court priests. This royal center, then, was surrounded by satellites governed by lords, under which sometimes sorted minor lords and, under all of them, the mass of peasants. While this model is not incorrect, it is also misleading in that it poses a hierarchy in the Dumontian sense of encompassment of the lower by the higher. The issues of Balinese kingship have been evoked at the level of the biggest rajas, with the assumption that the princedoms were micro kingdoms modeling themselves on, and encompassed within, the central kingdom which, in turn, was modeled on Majapahit. It should then be this that the princedom is harking back to today. Yet, beyond merely mirroring the larger kingdom, as an always lesser, dimmer replica through space and time, new facets also come to the forefront in the relationship between the rulers and the ruled when the issues of kingship are played out at the princedom level, refracted in the present day also through the impacts of further national and global developments.[38]

Though the modern princedom came together in ritual, this does not mean that its "government" is based largely on ritual display, anymore now than it was in the past. One surprise yielded by the Sidemen Princedom, given the way in which negara have been conceived by many previous scholars, is the extent to which people who participated in the ritual on the basis of precolonial historical connections appeal to land as material proof of such connection. The next chapter steps back from the ritual to look more closely at land relations in the realm of Sidemen. In addition, followers of the princes also emphasize the princes' populist politics and the mutuality in their relationships, with hints as well of the impact of the followers' own powers. Subsequent chapters will look more closely at these aspects by considering the daily work of the princes in securing the foundation for their power and for the possibility, in the first place, of staging the claim that they did through the maligya ritual, as well as at ways in which their powers are circumscribed. As we shall see, in order to effect the ultimately hierarchical system, there is also an incorporation of more "egalitarian" sentiments.

---

38. There is, in other words, a question here whether kingdoms and princedoms, kings and princes, conformed to a single ideological model, as reportedly do African chiefs and kings (cf Muller 1981), as well as Polynesian chiefs and kings (Claessen 2000:708).

PART TWO

RECASTING BALINESE HIERARCHY

CHAPTER FOUR

LAND MATTERS: OBLIGATIONS TO THE SOURCE AND THE ANCESTORS

From reading much of the literature on Southeast Asia and Bali, one easily gets the impression that land has been of little importance to kingship. Stressed throughout is how the ability to summon followers has been far more instrumental in determining royal power than has ownership of land, which until the twentieth century was not a scarce commodity and over which kings, moreover, did not have absolute command. Anthony Reid thus emphasizes "manpower not land" as being what "distinguishes traditional Southeast Asian states from feudal ones" (1983:8) and Tambiah characterizes the Southeast Asian "galactic polity" as "a politico-economic system premised on control of manpower as its chief resource" (1985:281). Also in trying to understand the perennial rebellions of galactic polities, he stresses that "We should not for a moment lose sight of the manpower shortage and of the low demographic densities in all the traditional Southeast Asian mainland polities, and of the fact that control over men rather than over land was the dominant principle of their political organization" (1985:268).

In Bali, royal edicts concerning village-state relations indicate that, likely, rajas sometimes were declared or declared themselves the owners of everything, but also that this should be understood in an abstract sense, much as deities were the owners of all of the land or all water, for example.[1] As Wolters

---

1. All-encompassing ownership of land was sometimes attributed to either gods or kings in an abstract sense. Liefrinck wrote: "The land, with everything that grows on it, the water that flows through it, the air that envelops it, the rock it holds in its womb, belongs without exception or limitation to the invisible gods and spirits who inhabit it...Also completely in keeping with this notion of overriding rights of the deity is the fact that land is never farmed before permission has been requested from the local deity and that as soon as cultivation has begun nothing is considered more essential than to erect an altar to the

observes regarding Southeast Asia, it is precisely when a realm is not territorially defined that "there need be no limit to a ruler's sovereign claims on earth" (1999:22). In Bali, it appears that while rajas may have had control of uncultivated lands outside of village territories, the land within these was owned not only by rajas, but by village institutions, including temples and village associations, or even by individuals, and irrigated land was managed through irrigation associations (cf. e.g. Alfons van der Kraan 1983:318; Stein Callenfels 1947; Lansing 1991). That land in Bali could be owned by any individual other than the lowest of serfs and slaves, meant that a villager did not necessarily have to be connected to a lord in order to cultivate. Even in the absence of reliable records of palace landholdings prior to colonization by the Dutch, it is reasonable to conclude that there was not necessarily a direct correlation between wealth in landholdings and power as reflected in one's ability to attract followers (cf. Robinson 1995:125).[2]

---

deity as an expression of gratitude. A part of the crops harvested from the lands should be presented to the deity as an offering, and whenever wood and other materials for the repair of temples or altars are needed they are taken where they are best to be found, regardless of whatever rights persons may exercise on the lands where they occur…All in all, the above removes every doubt that, in the view of the Balinese, the land is owned by the gods who inhabit the country" (Goris 1954:82). See also Lansing (1991) regarding how all of the water belongs to the Goddess of the Lake. Similarly, at times the ruler is declared owner of all the lands and resources in his realm, but this must be viewed in a symbolic sense. Geertz summarizes the issue: "The general relationship between the king and the material world was summed up in a deceptively prosaic word whose apparent ease of translation has been the chief bar to scholarly understanding of it: druwe…('to own,' 'possess'…)…The problem is that, used in connection with the king, it was applied to virtually everything…to the country as a whole, all the land and water in it, and all the people" (1980:127). Geertz points to the ways in which this has been misunderstood and adds: "When one considers that not only 'kings,' but also 'gods,' 'villages,' 'families,' and 'individuals' were said to own 'everything' - the same 'everything' - the necessity for a less elementary view of 'possession' becomes apparent. In particular, if the relation between ruler and the realm is to be understood properly" it must be understood that "it had to do with their role in the symbology of power" (1980:127–128). With the added complications of new forms of ownership, the issue is still evident today in how, for example, the land of the source in Padang Aji cannot be alienated from the god, and also in how there can be more than one legitimate claim to the same property (cf. the story of Padang Aji as well as Dangin's mediation cases in chapter 5).

    2. In the case of the raja of Tabanan, he was both one of the poorest and one of the weakest rajas in Bali: "In 1942 his puri owned a mere 14 hectares of 'very mediocre' sawah and a small amount of dryland, and by 1949 the total had been reduced to just 9 hectares.… The total amount of sawah and dryland could not support the simplest ritual obligations

And yet, however true it may hold that the ability to control human resources mattered more to kingship than did landed wealth, and although the extent of human resources any given raja could mobilize was not inevitably reflected in his landownership, the example from Sidemen indicates—as does that farther west from the former kingdom of Mengwi (Schulte Nordholt 1996a:60)—that land was central nonetheless to establishing your human resources. In Sidemen, land to this day remains implicated in retaining such connections: Inquiry into people's reasons for continuing to perform ritual duties to the princes, labor without which the royal ritual would not have been possible, has revealed that at the heart of much ritual participation lay historical connections involving land. Significantly, it is not a new form of land relationship that is highlighted as constituting the tie of followers to lords: People explained over and over that their relationship is based on gifts of land from the noble house from the seventeenth century on, a form of land called *pacatu*, land on which they live and from which they continue to draw sustenance.

Princes, Pacatu, and People

Historically pacatu was a category of land "belonging" to lords, but of which full usufruct was granted to farmers in return for loyalty and palace service (*ngayah*, as discussed in chapter 3). The main responsibilities of the workers of pacatu lands to their lord included maintenance of the palace as well as ritual duties. In addition, they were obligated to follow their lord in war, should the need arise. The obligations were primarily to their own lord, but sometimes they also had to work for the raja under which their lord sorted. Though there was some taxation of pacatu (*pajeg*) it appears that this was generally not a large amount and that there was variability in the extent to which the lord succeeded in collecting it (Schulte Nordholt 1993:298, 1996a:60, 130; regarding Southeast Asia in general, see Tambiah 1985). The produce of pacatu land, in short, belonged largely to the pacatu holders.

---

or even the normal material needs of the puri" (Robinson 1995:125). On the other hand, "according to official figures, the raja of Klungkung also owned only 9 hectares in 1949" (1995:125). As Robinson concludes, these figures "appear to indicate that landed wealth alone was not a major factor in determining political authority, since the Dewa Agung was easily the most powerful and respected of the rajas in Bali" (1995:125). But note that Robinson also mentions contradictory sources, including that, according to other figures, Klungkung in fact "was among Bali's largest landowners" (1995:125).

Meanwhile people could be farming other land as sharecroppers as well, from which they would get a much smaller part of the produce. With regard to the pacatu land, they had the right to pass this on as inheritance and even to lease it, though usually not to sell it. For any would-be local rajas, delegating out land as pacatu was the key to having followers for rituals and for war, and this—the labor rather than the produce that pacatu lands brought—was the major reason why pacatu was so valuable to the lords.

Geertz, however, has felt that the importance of the pacatu system "has been greatly exaggerated" (1980:177). Because there was "no systematic congruence...between the structure of political authority, the structure of land tenure, and the distribution of land tenancy" (1980:67) he emphasized instead what he referred to as the perbekel (district head) system as the political institution which had articulated the relation between village and negara and by which the theatre-state rituals had been accomplished. He still saw this to be about people with ritual and war duties to the perbekel who sorted under the lords, but duties based on personal, specifically not land, connections (1980:176, 54, 255). In fact, he says, "some lords...did give the right to work plots of their land to peasants, or sometimes organized groups of them in return for certain specialized services....But this, too, did not loom large anywhere" (1980:176). It is possible that the role of pacatu is more explicit when viewed from the princedom perspective; that is, from the perspective of the level of a local lord who may be perbekel to a larger lord. As mentioned, Schulte Nordholt found it to have played a central role in the Mengwi region as well, and the main example he cites pertains to a local-level lord and his relatives establishing connections to followers through pacatu (1996a:60).[3] A colonial estimate approximates that 35 percent of the irrigated rice (sawah) land in Southern Bali was pacatu, but Schulte Nordholt suggests that, given how rapidly the Dutch dismantled some pacatu lands, the precolonial figure more likely was around 50 percent (1996a:129–130). Whichever the figure, there is no doubt that there, concomitantly, were considerable quantities of non-pacatu sawah as well. Some of these provided for the palaces themselves, for since pacatu holders largely kept the produce of pacatu lands, a lord had non-pacatu lands farmed by slaves to provide produce to the palace. In addition, there

---

3. Note that Korn, too, had argued that there was not pacatu in Tabanan (1932:227), which is the main region on which Geertz's study is based. It should also be noted, though, that Boon in the seventies found that "current local lore and practice echo pachatu traditions to a degree which makes it doubtful they are a total fabrication" (1977:56).

also were lands owned by village and temple associations and by individual peasants. It is also important to take into account the other characteristic of the Balinese situation, that villagers had mixed land rights: The same villager might farm and harvest land given to him by his lord while also holding land in common with other villagers or fellow kin group members, and even outright owning some land privately. In other words, Bali did not neatly fit the classic theory of a linear succession of production modes; rather, there was a coexistence of various productive systems: There was slavery of people who could hold no land of their own, there was pacatu constituting lord-follower relationships, and there was freehold. The relative composition of these systems varied within and across kingdoms and princedoms. As a result, as also Schulte Nordholt has pointed out, even if 50 percent of land was non-pacatu, it does not follow that "50 percent of the total population was without some relation to the puri [palace]" (1996a:130) or, we might add, it does not follow, as has been assumed, that it was not through pacatu that relationships between lords and followers were articulated.

Pacatu in the Sidemen Princedom

Groups of followers of the Jero Gede Sidemen each date their land connections primarily to their initial entry into the area. When the *pengiring* followed the forefathers of the noble house to Sidemen, each group was assigned to various plots of land in the surrounding area, while a few others moved into the area later, and approached the noble house for an assignment of land. In the words of Tjokorda Gede Dangin:

> We controlled almost everything. We also gave them land: Here is a place to stay; here is land to cultivate [we would tell them]. We gave them everything from here before. This is also why they are loyal to that; they still remember that. That is what was important during the maligya ritual....They very much remember that it was us that helped them....From when kids are small, they are told these stories.

Dangin imagines how a conversation between parents and their children might relate the dispersal of people out from Sidemen:

> "How did we come to live here?" children may ask. "O, it's like this," parents might respond, "Previously when the Cokorda at the Jero

came here, he bid our forefathers here too. We followed the forefathers of the Cokorda at the palace. And so Cokorda placed the Pasek family here, here the Pande, here the Pulosari, and so forth; the Tangkas, like that. We were sent to settle here. Because they owned the land, now they have given it to us, and we have become a village."[4]

Again it must be recalled that although rajas did not have all-encompassing ownership of land, they did primarily "own" and could delegate out the uncultivated portions of forest, and that is what much of Sidemen was in the seventeenth century when the heirs of the noble house first established themselves in the region. When asked approximately how many hectares they had in the past, Dangin responds once more that they used to own it all; but, in the same breath, he reiterates regarding the land that "We gave it all to the people....That is what my father recounted." It is this that created the connections, some of which persist to this day. According to Dangin, pacatu is "land given to people to cover their basic expenses of living; it is so they will be able to eat." Previously to give pacatu, *nyatu* also meant to give food, to "give to eat."[5] As we have seen, *ngayah* was defined quite similarly to pacatu, as performing ritual obligations in return for food, and workers of pacatu in some cases were referred to as *pangayah*. Comparing this to the responsibilities of the noble house toward the lowest subject category, the parkan, Dangin explicitly states that "these are two kinds of eating here:" "In the case of pacatu it is in the shape of land; this is land to eat. In the case of the parkan living at the palace, on the other hand, they were outright given food, and they were also said to *nyatu*."[6]

There is sometimes reference as well to a form of land called *pauman* land, defined as the land given to an organization, whereas pacatu is private land, land given to individuals.[7] Says Dangin,

---

4. "They were given everything here, they were given it continuously. They were given four pieces of *sawah*," he says regarding his own group; "more than a hundred *are*" (an *are* is a unit of land of .01 hectares or 100 square meters; i.e. in this case they were given one hectare).

5. "A pacatu is a field of such size that it can be planted with one catu (ration, provision) of rice (=ca 2.5 kg of rice grains). It used to be ten ares or 1,000 square meters [i.e., 0.1 hectare], but by the mid seventies was reduced to five ares (Schaareman 1986:90). Schaareman reported that a minimal subsistence level requires ca. 20–30 are of rice fields per nuclear family (1986:102).

6. McWilliam notes that in West Timor "people will say that they 'eat' from the land of their wife-givers" (2002:163). In that case, unlike Bali, wife-givers are their superiors, from whom "in return for their political allegiance,...[they] are able to gain access to forest and cropping land" (2002:163), in a system that may be comparable to the pacatu system (cf. McWilliam 2002).

Pauman is via the *dadia* [kin groups]; it is more honorary. It is for the provisions of many people, so that they have something if they have a meeting, for the expenses of the meeting. The *pauman* is not a lot of land, just a bit owned by a lot of people.... [It is important to the noble house] for in their meetings they talk about this and that, so that they are ready for war and whatever. The land provides a form of proof that this is an organization from the Jero, an organization that belongs to the palace; this is the land.

Pauman land thus also serves to establish ties between the noble house and human resources. As in chapter 3, where we found that the ties between lords and followers in fact may be between kin groups, not just between individuals or houseyards, here, too, what we find in Sidemen differs from or adds a new perspective to Geertz's finding that "neither perbekels [district heads sorting under lords] nor punggawas [lords], nor even the king himself, held territories. Nor did they hold village political units (hamlets, irrigation associations, temple groups), to which they had no defined relationship as lords at all. They held, or as they put it 'owned,' the real political resource in classical Bali: people" (Geertz 1980:64). Again we find that not only do there appear to have been and continue to be defined relationships as lords to forms of village political unit, but this connection also was and is through land. As Dangin explained, "be it pacatu or pauman land, it is usually given by the raja to families close to the raja. They have the duty of helping at the palace—that means, if there is a work at the palace, they come. No matter what it is. Before, this included war, ceremonies, anything."

The land is viewed as a "gift" from princes to people, a gift that brought and brings returns. It is on the basis of these ties, that so many people ngayah'ed at the Jero Gede's big ritual work. Groups that in the past received land from the noble house continue to honor their historical connection to the princes, providing the resources to (re)create, boost and solidify their position, not only in the local area, but at the regional and national levels as well. As Tjokorda Gede Dangin underlines, "It was us who gave them a place to stay and gave them land to work. That is why they still honor that (*bakti*), why they still remember it..." "So it is with Balinese people," he adds, "no matter how many generations ago this happened, they still remember it." One farmer explained that "because Cokorda has been good to us here since a long time

---

7. Dangin explains that "paum" means "meeting." "Di paum" is to "become one" ("disatukan," "menjadi satu"). According to Korn, the yield of the pahuman land served to nourish the pahuman during their time in the palace (1932:98, 291).

ago, when Cokorda has a ritual work, we always want to ngayah at the Jero." Because people were given land, he explained, they remember it to this day, "whatever ritual work there may be at the Jero, they immediately want to ngayah, until it is completed."

Dutch Colonial Policy to Dismantle Pacatu

The continued appeal to pacatu ties is particularly interesting given that these have been targeted by both Dutch colonial policy and postindependence land reforms, all of which involved strong antifeudal sentiments. Though Dutch colonial policies in many ways escalated Balinese "feudalism" and entrenched Balinese hierarchy—in 1938 they ceremoniously reinserted rajas essentially as puppet princes in the main regional palaces and they codified and in various ways more fiercely enforced caste-related rules—they also sought to eliminate land-based lord-follower relationships in good part, through the issuance of titles, by transferring ownership of pacatu lands from lords to the pacatu holders. The system of productive relations facilitating the lord-follower ties, in other words, was supposedly dismantled by the Dutch, "done away with," Schulte Nordholt puts it outright (1996a:255): "In very short order, the old pacatu system disappeared. The BB [*Binnenlandsch Besturr*, Interior Administration] put an end to this through the introduction of individual landownership" (1996a:252). In some cases, when this happened, the land's cultivator gained title to the land and "noble families who, owing to administrative reorganizations, had lost much of their power, now lost their control over their old pacatu sawah as well....This, in turn, implied that a follower could suspend his service to the lord without running the risk of losing his land" (Schulte Nordholt 1996a:252). In other cases, however, powerful palaces managed to convert their pacatu holdings to property holdings such that the former pacatu farmers were reduced to sharecroppers (*pengarap*) and no longer had rights to the entire harvest. In these cases, the followers were "in fact burdened threefold: as sharecroppers they retained only one-third of the harvest, they were made to pay the land tax of their masters and, third, they were assessed for a new income tax" (landowners were exempted while landless sharecroppers were assessed) (Schulte Nordholt 1996a:253).

As did Reid for Southeast Asia in general (1983:8), Geertz has made the point all along, on the basis of his argument that the lords did not get their ritual and military service through land tenants, that the Balinese state was not feudal in the European sense. Even when a land connection is recognized—as in Sidemen and, by Schulte Nordholt, in Mengwi—it remains that the situation in Bali is very different from European feudalism. We have seen, for example, that the pacatu holders got to keep the produce of the pacatu lands and that there was not heavy taxation of this land.[8] Following Dutch colonization, meanwhile, as a consequence of colonial policies that redefined lord-follower relations and territorialized the organization of kingdoms, the Dutch "unwittingly," as James Boon says, "reconstrued" Balinese society "as a feudalistic social control based on landholdings" (1977:180). Geertz refers to this as the system becoming "pseudofeudal" when, in order to perform the royal rituals, the rajas on the regional level, reinstated by the Dutch, had to start levying the ritual duty on their sharecroppers (1980:255). What we are seeing in the royal ritual of contemporary Sidemen, however, is not the residual of this colonially shaped circumstance. Those with continued duties in the princedom and its rituals are not sharecroppers. The Jero Gede Sidemen does continue to have regular sharecroppers on the land the princes still outright own, but these are a separate category, "can be anyone" and do not necessarily come from kin groups, villages, or organizations with which the noble house has historical connections predating colonization by the Dutch. The princes estimate that they have approximately fifty such sharecroppers, all of whom also do ngayah and bring a share of their produce if there is a ceremony at the noble house, but they are not involved in the ritual duties in the same way. Their obligations are very differently defined than are those of the historical pacatu holders; they play a minimal role. Those with continued duties, former subjects of various kinds, now often are referred to as pengiring to stress the historical connection, but also are pacatu holders, tracing these connections back to the seventeeth century. It would appear, then, that postindependence land reforms, the effects of which lie closer in people's memories, did not abolish pacatu ties either.

Postindependence Land Reform

In looking at the background to Bali's postindependence land-related crises, Geoff Robinson has pointed to an ongoing problem of landlessness, which, he says, already had "reached serious proportions in the early 1920s" (1995:57–58). Since there are no data pertaining to landlessness in precolonial Bali (cf. Schulte Nordholt 1996a:130), we might also presume that the 1920s, along

---

8. Reid also emphasizes "manpower not land" as being what "distinguishes traditional Southeast Asian states from feudal ones" (1983:8).

with the colonial registration of landholdings, was when the problem was first recorded. People still recall that, at this time (1926), in accordance with colonial land or tax reform, there was "a clarification" (*pemataan*) with regard to land: "Land was mapped, and only then was it definite. It became outright possession" (I Dewa Gede Catra).[9] It is not that the idea of landownership up until then was altogether alien. As we have seen, not all land was the possession of universal monarchs. In addition to land belonging to rajas, lords, and temples, there were also village and freehold lands. But now this "clarification" also became associated with an intensification of the problem of landlessness, the situation deteriorating markedly during the Depression. It was an issue that came to a head again following the Nationalist fight for independence (1945–49),[10] especially when youth (*pemuda*) who had been fighting the war were reintegrated into society, increasing the demand for agricultural land (Robinson 1995:57–58, 251–252).[11] Population growth was a further factor aggravating the problem of access to agricultural land in the postindependence period. The population of Bali in the sixteenth century was, roughly, a quarter million, and at the beginning of the twentieth century still less than one million. But already by the 1950s it had expanded to about a million and a half and was rapidly increasing—by the end of the century, it was approaching three million. In 1963, the eruption of Mount Agung, moreover, resulted in the loss of productive land. The mounting and combined pressures of these factors spurred various phases in the call for land reform.

---

9. Schulte Nordholt writes of a situation in the kingdom of Mengwi: In 1902, when lords divided over whether to remain loyal to the Dewa Agung of Klungkung or give allegiance to the Dutch, "the Mengwi dynasty was ripped apart into a 'Dutch' camp and a 'Klungkung' camp" (1996a:206). Unlike any prior local practice, the Dutch proceeded to map this out, imposing territorial division on the situation of "dispersed groups of followers," such that people ended up having to uproot and move into the so designated territories (1996a:208–209). This process repeated itself.

10. During World War II, the Japanese occupied Indonesia for over three years between 1942 and 1945. Sukarno proclaimed Indonesian independence following the Japanese capitulation in August 1945, but the Dutch tried to resume their rule and sovereignty was not transferred to Indonesia until December 1949.

11. Following the 2002 bombing in Kuta and the subsequent decline in tourism and general economic crisis we see again increased pressure on land, as former employees of the tourism sector who have lost their jobs return to their villages. Regarding the situation in the 1950s Robinson explains further: "In the course of the Revolution, the families of many pemuda had been forced to sell or pawn their land, and still others had lost legal title…as a consequence of their 'illegal' guerilla activity. Those who had taken over these holdings during the Revolution with the blessing of the village assembly or of local officials were not inclined now to return them" (1995:251–252).

Though some land reform measures already had been undertaken in the early 1950s,[12] enforcement had proved impossible, in large part because of the extent to which people still honored their ties to the local palaces and nobility (Robinson 1995:252). It was only at the outset of 1961 that reform legislation really began to gain momentum. In a climate of growing economic crisis people were coming to rely increasingly on already scarce and disputed land for survival. In this context, Robinson points out, "the implementation of national land-reform legislation in the early 1960s, therefore, had a singular significance for Balinese politics, with, he assesses, "immediate importance for virtually every Balinese," as "most stood clearly to gain or to lose in the event of a straightforward interpretation of the laws" (1995:251). By the end of 1963, land reform became a major focus for the Indonesian Communist Party (PKI); it gained Sukarno's support, and "came to represent a genuine threat to landed interests" which were backed by the Indonesian Nationalist Party (PNI) (Robinson 1995:266).

An "ideal minimum" for universal landholding as well as limits on landholdings were set, the latter varying according to pressure on and demand for land in any given area. In densely populated areas, each household was allowed five or six hectares of land (depending on whether it was irrigated rice or dry land, respectively). In less densely populated areas up to fifteen and twenty hectares, respectively, were allowed. Anything in excess was to go primarily to the farmers of the land in question. Robinson points out that this particular reform actually affected surprisingly few, since few owned large portions of land: It turned out that holdings of more than the two hectare ideal minimum "accounted for only 11 percent of the total agricultural land in 1963" (1995:255).[13] The "ideal minimum" landholding of two hectares, meanwhile, was never realized. Instead, as more than a third of the agricultural land was cultivated by tenants, it was harvest sharing reform that stood to have the greatest impact on the greatest number of people. Here an ideal division of fifty-fifty was determined for irrigated rice and two-thirds (to the farmer) to one-third (to the owner) for dry land. In addition, the landowners were to be responsible for some of the production costs (1995:256, 253). Land reform

---

12. Laws were passed to improve tenants' harvest shares by establishing the legal minimum at 50/50; and for land-owners, land-tax exemption was granted for anyone holding less than three hectares, exempting at least 80 percent of landowners.

13. In Tabanan, Badung, Karangasem, and Gianyar, the total number of owners potentially affected was only about 1,500. In Karangasem a total of 1,629 ha, of 27,180 total farmland, were to be redistributed, affecting 127 landowners with an average holding of 10.07 ha (Robinson 1995:255, tables pp. 254, 256).

was halted in 1965, however, with the alleged coup and anticommunist countercoup,[14] which marked the end to Sukarno's reign and the beginning of Suharto's. Decades later, farmers in Karangasem still report receiving only a third of the harvest as well as remaining responsible for significant production costs. This is the case just as much when their landlords are wealthy Sudra as when they are palace nobles.[15] The land reform movement, meanwhile, became implicated in other political developments surrounding the regime shift.

Robinson writes of how, in the period from 1950–65, "the aggressive implementation of land reform in Bali—led by the PKI [Communist Party] and its peasant organization and assisted by key elements in the local state—contributed to an increasing political polarization along class lines after 1963" (1995:16). As he points out, "the struggles over land set the stage for a powerful and violent reaction by landowners and their allies in the PNI [Nationalist Party]" (1995:16), following the coup of 1965 that brought Suharto to power. It was a time of mass action on behalf of both the Indonesian Peasants' League (PKI/BTI) and Indonesian Nationalist Farmers (PNI/Petani). There were rallies and marches with slogans and songs "deliberately held...in 'enemy' territory" (for a marching song sung by the PKI/BTI members in Sidemen, see Robinson 1995:270):

> Activists burned government offices, stoned the houses of political opponents, and disrupted religious ceremonies or community meetings. Physical scuffles and armed attacks resulting in death were not uncommon.
>
> Particularly acrid confrontations developed over BTI occupations of temple (pura) lands and land attached to one of the more powerful puri. Unilateral BTI seizures of such lands were construed by their opponents as sacrilege, as challenges to the Bali-Hindu religion, and as disruptive of the cosmic order. Also considered offensive and sacrilegious were the refusal by some PKI and BTI members to abide by linguistic etiquette in dealings with their "superiors," and their failure to perform customary ritual obligations. Such interpretations were powerfully reinforced by natural calamities...confirmation of cosmological imbalance and spiritual impurity. And because these...co-

---

14. The coup to put Suharto in power was effected following the murder of six army generals, which Suharto's government said had been a communist coup attempt. The Indonesian communist party at the time was the largest in Southeast Asia.

15. Note that Schaareman reports that in the case of the village pacatu (pacatun desa or pacatun pahuman) fields in Asak, also two-thirds of the yield are designated for the banjar (or the desa respectively), and one-third for the cultivator himself (1986:90–91).

incided with the most militant and aggressively class-based PKI and BTI actions, it seemed plausible to argue that these actions were responsible for the imbalance. [Robinson 1995:270]

Ideas such has these, pertaining to the importance of maintaining cosmic order, are reflected as well in regard to the maligya ritual's role in stabilizing the world. They are also the very rationalizations most people continue to give for the eruption of violence that ensued the growing political conflict in 1965–66, when the escalating tensions described above culminated in the killings throughout Java and Bali of thousands of people accused of being communists (estimates range from half a million to one million; in Bali, 80,000 to 100,000 or up to 8% of the population; see Cribb 1990 for an overview). Now, decades later, when people talk about these killings, they still invariably leave out any alleged component to the accusations of communism, most frequently highlighting the sacrilegious aspects of the PKI actions and program. Given this, many people—people of all castes and in various unconnected villages in the Karangasem region—still hold the view that what took place was inevitable. It is not uncommon for people to express that it was regrettable, but that at least they did a good and righteous job of getting rid of the communists, and Bali has since been safe and peaceful. Many also express the rationale that, at the time, it was either "kill or be killed." Among those with whom I spoke of this, the person who appeared most troubled and perhaps even haunted by what happened was a Nationalist Party (PNI) leader, who, according to how locals in the area talk about it, did not do any killing himself, but presumably gave instrumental directives. One dynamic that he explained as to how this came about was that it was clear from the top echelons of the party that they were going to come from Java to eradicate the communists anyway. The feeling that he and his fellows had was that they, as Balinese, should and could take care of their own matters, not have outsiders come in to do so. It was a situation, it should be noted, wherein local leaders and communities were threatened by the military with reprisals if they failed to take the requisite action.

Another individual, however—a descendant of a former raja—portrayed vividly how he, as a child, watched when individuals were dragged to the hillside below the palace's balcony to be assassinated. Sometimes he joined more directly in the excitement, as he described it, descending to participate in hurling rocks and insults at "the guilty ones." He also recounted joining a mob with torches to burn down a nearby "traitor's" house. He appeared to convey exhilaration at these so vividly remembered events (see Colombijn 2002 regarding moods of lynching crowds). For him, as above, the "justification" was the sacrilege of "the communists," including an oft-repeated comment that "they wanted temples to be used as toilets, you know."[16]

Lest it be thought that only nobility and political leaders have or had the somewhat unapologetic attitude toward this era in Bali's history, a commoner man from a village north of Amlapura, a farmer and a midwife, explained, not without pride, that they had had only one traitor family in their village, but that they had killed these people good and sound, letting only a couple of their youngest children live. Ever since then, these children had been, and still are, carefully molded and monitored by the village to ensure that they do not develop tendencies such as their parents. So far they are model citizens, he expressed, and the village is quite satisfied with the thoroughness of the job they did. He was explicit that it had been absolutely necessary to kill the parents and keep a very close eye on the children who, more likely than not, could have turned bad as well. Such vigilance reflects Suharto's New Order State's surveillance and "clean environment" policies regarding anyone suspected of communist tendencies—or family and descendants of anyone so suspected—policies prohibiting them from political participation or even from access to the lowest level civil service jobs. This is part of how, as Leslie Dwyer and Degung Santikarma have put it, "the bloodshed of 1965 has soaked into Indonesia's social landscape," continuing to shape interactions and individual lives (2003:290). (See also Schulte Nordholt 2002, Dwyer and Santikarma 2003 for discussions of the events of 1965 and their aftermath).

Another significant form of mass political action not yet mentioned was land seizure, *pendobrakan*, as it was generally referred to in Karangasem, but also known as *aksi sepihak*. A Balinese scholar, Ida Bagus Gde Putra, in a thesis on the land reform process (1986) identifies several instances of such action in villages in the Karangasem and Klungkung regions, including the Sidemen area, many of which concerned the landholdings of Puri Karangasem. Puri Karangasem, the main palace in Amlapura, after all, was one of the biggest landowners on Bali and also, if contemporary attitudes are any indication, is considered less legitimate, thus less inspiring of loyalty than, for ex-

---

16. Far from always being a result of mob actions, there were designated people, referred to as *tukang bunuh*, in charge of assassinations. *Bunuh* means to kill. *Tukang* indicates a skilled laborer or craftsman; such as *tukang besi* (blacksmith), *tukang jahit* (tailor), or *tukang potong* (butcher) (though it can also be used to refer to someone with a bad habit, such as *tukang bohong* for liar or *tukang mabuk* for drunkard) (Echols and Schadily, *An Indonesian-English Dictionary*). These people, it is often said, are the ones more affected, the ones never to be the same again, haunted by the ghosts of those whom they have killed.

ample, the not so well landed Dalem line of rajas. But Ida Bagus Gde Putra also points out that, albeit that the land seizure actions were directed at the landowners, their immediate victims were not infrequently the tenant farmers. He cites examples from the surrounding area of Sidemen also, examples involving land owned by the Karangasem palace, showing that these, too, had tenants that remained loyal at great risk to themselves:

> In one case reported from Karangasem, a group of about forty BTI supporters from desa Rendang marched with flags and banners to seize a piece of sawah in Desa Sangkan Gunung owned by the Puri Karangasem. The tenant farming the land in question, one I Wayan Kenggo, was in his field when the group arrived, and reportedly died resisting their attempt to seize the land. In a similar case in Yang Taluh, Sidemen, the land in question was also owned by the Puri Karangasem, but the tenant, I Wayan Madra, was supported by other PNI farmers and was not killed. [Robinson 1995:269; see Putra 1986:110, 116]

These seizures of land were condemned by both the Communist Party (PKI) and Sukarno, as well as by the Nationalist Party (PNI); yet they continued into the mid-1960s.

The Jero Gede Sidemen's Relations in this Period of the 1960s

Needless to say, the issues of this era of escalating conflicts played themselves out in the Jero Gede Sidemen's relations as well. Members of the noble house were not active in the nationalist movement or in the war for independence—indeed, much royalty, not least those associated with the palace in Amlapura, remained supporters of the colonial government and, in fact, themselves were targets of the nationalists. By the 1960s, however, the noble house was a strong proponent of the nationalist (PNI) cause, and in opposition to the Communist Party (PKI). Communist Party leaders and adherents, meanwhile, emerged among some of their followers.

Cokorda Raka, who was a Nationalist Party (PNI) leader in Amlapura at the time, confirms that there were many supporters of the Communist Party throughout the Karangasem region and that they "often did their own land transfers (*dorbrak*):" "If it belonged to the palace...they wanted to take the land, or the produce....They attacked and took it for themselves....Of course it resulted in opposition." He explains that at for example Padang Aji, too, that is what they wanted to do: "there was a prominent PKI [Communist Party] leader there.... The PKI people at Padang Aji said that that land is not the property of the Jero, that it belonged to them." Cokorda Raka continues:

> At that time my younger brother was very angry with these people. Why do you do that? Who owns that land?.... Those who were fighting each other...were the nationalist party with the PKI. The one that was strong was the PNI. My younger brother was prominent in the PNI. PKI was defeated. So they submitted to our house again. They came to the house and asked forgiveness. Now they were sick.

When asked how they sought forgiveness, Raka explains, "All of the people there came, all of the elders. Balinese call it *matur siseh*. That is how it is, up until now."

The 1963 eruption of Mount Agung—which has become linked to the intensification of land reform and, to this day in Bali, consistently is related to the rise of the communist party and the subsequent strife and ultimately massacres—also is seen as the turning point in the relationship between the people of Padang Aji and the noble house. For example, an issue that came up when conversing with the elders at Padang Aji following the maligya ritual, concerned a keris they once had received from the Jero Gede Sidemen. This keris, they mused, might also have had connection to the Majapahit, as does the heirloom keris of the Jero Gede Sidemen; but, they went on, it had been lost in the 1963 eruption of Mount Agung. Tjokorda Gede Dangin confirms that Padang Aji got a keris. Keris are important, he explains: "To each group of people a keris would be given as they were sent to occupy their various areas of land." Upon hearing the story I was told at Padang Aji, he laughs, "Yes maybe they lost it when they had to run during the eruption!" The idea of the keris is used here, in other words, to symbolize first the connection to the Jero Gede Sidemen, but then talk of its "loss" in those very years of the sixties also is taken to indicate some degree of separation on behalf of Padang Aji from the noble house, a separation linked to a natural disaster and possibly also to that period's conflict over land.

In retrospect, the eruption is construed as an explanation as well from the side of the Jero Gede Sidemen as to why some aspects of the noble house's relationship with Padang Aji legitimately changed. The priestly brother, for example, explains that maybe there was a decrease in their responsibilities toward the noble house when Mount Agung erupted: "Because of the situation, the harvest did not make that responsibility possible. So we got the notification from them that there was no produce and what to do? 'Oh, Ok then' [we said]. 'The main thing is that you come to the merajaan [the noble house's high caste family temple] every year.'" This, he explained, "is to implant that they are my responsibility, my family...that we still remember them and they still remember us" (Cokorda Pemangku). Cokorda Raka also emphasizes that not everyone at Padang Aji became involved in the land strife, "just a few people." As he puts it, "there were also those that were afraid to do so because they do hold that agreement with us.... They could be cursed, that is the belief of people in Bali." Robinson, too, has written that

> In many instances, strong bonds of loyalty or close religious or familial ties between landlords and tenants did inhibit class based consciousness and action. Furthermore, because landowners who were immediately threatened by land reform often had substantial followings of clients and tenants, the effective size of the community that felt aggrieved by the reform was actually far larger than just the number of landlords who faced expropriation. This was particularly the case in the eastern kingdoms, where feudal relations remained deeply entrenched and very high rates of tenancy continued to prevail in the 1960s.

> Thus a poor peasant who had for years cultivated a plot belonging to the local puri may well have felt threatened by the redistribution of the puri's land, because he could not be sure that the new owner would permit him to remain on the land. Others may have felt that it was wrong or inappropriate to seize the land of one's lord. [Robinson 1995:263]

Robinson notes here that

> In one such case, reported from Sidemen...a peasant (I Wayan Pugleg) refused to join the BTI at a public meeting, despite a promise that as a member he would get to own the puri-owned land that he cultivated. According to others who attended the meeting, Pugleg refused on the grounds that it would "not be fitting to oppose the royal family since he himself had long been a dependent of the puri." [Robinson 1995:263; see Putra 1986:112]

When asked about the fate of the PKI leader in Padang Aji, Cokorda Raka initiates by saying that "to want to kill people is not so good," continuing that "in fact, at Padang Aji, only the house in the rice field, by the lake, was burned.... The prominent PKI figure was killed, but...not my kavla families there." He says also that the person who had become the PKI figure was not from one of "his" families there. About Sidemen, he says, "there were one or two [that were killed]. Because my younger brother is a good person, he did not want that sort of thing. There were also prominent PKI in Sidemen, but not so many," says Raka, continuing regarding the surrounding areas with which Sidemen has special relations: "There was someone at Kebung, but he did not die. There was also someone at Sangkan Gunung," a teacher. Raka does not know whether he was killed or not, but they did not seize land there. Nowhere else did anyone try to seize their land. There was just the unsucceful attempt at Padang Aji: "My younger brother showed up there, very angry...and it did not happen."[17]

In the end, although land reform was carried out in Sidemen, the present day heirs at the noble house do not feel that it was all that debilitating.[18] They were not extraordinarily large landowners and the brothers of the house emphasize that they already had effected their own form of land reform prior to this anyway. They are referring to the pacatu system and to the original gifts of land to followers. Again, though Dangin will say that they owned all the land in the past, to him it follows immediately that it was all given to the people: "Before [land reform], my forefathers had already given land over....We had already done land reform here on our own. Because we have to give all of the people here food and land. Since the sixteen hundreds it has been so." He adds: "Land was cheap before. That is what my father related." As he puts it, "For what should we just sit on a lot of land?"[19] In other words, confirming

---

17. When asked directly about land reform, Dangin responds that "truly land reform did not benefit Bali, it was just political. When there were communists here, one family could not own more than 7 1/2 hectares. So the Raja of Karangasem has become poor. I feel sorry for them...they have a very extensive palace....The PKI was toughest in Bali (compared to Java). Consequently the Balinese people also were toughest in wiping them out. They disturbed our religion. They disturbed the land." In no way by means of apology for actions against them, Robinson says: "Like their counterparts in Java, BTI activists in Bali appear to have gone well beyond a strict interpretation of the land-reform laws, thereby stirring up conflict. In Karangasem, for example, some BTI members reportedly demanded two-thirds of the harvest for tenants on sawah, with some proportion of that share to go to the PKI. Apparently BTI activists promised this kind of harvest-sharing arrangements at public meetings in several villages throughout Karangasem" (1995:269).

18. The Raja of Karangasem was much more heavily affected, as he, according to 1949 figures, was the largest landowner in Bali (Robinson 1995:256). Moreover, his uncle "also had extensive landholdings...so that together the two members of the family owned about 5 percent of the sawah in Karangasem" (Robinson 1995:256). Dangin says that the raja had just had a little land in Sidemen, however; he estimates "maybe two percent or so." This was given to the people, the people (rakyat) asked for it."

19. In Ubud, too, it was expressed to MacRae that "the raja of Ubud owned all the land from the sea at Ketewel to Taro in the mountains" (1999:128). But in this case, no indication is given that ties of land still bind people to the puri. During the depression of the 1930s, MacRae notes a kind of reverse land reform as "farmers...were afraid to own land because of the tax, preferring to work on land owned by the puri, in some cases even vol-

the conclusions of Southeast Asian scholars in general, why keep a tight hold on land when what was more in need at that time was followers.

Besides not having extensive landholdings, the Jero Gede Sidemen also participated in some of the many ways in which landowners worked around the reform requirements in the 1960s.[20] It appears that the noble house was able to hold on to what remained of its landholdings primarily by the common strategy of subdividing it between extended family members, including Dangin's four wives. Land could also be transferred into the names of deities (such as at Padang Aji) for, according to Dangin, "pacatu over time also became temple land;" that is, land to which restrictions resulting from the land reform (or land taxes) do not apply.[21] And, as noted, land generally is not alienable from ancestral gods.

The Role of Population Expansion and Bartering with the Lord

One explanation that comes up repeatedly in connection with changes in land relations pertains to population expansion. With fewer people, there had been plenty of land to go around. Even a few generations ago, there was ample open land. With land not in short supply and under abstract ownership of the the noble house, it could be given away easily. In this situation, it also was easier for people to sustain themselves on the land. Nowadays, the increase in numbers of people frequently is given as the reason why the noble house had to ease off on their expectations that pacatu holders would bring them even

---

untarily surrendering their land to the puri to avoid tax" (1999:133). In the sixties, however, "the main economic base of Puri Ubud remained its substantial estates of land which, although subdivided, had remained virtually intact since the 1890s" (1999:136–137). Since then, the puri has lost almost half of its extensive holdings: "Twenty-one members of Puri Ubud and related puri with the largest landholdings reported total holdings in excess of 1,000 hectares (1 hectare = 100 are) of which some 425 hectares had been redistributed to local farmers by July 1996" (1999:152).

20. Such tactics included dividing up land among kin and allies, misrepresenting land holdings, and so forth. As Robinson points out "These tactics had long-term consequences....Land transfers remained unresolved and therefore open to dispute. When the political balance shifted against the PKI and BTI in late 1965, the process of reclaiming lost land was therefore relatively simple..." (1995:269).

21. Also "pauman land is entered in the land register today. As the areas are mostly modest (usually less than one hectare), there is no friction with the land reform regulations" (Hobart et al 1996:230).

the relatively small share (compared to sharecroppers) of the harvest they used to. After all, points out Dangin, "If they cannot support themselves, if we remove their support base, then they will just come to us and it will be our responsibility to take care of them." An increase in population thus not only provides more followers, more human resources, for the noble house, but increases the burden of responsibility also involved in the lord-follower relationship. Sharecroppers, meanwhile, always must bring their regular share; for, again, this is a very different kind of relationship.

When asked if there still are people at, for example, Padang Aji who disagree with submitting once again to the noble house, Raka first refers to the threat of ancestral agreement, known as *bisama*:

> They would not dare; because they hold an agreement from long ago that they must honor. Such an agreement is strong for Balinese people; they do not want to betray that. And there is a certain agreement [*bisama*] between the family of the noble house and the people of Padang Aji. That land must be inhabited by the people of Padang Aji. The *bisama* confers responsibility upon the noble house too, and in a sense secures the land for the people of Padang Aji. Raka continues that "if the people of the Jero Gede Sidemen were to take that land, the people of Padang Aji would come to the noble house; they would ask for land and would have to be given food. That is hundreds of people. Where would we find it? So we must just let them stay there."

With regard to the kavla in the immediate neighborhood of the noble house, it was similarly when they became too numerous that the noble house gave them a plot outside of the house, so that they could "better stand on their own feet." This is even the story of the main Muslim population in Sidemen, whose forefathers originally were brought in as slaves, as gifts from a raja of Lombok to priests of Sidemen. The shift away from keeping people in relationships of servitude is perceived as gradual: "It is not entirely clear when the change began. It began after Independence, when knowledge was progressing more and more. By then there was no longer slavery and servitude,…these things already were changing" (Dewa Gede Catra). But there was also the factor of population growth, in some cases rendering people more of a liability than a scarce and sought after resource: "And also their population had grown. Who wanted to support them? It already was not possible. If there is just one couple, you can support them. But now there are a hundred couples. This is what makes it impossible" (Dewa Gede Catra).

Dangin is sometimes asked by people with immediate need for cash to buy their land. But he usually refuses their deals, telling them that he does not have the money. He does this, he says, "so that it is not bought," adding, "We give them a bit of money so they can at least eat....If they are [our dependent subjects] we help them. But we do not buy up their land. This would just render them poor. And even if we bought it, they would take it back later. That sort of thing is normal." Though the lord-follower relationship by no means should be idealized, one often does, by contrast, hear stories of other wealthy people buying up the land of desperate people. In these cases usually not even a pretense of mutual responsibilities exists, and often, without further thought, the impoverished are rendered more vulnerable. Certainly in some Balinese kingdoms, too, especially with land values soaring due to the tourist and expatriate market, there are stories of lords seeking in various ways to claim follower lands for themselves, with little concern for the consequences. A cynic might argue that the reason the members of the Jero Gede Sidemen do not do this has more to do with their lack of resources than with ideals; yet, the investigation of everything that lies behind the Sidemen Maligya should show that a cynical view oversimplifies the many-faceted lord-follower relationships as they exist here, including the reasons people on either side of the relationships may have to continue them.

Dangin tells of how it was always the case that villagers could be out of line (*nakal*), taking a good share of the palace's harvest for themselves: "They brought a little here. 'Oh, there isn't any more' [they would say]. 'Here is what we brought.' 'Oh, OK,'" they would respond at the noble house. Unlike sharecropper arrangements, which grossly have disfavored and, after the stunted land reform movements, continue to disfavor sharecroppers, Dangin claims that in Sidemen, to this day, "normally we do not keep careful account of what goes where."

> [With regard to pacatu lands] the raja does not think of these things....The important thing is that the raja has these people, and that they respect the raja. The produce of the land, they take all of it. It is still like that....If I have land, I get a little of the produce. I know there is cheating. Ok, never mind. The most important thing is a good morale....It is shameful for us [*malu*] to keep too tight of an accounting of material goods.

If things are in relative balance, all is well: "You're going to kill yourself if you think about all of those details," says Dangin (see also Schulte Nordholt 1993:298). In regard also to the precolonial kingdom of Mengwi, Schulte Nordholt says there were many ways in which people could avoid paying what he assesses to be an already "cheap" tax on pacatu (1996a:130). Referring to the basic pacatu terms of exchange of loyalty and service for land to cultivate, he puts it that the old pacatu system "was characterized by bartering between a lord and his followers" (1996a:252). "If we were to take it all anyway," explains Dangin, "all of those people would not be able to eat: Oh, if you are going to take it all, can I then come to the palace?" they could and would ask. "All of those people would want to stay here. [And the noble house would have to receive them], give them pacatu here; they would become kavla roban."

Dangin's explanations regarding the realm today accord well with what we have learned about the flexibility of early Southeast Asian polities in general. A contemporary western audience may continue to be skeptical of such claims, not wholly unlike the earlier European reactions to what was perceived as lack of governance in the relationship between lords and followers in Bali.[22] Also contrary to our expectations, as Schulte Nordholt has put it, in the Balinese case "commoner loyalty was a fairly expensive commodity" (1996a:130)—in other words, when loyalty was the main resource the ruler could not be too extractive. Dangin does admit as well that if there is too much cheating, he will confront people; and, again, there can be no question that in many cases a heavy price was exacted of people by both rajas and lords. Schulte Nordholt, in his article on the genealogy of violence in Indonesia, makes the point that precolonial authority was based more on *control* of violence (including through rituals) than exercise of it (2002), yet elsewhere he mentions, for example, a royal decree, which "ordained no less than the death penalty for theft of paddy from the rice fields, even if the offenders belonged to the dynasty" (1996a:129; cf. also Robinson's argument regarding how force as a vehicle has been underestimated in overly romanticized representations of Bali). Certainly the history of the Sidemen Princedom is not one of perfect accord, but as reflected and reinforced in the maligya ritual, pacatu-based ties, in spite of Dutch colonial policy and subsequent land reform movements, in some way continue. In part this may be because these policies were never thoroughly implemented; yet there is more to it than this. As we have seen, this area has

---

22. Boon points out that "[Korn's] view of the apanage-pachatu system...obscured how the process could happen the other way around; how, for example, factious village-areas might seek attachment to courts—or might even fabricate their own courts—to gain the upperhand on rival neighbors. Korn made it appear that the system inevitably worked from the top down and only to the advantage of the rajas; he underestimated any real appeal of courtly culture" (1977:54–55). Boon continues, "Rather than monarchs regally bestowing favors on local populations, it might sometimes have been more a matter of commoners evolving their own lord, a master of their water to help them compete with other locales" (1977:54–55).

not been exempt from historical change, including land related upheavals and transitions, but, interestingly, even in some of the cases where there have been title transfers, people still appeal to the land ties as the basis for their ritual duties. It remains that there is an ongoing material basis for the lord-follower kinds of ties exemplified in the pacatu system, and as land has become in shorter supply it invariably has taken on renewed significance. Along with this, meanwhile, there is a memory embodied in the land that continues to assert itself.[23] This is a religious component to the ties, connected to ancestral reverence and reverence for a gift, and the belief that if these relationships are dismissed, those that do so suffer sometimes dire consequences.

The Land Embodies a History: Ongoing Material Proof

First of all, what remains of the pacatu system in Sidemen does not depend on continued landownership by the Jero Gede Sidemen. It is not based on people serving the noble house because they live on land owned by it, but on the fact that the land they themselves own once was conferred to them by the noble house, and with increased pressure on land this only has gained in significance. The relationship based on debt to the source of land also has Eastern Indonesian resonances (e.g. Lewis 1988; McWilliam 2002). Douglas Lewis (1988), for example, describes a central ritual in Flores directed to the source of all the land. In the Flores case, obligations to the source of land exist without a king as distributor, whereas in the case of the Sidemen Princedom, the Jero Gede is the source of all the land. Regardless of any subsequent formal ownership reforms, the land embodies this history. This always will be land that at some point was given to its followers by the noble house. The land continues to be taken as material proof of the historical connection and moral obligations that, to this day, bring people to the Jero Gede Sidemen to offer their services. [24]

---

23. Cf. much recent work on the power of place, for example Waterson (1997), Pannell (1997), Fox (1997) regarding how "a landscape of places forms a complex structure of social memory."

24. It is the same principle as that about which Goris wrote when he pointed out that since village lands belong to ancestral deities, the living members of the community must maintain contact with them to ensure their livelihood and well-being (1960 [1935]:81). Note also that Bloch mentions regarding the Merina of Madagascar that "land is the clearest manifestation of the trust passed on by the ancestors to their descendants" (1986:35).

Dangin points out that certainly there have been changes in the relationships with their followers:

> We do not use them anymore. If we need to, we call them. Not because they are [people given pacatu lands]. Now it has changed, the term is *krabat* [Indonesian for relative or allied]. This is since just ten or so years ago. It changed slowly, on its own. And because of the influence of the government's politics, people do not want to be called feudal and colonial.....But the connection is still good with the people....When we had this maligya ritual, they all came. These were most of the [pacatu] villages that came.

Or, as one farmer put it,

> The obligation is there from before. For example, if there was a war, we had to depart from here. If there was a war in the past, we had to join it; we had to go along with the Jero Gede. Besides this [obligation to serve in war]...and ceremonies, there were no other obligations. Nowadays if there is a ritual work, at the merajaan [high caste family temple] for example, then we join that....We cannot forget, you know, because of the pact from before. Forever after we cannot forget because of the pact, because they gave us *sawah* (irrigated rice fields) in the past. That is why we cannot forget. This will continue for who knows how many years. The proof is there to this day. The *sawah*, that is the proof.

This is echoed in Dangin's comment that "they were given land as a remembrance that they have a connection to us, they have an obligation....For example, if there is an enemy or a war, they really have an obligation, or if we go anywhere, they mengiring, they follow." To this it is important to add these connections are kept alive not just out of respect for the past. There also are risks, not inconsiderable ones, involved in forgetting them.

Ancestral Oaths and the Risks of "Forgetting"

It keeps coming up that people "would not dare forget" their connections to the Jero Gede Sidemen, that they would risk bringing a curse upon themselves. Indeed, when asked outright what could happen if people were to forget their responsibilities to the noble house, people explain that it depends whether there is a *bisama* from their ancestors, an instruction from the ancestors of an agreement or oath between them: "*Bisama* is a kind of tie to

strengthen the connection from the past into the future. That is the purpose
of the *bisama*." So here, too, remembering the deceased, your ancestors, as in
the maligya ritual, is linked to remembering the connections that make up
even the contemporary princedom.[25]

It is a common argument concerning Bali that temples rather than palaces
should be emphasized as the locus of Balinese culture and power. Cokorda
Sawitri argues that it was an explicit policy of sixteenth-century Watu Renggong, taking as a lesson the vulnerability of the Majapahit Empire, to not center culture and power in the royal courts, and Lansing (1983) has pointed out
that Balinese cultural practices obviously did not collapse with the collapse of
the courts, but were carried on through their loci in Bali's myriad temples (see
also Hauser-Schäublin 1997, 2003). In the years of Dutch colonization and
following independence, moreover, there was growing and persistent insistence on behalf of Balinese that state rituals be reinstated at Besakih, which
Guermonprez (1989) has taken to illustrate that rajas could be forgotten while
temples could not. The principle that temples cannot be forgotten may be illustrated as well in the Padang Aji example of how all land, ultimately, reverts
back to the ancestral god representing the line of legitimate rulers. The raja
of any given time is only a representative of this collective; so, indeed, any individual raja can theoretically be forgotten, while the collective, symbolized
in temples, cannot. But Guermonprez' statement is misleading, nonetheless,
in that in most cases the two cannot be readily separated. It is precisely by
proving himself through various means as the current legitimate representative of the collective that the raja or lord derives his power (cf. also Tambiah
1985:326 regarding the developments of the Buddhist notion of reincarnation
of the *cakkavatti*). It is thus that the evidence from Sidemen also suggests that
remembering or forgetting the local raja—as representative of the collective—
is linked to remembering or forgetting even your own nonroyal deified ancestors, whose existence was intricately linked with the ancestors of the raja,
an infraction of greatest consequence to just about any Balinese.[26] When asked
what it would mean if they were "to forget," one village leader explains:

---

25. Hobart refers to "forgetting and remembering" as "possibly the most important
pairs of terms:" "Where the living go beyond the normal course of duty in remembering
the dead, the dead are enabled to respond by energetically helping their kin…Inaction,
similarly, brings about a passive response: the dead are reminded, *kaelingang*, that the living have not remembered" (1978:329).

26. See also Guermonprez (1989:197–200) regarding "remembering the sanctuaries,"
"the temples." But the insistence for rituals at Besakih may have to do rather with the pressing need to gain Indonesian state recognition for Bali Hinduism.

That would be doing a great wrong. *Bisama* is ancestral. It is called a *bisama* between us, a command from them, from those *Dalem*, toward our family.... That means that, to this day, if we were to forget that they gave us a place, that they asked us here, if we forget that, we will suffer a curse, as it is called. [Sukayasa]

When asked whether this ever happened, the response is, 'I am sure it has, but with our family here it is not possible to forget (Sukayasa). At the noble house, Cokorda Pemangku responds to the same question—What could happen if people were to forget their historical connection to the Jero Gede? "In Bali this often happens," he says. "It very often surfaces as the reason why people suffer ill fate, be it disease, be it a business that does not succeed; this is the conviction, the belief, because they already too often pass by or forget the historical connection from before." The term in Balinese for getting sick if you forget the historical connection is *kepongoran;* you *kepongoran* with your ancestors, you are struck by their wrath. "*Kepongoran* is to remind those that forget historical connections of their descent; it is a sign to return to remembering.... They are given a condition to remind them of their position." Cokorda Pemangku gives an example from Kebung:

Formerly there was someone that forgot. Maybe because he suddenly fell ill—something happened, maybe in accordance with the bisama conviction—he went to a *balian* [spirit medium] and that *balian* told him to come here. It appears that after coming here, he truly experienced some changes, according to his conviction.... [Now] all of them still remember. What I have seen at Kebung is that the elders truly, up until now, still consistently tell the new generations about it. The proof is there whenever I go to Kebung, even if I do not know who a certain person is, he already knows me: "Oh, Cokorda from Jero has come...." With that I am convinced that the elders are still telling the new generations. It is a connection of history.

Indeed most people can relate stories of the consequences of "forgetting."[27] An elderly man from Sangkan Gunung, for example, on an unrelated occasion, brought up such a case of forgetting. He told of a family that he knew that had started getting sick often and becoming very poor, all because they "had

---

27. See Howe (1995) for a variety of examples. Also see Pitana (1997) for examples of the Pasek movement to assert its own clans in relation to the triwangsa castes by claiming Majapahit descent as well. There are no studies yet focusing on the spirit mediums facilitating all of this.

forgotten." In this case they had been alerted to the nature of the problem through consultation with a spirit medium with a specialty of divining (*balian tenung*). "Because this man was in the state of always being sick," he explained, "his thoughts became blurred. He did not get work and meanwhile his savings were used up due to illness." One example manifested in the maligya ritual concerned a group of people from the north coast. These are Pasek Nukuhin who had come originally from Gianyar to Sidemen and then, in the 1800s, followed a forefather of the Jero Gede Sidemen to the north:

> That was Ida I Dewa Ketut Panji. [Assigned by the raja of Karangasem, Anak Agung Made Karangasem] he became punggawa in Tejakula at the time that there happened a rebellion and war between I Gusti Ketut Djelantik, the *patih* [chief minister] of Buleleng who expelled the Dutch. The minister Djelantik was defeated, he was defeated by the Dutch. Now, because he was a punggawa, I Dewa Ketut Panji joined in war. Then he also died in the war. Many people from Sidemen died. Maybe some of those from Sidemen who did not die, maybe they ended up residing in Tembok, those pengiring.

> At one point, then, they forgot their connection to the Jero Gede. Afterall, the distance between Buleleng and Sidemen was far and transportation was not as it is now. There was thick forest to travel through. People went to Buleleng for weeks, not just to spend a day, for it might take them three weeks to just get there. They would go by foot. So the connection was not kept up....Now, this is according to people's stories. Then it happened that those people would get sick. They went to a spirit medium [*paranormal*]. The story of the spirit medium was, "Oh you never go to Sidemen, never go to the *merajaan* [high caste family temple] there." It appears that that spirit medium [*sedahan*] reminded them that they originate from Sidemen. You have people there that are called Gustis; go to the Jero. After that they were not sick any more! Now they come when there is an *odalan* [temple ceremony] at home and request holy water at the *merajaan*. [Raka]

The story of the people at Blimbling between Tabanan and Buleleng is the same:

> They say these people often were sick, often had mishaps and were exposed to dangers. They were wealthy, but did not hold an *ngeroras*, a kind of maligya ritual [i.e. the low caste version]. They never could. Whenever they were about to, someone would get sick. Or when they

were just about to plan an ngeroras, they'd have a car accident, and so forth. Then they went to a spirit medium. Just go to Sidemen, ask there, ask there about the forefather for whom you are going to have that ngeroras. So they came to my house. Finally it happened. After they realized that connection, their life now is good. Believe it or not. [Raka]

Then there are the people from Negara and the people from Aan and Akah (north of Klungkung). These, too, ended up remembering their connections because they met with misfortune and sickness. "This I saw myself," says Raka.

When the people from Akah came to the merajaan at Temege [where the forefather of the Jero Gede Sidemen had established himself after fleeing Gelgel, a temple for which Raka now takes responsibility], this is what they said; they said it was because of their illness. According to the *sedahan*, the *paranormal* [the two words he uses for spirit medium], they had to come here to pray and ask for holy water. It is said that those people now are healthy.

Also in the time period leading up to the maligya ritual, there were people who had reminded the princes of the Jero Gede Sidemen that they, wanted to be included. About this Raka explains,

Yes, those were people that I indeed notified late. So they came. That happened with many, too many for me to remember exactly who. "Why was I not notified?" they wondered. "But now I am here," they said. I extended my apologies because I had been too late, conveyed to them the happiness of my family, and thanked them, that they could help. I expressed that we were grateful that they had come and for their help, be it materially or morally. I only pray that hopefully my deified ancestors know this, everything that they offered, from their tiredness to the sincerity of their help.

Cokorda Pemangku points out that "sometimes it is the people that inform us that they belong to us, and admonish us to not forget. Then they tell me, this is the history, this is the origin of it. So I belong to you and you also belong to me. It comes from their acknowledgement too." In keeping with this, it is believed that there also are consequences for the noble house if they fail to remember a connection, including, as seen in some Balinese kingdoms, not being able to draw on the voluntary labor of followers to perform their royal rituals. People in the Sidemen area agree on examples of this both to their east in Karangasem and to their west in Gianyar (cf. also MacRae 1999 regarding the latter).[28] And so, "for the most part people always remember," iterates the priestly brother of the Jero Gede Sidemen; "no one dares forget" (Cokorda Pemangku).

Whatever the historical changes in titles and rights, the land often remains as physical testimony to the fact that it once was given and, through this, constitutes ongoing testimony to originating relations and the entailing responsibilities—the connections and duties which make up the princedom. Central to the evidence embodied in land, and thus also to the question as to why the system persists, is the importance of "remembering the ancestors." Thus, while ancestors may be invoked to make egalitarian arguments, ancestor reverence here becomes another significant religious basis for buttressing hierarchy, even as the importance of mutuality in the Balinese system of lord-follower relationships also is stressed. Of course, on the part of the followers, it is not a genealogical tie to the ancestors of the princes that is recognized; it is remembering them as the source of the land.[29] In other words, at the heart of this is a reverence for a gift, but it is expressed in an idiom of ancestor reverence: "Because we remember our ancestors [who stood in this relationship to the palace's ancestors], we cannot forget the palace today."[30] In the different

---

28. Thus, Anak Agung Ketut Agung, who was a central organizing figure for the 1985 maligya ritual at Pura Madura (a section of the Amlapura palace), explained that he made sure to invite the deity of the *Selonding* (a sacred orchestra) from the old village of Bungaye: "The *bhetara* (deity) of the Selonding must come here, as well as the Trune [youth society]. When the selonding orchestra plays, this calls the bhetara. One day, at the 1937 maligya ritual, they were not invited, and there was a fire. One part of my house, crowded with material went up in fire" (See also Mershon, 1971, and Schaareman 1976:40–41). Anak Agung states that there is a historical connection with Bungaya, and suggests that the deity of the Selonding may even be son of the divinely conceived "Bhetara Bukit" (1991).

29. In Hawaii, by contrast, every time a king died, all land would revert to the new king to be redistributed anew (Valeri (1985:154–155). In other words, land relations theoretically started again at zero: "Since the relationship to a piece of land depends on the relationship to a superior that is contractual in nature, no right to land is permanent or hereditary in principle. On a man's death his land goes back to his overlord, who can give it to whomever he pleases. On the overlord's death or disgrace, his dependents automatically lose their rights and must renegotiate them with his successor" (1985:154–155). This is a different kind of system, with more absolute power to the king than the power of the Balinese princes, and a system not based on the power of the gift of land to extend through generations.

30. On Sumba, land and wives are the two supreme categories of gifts. Both are sources of life; both gifts produce offspring, in other words, children and crops. The people who give you a wife also give you land, two gifts that never can be fully repaid (Janet Hoskins, personal communication). In more egalitarian societies, wife-giving indicates higher status. In Bali the Jero Gede gives land, but it is the people who give wives as an act of fealty to the raja. So both are life-givers, but generally and quite adamantly, high caste people

mediations of connection between lords and followers via originating land and historical relationships, people may, as Stewart and Strathern have observed with regard also to mythic narratives about connections between people and land among both New Guinea Highlanders and Australian Aboriginals, creatively reconceptualize such connections under changing circumstances, in those cases, transforming myths into "arguments about 'evidence'" in present-day land conflicts (2001:97–98).

In Sidemen it is those followers who continue to adapt the stories of their connections to the princes to shifting circumstances, or continue to accept or co-create the princes' stories of connection, that also continue to fulfill their obligations to perform services to the noble house, the members of which they still in many ways consider their lords. In return they have not only the ongoing harvests of their land as well as ancestral approval, but they also receive other benefits. Continuing to unravel what lay behind people's voluntary participation as the princes' subjects in the maligya ritual, the chapters to come shall round out further the picture of why people may choose to participate in a hierarchical princedom, even in the absence of force to do so. Chapter 5 deals with the various ways in which the Jero Gede Sidemen works for the people within the princedom, providing another perspective on what people would stand to lose by "forgetting" their connection and obligations to the noble house.

---

would rather see their women unmarried than given in marriage to anyone of inferior caste. To Ksatria, for example, that can very well mean excluding from the pool of options for their daughters other Ksatria, whose heritage may be considered inferior.

CHAPTER FIVE

POPULIST PRINCES: THE HARD WORK OF HIERARCHICAL PRIVILEGE

We have found the modern princedom to be based in pacatulike ties, relationships rooted in ongoing reverence for ancestors and ancestral oaths surrounding ancestral gifts of land and involving mutual responsibilities between princes and people. We have also seen how followers of the noble house, when asked why they continue to serve the princes, invariably bring up in some way the theme of what they get in return. This chapter will focus on the characteristics of the leader within this system and the work of maintaining hierarchical privilege, pointing again toward mutuality between leaders and followers. Most observers of Bali recognize primarily the penetration of hierarchy into Balinese society,[1] but concomitant with concern to uphold caste distinction and privilege, there has also been an adaptation to, and even an adoption of, a measure of more egalitarian values by the princes. The members of the noble house continuously have had to rework their relationships with potential followers, as they craft modern roles for themselves.

Divine Kingship Revisited

Integral to the theory of the Southeast Asian negara as a cosmic state constructed around the cosmological principles of a Meru-centered universe was

---

1. Warren (1993) and Lansing (1991, in press), focusing on more egalitarian and non-court-related aspects of Balinese society, are significant exceptions. But whereas Warren tends to emphasize parallel or oppositional political structures (egalitarian and hierarchical) and Lansing (in press) shows ways in which villagers appropriated caste (see also Pitana 1997, 1999 regarding the Pasek movement), the focus here is on how the influence of political values and exigencies has worked in the opposite direction as well.

also the idea of divine kingship, the *Devaraja* cult inaugurated by a ninth-century Cambodian ruler (Wolters 1999:19; Heine-Geldern 1956, Coedès 1968 [1947]). The *Devaraja*, or "God-King," was considered an incarnation of a god. The fourteenth-century Javanese court poem, *Nagara-Kertagama*, for example, claims all kings to be incarnations of Siva, including the Majapahit Emperor, Hayam Wuruk, who gave the keris Bangawan Canggu to the Balinese raja (see Pigeaud 1960). Kings were also presented as incarnations of other gods, including Buddhist deities, and as compound incarnations of more than one god (Heine-Geldern 1956:6–7). Balinese rajas, too, have been associated with gods. To Hayam Wuruk, Ketut Ngulesir, appeared as if he were an incarnation of the God of Love (*Dewa Asmara* or *Sang Hyang Aswino*); the dynastic chronicle, *Babad Dalem*, describes him as such; and, indeed, an identification with the God of Love, following the successful example of Ketut Ngulesir's rule, came to be closely linked to good kingship (see Wiener 1995:116).[2] Beginning with Dalem Ketut Ngulesir, there also in Bali has been an identification of the Kapakisan raja with the God of Mount Agung (*Tolangkir* or *Mahadewa*), and, in some myths, of the mountain with Mount Meru (Stuart-Fox [1991] 2002; Wiener 1995:115). Whatever the incarnation, it was often assumed by scholars that "deification of the king [raised] him to an almost unbelievably exalted position with regard to his subjects" (Heine-Geldern 1956:9).

Guermonprez (1989), by contrast, has presented a series of arguments why Balinese rajas cannot be considered divine at all. First of all, he reminds us, Balinese do to some extent follow the Dumontian distinction whereby Brahmana priests rank higher than Ksatria rajas. Guermonprez finds also that the *abiseka ratu* ritual of royal consecration does not treat the raja as a god, but rather reinforces the Brahmana as elder kin to the raja, leaving the raja as elder only to his subjects. Furthermore, he argues, the overall Balinese response to signs that "the gods were leaving Bali"—such as the devastation resulting from colonization and earthquakes—reveal that it is temples, not rajas that matter most: Through decades the Balinese pressed first the colonial then the nation-state for support of Besakih, until the latter sponsored the Eka Dasa Rudra ceremonies in the 1970s. Concludes Guermonprez, "Le roi est mort! Vive le tem-

---

2. Coronation ceremonies thus involved a "large offering…to imbue a new king with Smara's qualities. Further connections with Smara were sought through study: Klungkung rulers had a great many texts on pengasih, the power to attach through attraction…the Klungkung court was even named Smarapura…" (Wiener 1995:116). Note that based on the *Babad Dalem*'s interpretation of Kapakisan kings, Wiener modifies the image of the Divine King by balancing out divinity with demonic aspects (1995:134).

ple de la montagne! In other words," Guermonprez continues, in an argument somewhat parallel to Geertz's that "power serves pomp, not pomp power," "Temples do not serve kings....Rather kings serve temples as all householders do in Bali" (1989:199). Guermonprez' image for the king (raja) is as "householder," a householder among householders, ranking above his subjects and below Brahmana and gods. Yet, when a raja serves a temple or, for that matter, deities through rituals, it reflects back on him in a categorically different way than is the case with the ordinary householder, and thus temples do serve rajas as well. By proving himself legitimate and more divinely imbued than most, moreover, the raja can become a revered manifestation of the collective. Perhaps most convincingly, Guermonprez finally points out that the fact that rajas are cremated and, we might add, as in the maligya ritual, must undergo a series of rituals in order to reenter the sphere of the divine, underscores that they were not gods but mere humans (1989:202), albeit, as we have also seen, humans with particularly auspicious connections to the divine.

Resurfacing here are the issues pertaining to the practices of deification (see chapter 2), recalling that deities are different entities to Balinese than is the image of a god to adherents of monotheistic, universalist religions. There is a subtle gradation in Bali between gods and humans, reflected in the life and death cycle rites transitioning all people through their passages in and out of divinity. A substantial part of the issue has to do with how you define "god." Indeed, following Guermonprez's arguments, it appears that the gods are not too "godly" either: "The gods are the primary food givers and, thus, merely the ultimate elders of the universe" (1989:195) and "gods and ancestors...are the social partners of the highest status in a system of vital prestations," though there remains the fundamental distinction that "humans have bodies and gods do not" (1989:201).

Linked to the question of divinity is also Geertz's presentation of the raja as "passive object"—a raja at the center of his realm, who "with holy water, hymns, lotus seats, and daggers,...was a ritual object." Geertz does allow that the "king as object" also had to be a "political actor:" "It was not enough just to sit still, even passionately still. To be the master representation of power, it was necessary also to traffic in it" (1980:131–132); yet, Geertz does not show the raja to do much "trafficking." Rather, this was done through others—especially his "most immediate associates"—who "were concerned to see that the king's ritual deactivation was literal as well, that he became so imprisoned in the ceremony of rule that his practical dependency upon them was maximized" (1980:132–133). The raja, meanwhile, was seen to seek the same "deactivation" in his quest to become ever more like a god. To Geertz this was the situation of every would-be raja and thus should have applied to the level of the Sidemen Princedom as well, for as he said:

Each lord, at whatever level and on whatever scale, sought to distance himself from his nearest rivals by expanding his ceremonial activity, turning his court into a nearer Majapahit and himself into a nearer god. But as he did so he laid himself open to becoming a locked-in chess king, separated from the intricacies of power mongering by the requirements of his own pretensions: a pure sign. [1980:133]

While this may have been true at most for a few royal individuals, it is more likely that the majority of rajas and princes in Bali's political landscape sought to and had to be successfully involved in real politics, pretending to much more than signs and with aspirations that went far beyond "active passivity," a "forceful sitting still" (see Geertz 1980; see also Tambiah 1985).[3]

Through the contemporary example and inherited tradition or memory of the princes of the Jero Gede Sidemen, we may consider qualities of the ruler at this level, beginning with the issue of succession. While kingship, embedded in caste as it is in Bali, invariably is associated with ascribed hierarchical positions, the position of leadership here, as with the notion of power implied in kesaktian (chapter 3), also entails a strong component of achievement, which already emphasizes political activity over passivity. Certainly the royal power we find at the princedom level in Sidemen has components of that which is "divinely imbued" and even today a few people may be heard referring to the head of the noble house as Dewa Raja (God-King). But any would-be rulers also must activate these powers through their actions. The emphasis on combining birth with achievement corresponds to notions that came to the fore through the by now famous published caste debates of the 1920s,[4] when there was emerging modern consciousness as well as reaction to the inflated caste privileges accorded to the triwangsa (Brahmana, Ksatria, or Wesia) through colonial policy, debates which have continued with varying degrees of intensity. Appealing to ancient Balinese and Indic teachings (such as the *Sarasamuçaya* and *Bhagavadgita*), one group forwarded a notion now heard frequently in Bali, that it is your actions not your birth that determine whether you are a true Brahmana, Ksatria, and so forth. At the time of the maligya ritual in 1998, and on several occasions since, I have heard Tjokorda Gede Dangin present almost verbatim the viewpoint of propo-

---

3. Cf. Fox's article, "The Great Lord Rests at the Center." Wiener shows the colonially perpetuated dichotomy between spiritual and real/political power to be false. Schulte Nordholt (1996a), meanwhile, based on examples from Mengwi, brings across the dynamic political qualities necessary for establishing royal authority.

4. This happened especially through the publications of two organizations, *Surya Kanta* and *Bali Adnjana*, (see Picard 1999 and his other publications).

nents arguing against automatic caste privileges for the triwangsa; in other words, that "the aristocrat in the age of progress"—and Dangin, having embraced this notion, would say always—"should be a person whose nobility stems from intelligence and character (*bangsawan pikiran*)" (Picard 1999:28). That is, "aristocracy should be based on merit, not on birth" (Picard 1999:28). From the perspective of those of high birth at least, and not infrequently others as well, it would also be understood, however, that a person of category matching birth would have more of the qualities and predispositions for aristocracy. Still, far from revealing the vestiges of a godlike raja passively emanating power, also a populist value of *memasyarakat*, connecting with and working for the people, emerges in Sidemen as particularly salient to the role of the prince.

Characteristics of the Ruler: Leadership of the Sidemen House

To look first at who becomes "raja," there is a component of ascribed heritage, and those of Dalem descent and their followers would emphasize the importance of being from this line of Bali's historically most prominent rajas. Within the kin group, however, the position is not ascribed. There is a certain theoretical emphasis on primogeniture in Balinese kinship and kingship, but, in practice, primogeniture does not seem to have figured prominently in determining kin group leadership.[5] Certainly this is the case in the Sidemen

---

5. In Geertz's view, *dadias* (kingroups) were internally integrated by a system of "agnatic kinship and primogenitural succession," where every upper-caste dadia had "a core line of eldest sons of eldest sons, stretching back in unbroken purity to the original Majapahit-period founder, the present representative of which was viewed as the ranking figure of the dadia...the dadia's nominee for exemplary kingship" (1980:30). Primogeniture is seen by Geertz to permeate the whole system, for as this kicked off into the "sinking status" pattern (see 1980:31), "there took place...the generation of a number of peripheral or cadet lines, each founded by one or another of these junior brothers. These lines continued thenceforth by a primogenitural succession pattern of their own, formed separate sub-dadias" (1980:30). Wiener agrees that "anthropologists would regard aristocratic semetonan [kingroups] as conical clans, organized by a principle of primogeniture that creates ranked lines [wherein] [t]he senior, highest-ranking line in the clan in theory traces descent through eldest sons of eldest sons back to the pivotal ancestor" (1995:97). Wiener notes that the primogeniture theory ignores polygyny and the fact that sons of lower ranking women were not considered even if older (1995:386 n. 2). However, as the first marriage often was arranged with a woman of high rank, the first born children, in practice, often were of the highest ranked mother; and, at any rate, sons of lower ranking women did become kings: Schulte Nordholt mentions such an example from Mengwi where sons

noble house, where the present head is Tjokorda Gede Dangin, the sixth born, fifth surviving child, and third son of the family. The two oldest children were women and the two older brothers to Dangin chose teaching and national careers, perhaps a modern version of how older brothers, in the past, might have chosen religious study as an alternative option to lordship. Of these two brothers, the oldest lives in Amlapura and remains very active in the kin group, while the second oldest, a now retired teacher in Java, also remains involved, as do their children. The noble house furthermore provides recent examples of dual leadership, for prior to Dangin, his father and his uncle jointly headed the house; and before them—a relatively rare, but not unheard of solution— a woman was considered its head, though her male relatives took on much of the public role of leadership.[6]

Some people indicate that Tjokorda Gede Dangin's father singled him out for the position of head, but when Dangin is asked how he became head, he responds:

> You can become [head] without being designated…on the basis of your abilities. In that case it happens automatically, within the family. They will notice, oh, this one already [is performing the role]…. If that happens, that is very good. There is no need for saying that "this one becomes [head]"….It is picked automatically by the family. And we do not even say "pick," but that it "becomes agreed to."[7]

---

of noble women were passed over, surmising that "age, and especially personality must have been decisive" (1996a:30). As Tambiah was quick to note regarding royal dadia, "the line of kings provides no evidence on orderly succession according to descent rules" (1985:334-5). Wiener also recognizes that "in practice the core line was constituted by the series of persons who occupied the status position, regardless of genealogical relationships" (1995:97), and Schulte Nordholt has remarked, that succession to the status position "seldom went smoothly" (see further 1996:62). Heine-Geldern mentions that for divine kings, too, there was "vagueness of the rules of succession" (1956:10), and Wolters (1999) makes a similar point for early Southeast Asian kingship.

6. There are several examples of widows assuming power (cf. Schulte Nordholt 1996a:87ff, 118, Vickers 1982b:492, Vickers 1989:66-8, Creese 2000:29), though in all cases they ruled in some arrangement of dual leadership with a male. Again, the theme of female authority with male executive power has Eastern Indonesian resonances. Cf. Francillon's article on Wehali, a small princedom in central Timor (1980), for which he relates also the image of an unmoving female center, surrounded by masculine executive power. Cf. also David Hicks (1984), also from central Timor, where he, too, presents an example of a matrilineal center of the great motherland, with an unmoving female ritual specialist, around which are scattered patrilineal groups (i.e. matrilineal at the center/unmoving; patrilineal at the edge/a more virile type).

7. This is not unlike how the process of reaching consensus (*musyawarah*) in the more "egalitarian" institutions of the neighbourhood and irrigation associations is talked about.

It was thus that he, himself, emerged as head, gradually assuming a leadership role within the family and then without. Prior to the maligya ritual, word was that he was a little disconcerted that none of his sons seemed a likely candidate to succeed him as cokorda (lord) and there were musings as to which candidates, not necessarily his own sons, may or may not be proving themselves suitable. Following the ritual, one of his sons emerged briefly as a political player on a regional scale, as it happens, his first-born son by an arranged marriage to a high caste relation. Some were quite confident that this was who he was grooming to succeed him, but Dangin did not say as much. Options continue to be kept open as the development of all potential candidates is monitored. Though sons are looked to more readily as potential leaders, and possibly the first-born son especially so, it appears in Sidemen that indeed, as historically is the more common Southeast Asian pattern, " 'personal' charismatic claims of kingship are as important as, or even more important than, succession through strict lineal counting" (Tambiah 1985:331). In some, still rare, cases such claims can transcend gender. Thus Cokorda Raka explains of his great grandmother, the woman who was considered head of the house:

> She was very influential. Her charisma was great. Nobody dared contradict her, not my father, not my uncle....If, for example, an uncle of mine would sell off sawah, she would be angry. Do not sell that sawah. And the sale would not be completed. [Furthermore,] if, for example, she were to say, do not marry with that family...it would not happen....It was she that, until her death, determined the family....She died when I was about four years old. I still remember her. It would have been around 1935 that she died.

Generosity, too, is revealed as an important attribute: "She would be one to give a lot,...to look out for the life of the family. Whoever did not have anything, to that person she would give." In all, there is a strong emphasis on the notion of "natural leaders," leaders whose lives indicate, to both the family and potential supporters, that they are favored by the gods and by the ancestors; they have *kesaktian*, power rooted in connections to the invisible realm. This is similar to the Javanese notion of power as being reflected in the world around the power holder (Anderson 1972); as Soedjatmoko phrased it, the notion that there is a "direct relationship between the state of a person's inner self and his capacity to control the environment" (1967:266). Regarding Southeast Asian kingship in general, Wolters, in a like vein, explains that the leadership of what he prefers to call "men of prowess" "would depend on their being attributed with an abnormal amount of personal and innate 'soul stuff.' "

A person's spiritual identity and capacity for leadership were established when his fellows could recognize his superior endowment and
knew that being close to him was to their advantage not only because
his entourage could expect to enjoy material rewards but also, I believe, because their own spiritual substance, for everyone possessed
it in some measure, would participate in his, thereby leading to rapport and personal satisfaction. *We are dealing with the led as well as
the leaders.* [1999:18–19, emphasis added]

In keeping with this view, the present leader of the Jero Gede Sidemen, Tjokorda Gede Dangin, is typically described as a man who never met with adversity, never encountered opposition or difficulty in his life. Referring to tensions between his four wives, his brother once added that only when he
married did he start learning about complications. Yet Dangin's history of having been a lady's man, reflected in stories about how he came about some of
his marriages, merely indicates another desirable characteristic of the ruler
and certainly has not hurt his standing in the family or community.[8]

The connection between sexual prowess and power is a common theme in
Southeast Asia and in Bali no less.[9] Yet some tension exists between the value of
prowess and abstinence, for both men and women may concentrate power by
reserving their sexual fluids (cf. Anderson 1990:40). The prowess, meanwhile,
fits the theme mentioned earlier, that it is not enough merely to embody power;
it also must be activated. However, unless she is gaining by joining with a man
of higher status than herself, a woman's chances of being powerful remain
linked more commonly to abstinence and even to refraining from marriage.[10]
Regarding the large majority of rajas, the male rajas, Dangin reflects that "pre-

---

8. Though by 2000, his polygamy is mentioned by a follower of the house as one reason why Dangin did not want to pursue his ticket for Bupati (regional head) in that year's
elections.

9. Arguably it also had to result in procreation. As Anderson has commented: "The
ordinary [person] has no means of gauging the ruler's virility except by the number of children he produces" (1990:40). Of two kings in Gelgel, for example, the infertile Bekung
came to be emblematic of poor kingship, by contrast to his virile younger brother, the good
king, Segening.

10. Schulte Nordholt writes about the leadership in Munggu/Mengwi of the widow
queen Ayu Oka who started losing her power when she became besmitten with Dewa
Manggis DiMadia a seductive Panji playing Gambuh dancer and a rising ruler to the east
of Mengwi: "Ayu Oka was so taken with her lover that affairs of state were forgotten; she
became careless even about her position as queen of Mengwi. One source reports that she
acted like a smitten village maiden and thus endangered the negara. For example, she gave
Dewa Manggis two priceless heirlooms of the dynasty, one of which was the headdress worn

viously, in the times of rajas, every woman as she matured would think, I am grown now, does the raja want me?" Only if he did not, would she think, "Okay, I can meet someone else. I can marry within my family." "Previously all people were the possession of the raja. Women were the possession of the raja," adds Dangin (using the word *milik* or *druwe* to indicate ownership, the same term use for land and followers).[11] With regard to the Kapakisan lineage, from which the members of the Jero Gede Sidemen trace their descent, stories are still told of sixteenth-century Watu Renggong who could not control his desires for beautiful women he might encounter on his way, hence advising his subjects, for their own protection, to keep their most attractive wives and daughters out of his sight.[12] And it was Watu Renggong's "father," Dalem Ketut Ngelusir, the original recipient of Keris Bangawan Cangguh, who was seen to be an incarnation of the God of Love. There is a strong connection, in short, between being a raja and a lover. Sexual prowess may even be linked in a very concrete way also to drawing followers to royal rituals. As seen in chapter 3, many of the groups that participated in the ritual work stood in some form of wife-giver relationship to the noble house (*beraya*), a relationship that entailed ritual responsibilities. The sexually imbued kind of power, furthermore, is attractive to invisible forces, forces which were so important to the maligya ritual. Illustrative of this theme was the prominent presence at the ritual enclosure's ancestral platform of the *Smara Ratih* offering, symbolic of the God of Love.

Dangin explains that in his own case of ascendance to leadership, he "started taking responsibility for things, for anything and everything—the name of the family, advising the kids so that they would act well, and so forth. The one that assumes this position," he continues, "is one who takes care to remember the ancestors, one who does not step outside the stipulations of the rules of the family." Moving beyond inter-family dynamics, Dangin adds, "one who is *alus* [refined] to the people, who behaves well toward the people." When Raka explains why his younger brother and not he became head of the house, "the people" feature again. Dangin became head in connection with assuming the village leadership position, he said, when, after returning to

---

by Panji during gambuh performances" (1996a:89). It should be said, though, that in the case of men also, kings should not lose their bearings to love (cf. Wiener 1995:298).

11. Regarding Fiji Sahlins writes: "The specific quality of Fijian chiefly power (kaukawa or mana) is masculine potency, a virility that has more than one representation in common custom. It appears directly, for example, in the paramount's privileged access to nubile women of his domain" (1968:26).

12. President Sukarno also was particularly noted for having this quality.

Sidemen from his schooling elsewhere on the island and in Java, the people of Sidemen requested that he do so.[13] Dangin laughs, talking about how he started in leadership positions while still very young, but that this is because his family had been lords here from way back. He adds that Cokorda is a name conferred by the people. "We do not create it on our own here." Dangin explains that his father was very diligent in working with the people: "Although there were not yet many people here, he was already a leader, a *punggawa* [lord], and people followed him....My father, according to the people of Sidemen, was a person who liked giving, liked helping." This characteristic was emphasized whenever people outside of the noble house spoke about them too: the extraordinary extent to which Raka and Dangin and their family *memasyarakat*: connect and work with the people, work for the people, or, if you will, work the people.[14]

Working the People: Populism and Philanthropy

The term *memasyarakat*, denoting characteristics desirable of any community member, was used of the members of the Jero Gede Sidemen to refer to their practice of populism or philanthropy, to how they do not excessively elevate themselves above the people, and, above all, the extent to which they are involved in people's organizations and endeavors, making themselves available to help when needed, and establishing personal ties to as many people as possible. Raka explains the general concept:

> People that *memasyarakat*, this means people that have a lot of associations and social intercourse, people who like to associate with people. Society or community [*masyarakat*], this is very important in Bali. For example, I, here in Karangasem, if someone dies, I go there, I help. This is what is referred to as *memasyarakat*. If I have even just a little bit, I give it to others....People like that usually are respected by the people. Take one example, such as Dangin in Sidemen. He likes to come if there are people in difficulty. People like it that he comes.

13. It is interesting to note that it is the brother who returned to Sidemen, to remain local rather than seek a national career, who now has extensive national and global connections, being host to personages ranging from the likes of Mick Jagger to Megawati.

14. Though *memasyarakat* is a New Order term, the practice itself is likely old. The term given in Balinese is *menyamabraya*.

At this point Raka, in keeping with the spirit of the principle, denigrates himself, laughing that he, on the other hand, is lazy—far from the truth and far from how he is perceived by others.

Dangin, as head of the Jero Gede Sidemen, feels that it is incumbent on him to *memasyarakat*, that it is more important than any wealth he might offer:

> When there is any kind of ritual work, I come if I am invited, I have to. If there is a death, cremation, no invitation is necessary, I come on my own. . . . If for some reason I cannot come, someone else goes on my behalf, carrying a little rice. This means that we are participating, and they understand that we are remembering. That is what is most important. . . . Even if I were to give a lot of money, if I would not want to visit, would not want to help at difficult times, they would not like that. . . . The important thing is that we come and remember the people. This is the Balinese way.

To *memasyarakat* is an imperative of the civic diligence characteristic of Bali's relatively egalitarian institutions, especially the neighborhood but also the irrigation associations (*banjar* and *subak*), and its presence among the princes is influenced as well by the various pressures to not be too feudal, both during the Dutch colonial times and into the post-Independence era. Yet, the understanding handed down through generations is that these kinds of characteristics also have been desirable for kingship in the past and they correspond well to what has been emphasized more recently regarding precolonial Southeast Asian polities generally (Tambiah 1985; Wolters 1999).

In Sidemen, people, variously situated and in a variety of contexts, high caste as well as commoners, insisted that it is—and was—important for the raja to give to the people in more than a material sense. Then the people will—and would—support him; "otherwise they would not receive him." The senior head of one group of followers is convinced that it was like that before too; even if it was a raja, he still had to "descend," to *memasyarakat*: "Even though he was a raja, they were his; the people belonged to him ["rakyat ini kan milik beliau"]. That is the understanding. If a raja just sits in a chair, no that cannot be. He descends." The contemporary heirs of the Jero Gede Sidemen, too, insist that even a big raja had to *memasyarakat*: "Especially if he wanted to come to people who are sick, who are poor, and so on; he would be more praised, more respected. For example, the raja of Klungkung was like that, the last raja. If someone died, he came. And people respected and feared him" (Raka). Wiener, too, talks of people reminiscing about characteristics of Klungkung's last raja indicating his "common touch" (1995:114). In Sidemen, older people who remember an earlier maligya ritual at Klungkung note how many common people (*orang rakyat*) participated there.

> The distinctive feature was that the raja of Klungkung was close to the people [unlike some rajas] disposed to glamor; in Klungkung he had greatness. This was seen also in the sheer numbers of pengiring, numbers of people who participated. And it was they, the people themselves, who financed it in the case of Klungkung, because the raja was not that rich. But he had many people. These people, so extraordinarily did they love the raja, in the case of Klungkung. [I Dewa Ayu Alit, the unmarried sister of the noble house, who lived most of her life with a female relative married to the raja at the palace in Amlapura, Karangasem]

Raka, in a different conversation, points out that the last raja of Amlapura was also like that, also had good connections to the people, but the others less so. At the palace in Amlapura today, they do tell stories of that last raja and his interaction with the people, including how he would tuck up his sarong to work among the workers constructing his water palaces. Among the women in Sidemen, however, talking of Klungkung leads to discussion of the loss of any real status in certain other palaces: "They just have a palace now, no longer the emotional connections." In Klungkung it remains, they say, that it holds true "up until now even, with the family of the raja" that this palace is characterized by being loved by the people.

There are stories of rajas in other realms as well who were distinguished by their connections to the people, and it is interesting to note the description, by an Assistant Resident of the Dutch administration (A.J.L. Couvreur), of the old raja of Gianyar in the face of colonial rule:

> This regent loathes modernity. The old man does not really administer, but he knows what is going on. Every morning he ensconces himself in front of his puri under a pala tree on a flat rock—which he has had recast into a horrible, cemented monstrosity—and listens to what passers-by can tell him of the day's affairs. Meanwhile he carves little wooden statues. [Schulte Nordholt 1996a:256]

Elsewhere Schulte Nordholt has argued an important point that Western scholars with preconceived notions of kingship often miss, that in Bali "there existed no separate worlds of elite and village in the 18th and 19th centuries, because the very nature of the political order implied many intensive and personal contacts between lords, followers and wider circles of clients within the framework of a dynamic hierarchy" (1986:19).

In Sidemen, the present day heirs have inherited the stories and values, according to the explanations of their elders, that their forefathers in general liked
to *memasyarakat*. From the seventeenth until the early twentieth century, the
princes describe their forefathers as "big rajas" ("until 1912; my grandfather was
the last of them"), some of whom also would spend much of their time smoking opium, feeding the image of decadent royalty. But Raka and Dangin insist
that even then they "certainly had to get around,...they still had to be diligent."[15]
Dangin continues, "even if there was no ceremony, they would look,...go see
how the *sawah* was, see how the people were doing. Could the water flow or
not?" Raka adds a couple of other examples of diligent forefathers:

> One of my forefathers became a 'Balinese doctor' [*balian*].[16] He liked
> to help people. And this, too, is to memasyarakat...I also had forefa-
> thers who liked to help people; if people were very poor, they would
> help out....And that is the case up to this generation. Take my younger
> brothers Dangin and the *pemangku* [non-Brahmana priest], for ex-
> ample; their level of working for the people [*memasyarakatnya*] is great.
> They like being like that; they are not egoists. They like to help people.

Of course when it is princes, rather than "ordinary people" who memasyarakat,
there is a clear connotation of philanthrophy or social service, still implying hierarchy rather than equality. In talking of his father, Dangin thus also had used
a term that translates as philanthropist (*dermawandau, dermawan,* where
derma is alms or donation); and it was said that it was because "the people belonged to him" that a raja had to memasyarakat. In the end, to memasyarakat,
on behalf of princes, still underscores their ultimately higher position, for they
are not thereby relinquishing their status to in true populist fashion become
one with or of the people, to whom they may still refer as "ordinary people" or
"lower people." The implication of the practice of memasyarakat—when by
hierarchical superiors—is that of "noblesse oblige." Though in a sense at odds,
populism and philanthropy, with such tension between them, coexist in this
way in the contemporary value and practice of memasyarakat.

---

15. Compare this to what Wolters finds Prapanca's poem, Nagarakertagama, to reveal
of Hayam Wuruk's fourteenth-century style of government: He finds that the poem "throws
credible light on the style of government," which he also describes as a "relaxed style of government," and "associate[s] with the projection of the ruler's prowess in order to control
his mandala." "Every time at the end of the cold season he sets out to roam the countryside," explains Wolters and goes on to describe "the numerous things he does" (1999:139–
140).

16. Cf. how Raja Horo on Sumba derived part of his prestige by providing medical service, in his case with a specialty in fertility (Hoskins 1998).

Today the combination of acquired and ascribed status extends to caste privilege too. Though it supposedly is something you are born into, it is for giving
of yourself to the people that you in return receive the recognition, including
caste privilege, that you care for them. One follower says regarding Raka, for example, that, although he is a person from "feudal surroundings," he does not assert his own title. He is not pretentious. In return people do address him with
his full title of honor and accord him the corresponding respect. Dangin points
out that "you never used your title about yourself anyway; people already knew
who you were." As we have seen, people in fact even sometimes refer to him by
the title "Ida I Dewa Agung," normally the title of the raja of Klungkung, Ida I
Dewa Gede being the title of the raja of Sidemen (again, it is raja in local, punggawa in regional perspective).[17] This is just to pay respect, explains Dangin. "In
Klungkung it is [Ida I Dewa] Agung. Here, officially it is Ida I Dewa Gede. That
is if I become raja again. Only then will I use that." In this way, some people actually elevate the title of the heirs of Sidemen to show deference and respect, but
they also expect of them to act in keeping with the status that is accorded them.
With regard to the ritual of the maligya, for example, the Jero Gede Sidemen was
not just emptily asserting itself by holding a large ceremony. As pointed out by
a local Brahmana priest, if the Jero Gede were to have "taken a small ceremony,"
it would have been the people who would have judged and condemned them.

The importance of having to earn the role of prince who leads through
what can only be described as "big-man-like" characteristics and actions, or
what Wolters calls "men of prowess" (1999)—even with the inherited caste
status predisposing and legitimizing you for it—is emphasized by how, conversely, the lack of a leader with these characteristics could put dynasties out

---

17. The titles of Balinese nobility can be traced, as does Geertz, to begin with gods.
From there the title *Batara*, "descends through various semi-divine figures who bear the
title Mpu," to the Dangiang title of Kapakisan's father, the Brahmana priest. Kapakisan
could not as king of Bali remain a Brahmana, but became Ksatria, with the title of
Dalem—"a title that all the Gelgel kings who followed him bore as well." After the fall of
Gelgel, however, and the establishment of Klungkung, the new king's title became Dewa
Agung, "a still lower title by which all the Klungkung kings were subsequently known." The
pattern continues for the regional, as Geertz calls them, 'secondary' kings: "As they were
descendants not of the (originally) Brahmana Kepakisan but of the Javanese Satrias in his
entourage (who had also dropped a notch in transit), they started out lower to begin with
and also subsequently sank....Thus the general picture...is one of an overall decline in status and spiritual power..." (1980:17). But from there, as we continue to see in Bali, there
is both variation and contestation of titles, and not just in a declining pattern. Even the
peripheral princedom of Sidemen is in the position of claiming to be Dalem and though
it is not every day fare, they even experience being referred to as Dewa Agung by followers.

of the running. A dynasty cannot rest on the laurels of caste and descent alone. In a historical example, when the Mengwi dynasty by 1823 "had dropped from the highest to one of the lowest rungs," Schulte Nordholt points this out too: "It would have to wait for a new 'big man,' one able to restore royal authority to its former glory" (1996a:110). Involved in being a raja in Sidemen, then, where you have to "work (for) the people" to retain your hierarchical privilege, is diligent everyday activity.

The Everyday Work of Maintaining Hierarchical Privilege

The Indonesian government has taken over the reorganization initiated by the Dutch colonial state, such that an administrative structure (*dinas*) parallels the customary institutions (*adat*) (see Warren 1993a). In 1963, Tjokorda Gede Dangin became head of the administrative village (*desa dinas*) of Sidemen, a position he held until 1977, at which time he "resigned" and what he refers to as "a military person" was inserted. He continues, however, as "honorary elder" and leader of the customary village (*desa adat*).[18] But beyond and above that, he is the cokorda or prince to his people, and as such he is kept continuously busy. Every day people seek him out. They most frequently come with issues concerning ceremonies, especially to invite him to their life-cycle or temple ceremonies. If somebody dies they want him to come and read lontars at night. His presence is considered essential to the success of any large ceremony. They might also come to ask for help with a construction project or if they are dealing with illness in their family. And they come for Dangin's help to resolve conflicts or for him to provide advocacy.[19] Dangin's assistance might be needed in the event that someone is trying to exercise pressure on the villagers or is asking them for bribes, such as is sometimes the case with government agents. Dangin explains,

> In such cases [the villagers] come to me, and I talk to the people in question. If, for example, there are police that are out of line, or any-

---

18. See especially Warren (1993a) for an explanation of the parallel administrative and customary structures, dating to the reorganization of Balinese society by the colonial administration.

19. This kind of practice of "working the people" is not unlike that of U.S. congressmen and women who have values of "serving the constituency" and always, in a sense, are campaigning for office, even when not in actual election process.

208   PART TWO: RECASTING BALINESE HIERARCHY

thing like that, I show up and ask them what is going on.....The people of the village are afraid. They do not dare take this up on their own, so I go. There have been times when I have stirred up the government. I do it in a smooth way; my protest is polite. Why do you do such and such? Don't do it. Like that....So I use it as an opportunity for politicking, to assert the people's rights.

One recent case of Dangin rising as advocate for his people happened when the inhabitants of Kebung were prohibited by police from selling the alcoholic brew of *tuak*. A few individuals were seized on the grounds of a national law forbidding the sale of hard liquor, whereupon representatives from Kebung went to Dangin with their dilemma, since this is their primary means of making a living. He brought their case to the regency level, arguing on the grounds of tradition that this is their livelihood and that *tuak* even is required for ceremonial purposes.[20] Sometimes, he says, people think he can work out anything. If they are trying to become civil servants, for example, they may also come to him, but "I cannot make that happen; I say that to them, straight forward, even as I try to talk about it, to discuss it."

Given his position as village head, people of course once saw him as representative of the government, and probably still do although he withdrew, in his own account, due to conflict with the head of regency of the time, the heir of the Amlapura Palace. Dangin explains:

> Politics do not suit me. I didn't want to [deal with the way the regent was behaving] "Ooy I am the raja...I am the *bupati* [head of regency]" [he mimics, inflating his voice as does the puppeteer in Balinese shadow puppetry]. I don't like that. Then I just responded [again inflating his voice] "Ooh this is the *perbekel* [district head] speaking" [laughs]. What is with this? It is very pompous. All of the government was arrogant then. I didn't like it.

Yet he also pulled out of government, he says, because he found that he had more power that way. Now the government comes to him for assistance with projects and disputes. And so it remains even now that he is the best hope of most local people for a voice at the extra-local level. Any extent to which the princes have influence with government of course also implies risk to the peo-

---

20. This replicates the argument that Balinese authorities made regarding cockfights in response to a nation-wide ban on cockfighting and other gambling, viz. that it was an essential component of ritual sacrifice. In 2003, the new police chief, of Kuta Bombing trial fame, denied the validity of this line of argument and crackdowns have since started.

ple that assistance might be withheld. This possibility is suggested in the story of an earlier issue of contention involving Kebung, estimated to have happened in the 1950s, when people refused to harvest the rice at the site that decades later became the maligya ritual site. According to Cokorda Raka, "This is what happened:"

> There was a *provokator* [provocateur], not someone from Kebung but a person from Sidemen, who, among other things, said to the people of Kebung that they did not need to go there anymore. So they did not want to harvest any more. They severed the connection and rarely came to the house. But eventually, as time went on, my younger brother, Dangin, became *perbekel*, became the head of the village....The village extended to Kebung. It was under his jurisdiction; he was in control there. Then he went to Kebung to clarify why they were doing as they were. They apologized. In the case of the people of Kebung, many were confused after that. Some were in agreement, some not. Why do we have to remember? Must we? But this is good again now. And the *provokator* has passed away. None of his descendants is doing this sort of thing.

People also come to Tjokorda Gede Dangin with issues of conflict with family and/or neighbors. According to Dangin, people frequently seek his assistance with marriage issues. In the not too distant past, this often would involve marriages by capture and it continues to involve arranged marriages. "Then I am brought into the picture," says Dangin: "Look, you are one family, you are related to each other, it would be very good for you to marry," I say. "Through you there will be a good connection; you will have a family." A man from a village just south of Sidemen, gives a different example of a marriage issue that his kin group brought to Dangin, an example, interestingly, of a caste-type struggle between commoners:[21]

> I had a niece who married to [a nearby village]. You might say that their *adat* [customary law] is fanatic...For example, if an outsider marries in, they will not eat her offering "left-overs" from the ceremony....It went so far that even the husband who took her did not want to eat it....What this means to us is that our family is dismissed, as we put it, by their family. [Sukayasa]

---

21. The notion of a completely "undifferentiated caste of 'egalitarian commoners'" is, as Schulte Nordholt points out, a misconception (1999:251).

"So," explains Sukayasa, "we asked for [Dangin's] judgement and he advised us as to how we might seek a rapprochement with the family there." The basic point made was that nowadays it is uncalled for to adhere to such fanaticism, that within the family you can do as you like, but if you take someone from outside, there is a "model of *adat* [customary law] that is in general effect." He begins to explain that "if the marriage is between peers, people of the Sudra caste," but stumbles to clarify the Sudra concept: "that is people of no caste, or, no, not with no caste, but whose caste is Sudra; you know, Sudra are at the bottom, like me; that is, they are not Ksatria, not Brahmana." That said, he continues, "If they marry each other,...it is already in general effect in Bali that the ritual leftovers ought to be eaten. That ceremony is enjoyed by all families. That is what is in general effect."

In the end this particular matter was resolved; the wife-takers conceded to eating the ritual leftovers of the bride and the marriage proceeded smoothly. In terms of Dangin's role, this man concluded:

> When there is no way out for us, we automatically bring it to Him, for Him to give a judgement. Whatever the problem, we always put His judgement highest. Everything we experience here, like I said before, be it good or be it bad, we approach Him to discuss it and ask advice. If we can take care of it ourselves, between our dadia family here, we do that. But if we really cannot, clearly we ask Him to show us a way out....We always ask guidance of Him, of Tjokorda Gede Dangin. That means that we, here, still place Him high and respect Him, and recognize that He is constituted from before, from our forefathers; ongoing you could say that we are *markan* to him. Be it the bad or be it the good in the course of life, we always seek the connection, be it in the manner of birth, be it in the manner of service and loyalty to him at Sidemen. [Sukayasa]

Richard Berg, an American law professor and a long time friend of Dangin's, specializes in dispute resolution. As he is married to a Balinese woman and spends most of his summers in their house in the vicinity of Sidemen, he has since the 1970s witnessed several of Dangin's cases. He offers an example involving domestic relations:

> There was a young girl who was pregnant and she was carrying on with two different guys. And neither would marry her. Generally in Bali, if you're carrying on with somebody, and it becomes public, or somebody gets pregnant, you marry them, that's it, that's custom [see Sawitri (2001a) regarding the issue of pregnancy outside of marriage

in Bali]. You may or may not be happy about it, but you do it. Almost always. But here there are two guys, and each one says, it's not me…So they go to the Cokorda…She wanted to marry either of them and both of them said, not me. So he was the one who had to impose his will.…The way it came out, the first one that slept with her had to marry her, the second one still had to pay for something, and all three of them lost a rank of caste.[22] And they all had to have a big ceremony.

Dangin offers that land ownership disputes would be another reason for people to seek him out.

"Oh, I own this up until here," someone might say. This happens a lot, and it is very difficult. If it is brought to us, I say, "Oh, is that so. May I ask for this then?" I ask the one party. "Yes, you may—take it." Then I ask the other party. "May I ask for this?" I ask for this. "Yes, please take it." "Ok, now I have this and I have that. Now I am going to give it to the two of you." So it is no longer their dispute. The land is now my possession, and I want to give it to each of them. "*Gaja ketcapa*" this is called.

This makes for a good story, and Raka, in a different context, tells of another example applying this principle:

It once happened like this. There was a large tree, where part of it was in "A's" yard, the other part in "B's." The one wanted to ask for it, and—*wah*—it developed into a dispute. My younger brother was very clever: "I ask you for that tree," he said. Ok, it was given to him. He then had it felled and divided it in two, giving half to each party. That was the end of the matter. He, himself, did not take any share of it at all. The people were confused!

Dangin explains that he uses this method often. "Now it is mine, you cannot argue over it. But I do not really want to take it, so I give it back to you. Now

---

22. Being expelled by your dadia might be compared to expulsion from the village community (the banjar or the desa) the ultimate sanction applied against violations of local customary law, the direst implications of which are the loss of right to burial and cremation at the village cemetery as well as to the assistance of banjar members in the performance of death rites. Expulsion from the caste and kin group would at the very least have implication for terms of address and would be marked by people not being willing any longer to partake in your offerings.

if you have any argument with your share it is with me, not with each other."
Berg, too, gives an example of a land dispute:

> Land is worth more [than it used to be], people are fighting about it
> more, and it's only been the last couple of decades that most of the
> land has been given into somebody's name, into an actual land cer-
> tificate. Before that it was just in the family....A lot of times somebody
> sells a piece of land and then they deny it. But by then it's already sold
> to somebody else....I've seen situations where [both sets of people]
> have a plausible argument why it's their land. Somebody says it was in
> the family and I have the paper, and somebody else says, yes but you
> said it's mine and I've been farming it for 20 years. I saw Cokorda one
> time, it was really interesting..., it was not really an adverse posses-
> sion, but a religious issue: The central issue that Cokorda brought up
> was who's making the offerings for the land, who's praying to the tem-
> ple on the land, who's got an offering place on the land? That's the per-
> son who has a relationship to the land....Both have claims to it, but
> that's the...true one. That was the basis of resolving the dispute.

Berg relates also a situation that happened at Sangkan Gunung several years ago:

> There were some kids who were partying and they broke the wall of
> a temple, and they didn't want to take responsibility, because they
> were young, they were kids...probably teenagers....The people from
> the temple wanted them to fix the wall but the kids didn't want to do
> it, so finally they went to Cokorda....It was one of these things,
> [where he says] we've all failed ... but at the end of the day what I re-
> member most about it is that Cokorda supplied the cement out of his
> own pocket to fix it, and the kids and the temple people both had to
> work together to fix it. And then they had to have a big ceremony, be-
> cause it involved the temple. That was the solution.

> So then you might say, why would he throw in the money and whose
> money is it really, and where does it come from? I would say that
> because he's the Cokorda he's also the rich guy...more money is
> coming through him and a certain percentage of this money is re-
> ally to help for this project and help for that project, and to help re-
> solve people's problems. And I don't know if he'd be as gross as I am
> about describing that, but I think that's probably what's going on
> there. So that's one example. Now did he order that? No, he said,
> now I'll throw this in and...it never got down to, OK, I've heard

you both and here's such and such and such. They just all worked it
out, and probably the most expensive part of the whole thing were
the offerings, which took not necessarily money but tons of time
and energy.

Raka confirms that his younger brother is very skilled at resolving disputes and
that people also would come for these forms of assistance during his father's
time. Sometimes the government would not be able to resolve an issue, whereas
his father would. "My father was very persuasive. And Dangin is like this."

Though his duties toward the people keep Dangin busy always, this does not
mean that any given individual or group goes to him all the time. In the surrounding villages, they confirm that, absolutely yes, they would go to Cokorda
if they had a dispute they could not resolve internally. Then they generally will
recall a case maybe as much as a decade ago to make the point, for people do not
come to him lightly with small matters. Not only can they not be going to him
all the time, but they do not want to establish a reputation as a family fraught
with problems, rather than as someone for whom things go smoothly. There is
not a high cultural value placed on pursuing your rights at any cost, and to have
to approach your cokorda because you are unable to resolve your own problems
already has negative implications. Moreover, the solution often requires that
everyone give something, to the extent that it is sometimes a lose-lose situation.

The above mentioned *gaja ketcapa* principle of course brings to mind the story
in Christian tradition of King Solomon and the baby. The principle, as we know,
does not work well for a child, nor would it for anyone in the above Balinese example who might have wanted the tree for shade. Richard Berg provides further
insight from the perspective of a western law professor, when he explains how
Dangin's role differs from the various forms of mediation employed in the U.S.:

In America we have arbitration where you empower a neutral party
who doesn't know what is going on to hear the evidence and make a
decision, and it is binding. And we have mediation where a nonin-
terested neutral party is there to assist the parties to reach their own
solution, a facilitator. It's not somebody who has a stake in it or
power in it. Neither of those are the role of Cokorda.... We also have
a process in America called 'med-arb,' where it still is a non-knowing-
neutral that will go through mediation and if that doesn't work out,
the parties empower that person to reach a decision. What we have
here is a little closer to that, but it's still not that, because the biggest
difference is that Cokorda is in the know, he's a person with knowledge, he's not a real neutral in the sense of a western neutral.... He's
not an outsider. And if push comes to shove he's got the big hammer,

whether or not the parties agree in writing. By tradition, and by the way things work, if he says this is what's going to happen, believe me that's what's going to happen. So he's got the power of an arbitrator, but he's not really a neutral and in most cases, the people work on consensus not on command, *but the consensus stems from knowing what the command would be.* So as soon as it's clear which way it's going, everybody agrees without saying what you have to do (emphasis added).

Berg explains the process that he has observed many times over the decades (see MacRae 1997:115 for a description of an audience with a Cokorda of Ubud):

They come to Cokorda with a problem and they sit down. At first they're going to just laugh and talk and have peanuts and not even talk about the problem. But Cokorda has already been told,...he already has got a few sides to the problem and he's already got in his mind where it's going to go. He works fast by the way...he comes to where's it's going to happen and boom, it's done. But they still have to do the ritual dance. So they'll talk real slowly and then they'll get down to talking about what they're there for, which he already knows, but they'll talk about it as if he doesn't and they may just talk around it and talk around it and talk around it, and Cokorda at that point may just suggest a solution. Generally at that point his solution will be built upon by them to form the consensus. Now is that command or is that consensus? It's closer to command. Believe me. Because with his suggested solution, it's hard for them to say, "no we don't want that," because they've come to him. But the solution usually is a facilitative type of solution. It's got something for everybody. It's not necessarily a compromise. It's principled in that he'll draw upon lontars, he'll draw upon adat, he'll draw upon religion, he'll draw upon all these principles, so in this sense it's not a split the baby kind of thing....

Everybody has to take part in the fact that there's been a dispute. There's almost always going to be a ceremony and the ceremony is going to be expensive; there's a cost to doing this whole thing. Oftentimes Cokorda becomes a player in it, and he'll say, look we're all wrong, because there is a dispute. You're wrong because you haven't been able to resolve your problem. I'm wrong because I'm your leader and something like this could come to be. He'll say that....So we're not talking about who's good and who's bad anymore, who's right and who's wrong. We've all got a problem. Even the leader has failed here.

Dangin also stresses the role of oaths in this process of resolving conflicts. If people are squabbling over something, for example, he will take them to the temple to take an oath, to swear to God. Alternatively, you can speak a curse on someone. This is the way with Balinese people, he says:

> You have to apply oaths, in a ritual manner, for people are very afraid of the possibility that [an oath] might work. If a person has been honest, things will go well for him. If not, he will come into difficulties. God will bend him (*menunduk*). He will never have any success in his work. It often happens that someone is thus endangered. People who have taken an oath often fall into poverty, for example. Sometimes they die as by a stroke of lightning. Sometimes by a grave illness, an illness that will respond to no treatment. It can drive people insane. They lose their way. You may see people of noble birth fall. They lose their caste standing. These things can happen to people that are struck by an oath. People are very afraid of that, not least because their offspring can be affected by this too. And it is not just the consequences of oaths. If we lie, we will be affected. It is very dangerous. If we are truthful, on the other hand, it will bring happiness. So just speak the truth.

Besides in this way ensuring peace in the community, Dangin has concern also with its material well-being. He admits that of course the noble house also still has and needs a material base to maintain its role in the area: "One must have in order to give." He does not need much, he emphasizes. "Much would, of course, be great, but in the meantime…as long as you cannot offer a lot, do a little, do what you can. It is the will that is important." In the villages that participate in the Sidemen Princedom, they expressed that if they have a need, they just complain a bit to the Jero Gede Sidemen to indicate as much and the Jero Gede Sidemen invariably helps. In addition to owning well more than the average holding of land, the Jero Gede Sidemen also benefits from tourism-related income. Two of Dangin's wives hold and manage very valuable "home-stays"—the homes of former notable expatriates that continue to draw artists and writers for long-term, lucrative rentals, not the Bali-on-a-shoestring options that abound in other Balinese tourist villages.

Dangin has been involved in stimulating local industry, especially weaving,[23] and he will also ask for donations on behalf of his people. Through his contacts with scholars and artists, he has helped secure various privately spon-

---

23. For a case study of the small-scale Sidemen weaving industry, see Nakatani (1999).

sored foreign aid projects. These include a drinking water project, improved health care facilities, as well as a cultural school built through Swiss philanthropy, which has operated in various incarnations since 1970. "Those are not gifts for me," says Dangin of these projects, "they are for the people from Swiss donations. I just help." As Richard Berg explains: "Cokorda [Dangin] gets his fingers in a lot of fires....There is a project here and a project there....He's got a lot of family now out there doing things too, and he's involved with it all. At the end of the day, he's the main man in the network...."

Dangin reiterates:

> Now we can improve ourselves together [the Jero Gede and the people of Sidemen]. The one most important thing is to love the people, even if you do not have anything, they will still receive you....That has always been what is important, to serve the people. Extend good thought, intelligence, good education, set a good example. If we are harsh [*kasar*], the people will be so too. That is the key. To set a good example. Even if there is something they do not understand, do not render them too lowly; give clarification.
>
> We ask God for strength. Hopefully my children, my family, will be able to continue this. This is what is important, and then maybe we will grow strong materially again too. Obviously if we are too poor we cannot do anything, so it is not that we seek wealth out of greed. We have money so we can carry out some project. It is the same with the government. If they have no money, how can they build a state?... This is written in lontars too. There have to be sufficient means.

As Cokorda, then, Dangin has a role in ensuring peace and some level of prosperity in the community. He has a role also in Sidemen's connections to increasingly global systems, in development and in politics. He has been the local leader in times of major national transition. He was so when Suharto came to power, during the upheavals of the sixties. Although there was, and now again is, as it is expressed, a lot of love for Sukarno, the Jero Gede Sidemen supported his removal at the time, and also fought against the PKI (Communist Party):

> Dangin was the leader. People died at his hands. He was the leader of the troops when that was going on in this area....It was never official. But he's the leader. It is much stronger than an official post.... He led the troops, not because the government said you're the leader, but because the people said, you're our leader.

Similarly, Dangin was on the leading edge of Sidemen's shift from Suharto and the Golkar party to Megawati and her Democratic Party of Struggle, which happened, as we know, in the context of the maligya ritual. When Dangin indicates what the community needs to do, and that they need to do it as one, many people follow.[24]

In all of this it also is stressed that a cokorda is brave: "when everybody else is running away, he's in the front....A cokorda will say, I don't care if I die; I'm ready to die right now....It's part of their role. It's also part of the reason people fear them, because they play that role"—and indeed fear, to the extent that the cokorda is powerful both materially, physically and spiritually, undeniably plays a role in the princedom's relationship to its followers as well.

Dangin does not stand alone in effecting the position of his family and the Jero Gede Sidemen. The literature is replete with the persistent and influential role in Balinese history of internal kin group strife. Says Geertz, "outward political success brought inward political strain. When a powerful dadia declined it was more commonly from weakness within than from pressure without" (1980:28). It is also the case, however, that there is a strong dynamic within the kin group to enjoy power by association to those in the more prominent positions, and there certainly by now is a firm awareness that internal strife, as recounted in many a dynastic chronicle and oral history, can lead to the demise of whole palaces and lineages, providing a not altogether dismissible, even if not always realized, incentive to stay integrated. This may be especially so when pressure from the outside is a considerable factor to contend with, and such has certainly been the history of the Jero Gede Sidemen. As Dangin said, they were pressured by Karangasem and forgotten by Klungkung. But he also continues that, ultimately, this just made them stronger by bringing them closer together in family strategy, a strategy that, as we have seen, emphasizes their links to the people. "In all areas we struggle," says Dangin, who instructs the members of his family:

> I have told them to do this, to help the people, with their knowledge and ideas as well as materially. For in the past they helped us with their souls [i.e. lives], wherever we went. We urged them to go to war everywhere. This is the history and we must remember it. This is what is important; this history has to be told to the young....The people also can get very angry with us, if anyone here forgets, if any-

---

24. As disillusionment with Megawati's presidency grew, however, and as there was a growing diversification of political options, people in the area of Sidemen, too, were divided in their affiliations.

one from here is out of line....For example, if there were to be a
death and we did not go there. If they were to invite us and we were
to refuse to come. Or if we were to pressure them, cheat them, they
would be very angry. So, I say, definitely do not act inappropriately
with the people. It has always been so. If they have difficulties, we
help them.

In the contemporary case of the Jero Gede Sidemen, you see a whole family
system at work. It is not without its share of tensions, but for the while at least,
there is more to be gained by cooperating than by giving in to disruptive tendencies. It seems that the Jero Gede Sidemen has managed to keep enough of
a core of its people at home to retain its position in Sidemen and that it is only
strengthened by the tentacles stretching beyond the local realm, for most, if
not all of these, still connect back to the house. It is also through its different
characters that the noble house effects its connections to the people. As Sawitri said regarding her own immediate family within the kin group: "People
like my father, Cokorda Raka, because he is wise. People like me because of
my activism. People like my brother because he will drink with them."

Roles of Other Men of the House[25]

Cokorda Raka is the older brother of Tjokorda Gede Dangin. While there
is no acrimony on his behalf over the fact that his younger brother is head of
house, the story of how he himself came to assume responsibility for the family temple at Temege near Amlapura does have overtones of potentially resulting from his need to find a separate niche of prestige. As he tells it, it was
as result of a bout of illness and a subsequent dream that he came to realize
that this temple was being neglected and that it fell upon him to take charge
of it. After all, this was the temple of the father of the man sent to govern in
Sidemen, and thus has a form of senior status.

Raka is, himself, highly respected, both through his positions of political
regional leadership and through his career as a teacher. Most of the currently
well-positioned civil servants, including the post-regime-change bupati, were
at one time his students. Raka is also well known for having helped several

---

25. As mentioned, one of Dangin's sons, following the maligya ritual, became a political player at the regional level, active in Megawati's party PDI-P. During the era reformasi,
he was installed as representative to the people's assembly (DPR) in Denpasar. Notably, he
still lived in Sidemen, maintaining strong local ties while commuting to Denpasar, but due
to his responsibilities elsewhere was not one of the most active men on the local level.

poor people through school, more than he can give an immediate figure for: "That is why I never became a wealthy person! But I have many friends. I can go many places and ask almost anything." Raka explains that parents sometimes would seek him out, pleading with him to help their children. In some cases, he even ended up arranging their marriages for them, he laughs. Helping children through school remains one way that at least some of the members of the Jero Gede Sidemen, as well as other palaces and priestly houses, continue to give in ways that put people in service to them—or, one might say, that engender obligations not unlike those of earlier *parkan* ("slaves") or, in some cases, of the *pacatu* land holders. In fact, with regard to such people who still can be found helping at the larger regional palace also in return for school fees, Raka will say, "actually those are *markan*. The palace has to feed them, give them a place to sleep, and also send them to school," adding that this happens at priestly houses too. "Usually the people that become *sapangan, kavla, korban* [various forms of subjects, "slaves"], have a historical connection with the palace." Though, as he also points out, "nowadays people do not want to be called by these terms.... These words have disappeared in this modern age. Nowadays a *markan* can acquire the title of professor or doctor." Raka, himself, does "not consider [those that he helps] *markan*; I consider them as my children. They always come here, they sweep and so forth. But they eat the same food that I do. When they were *markan* their food was certainly inferior."

Those helped by Raka include a member of the descent group that summoned the forefathers of the Jero Gede to Sidemen. Gusti Ngurah Sidemen lived three years with Raka in Amlapura and extols his selflessness. By 1977, Ngurah Sidemen explains, he had become a teacher, was able to put on the cremation ceremony for his parents, and subsequently to marry—none of which, he says, would have been possible had it not been for Raka, as a representative of the Jero Gede. Another man, Nyoman, now a school principal and neighborhood leader, stresses that he would have been in the streets amounting to absolutely nothing, had it not been for Raka. He started coming to his house when he was six or seven, and it was only because of him that he got to go to school at all. He was welcomed and made to feel very comfortable in the house, free to help himself to food whenever he wanted. When asked about language, he explains that Raka uses a low level Balinese to him, whereas he uses a high level when speaking to Raka. He feels just fine about receiving the low level language form, he assures. Raka's now grown children would not be brazen enough to use the low level, but rather use a medium level when speaking to him, while he still addresses them in the high level. Repeatedly and consistently this man, who has a busy job, civic duties,

and a family of his own, puts being available to do things for Raka above anything else.

Cokorda Pemangku, the younger brother of the house, studied in Java for
his teaching degree and later to specialize in religious studies. Like Dangin he
returned to make his life in Sidemen, serving first as a teacher and a holy
dancer at sacred performances and, more recently, has become a non-Brahmana priest (*pemangku*). Formerly pemangku of the Pura Dalem, the village
temple associated with the cremation grounds and dedicated to chthonic
forces, in 2000 he became consecrated as pemangku of the Pura Puseh at
Tabola, the main village temple with connection to Besakih. His return to
Sidemen in 1981 was secured by a concerted effort on the part of the family,
including the arrangement of a marriage for him. Apparently there was concern that he would otherwise have stayed in Java:

> Maybe the old folks were worrying, maybe I belonged at home, maybe
> that was the hope of the elders, and also of my older brothers. Maybe
> this was for the sake of the people and to help with the matters con-
> cerning the people....I was not aware of it then, that the people re-
> quested me. When I went out into the villages, it became apparent;
> only then did I understand....But, excuse me, it is not that I put my-
> self forth, suggesting that I am considered important. It appears that
> they truly put me forth from the side of the people....They needed me
> home, from the perspective of relations with the people,...as an in-
> strument of communication, to benefit from the good connection that
> we have, both historically and privately..., the connection between
> my extended family and the extended families of others.

He does it, he says, because he wishes to reach out to help others with their
works, however he is able to: "This is my responsibility."

> Even when my uncle...still was pemangku, he told me that I would
> be so one day. He told me not to eat certain things. Since I was small,
> I was not allowed to eat the offerings from death ceremonies, for ex-
> ample, or from marriage ceremonies. When I disregarded that it be-
> came apparent that it was true [he became ill]. This happened sev-
> eral times, so I stopped. So I was automatically designated as
> pemangku of our family temple.

> I just go about this according to my abilities. For example if someone
> has a ritual work, I try to go. I go to help according to my ability, with
> whatever I can. That is what I do. I do so without thinking of my
> standing [lit. seating] as a cokorda person. Because their work is my

work. As long as they submit their work to me, it is my work and my responsibility.

Cokorda Mayun, a nephew of Dangin and Raka, is an emerging contemporary male player in Sidemen on behalf of the Jero Gede who, in the post-regime-change period following the maligya ritual, was elected interim village head (*kepala desa*), formalized with an actual election in July 2000.[26] In connection with this role, a role that he plays for his family as much as for the village, Mayun is very diligent in getting out to surrounding villages, maintaining strong personal connections with "the people." In his estimation, the office of village head consists of spending 25% of your time in the office, 75% of it out in interaction with your constituents. It is an aspect of his position that he obviously enjoys; he walks through town, recognizing and talking to people in an affable though distinguished way. Sometimes when he visits people in surrounding villages, he ends up staying so late that he spends the night. In the past too, he says, such mutual visiting was common. Elderly people in the villages remember coming frequently to the Jero Gede Sidemen as well, to "exchange ideas" (*tukar pikiran*). Wherever he shows up, people bring to him issues with which they are dealing. These may include seeking assistance to try to lease out attractive land, talking over water sharing or local leadership problems, electricity and road improvement projects that Mayun is facilitating for them. Five years after the maligya ritual, notably the road to Kebung extends all the way to the village and the bridge to Sangkan Gunung has been fixed (cf. chapter 3)

Mayun talks of all of these people as any village leader might, as "his people," using phrases such as "my people" ["masyarakat saya"] and "I have people" here and there ["saya punya orang" or "masyarakat"], and "descending to the people" ["turun ke masyarakat"]. Generally he speaks medium or low level Balinese to them, they high Balinese to him. Sometimes, however, he too speaks high Balinese to them—"So they know," he says, and to put them in a position of shame were they to not uphold the high level themselves.[27] It is obvious that there is no clear-cut distinction between his governmental position and his "traditional" position as representative of the noble house, as also evidenced in the election process that led to his assumption of the position of village head. This election was remarkable in that it was the first of its sort,

---

26. Theoretically he and other men of the Jero Gede now also participate in the local banjars.

27. His wife is a gusti and speaks an elevated language to him as well as to their children, while he responds to her in kasar (low level) and her children do so in madia (a medium level).

for apparently in the past, village leaders had been appointed rather than, as officially should have been, elected. Yet, even now, it was evident, leading up to the election, that Mayun at no point was in doubt as to who would win. Afterwards, regarding one village for example, he explained that because of the historical connection, when he goes there at least 80% of the people recognize him: "I went there during this recent election. All of them voted for me. There were maybe just five people or so who did not, maybe because they had misunderstood."

Women of the House

I Dewa Ayu Alit, the older sister of the cokorda brothers, never married, for, according to Balinese marriage principles of hypergamy, though men may marry women of any caste or title status, a woman may marry only men of equivalent or higher caste or title status. The movements of high caste women were highly restricted (cf. Pedersen 2002). As Dewa Ayu Alit explains, "women of caste were not allowed out by their elders. They were not allowed to go off to school. I went to school three years in Sidemen only. The women did not get to meet and talk to people. They only got to weave." From the age of eight she lived with her great aunt (her "mother") who was married to the raja at the palace in Amlapura, and only would go out when helping her accompany him on visits, such as to ceremonies. She, as did some of the men of the house, spoke of the family saying that the daughters of the house generally have ugly faces so no one will carry them off, and that this is a good thing, as there is prestige in high caste families to having your women unmarried. [28] The men, by contrast, are considered irresistible to women outside the house. Since she did not marry, I Dewa Ayu Alit says, her father always gave her anything he could. She says she also got an inheritance, though not as much as the men, as she would get one share to their two. She added that she also was

---

28. Due to this proclivity for keeping high caste women unmarried, women of very high rank end up having low fertility. Janet Hoskins points out that this is in contrast to the example of Raja Horo, installed as raja by the Dutch (see Hoskins 1998, 1993). Still a product of more egalitarian Kodi (West Sumba), where wife-giving reflects and confers high prestige, he did not want to see his daughters linger on unmarried, and would give them away, some complained, "too easily." These critics were from East Sumba, where, as in Bali, they were proud of having spinster sisters "too good for any of the local men" (personal communication). Sawitri, in an article on "Women in Indonesia's Military" (2001b), makes the interesting point that "should a woman soldier wish to marry a male soldier, his rank must be higher than hers."

given land "so she could eat."[29] Mostly I Dewa Ayu Alit spent her life weaving, doing quite successful business with island-wide nobility. Through this, she was instrumental in raising the money to support her brothers in their schooling. This they never forget and she retains a voice in the house to be respected.

Cowives. Other women who remain in the extended household of the Jero Gede Sidemen include Dangin's various wives. His first wife, a high caste cousin, owns and runs a homestay, as does his second wife, a Brahmana woman, who also holds an official post as head of administration in the subdistrict (*camat*) office. His third and fourth commoner wives work at each of their separate homes, the third one living at the Jero Gede Sidemen where she is in charge of the daily upkeep. They all in various ways help support the position of the noble house, financially, practically, and also by diligently attending ceremonies in the realm.

Cokorda Sawitri, an unmarried woman in her thirties, is Cokorda Raka's daughter. She lives in Denpasar where she is a civil servant and a poet, writer, performer, and, when I last visited (five years after the maligya ritual) was a graduate student and had immersed herself in painting too. She has an established reputation as an activist, albeit one that talks a lot about the importance of taking the "middle road." It caused some perplexity in the circles of her progressive friends when she shifted careers from being a writer for the main Balinese newspaper to becoming a government accountant. She did so as the result of parental and wider family pressure. Her father, in talking her into this, stressed the importance of serving the people and doing something useful. But her mother, she says, was smart, pointing out to her that it would still give her time to write and that she could always stop if it did not work out. Thus an accommodation with the family was reached, for, as she also stresses, she very much needs her family and therefore cannot and will not just break these ties by going her own way.

In retrospect, she does feel that her time has been freed up now that she is a salaried civil servant. She no longer feels that she has to compromise the work she really wants to do, as was the case when on writing assignments for the paper, always under deadlines. She still leads a disciplined writing life, sometimes secluding herself in her time off to work on her projects. Even as she was diligently participating in the maligya ritual preparations, she was also responding to the national events by writing poetry (Sawitri, n.d., see Sawitri 2003 for a published poem). One of her projects following the maligya ritual, first

---

29. According to Van der Kraan: "One of the most important social consequences of the individualization of land rights was the enhancement of the power of men over women. Individual land rights could be vested only in men, and therefore could be inherited only through the male line" (1983:323)

performed in Karangasem in 1999, was a retelling of *Calon Arang*, the story of Rangda or, less commonly, Dirah, the widow figure associated with witchcraft and destructive powers. Her piece was entitled *Pembelaan Dirah*, the Defence of Dirah (see chapter 8). Interestingly, it turns out that Sawitri was one of three women who, independently of each other, reworked the Calon Arang myth in 1998, at the time when Indonesia was in the throes of regime change. Their works are described by Barbara Hatley in a recent volume on *Women In Indonesia* (Robinson and Bessell, eds. 2002): "The three authors," explains Hatley, "have each approached the Calon Arang/Rangda figure in a different way—explaining and justifying the witch's fury; refuting, as male slander, her standard portrayal; making strategic use of the fear she evokes" (2002:139). As Hatley points out, it is a remarkable coincidence "that their works should have appeared almost at the same time, embracing the most hated and feared, but also the most powerful, of mythical female archetypes" (2002:139). These three women "publicly identify with and defend the horrifying male fantasy of powerful woman, Rangda, unafraid of such association" (2002:139), not a small feat in Bali, where some would not dare so much as to watch a Calon Arang performance.

Following the October 2002 nightclub bombing in Kuta, one of Bali's major tourist centers, Sawitri was intensely involved in clean-up, community healing, and purification efforts. She frequently is sought out by various youth and does a lot of civic work with poetry groups, mentoring and jurying young poets. She organizes arts festivals. She was the only Balinese woman to speak on a panel at the 2000 meetings for the Society of Balinese Scholars, where she spoke not of women's issues, but of politics. And her activity continues at home in Sidemen too. Most recently, she is strongly involved in an initiative within the princedom, working closely with her uncle, Tjokorda Gede Dangin, to organize local village associations to respond to Indonesian decentralization legislation by taking matters into their own hands, envisioning that they may be devising a pilot project for the rest of Bali (Pedersen 2004).

Her various forms of activism notwithstanding, Sawitri also remains caste conscious. She has no intention of marrying, but thinks she may, if anything, one day become a priest. By many within the family she is already regarded as a healer. They sometimes feel they have a need for her touch and come to her if they are afraid of witchcraft. Sometimes she ministers mantras over the phone. For her to ever marry would almost certainly mean relinquishing the special somewhat androgynous niche of power that she has established for herself. As for the official leadership of the house, it is noteworthy that in the speculation as to who might succeed Dangin, no women were ever mentioned. It appears that a woman becomes leader more by default, or in some arrangement of dual leadership by virtue of her personal charisma and power. But Sawitri did once in partial jest suggest that maybe one day she would become bupati, government head of regency.[30]

The Role of the Jero Gede Sidemen in Village Temples and Agriculture

It has been said often that those of high caste will not pray or participate in ceremonies at village temples, yet in Sidemen the presence and prayer of the princes may be prominently marked in such contexts. Consider these field notes of the arrival of deities and princes to a village festival in the beautifully situated *Pura Puseh* temple overlooking rice terraces and Mount Agung. The occasion is *Galungan*, the day on which all deities and ancestors descend upon Bali; the temple, the Pura Puseh is the "temple of origin" associated with the ancestral founders of the village:[31]

> Two gods have arrived from [the temples of] Kikian and Gunung Sari, and the one from Dalem Cepik is about to.... The Deity from Gunung Sari, apparently is very "strict" and gets mad if anyone stands in her way.... Intaran [Dangin's fourth wife with whom he now lives] just arrived, relatively late, 5:15 [some people have been here a couple of hours already].... Now Dangin just walked in as well.... Intaran seated herself in the courtyard, Dangin goes to sit with the priest in a small raised platform.... 5:30 The bells are beginning as is the gamelan.... 5:45 Sutedje just arrived, the current most likely candidate to become the next Cokorda. Once he and his wife are seated, Dangin moves forward.... Dangin sits prominently in front of the seated crowd, with

---

30. It is hard to resist quoting the description in the Alam Indah hotel's newsletter of Sawitri when she recited a poem at a multicultural "Bali Peace and Unity" event in Ubud. Upping her bupati comment, the newsletter reports: "She has a voice that was so passionately strong, one would think she should be the voice of Megawati! It is what the masses of Indonesians need to hear in their leadership" (www. Alamindahbali.com 01/15/2003).

31. Sidemen's Pura Puseh (the Pura Puseh Tabola, Tabola being the name for this area of Sidemen) has special connection to Besakih. When the gods of Besakih make the trip to the ocean for the *malasti* ceremony, they spend a night at this Pura Puseh. The Pura Puseh also has some features in common with the Pura Panataran Agung at Besakih: It has a triple lotus shrine, which bears resemblance to that at Besakih. Also it has shrines dedicated to some of the same deities. A large pavillion recently was constructed outside the Pura Puseh to shelter the people making the trip with the gods.

Sutedje and his wife behind him. Dangin's own wife is a little further back with their two sons....The priest has started with the holy water....6:15 Time to pray. Everyone makes sure they have their flowers and incense sticks.[32]

The central position of the Jero Gede, Tjokorda Gede Dangin, and his, at the time, emerging son, Sutedje, is clearly displayed at such ceremonies at the local village temple and indeed is required for the well-being of the village. Following the prayer in this case, there was a communal meal of eating from shared platters of food (*magibung*), commensality for the entire village. Some of Tjokorda Gede Dangin's younger sons participated in this event, arriving back at the Jero Gede Sidemen with the procession escorting the visiting gods back to their respective temples.

The members of the Jero Gede Sidemen also pray at the Pura Dalem, a practice which Wiener heard of regarding palace members in Klungkung as well, for in that case, she says, while "it is striking that in Klungkung members of royal and Brahmana clans did not traditionally support or worship in local village temples (Pura Desa), [they] did worship in their locality's Pura Dalem" (1995:111–112). Toward explaining this, she reminds her reader of "the obligation of rulers to placate demonic forces that could or did harm their realms, forces ultimately subordinate to the Goddess of the Pura Dalem. Rulers could only ensure prosperity with her aid" (1995:111–112). The same logic can be extended to other village temples. Certainly rulers need the help of Durga, the goddess with power over demonic forces, to ensure prosperity, but they need also the help of Dewi Sri, the Rice Goddess, as well as of other deities. And toward the purpose of fertility, as it turns out, the village needs the Jero Gede, all of which came together at the Pura Puseh at the *Galungan* ceremonies. Tjokorda Gede Dangin explains:

My temples at Gunung Sari, Kikian and Cepik have to descend to the Pura Puseh in the interest of the subaks [for a three day ceremony once a year and also at *Galungan* for one day]. Because they are my temples, because I [i.e. his forefathers] built those temples, this means that I have given fertility to all of the people; it means that I have provided them with food. So we are asked that my gods at those temples come to bless the ceremony. [Elsewhere he phrased it as his temples "becoming" the village temple].

---

32. Even village temples, as well as lower caste family temples, can host the supreme gods. It is to them that those of higher caste pray when they do enter these temples, not to the lower standing ancestors of the lower caste villagers or affines.

He explains the significance of the three temples from which the gods that day were visting the Pura Puseh: "Gunung Sari gives the essence, the *amerta*, for fertility. The dam is near Kikian and they ask the help of the Goddess there to guard it, to guard that the water enters the *subak* (the irrigation associations; here referring to the land farmed by the members of one *subak*). And Cepik gives purification, for good growth." This last temple, Cepik, is what is known as a Pura Dalem *Suci*. Whereas the Pura Dalem, or Pura Dalem *Setra*, is the temple associated with the cemetery and with death, the Pura Dalem *Suci* is associated with fertility and with agriculture. Dangin explains further, "If there are pests, at Pura Puseh these gods fight the pests. It is like the inner desire of the gods to go there to bring fertility to the people of Sidemen. If it were not for the fact that they go to the village temple, there would not be fertility."

Kingship here, in other words, is an important component of the relations between ancestors, earth and fertility. The connection between the noble house and the village and *subak* associations continues on the ceremonial level, not just in terms of ritual obligations to the noble house, but also in terms of obligations of the noble house to play a central role in village and *subak* ceremonies. Talking specifically of the subak, Dangin says: "If there is a subak ceremony, we still participate; they ask us to do so. We participate in offering prayer to Dewi Sri, asking for fertility. We cannot completely sever that connection. This is what is most important. If there is a subak ceremony, I must attend, sit at the front, and pray."[33] Danker Schaareman reported, too, that "it is the king who has to be present at the village rituals in order to pray for fertility of the land" (1986:40). And Boon mentioned that in Tabanan, "a now powerless raja is still occasionally borne aloft to the paddy fields of his voting subjects to beckon rain during drought or to turn back the rats during plague" (1977:165). In Sidemen, moreover, as do other subjects of the realm, leaders and members of the subak associations may still come to the Cokorda should there be issues they cannot resolve internally, including issues pertaining to water sharing. His role is not to help work things out technically, but rather to appeal to the moral obligation to resolve conflict, ask questions, and likely make a principled decision that they will have to abide by.

On the basis of current practice and received local history, the example from Sidemen bears on a recently renewed scholarly debate concerning the

---

33. Schulte Nordholt observed regarding Mengwi: "Once the overarching royal hierarchy disappeared, the great rituals to promote the well-being of the negara disappeared as well. In this way the progress of agriculture was in jeopardy, and even life itself was endangered" (1996a:254). In Sidemen, neither royal hierarchy, nor the rituals to ensure well-being and fertility of the realm have disappeared.

precolonial role of royalty in irrigation matters.[34] Lansing long has argued that
irrigation and agricultural management was in the hands of subak and water
temple associations rather than rajas (1991, 1993). Hauser-Schäublin has challenged this, emphasizing instead that the raja not only had a significant "reli-
gious-ritual role," but also an important role in "the coordination of the organization of irrigation" (2003:169). On the basis of regulations from
Northern Bali associated with royal irrigation agriculture, she concludes that
"coordination of water distribution...rested in the hands of the king"
(2003:160). Aside from the royal regulations, Hauser-Schäublin's argument is
based largely on incidents that show that rajas did, as we have seen also in
Sidemen, play a role in irrigation and fertility related ceremonies and could
be involved more concretely as well. She cites an example from Schulte Nordholt's work on Mengwi that the raja could seize and manipulate control of irrigation systems for purposes of war (i.e. "control over water could be used as
a political instrument in a battle against another principality" [2003:156]). In
the Sidemen area we have seen that the noble house is said to have owned the
source of water at the village of Padang Aji, and that control over this source
has been manipulated by different players at different times. Yet there is nothing in the evidence cited by Hauser-Schäublin or in that from Sidemen that
would indicate that it was the raja who had devised the distribution scheme
he sometimes decreed or was involved in disrupting, nor does Hauser-
Schäublin elsewhere present evidence of how the raja is to have arrived at and
effected what—and this much is inarguably demonstrated by Lansing's
work—is an intricate agro-ecology involving complex planting, water, and
pest management. Lansing has presented a plausible scenario for how this system may have developed from the ground up rather than have been designed
and implemented according to a master plan from the top down, and he has
shown convincingly how it worked ecologically, with the tasks of irrigation
and rice production being coordinated through subak associations. Other evidence so far adds perspectives on the roles that rulers played within and in
relation to this system.

One of the main flaws in the way the debate is currently framed and thus
in the conclusions drawn from the available evidence is the apparent assumption that the answer has to be either or: either rajas were involved in and
in charge of agriculture or they were not involved in and not in charge of agriculture. There certainly is evidence of rajas playing a role in regard to agri-

34. See Lansing 1991, 1993; Schulte Nordholt 1996a; Scarborough et al. 2000; and regarding the renewed debate, Hauser-Schäublin 2003; Lansing 2003, in press.

culture—ergo, it is concluded by Hauser-Schäublin that the scenario presented by Lansing cannot be true. As the evidence from Sidemen suggests, it is more likely that rajas were involved in agriculture—in fertility rituals, in announcing management plans, as occasional arbiters, and as rulers who could make use of water for politics. But there is no evidence that rajas were in charge of the organization and management of irrigated rice agriculture.

A final word now with regard to fertility in Sidemen: Recall the story of the noble house ensuring human fertility at the village of Kebung (chapter 3). Recall also that, in each village, people pointed out that in addition to being wife-givers, they had turned forest into fields of rice or plantations of *salak* fruit. So while fertility may be bestowed from above, from the gods and the princes, it also is created from below, from the forest and the people. The fertility of the realm depends on both.

Conclusion

What we find among the princes of Sidemen is a form of both ascribed and achieved leadership, according to which the leader, to maintain hierarchical privilege must exhibit some degree of egalitarian values. The importance placed on achieved leadership, the importance assigned to nurturing relationships with the people, the work involved in this, and the role played by the Cokorda in commoner village rituals to ensure the fertility and well being of the realm—all point to a different image of the local raja figure than the passive king-as-icon. Indeed, also Wolters writes regarding early "mandala management," that "strong government was literally on the move all the time. The sinews of government were the ruler's personal energy and surveillance" (1999:30–31). The characteristics of this ruler begin to resemble more those associated with the Austronesian chief or Melanesian Big Man than they are reminiscent of aspirations toward the old stereotypic Southeast Asian King Divine. Indeed, mortuary ritual, which the maligya ritual is, tends to be stressed in societies where there is a significant achieved dimension to rank. In discussing "cultural factors which promote leadership and initiative beyond a particular locality" (1999:18), Wolters, too, has recently suggested that the achieved rank of "Big Man" is a wider Southeast Asian phenomenon, [35] for

---

35. As Sahlins has outlined it, a Big-Man is a man who "personally acquires dominance over certain other fellows, a man who rises above the common herd...who makes himself a leader by making others followers: a fisher of men, inducing compliance by the strength of his personality, by his persuasiveness, perhaps by his prowess as a warrior, magician, or

which he prefers the phrase "man of prowess" (1999:18). It was as a part of this that Wolters argued that "other and more palpably religious aspects of his authority were also important...signs that people were able to read as verification that government was in the hands of one who was destined to be a prince among men in his generation" (1999:30–31). Yet we cannot presume to *equate* a Balinese prince with a Big Man—for example, genealogy and hereditary rank are also important in Bali. Indeed in other aspects, the Balinese Prince is perhaps better compared to the Austronesian chief than to a bigman. If we take as a point of departure Nicholas Thomas' model of Polynesian chieftainship, we can by now see that he is so by the following defining characteristics:

—A genealogical and mythological construction of rank.

—The hierarchy is linked to an iconography of food production (conditional upon ritual work associated with specific ancestor-gods).

—Abstract titular ownership of land on the part of the chief, and contingent but immediate tenure on the part of the users.

—This general, abstract ownership was associated with a flow of goods towards the chief: first-fruits and others.

—Since the survival and regeneration of the group as a whole was dependent upon the work of the chief there was a sense in which everyone was indebted to him. The well-being and productiveness of the land were seen to flow from a generalized condition of chiefly well-being and chiefly ritual in particular.

—Because the chief had a kind of overarching if partial ownership of everything, and because of the condition of the open-ended indebtedness to the chief as the giver of life (or at least the living mediator of divine life-giving forces), the system entailed asymmetrical rather than mutual reciprocal dependence, and prestations to the chief had the character of offerings rather than of the stereotypic debt-creating gift. [Thomas 1990:28–33;][36] [This latter characteristic, points out Lutkehaus, differs for Melanesian chieftainship, personal communication; on Big Men and/or chiefs see also Sahlins

---

gardener, and often by calculated disposition of his wealth, which puts people under obligation to him and constrains their circumspection. This is the prince among men: men heed him because he is princely" (1968:22).

36. There is difference however regarding the monopoly of ritual knowledge and practices, which in Thomas' model "were generally monopolized by either single chiefs or groups of chiefs," based on the special genealogical link between the chief and the deity (1990:7–8).

1963, 1985; Weiner 1976, 1988, 1992; Godelier and Strathern 1991; Lutkehaus 1990a, 1990b; Mosko 1992a, 1992b, 1995.]

Based on historical sources for Tahiti, H.J.M. Claessen evaluates Thomas' model favorably, but adds a point that also concurs better with the Sidemen example: He is not so sure, he says,

> that the relations between the chief and the people—as Thomas suggests—were wholly free of reciprocal expectations. The chiefs guaranteed (or created, or promised) fertility and well-being...and the people worked for the chiefs and handed over their products and daughters to them. The system worked satisfactorily—as long as the chiefs fulfilled their part of the "deal" by procuring fertility and well-being. Where this was not (or no longer) the case, a chief could be rejected. [2000:709][37]

We shall see in the next chapter that such was the case for rajas in Bali too. Applying such a model over time, it also becomes evident that this was and is an area of shifting negotiation.[38]

The case of the Balinese princes may be compared not just to earlier Austronesian forms; there are also contemporary parallels. In the Sepik area of Papua New Guinea, for example, in a society with hereditary chiefs, Nancy Lutkehaus (1995) examines the ways in which hierarchy and hereditary prerogative continue in the light of colonial and national state discourses of democratization (see also White and Lindstrom 1997, McWilliam 1999). As Lutkehaus (1995) discusses, it was predicted in the 1930s that the chiefs in

---

37. Claessen cites Douaire-Marsaudon (1998:77ff., 101, 114), who "asserts that no such idea of reciprocity was found on the Tonga Islands, but that on nearby Futana and Wallis a chief could be removed if he did not (could not) meet his obligations" (2000: 709; see also Sahlins 1968 for Fijian themes of reciprocity).

38. At this point, we should take note also of Denis Monnerie's argument against this very sort of exercise in mixing and matching typologies of Melanesian Big Men and Polynesian chiefs. In his work on the Mono-Alu in the Solomon Islands, Monnerie, too, found status and rank to be but "potentialities" (1998:94), "a combination of ascription, generational order and achievement, combining features which at the same time echo some criteria in the Oceanian typologies—again, of both Melanesia and Polynesia—and features which contradict these criteria" (1998:93). But "rather than attempt to create a new type, or compare unlike things," he urges instead that we find new paths. He proposes that we strive to understand social orders "in their relation to the entire social system;" more specifically, emphasizing status and rank not just at points during a person's life, but through death and death rituals into ancestorhood as well (1998). Here, in other words, we have yet another comparison to Bali.

Papua New Guinea would disappear. So why, she asks, have they not? An intriguing component of the answer is that they never were what those making the predictions had presumed. The chiefs were seen by outsiders "as leaders who had fallen from greater heights of autocratic rule than had actually existed in the past," and their power was therefore seen wrongly to be on a serious decline (1995:278). Regarding the authority and status of these chiefs over time, Lutkehaus points instead to "an ongoing process of reinterpretation and renegotiation," which allows them a continued role as chiefs (1990a:307), an argument similar to that made here in regard to the Balinese princes of Sidemen as they strive to re-create or recover their perceived former stature, even as they respond to variable circumstances.

Chapter Six

Circumscribed Royal Power

The emphasis on mutuality in the princedom notwithstanding, rulers, including the more populist ones, also could and still can have autocratic tendencies as well. As we have seen, even in the contemporary story from Sidemen, there are indications of the ruler's power to appropriate anything he wants. He could pick any woman of the realm he desired, and in examples of Tjokorda Gede Dangin assisting his people, it emerges that they will not or cannot deny him anything he might ask, a method he sometimes uses to assume and then redistribute disputed possessions. We have also heard contemporary followers define their relationship with their raja in part by the theoretical possibility that he could in the past have sold them as slaves, if he had so wished. Yet the raja could and cannot get away with just anything. Linked to and concomitant with pressures for rajas to work for their people, they also have had to contend with what we might call powers of the people. People are quick to point out that even in the past, if a raja did not work well enough for and with his people, people did not heed him and once in a while he was in fact destroyed.

What we see in Sidemen in this regard again turns out to correspond to newer scholarship on Indic kingship in Southeast Asia, which now brings to the fore that Southeast Asian kings, in general, were far from omnipotent (cf. Tambiah 1985; Wolters 1999; Schulte Nordholt 1996a regarding Bali). Upon a more careful reading of the earlier literature, it also becomes clear that even in the old mold of Heine-Geldern's representation of divine kingship, deification of the king did not circumvent power struggles. Even here "the empires of Southeast Asia from the very beginning were torn by frequent rebellion, often resulting in the overthrow of kings or even dynasties" (1956:10), for "the theory of divine incarnation could be used not only to exalt the position of the legitimate king, but equally well as a justification for usurpation of the throne" (1956:7).[1] In

---

1. Cf. also Quigley's point (2000) regarding regicide as a device for asserting kingship.

other words, in this interpretation, the kings were indeed believed to have spiritual and divine power, but by the same token, if they in some way failed—if a king lost in battle, for example—this could be taken as a sign that the given king no longer had to be followed. Furthermore, anyone who succeeded in seizing the palace that represented mount Meru, or, in some cases, the regalia representing kingship, by that act alone could become ruler. Heine-Geldern includes as a reason for the overthrow of kings also a suggestion of powers of the people in the face of a king raised to such an "exalted position:" "the immense power and the lack of restrictions which the king enjoyed invited to abuses which in the end made the monarch obnoxious to his subjects and hastened his downfall" (1956:10). There is no doubt that much resistance either never was publicly expressed or, as Dirks puts it regarding village leadership examples in India, never "leaked into official view, usually because the disputes were dealt with in summary (and no doubt brutal) fashion by the dominant groups" (1994:494). But it is also the case that, in the context of the fluid negara, the process of keeping in check the powers of kings is likely as old as Southeast Asian kingship itself, even if it does take on new dimensions within shifting political contexts.

Divinely Imbued Powers of the People

In Sidemen, princes and followers alike appeal to precolonial tradition when emphasizing that rajas had to heed their people. To make their points, both Dangin at the noble house and Pak Komang, his follower at Kebung, separately volunteered the pre-Majapahit story of the Illusion Demon, Mayadanawa, who ordered people to worship him instead of the gods at Besakih. What follows is Pak Komang's story:

> Dalem Maya Danawa was hostile with the people. At Bedaulu, Gianyar...He competed against the people...because He used power at his whim. It was not just in Gelgel. Not just in Gianyar. There were many rajas that were called Maya Danawa. *Maya*—at first glance it is seen, then it is not seen. From time to time it is not seen....The material/the immaterial [*Sekala/niskala*], it is called Maya Danawa....In the case of Maya Danawa at Bedaulu, this led to war with the people because he was too arrogant; his arrogance was out of the ordinary. He was seen momentarily, then gone again; [he could make himself disappear and reappear]....Because of his abilities, his ego grew...and the people grew hot. They were oppressed. They were told not to do this and not to do that. They were oppressed...to the point

that the ceremonies at Besakih for so many years were not held. [The people] did not dare [because he would stop them]. Do not go there [he would admonish them]; where are the deities? I am God....The people really got hot. They opposed that. They were helped by invisible forces. Those gods descended to go amuck against him. In the end he disappeared. He burned up, without a trace....Maya Danawa disappeared.

This account of the story is interesting in comparison to how it is usually represented (cf. i.e. Wiener 1995:102–104). Other versions of the story do also contrast Maya Danawa, along with Bali's last indigenous raja, Bedaulu, as demonic as opposed to just rajas, the latter being the Majapahit derived rajas who are represented as liberators of the Balinese from unjust rule,[2] but in those versions Maya Danawa angered not so much the people, who are not even mentioned, but the God of Besakih, whose place he usurped. Wiener does mention as well an example of the Maya Danawa story being used as "cultural precedent for rejecting the suzerainty of supreme rulers" (1995:260– 261). This happened in the context of trying to account for one kingdom's resistance to the authority of Klungkung, and its subsequent willingness to align itself instead with the Dutch: "His enemies could tell themselves that the Dewa Agung's [of Klungkung] power had taken an ominous turn and that his actions suggested he was a Bédaulu or Mayadanawa—*sakti* [charismatic and powerful] but greedy" (1995:260–261). By both Tjokorda Gede Dangin and Pak Komang, however, the story is viewed as a mythical precedent for the rights of "the people" to curb the arrogance of their rajas. It is a story that is taken to show both that the raja cannot behave as though he is a god and, moreover, that the gods will side with the people against any such pretender. Note also an interesting point made by Rubinstein, that Brahmana, too, beyond merely being aligned with rulers and in addition to sometimes having political ambitions of their own, may align with their *sisya* or followers in curbing the excesses of rulers (1991a:70–71). In terms of actual practices in historical and contemporary society that might bear out the license of people to challenge rulers, meanwhile, Bali is known for especially two practices that indicate empowered villagers: the rights of followers to desert a lord (*matilas*) and the tradition of disrupting cremation ceremonies (*ngarapngarapan*).

---

2. All of these versions contrast with Bali Aga representations of Bedaulu as a just raja who is unjustly usurped by Majapahit conquerors (Reuter 1999:162).

Matilas. Balinese followers of a lord, by tradition had the right to *matilas;* that is, in the face of misgovernment, to become "unfaithful" by abdicating from one lord to seek the protection of another. That there at least theoretically were alternatives for followers to choose between is perhaps one facet of the situation of unconsolidated kingship in Bali following the seventeenth-century dissolution of the kingdom of Gelgel, which resulted in a multitude of kingdoms and princedoms competing for the loyalty of followers. The situation, conversely, also allowed followers to take advantage of the rivalries among the lords (cf. Van der Kraan 1983:321; Stein Callenfels 1947:194–195; see also Schulte Nordholt 1996a; Korn 1932). To an outsider such as Van Bloemen Waanders, the first Dutch colonial officer to Bali, the result was anarchic:

> In Buleleng [north Bali] there is not a trace of an ordered adminis-
> tration....The population has been able to free itself from all con-
> straints, giving rise to a situation contrary to all principles of gov-
> ernment....Nearly everyone seems to be of the opinion that he can
> choose his own punggawa [lord]. Every desa [village], and even parts
> thereof, assume these rights and choose their punggawas [lords] in
> order to dismiss them as soon as they grow tired of them. [Van der
> Kraan 1983:320–321]

The availability of the option to *matilas* should not be exaggerated, as it would not always have been a practical solution for the general population. The practice also had the potential effect of weakening the village community by "[giving] rise to political division within the desa which prevented the village from confronting the Raja and punggawas as a single, unified entity" (Van der Kraan 1983:321). One might further wonder how people, if they feel as bound by ancestral oaths as we have seen to be the case (chapter 4), could be free to take advantage of the option to *matilas.* Yet this is not as much of a contradiction as it may seem for, again, the oaths tying followers to lords are mutual. If the lords do not live up to their responsibilities toward their followers, it is they who have breached the agreement. Balinese scholar, Ide Anak Agung Gde Agung, describes such a case in nineteenth-century Bali:

> An important village situated at the border of both princedoms
> Bangli and Gianyar revolted against the authority of Dewa Manggis
> VII as a result of misgovernment of the punggawa or district head
> there who happened to be the son of the prince....This district head
> Dewa Ngurah Ratnakania was so much hated by the people because

of his extortions that he had to flee from his post to the capital of Gianyar. This opportunity was utilized by the foremen of the village of Apuan to gather the population for a meeting in which they decided to renounce the authority of the Dewa Manggis VII and to place themselves under the protection of the prince of Bangli Dewa Gde Tangkeban, the arch enemy of the prince of Gianyar. [1991:119–120]

The sometimes strong and sometimes waning resistance that the Dutch encountered in their nineteenth-century expeditions against Bali may also in a few cases be linked to these kinds of powers of the people. At first there was determination on behalf of people to follow the rajas in encounters where they resisted the Dutch (Van der Kraan 1995); yet, later it made for some of the turning points in the course of events when people defected from the armies of their rajas, first the raja of Buleleng at the famous Jagaraga site, then the raja of Karangasem. Though the lords, on the face of it, made the critical decision to walk away from the battle in Jagaraga, there are indications that they were acting on the basis of pressures from their men. Abandoned by their followers, these rulers were forced to flee, later to be hunted down and killed (Van der Kraan 1995). Its limitations notwithstanding, there can be no question but that *matilas* could be an empowering practice and an important theoretical possibility that sometimes had consequences for the careers of rajas and the course of history.[3]

In Bali, challenges also could be expressed in a way that did not necessarily reach the breaking point of *matilas*. Thus the popular Balinese theatrical tradition of *topeng* (masked dance) provided and continues to provide an arena of potential criticism and ridicule of rajas and courts (see Jenkins 1994), and the popularity of cockfights indicates as well a site of potential counter-hierarchy, wherein commoners might rise over nobles (see Geertz 1973b). Another notorious practice that still exists is the disruption of cremation cere-

---

3. Van der Kraan (1983:327) cites a Dutch colonial official, Dubois (1837), to assert that even would be slaves had some clout - "The rajas and punggawas who agreed to sell some of their slaves had to proceed with the utmost caution because the Balinese people 'consider it one of their privileges not to be *undeservedly* [Dubois' emphasis] shipped outside of Bali" (Van der Kraan 1983:327). And: "Although ruled in a tyrannical manner, the Balinese people have retained certain privileges which cannot be transgressed upon without danger of rebellion....A lord would commit the worst offence if he were to arbitrarily seize one of his subordinates' daughters, especially if he were to sell her to foreigners. If he did this he would *at the very least* [Dubois' emphasis] risk losing all his subordinates through flight" (Van der Kraan 1983:327).

monies. Although this is a practice not exclusively reserved for rajas, it does extend into the relationship between these and their followers.

Ngarap-ngarapan: Disruption of cremation ceremonies. Given the central role of a death ceremony to the manifestation of the princedom as discussed in this study, it is interesting to note that it is precisely in death ceremonies, though in cremation rather than postcremation rites, that not only status is asserted prominently, but that also the disruptive potential of followers is displayed. Bateson and Mead had described this in the early forties:

> This activity, called *ngarap bangke* or *ngarap wadah* (literally, "work-ing the body" or "working the tower"), is noisy, riotous, and mischie-vous. When the carriers excel themselves in excitement, laughing and shouting, splashing up the mud in every stream and almost upsetting the cremation tower or tearing the corpse to pieces, it is usually said that they are "very angry with the family of the deceased." Our obser-vations indicate, however, that the degree of intensity of this riotous behavior increases with the social status of the deceased, the size of the tower, the newness of the body, and the number of carriers. [1972:243]

Geertz, too, described it, providing an example precisely of a royal event of highest status:

> The procession was a clamorous and disorderly affair throughout. It began with a mock battle between the men trying to carry the corpse over the palace wall to place it on the tower and the crowd outside seeking to prevent them from doing so. It ended a half mile or so far-ther on, with a series of similar battles as the corpse was brought down from the tower to its animal coffin and set upon the pyre. In between there was near-hysteria. [1980:118]

To Geertz, in the end, the disruptive behavior only shows up the hegemony of the center. As he concludes, "Yet for all that, the procession had a rigor-ous order: it was as calm and unruffled at its apex and center as it was tu-multuous and agitated at its base and edges" (1980:118). In this, Geertz con-cords with what until recently was the typical anthropological practice of interpreting rites of rebellion as serving ultimately to reinforce the position of those in authority. Arguably, however, there is real potential for disrup-tion being displayed in *ngarap-ngarapan*, as it can and does, albeit on rare occasion, result in outright destruction of the cremation tower, the sarcoph-agus, or even the body, and can culminate in the outright refusal, in the end, to get the body to the cremation ground at all. As Dirks has pointed out, although Van Gennep, almost a century ago, recognized well "the danger and disorder that was part of ritual," as evidenced in the attention to liminality in his framework for analyzing ritual, which, via Victor Turner, lies behind much anthropology of ritual, his theory nonetheless "has a tendency to contain danger too readily, too automatically, and to assume that disorder is ultimately epiphenomenal" (1994:498). For Balinese, dangers posed to the journey of bodies and souls are not a merely symbolic matter; they are dangers to which the center or the apex certainly would have had to and still has to adjust itself.

That disruption of death ceremonies be recognized as a true mechanism of leveling is strongly argued also by Carol Warren, who presents several examples of such events (1993a, 1993b), noting that the "celebrated instances of disruption in local lore invariably involved individuals of title or wealth who failed to demonstrate their equal obligations as banjar [neighborhood] members and/or to pay adequately for their claims to status through appropriate redistribution" (1993b:48).[4] Clearly this practice can be a way of expressing resistance to autocratic and stingy rule. Furthermore, it was on occasion an avenue of action taken by the Indonesian Communist Party (PKI) in the tense political climate of the 1960s, the most notorious case reported being the impending disruption of the cremation ceremony of Dewa Agung Oka Geg, the "last raja" of Klungkung:

> His cremation was to be an event which would be a tribute to his standing. The whole of Klungkung was mobilised and donated its labour and materials, and the highest level of cremation tower, with eleven tiers, was prepared.... On the eve of the procession the PKI massed its supporters outside the palace, ready to rush in and burn the tower and perhaps even the body, the ultimate insult which would totally destroy the ritual. [Vickers 1989:170]

---

4. One of Warren's friends, from a family with ritual ties to Puri Tarian, had remarked after a large cremation ceremony of Puri Tarian ("the most elaborate since the 1950s") that she was surprised that it had not been disrupted: "I thought the carriers would do something to the tower. Lots of people were peeved that the puri wasn't as generous as it ought to be. They cut down on the meat served to those helping, and they should have given presents of clothes or jewelry at least to those of us who came every day" (Warren 1993a:79). And, as MacRae notes regarding a prince of Ubud who is said to have lost the connection to the people, Cokorda Gde Raka Sukawati: "the turbulent carriage of the Cokorda's corpse, borne reluctantly by the local community to its place of cremation, bears witness to this reputation. He is remembered on a larger stage primarily as a political opportunist, collaborator with the Dutch, and instigator of repressive violence against his own people" (1999:151; see also Robinson 1995:169–178, who gives an account of Sukawati's actions especially during the nationalist struggle).

Apparently the threat to the event and everything implied thereby was averted when people loyal to the palace summoned military support and members of the PNI [Nationalist Party] to the scene: "After a brief skirmish the PKI fell back and the ritual went ahead" (Vickers 1989:170). The choice of the cremation to express the political protest of the PKI testifies to the power of this arena as an expression of the potential for genuine dissent, which may also be reflected in the more licensed practice of *ngarap-ngarapan*.

The above incident happened in 1965, only shortly before the supposed coup and counter-coup which ousted President Sukarno and put Suharto in power. Within months of the Dewa Agung's cremation and Suharto's new presidency, a spree of killings broke out in Bali in which the power of the disruption of death ritual was to be borne out in much more lethal fashion. On the basis of fieldwork in a Southern Balinese village, Leslie Dwyer and Degung Santikarma have learned that most people interpret the practice of dismembering and dispersing bodies beyond recognition and retrieval "as tactics designed to ensure continuing distress to victims' families by upsetting established ritual practice regarding the dead, leaving emotional effects that linger in the present" (2003:300). As the authors note, the symbolic and ritual violence inflicted was more traumatic than simply death (2003:300).

In 1998 in Sidemen, one cremation still required completion prior to the maligya ritual, the cremation for the wife of a cousin of the core line of the noble house who had died two years earlier. During the procession to the cremation grounds, the carriers were very riotous indeed, one so drunk that he was escorted to the police station. On several occasions in the mayhem, Cokorda Raka exclaimed, "Awas masyarakat!" "Be careful people!" as he semi-jogged along with an expression of concentrated concern on his face. The whole procession came to several screeching halts and near collapses.[5] Aside from a few personal jabs at the deceased, any display on this particular occasion of potentially disruptive power on the part of the people of Sidemen would be understood to be directed at the noble house performing the cremation, rather than at the individual person herself. Drinking and riotous behavior is customary, a part of any cremation, but through this there is a reminder of the potential always for more poignant disruptions. In this case, there was an incident shortly after the procession arrived at the cremation

---

5. Various female relatives made mildly disparaging comments about the deceased and her offspring, pertaining for example to her daughter being slow and she being a spend thrift. It is a quality of these occasions also that they provide the opportunity for leveling between relative equals as well (i.e. between family or fellow banjar members if someone has been lazy or has not participated equally in community life).

grounds: "An accident happened to the body," sending the deceased's son-in-law into a trance and requiring the staging of a special corrective rite. It was unclear exactly what happened and who had been responsible for the accident; some even denied later that anything had happened at all.[6] Overall, despite the high level of excitement, this was a fairly mild expression of disruption or potential disruption. It remained within the bounds that allowed Raka to make light of it afterwards, saying that it has to be so. And indeed it does, for the power of the people is a reality in the Balinese princedom and the cremation procession is a ritualized arena in which to display its potential, revealing at once the importance on behalf of the rulers of engaging possibly unruly forces to demonstrate their power and the often ambivalent attitude toward privileged people.[7]

Though these events do not usually spiral out of control, there is always the inherent tension present and the suggestion that they could do so. John Pemberton writes of a similar phenomenon on Java, *rebutan*, ritualized disruptive events, which used to "occur within many occasions emblematic of 'tradition'—village annual observances, acts of ascetic pursuit, and, sometimes, weddings" (1994:18). Such ritualized disruptions always imply that something irregular could happen, or, as Pemberton puts it, that something might not *not* happen (1994:257). Their power is attested to by the New Order government's strong discouragement of these events, which certainly do not fit with the program of portraying only a beautiful and secure Indonesia (Pemberton 1994:253). In incidents of extreme corpse abuse in Bali, there have been legal prosecutions charging disrespect toward the deceased (Connor 1979), but because cremation disruptions also are "ritually legitimated forms of play" and, perhaps more importantly, are

---

6. Warren conveys a story she heard from Doug Miles of the disruption of the cremation ceremony in north Bali in 1963 for the daughter of a wealthy building contractor who "had made no effort to establish himself as a good local citizen through active participation or redistributive gestures" (1993b:47). In this case, "when the body was brought out by the banjar and passed about in the customary mock play-battle...they began throwing it about until it was literally torn to pieces. At this point the mother, apparently possessed by the spirit of her child, began screaming expressions of agony. In the end the banjar walked off, refusing to continue its part in the ceremony" (Warren 1993b:47).

7. In some places, including parts of Africa and Polynesia, chiefs and kings were subjected to ridiculing rites-of-passage when assuming kingship or chieftainship (cf. Turner 1969; Quigley 2000; Claessen 2000), but in Bali there is no evidence that ridicule was a standard component of the rite-of-passage to kingship. Here the rituals of disruption surrounding cremation, in the rite-of-passage from king to deity, appear to come closest to including this component. (In addition to Warren regarding death rite disruptions, see also Connor 1979 on corpse abuse.)

integral to the imperative that the collective transport the corpse to the cremation grounds, it has not been possible to banish them (Warren 1993b:48).

Events of *rebutan*, reported by Pemberton still to occur in Java, include a rite
of scrambling for food that has been offered to various spirits as well as an annual rite of doing so for magically charged pancakes at the tomb of a particular
ascetic (1994:244–245, 253–254).[8] In Bali, too, there are occasions for rushing
to get "empowered booty:" offerings on the ground get rummaged through after
having been dedicated to the demons or chthonic spirits, as do cremation towers and goods that are thrown to the waves. At the maligya ritual, the items to
be returned to the ocean included gold and gems and boats were hired to take
them out to sea to be released beyond the reach of eager hands. Another event
was incorporated in the maligya ritual, however, where tall poles were erected
with various items tied to the top, such as umbrellas and flashlights. While these
were many of the same items that were given to each priest in the thanksgiving
feast, the young commoner men had to compete with each other, albeit play-
fully, to reach and make off with the goods. By contrast, offerings of fruits and
rice cakes which have been dedicated to deities or to living persons are distributed in a very orderly fashion, their system of distribution remaining one of the
strongest caste and title groups markers in Bali, for one only accepts offerings
from persons that one recognizes as one's kin or superior. Refusing to partake in
someone's ritual leftovers can constitute a statement of resistance to equality, or
indeed to hierarchy, that can result in major discord (cf. the mediation example
mentioned in chapter 5, where a husband refused to eat his wife's ritual leftovers).

Death rites frequently also are the sites of trances, another reminder of potential disruption and discord in what might otherwise appear to be beautifully orchestrated rituals—and reminiscent of the story of Mayadanawa in
which invisible forces and deities helped people go amuck in reaction against
an unjust raja. People are not held personally accountable for what they utter
in trances, and what is uttered almost invariably reflects dissatisfaction with
the state of affairs represented through the ritual action. Take, for example,
the trance mentioned in chapter 2, where a woman married to an Amlapura

---

8. Pemberton remarks that "[conversations] with villagers after the day's events revealed
little sense of a contradiction between the acutely orderly scene of struggle at the site of the
guardian spirit." He, too, finds that "this apparent compatibility is striking in light of the
considerable analytic emphasis given slametan as an expression of cultural order in ethnographies on Java" (1994:245). Very similar to his interpretation of the cremation in Bali,
Geertz wrote regarding the slametan in Java: "The slametan represents a reassertion and
reinforcement of the general cultural order and its power to hold back the forces of disorder" (1976:29).

prince was entered by her husband's deceased mother. The mother-in-law who spoke through her was from the noble house of Sidemen, but had been married to the last raja of Karangasem in Amlapura. She was now in a situation that the trancing woman might find herself in posthumously—at once dissatisfied with not being included in the Sidemen ritual and dissatisfied with the ritual treatment accorded her at the larger palace. Behind this lies also a broader issue between the palace and the noble house: Despite the affinal connection between Amlapura and Sidemen, and although Cokordas Dangin and Raka each have lived at the palace in town, as has their sister, it is ultimately a relationship of conquest with some degree of underlying tension. Aside from the Amlapura prince whose mother was from Sidemen, no other members of the Amlapura palace participated in the maligya ritual. In part, said a member of that palace, this was because Sidemen did not invite them to do so, yet various members and followers of the Jero Gede Sidemen nonetheless made note of their absence, commenting on how good it would have been for them to witness real royal power in action. They were referring to the noble house's power in other words, and to the power base of loyal followers, which is deemed lost in the larger regional palace. That the daughter of Sidemen who had married into the Amlapura palace, as manifested in the trance, had complaints concerning her ritual treatment in Amlapura and desired to be included in Sidemen's ritual, served to imply the superiority of the latter.

Examples of the highest ranking raja of Bali and of the removal of a raja. It has been suggested that even the Dewa Agung of Klungkung may not have been as powerful or as readily obeyed as is sometimes imagined. Schulte Nordholt points, for instance, to a form of passive resistance when another raja sent troops to support him, for the men "arrived deliberately too late" (1996b). He mentions an example also from the 1880s when "royal servants of a neighboring kingdom ridiculed the Dewa Agung by kicking a straw puppet, representing the paramount ruler, at the entrance of the local market" (1996b; see also Geertz 1980:43). In the presence of certain indicators, people could, as mentioned, be justified not only in abandonment or disruption, but in outright removal of a raja. Natural calamity, in particular, could be seen as indicative of a raja not doing well by the people. Schulte Nordholt provides the following example:

From March 1827 to November 1828 southern Bali was visited by the scourge of a smallpox epidemic; many succumbed and public life was lamed. No rituals were conducted, no war was waged, no music was heard. People did not go out; they remained inside, if at all possible, until the doom should be lifted. Disaster was added upon calamity when eastern Badung was hit by a great flash flood that washed the crops away. Epidemics and nature gone berserk were seen as the wrath of the gods, and this in turn created a climate in which removal of the king was at least thinkable, since the condition of the negara was held to be causally related to the person of the king. On this view, the king was responsible for the misfortune that visited his negara, and murder justified. [1996a:112]

In the twentieth and early twenty-first centuries, too, leaders can be brought down by what in Southeast Asia has come to be referred to as the phenomenon of "people power." The Philippines has provided the most prominent examples of this, at the time through the Philippine people's movement that under the leadership of widowed Corazon Aquino felled the Marcos regime. Though there may be argument as to its applicability to the Indonesian example, the phrase of "people power" was in fact applied, both in international media and locally, to the events forcing Suharto to step down in 1998, the same events that were to lead to Megawati's rise to a position of intensified popular support.[9] The phrase has been applied as well to subsequent cases of local mass action in Indonesia.

Contemporary Examples of People Power: The Rise of Megawati and the Threat of Mob Actions

Megawati rose to prominence within the Indonesian Democratic Party (PDI), which was formed in 1973 as an outgrowth of the Nationalist Party founded by her father, President Sukarno. In 1993, the party succeeded in electing her over the government's favored candidate to the post of its chairmanship. By 1996, it became apparent that she was being positioned as presidential candidate for the 1998 elections by the People's Consultative Assem-

---

9. As with Aquino, who also followed in the footsteps of a felled popular leader—her husband, the assassinated senator Benigno Aquino—Megawati is often referred to as the housewife turned politician. Megawati herself brings up this similarity even as she discourages other comparison: "Our social and cultural context is different. There might be some similarities at the personal level—at least we are both housewives! What I don't agree with is the easy equation that can be engineered....It is an attempt to label me as a revolutionary" (Sailendri 1996). Even as she became president, Megawati was sometimes still referred to in the press as a housewife lacking qualifications. Although there was much skepticism as to how she would perform as president, the appellation of inexperienced housewife surely could have been dropped after what already had been a decade of political leadership.

bly (MPR), which as the highest state institution determines the mandate of the President. "It would be the first time," wrote the editor of the Australian-based magazine *Inside Indonesia* that year, "that someone within the system has challenged the incumbent" (van Klinken 1996a). And another commentator, Ed Aspinall, expressed that since its formation, the PDI had been nothing but "a weak and mostly docile component of the New Order's corporatist political system:"

> The party represented no threat to the government. It always made clear its support for the key pillars of the political system, such as Suharto's next candidacy for President.... The election of Megawati as Chairperson in late 1993 changed all that. For the first time in the 30 year history of Suharto's New Order, a political party was headed by a leader who had not been groomed by the government, indeed, who was elected by party members in defiance of government instructions. [1996]

Megawati herself said, "I am the only party leader in the history of the New Order [Suharto's reign] who has been elected from the grass roots. This is what the government does not like. Thus far all other leaders have attained their position mainly through the blessing of the government" (Sailendri 1996). In response, the government orchestrated her ousting from the PDI leadership by manipulating other PDI leaders to set up an "extraordinary congress" in Medan, Sumatra, in 1996, prior to which "the press ha[d] been instructed not to describe the events as 'displacing Mega,' and not to call her 'Megawati Sukarnoputri' (i.e. daughter of Sukarno) but by her husband's name Kiemas" (van Klinken 1996b). On June 20, Megawati was removed as leader of the PDI. Already, says Aspinall, "the spectre of Manila style 'people's power' haunted Jakarta:" "A large demonstration took place in Jakarta. Cheered on by construction workers in scaffolding high above their heads, and watched by thousands of business district office workers, a large crowd marched through the centre of the city. Estimates of its size varied from five to twenty five thousand" (1996).

When the Medan conference was followed in July by a government and military backed attack on Megawati's supporters at party headquarters in Jakarta, resulting in several deaths, severe riots broke out. While all of this, as Stefan Eklof assesses, "exposed the government's heavy-handedness and manipulative methods, it also served to boost Megawati's public reputation for justice and incorruptibility" (1999). Even so, commentators doubted that she stood a chance of posing a real challenge to Suharto (van Klinken 1996a). Van Langenberg doubted that her repetition of Sukarnoisms—that is, "present[ing] herself as a representative of 'the people,' principally echoing her father's earlier construction of himself as the 'voice of the people' (*lidah rakyat*) in the late 1950s"—could "be a focus for a populist 'people's power' movement that may replace the present Suharto government." He felt that "discourse of 'Sukarnoism' is not one that sits easily with a commitment to a democratic polity, certainly not one with a primary concern for human rights" (1996), but then human rights may not be the foremost motivation of every people's movement. At any rate, Van Langenberg did not believe that conditions in Indonesia or surrounding Megawati were such that a "people's power" movement would be instrumental in the transition to a post-Suharto presidency (1996). And yet, Aspinall proved right. As he said later: "This is the irony of Indonesia today. The regime—like many run by ageing strongmen—is determined to prevent the development of institutionalised opposition, no matter how moderate (and Megawati is very moderate indeed). This policy has had the unintended consequence of inflaming mass sentiment" (1997).

Megawati became a unifying symbol, not just for her newly founded party, the PDI-P or Democratic Party of Struggle, but for a whole array of nongovernment organizations, student groups, and others in opposition, including a broad base of disillusioned middle and lower class citizens. Prior to the Medan conference, thirty pro-democracy organizations had issued a statement in support of her and it was activists connected to these that led the demonstrations (Aspinall 1996). Megawati, meanwhile, appealed to her supporters to avoid violent confrontation, as she moved ahead with a court challenge to the decision to dislodge her as chair of the PDI. (It was the unfavorable decision of this that was handed down when she was in Sidemen for the peak of the maligya ritual in August.)

Meanwhile the presidential election drew closer and Megawati's base of popular support only grew. By January 1998, Pijar, an activist group consisting mainly of Jakarta students, in joint action with PDI Megawati supporters, read a statement to the People's Consultative Assembly (MPR), urging the assembly to withdraw its support from Suharto, who, they proclaimed, "has used his political position to enrich himself, his family, and his colleagues," as a result of which "the Indonesian people are now suffering from the collapse of the economic and political system" (Pijar 1998). They urged the nominations of Megawati and Amien Rais, leader of a Muslim coalition, as president and vice-president, respectively, stating that "behind these two leaders for renewal stand six million angry people who have lost their jobs, 30 million PDI-Megawati supporters, tens of millions of Amien Rais supporters, and many more anxious people in the cities" (Pijar 1998). A few months later, riots and a form of people power movement were to bring down Suharto, in what came to be known as "Jakarta's May Revolution." May 12, following weeks of student protests, the shooting of four Trisakti University students in West Jakarta was to trigger the worst Indonesian riots ever. Approximately twelve thousand died, hundreds of Indonesian-Chinese women were raped, and damages were estimated at about two hundred fifty million U.S. dollars (cf. van Klinken 1998; see also this article for a step-by-step account of the progression of the riots).

In 1999, although there still was not actual popular vote for president under the Indonesian electoral system (the 2004 elections were the first elections where Indonesians voted directly for their president), Megawati clearly enjoyed the popular support of the nation, including that of the vast majority of the Balinese population. She could not secure the vote of the People's Assembly, where there were concerns surrounding her being a woman and not being a sufficiently devout Muslim, but she was appointed Vice President to Adurrahman Wahid (Gus Dur). By July 24 2001, Wahid, after months of maneuvering by his opponents, was dismissed by parliament, accused of having become a dictator. Megawati was unanimously elected president by the 591 member Assembly and a peaceful transition was made, Gus Dur having failed to rouse people to take to the streets on his behalf. Members of the Jero Gede Sidemen indicate that Megawati during these days of transition had telephoned to Sidemen, that they may join in praying for her presidency.

Many agree that Megawati's popular support and charisma in large part derive from her father, first President Sukarno. Yet, Sukarno, who became linked to the perceived threat of communism, is sometimes remembered in the West as mainly a dictator and a debauch. To give but a single example, one American guidebook to Bali states:

> Though Sukarno was half Balinese, he showed little empathy for the Balinese and their plight....Bad government led to the disintegration of the island's economy. Sukarno meanwhile treated Bali like his own private playground. He and his entourage visited the island constantly, demanding special dance performances be staged, abducting Balinese women for sexual favor, commandeering without payment vehicles, paintings and whatever else seized their fancy. Advance squads of soldiers would sweep in to shoot dogs and pigs so parties of devout Muslim visitors would not be revolted by the sight of the unclean creatures. [Dalton 1997:29–30]

Were this indeed the legacy of Sukarno, it would be odd that the Balinese voted so overwhelmingly, albeit indirectly, for his daughter in the 1999 popular elections. The Indonesian author, Pramoedya Ananta Toer, in a 1999 *Time In Asia* article, expresses what locally are more widely held sentiments of "Bung (Brother) Karno": "He gave unity to Indonesia, dignity to the down-trodden and anxiety to the powerful, who finally brought him down.... Sukarno was the only Asian leader of the modern era able to unify people of such differing ethnic, cultural and religious backgrounds without shedding a drop of blood." As Ananta Toer points out, Sukarno's reputation began to be reexamined. He echoes the sentiment of many when he concludes that when "Sukarno's daughter Megawati triumphed in the first truly free general election in 44 years it was, in a way, Bung Karno's triumphant political comeback" (1999). Cokorda Sawitri, meanwhile, makes the point that Megawati gained the support of Balinese people, not so much because she is Sukarno's daughter, nor, she agrees, because there is a strong sense of support for her party, the PDI-P (though this was where the popular vote was cast), but because she had become a symbol of affiliation to Hinduism, something she was strongly criticized for by some Islamic leaders, especially following what Sawitri refers to as her "prayer safari" through Bali the year of the Sidemen Maligya (personal communication; this is the viewpoint she presented in her Society of Balinese Scholars conference paper in 2000).

Eklof found that in Bali Megawati assumed the status of an idol:

> For Megawati's young followers, she is much more than an opposition politician, she is an idol. One Balinese high school student said: "Megawati has been my idol ever since junior high school. [...] Because of her self-confidence, Megawati dares to be oppositional [and] to fight continuously to defend the truth." Another student said: "Mega is a super woman. She dares to face any obstacle whatsoever. I hope I can become like her." [1999]

As late as 2001, Cokorda Raka at the Jero Gede Sidemen, too, was still saying that "Megawati is the idol of Balinese people, especially the people of Sidemen." Marked disillusionment among many Balinese set in only a couple of years into her presidency.

People power on the national level notwithstanding, throughout the events of 1998 and ever since — including in the aftermath of the 2002 terrorist bombing of a night club in Kuta — Bali's media and indeed most Balinese people continue to promote the image of Bali as an idyllic island of peaceful inhabitants that will remain so no matter what. In 1998 and in 2002, Bali did remain relatively peaceful, and the reassurances to tourists to keep coming are undoubtedly well placed. And, yet, the current situation does also show signs of an increase in people's vigilance and of mob actions. Not long after 1998, some Balinese, referring to the mass killings in 1965, even put it that in a small way killings have started happening again—not of masses of people, granted, but sometimes by masses taking the law into their own hands. Horrendous stories could be heard especially of mobs going after thieves, but also, for example, in one village after a man who would not marry the girl he had impregnated and in a different village after a man who had accused another man of witchcraft, while, in a third village, a woman accused of witchcraft was put to sea tied down by rocks.[10] Such incidents were happening elsewhere in Indonesia as well. In a recent volume on the *Roots of Violence in Indonesia* (Colombijn and Lindblad, Eds. 2002), no less than three of the articles highlight this surge of mob violence, which, although incidents grew in frequency in the period surrounding and following Suharto's fall, also predate it (see Schulte Nordholt 2002, van Dijk 2002, and Colombijn 2002).[11] Schulte Nordholt traces the genealogy of violence to the Dutch colonial state while Colombijn looks at historical continuity of mob justice from the earliest recorded case in 1787 through each political order until the present. While no definitive answers are found, the three articles explore a range of explanations, including the one most frequently offered in eastern Bali: People are so dissatisfied with the effectiveness of the police and legal system that, at a time when they are likely to get away with it, they will take matters into their own hands. But as also emerges from the range of accounts, the actions are not necessarily about "rationally" meting out justice, but take on mob dynamics. According also with some of the ways in which people talk about such incidents in the 1960s, several of the descriptions denote an atmosphere of excitement (van Dijk 2002, Colombijn 2002). As for consequences for the participants, Colombijn reports variation in the inclination of the police to pursue perpetrators of mob actions. In eastern Bali, where the cases I heard of happened, people say, they typically are required to go to the police station to file a report,

---

10. In Robinson and Bessell, Eds. 2002, Baso and Idrus find that there is "evidence that sexual violence against women is becoming less tolerated" in Southern Sulawesi, for example. They cite a case from 2000 where a "widower accused of kidnapping and raping a girl had been burned to death by a 'crowd of people'…The act of mass punishment occurred not only to defend siri [a word of many meanings, including honor], but also because many previous such cases had not been treated seriously by the police" (2002:205). In other cases, it should be noted, stronger restrictions on women are being enforced on the local level. In all, the chapter in which the above example appears still calls for national-level responses to the problem of violence against women (Baso and Idrus 2002:198).

11. As Colombijn notes, "although the weakening of the state during the Reformasi explains the increase in mob justice, a weak state cannot explain the existence of lynching as a sign of state weakness" (2002:313).

but they will do so en masse, thus sharing the responsibility and rendering it impossible for the police to apprehend any individuals.[12]

Probably the most impressive case of mass action in eastern Bali that was talked about in those years was class related and happened at the exclusive Amankila resort, located on the road between Amlapura and Klungkung. Set on the edge of a high cliff, this hotel has a serenely spectacular vista of the sea and along the coastline of promontories and white sand beaches lined with groves of coconut trees. From the cool, tranquil verandahs of the Amankila, you do not see the trash lining the beaches, nor the cars and soot-spouting trucks barreling along the relentlessly busy roads. From here it is easy to imagine that you are in a worldly version of paradise, as Bali is so often billed. A passage from the Amankila pamphlet reads that "the resort's design reflects elements of Ujung, the water palace built by the last raja of Karangasem," while "Amankila's recurring design motif, a series of inwardly curving shapes, echoes the ornate entrance doors to Maskerdam, [a structure] at the Karangasem royal palace." But whereas Ujung lies in ruins and Maskerdam stands somewhat less than glamorous, Amankila rises with all of its more recently constructed features of palatial architecture intact. The view from Amankila looks down on what it describes as "the Manggis village family temple, which claims the rugged promontory next to Amankila"—Manggis being the nearby village, whose nobles once owned the land on which the hotel now sits. Only Mount Agung towers over Amankila and its seaside setting. Indeed, in interesting ways, the pamphlet distributed by the hotel imagines Amankila as an elevated center from which the rest of Bali emanates. For example, it is a "downhill route" to Sidemen," on what is apparently "among the most popular" of the mountain bike "countryside trips...to the many villages and the rural life that *spreads out from Amankila*" (emphases added). In fact, the pamphlet continues, "a hypnotic mix of religion, royal culture and architectural splendor *spreads out from Amankila*, in the area often referred to as 'old Bali'" (emphasis added).

To this modern palace of Amankila, "Peaceful Hill", a crowd ascended from Manggis one evening in April 2000. They carried knives and sickles, cutting down flowers and vegetation on their way. They presented the hotel with a

---

12. As for employers, even Balinese employers who have established business outside of their home area, these report that they are conscious of the need to not cross anyone. There is an expressed fear of confronting employees too directly with any transgressions because in many such cases, they say, the employee would be prepared to simply depart. As in the matilas option, it empowers people when they do not feel more dependent on the employer, or the lord as it were, than to be able to walk out on them.

number of conditions, including, word has it, that a specific number of people be hired from their village and that all groups hired for entertainment at the hotel likewise be from Manggis. The police was summoned, but could only stand by. Since the road out was blocked, hotel guests, who pay between six hundred and one thousand seven hundred U.S. dollars per night, plus an additional 21% service charge and tax, had to be evacuated by boat from the beach, in a torrential down-pour as it happened. The hotel remained closed for three days as negotiations were carried out, until the management finally conceded. The requested number of people from Manggis, over a hundred it is said, were indeed hired; though, as these were largely untrained, Amankila apparently also had to retain its existing staff.

In Bali, with its proliferation of small kingdoms and the contestations between them, reckoning with people power may always have been more of a component of kingship than often is allowed. As indicated in the introduction, Tjokorda Gede Dangin, when asked to estimate the number of people that the Jero Gede Sidemen could count among its princedom (one approximate figure heard elsewhere was around twenty-five to thirty thousand), gave the following answer: "It cannot be counted. It depends on our deeds, on our performance." He continued that "This is not a problem, it was already so in earlier times. Even in earlier times, people's ideas were already like that. Not everyone followed." Pak Komang at Kebung, as did others, explicitly drew a parallel between contemporary ritual service to former service in war: "If [the raja of the Jero Gede] said—Go to war! We went to war. Die! Well, we'd die. That was the raja system. You can ask around, keep asking, up to this day, with them there is no-one that would dare cross them." "But," he added with a laugh, "They also are not bold with the people. It works both ways. I have self-esteem."

In many cases, of course, rajas were "bold with the people," and, in many cases, even an unpopular raja, "because he was a raja, would still be honored." Dangin admits this too, concluding that the system, in a sense, becomes very pure now by virtue of people having a greater sense of their own power: "Sometimes people went along before because they were afraid. And that is different now of course, because there is a different understanding. Now, whether we are followed or not really depends on the level of our conduct. So it is very pure now." It is not surprising that images and strategies of kingship should vary, and presumably always have varied, not only incidentally according to individual personalities, but also according to historical circumstances and developments within which any given kingship must be exercised.

Historical Shifts and Conscious Strategy

Just as the first would-be Indic rajas in Bali would have had to define their pretensions in the context of existing social structures of elder councils and chieftainship, so too after the seventeenth-century fall of Gelgel when new rulers established themselves as rajas throughout Bali. Although the absence of authoritative consolidated kingship in Bali often is attributed to the ensuing competition between princes,[13] dynastic dissent alone cannot account for the fact that powerful rajas did not emerge to take hold of larger regions, nor can it account for power sharing between princes and people; there are also real powers of the people to which rajas had to accommodate. New rajas had to insert themselves in new ways in the territories beyond Gelgel, where they had to work out relationships with existing local leaders and lords. The colonial and postcolonial, postindependence situations have continued to bring about circumstances to which princes have to adjust their claims and their exercise of power. Under direct colonial rule prior to World War II, for example, royal power in the larger palaces in many ways increased when the colonial administration, after in 1921 having changed the status of the lords (punggawa) to district heads (perbekel), in the 1930s reinstated some of Bali's rajas. Although Dutch force prevented these rajas from using their powers to mobilize for war, Dutch policy also reified rules that privileged these same rajas, and applied Dutch force to uphold them. In other words, while the smaller-scale rajas found themselves demoted, reinstated rajas of the large palaces found themselves in unprecedented positions of power. Ironically, the Dutch not only made caste more rigid by forcing certain caste-related rules, Dutch policy also opened up avenues for non-caste-based acquisition of status, for example by instituting administrative and educational reforms. Here, too, the minor palace was somewhat lost between the two.

Although Cokordas Dangin and Raka describe the situation in Sidemen when their father was head of the house as having been peaceful and characterized by very good relations with the people, their family was consider-

---

13. Vickers, for example, describes a historical shift toward more power for commoners in the course of the nineteenth century: "The Balinese rulers had consolidated their kingdoms and strengthened their images of ancestors. These rulers, drawing on the expertise of the Brahmana priests, sponsored the writing of extensive genealogies which linked them to the ancient kingdoms of Java. While they were doing this, dynasties were splitting and warring internally, and increasingly power had to be shared between aristocrats and commoners....Combined with the diffusion of the aristocracy was an increase in the power of commoner families, meaning that the aristocracy had to share power" (1989:65).

ably affected by the development surrounding colonization and an increasingly difficult economic situation. By the time of the Japanese occupation of Bali, between 1942 and 1945, they recollect that, for them as for other Balinese, there was little food and that they often would go to bed hungry. The brothers of the Jero Gede Sidemen did not participate in the growing nationalist movement, however. They say they were not educated, in the sense of being enlightened, and also had been eviscerated:

> We were all ignorant.[14] Upon the request of the Dutch, we were sent to Singaraja [North Bali] for schooling, but we did not know to, nor did we dare to stand up against the Dutch or the raja of Karangasem [who was allied with the Dutch]. At that time we really were afraid, afraid of the raja, of the Dutch....Truly the politics of the raja at that time was to always consider us lowly....And because we no longer had good connections with Klungkung, Klungkung neglected us; they left us alone. [Dangin]

This reflects, from the perspective of the peripheral kingdom, the unprecedented power gained in the course of the colonial era by the Dutch reinstated rajas (see Schulte Nordholt 1999:253, 261, 272). Dangin continues, "we were eroded as a family; our status and prestige were eroded...the level of respect, our acknowledged rights as rulers were eroded."

Following Dutch policy which required of Balinese rajas that they find ways to resituate themselves, there have been a few further critical historical periods of transition, times of social revolution that were characterized by an accentuation of powers of the people: in 1945, when Indonesians fought against the return of the Dutch and the Nationalists against the pro-Dutch loyalists; and in 1950, when independence was finally won and the Sukarno era began, as well as in the years leading up to and the aftermath of the alleged coup and countercoup of 1965 that resulted in the fall of Sukarno and the rise of Suharto to the presidency (see Robinson 1995 for an excellent analysis of the power struggles of these time periods). It was in the course of these times, when nobles again were under pressure to become less "feudal," that the Jero Gede Sidemen started finding a footing again. Dangin explains:

---

14. Note that this self description, "bodoh," was used prolifically also in correspondence with the Dutch. Cf. the letters of the Lombok raja, in van der Kraan 1980, who translates it as "stupid." Later President Suharto also was to use this term about the "common people."

My father realized that we would not be rajas again, but he also realized that our "noncooperation," outside of the government, outside of whoever was in power, that this was what was important. This is why my father...would participate [with the people] no matter what the activity was. Now this brought sympathy. Earlier nobody from the Jero had ever carried the dead body of a person from outside the Jero. My father descended to the people. This engendered sympathy. This was the way to take a hold of the people's hearts again, because we had already been discredited by the Dutch government, by the Raja of Karangasem, and there were others too. Because these really feared us, competed against us, we were discredited, and we were still not on good terms with Klungkung. That only helped our family here. After that we consolidated in a good way. And now we are on good terms with everyone.

When "rights of the ruler" eroded there was an adaptive turn to *memasyarakat*, to connecting with and working for the people. As it is told today, a local leader, a man with genealogical connection to the Jero Gede Sidemen, had been speaking up against their hierarchical privileges. Village leaders who remained loyal, however, had asked Dangin's father himself to preside at the discussion of this matter in the village organization. He had acquiesced and, realizing that times were changing, had preempted any discussion by his own declaration that his family would start participating in the local neighborhood organization. In this case, the head of the Jero Gede Sidemen had the foresight to give enough to prevent serious dissent against his house, allowing the princes instead to retain their special status and, in the eyes of many, even gaining an increased level of respect.[15] Gradually the princes have been defining new spheres of royal power for themselves, by also increasingly incorporating elements of egalitarian practices and values.

In the course of the twentieth century, the presence of resident Westerners not connected to the colonial government also has impacted the situation in Bali. The artist colony of Ubud and spiritual center of Sanur are particularly well-known for their Western expatriates, but Sidemen, too, has been frequented by a few personalities, including artists and anthropologists. Dangin tells of spending considerable time with some of these and talks openly of how their exchanges have influenced, even changed his own perspective of Balinese culture and its importance. These expatriates in many ways have also reval-

---

15. See Hoskins (1998) for an example of how a Dutch installed Sumbanese Raja reconceptualizes himself in response to changing circumstances.

orized and, some would say, helped reinvent local culture and tradition. The market value of foreign presence is obvious, but Balinese also see the respect and sometimes admiration that others have had for their culture. Conversation with Dangin indicated as well that exposure to liberal Europeans, in this case especially Swiss and German friends, has influenced his house toward certain democratic values, even as it maintains its own distinctiveness and overall sense of inherent Balinese "superiority."[16]

At a time when there was neither road nor electricity in Sidemen, Dangin's law professor friend admits having been struck when he first came to the region in the late seventies, with a feeling that he was in the sixteenth century with what looked like a lord of the realm with almost absolute power. Now that he has come to know the situation more intimately, his perspective has changed:

> When I look at Cokorda, not necessarily every Cokorda, but when I look at this man, I see somebody who was born and bred to love the people with a sense of absolute duty to take care of the people, to play that role, not just a title; it's a love and a reciprocal agreement that he will do everything he can to be community minded and to take care of them, as they support him and give him the respect that is due to that. And it's a very beautiful thing when it works, and for the most part it works here. They respect him, they fear him, they support him, they gossip about him. [Richard Berg.]

Undoubtedly, people do have more power vis-a-vis their leaders now than they did before; in which case, conversely, what we see in the princedom is an increased pressure to *memasyarakat*. The politics relying on memasyarakat are more fine-tuned and important now than when matters could be effected by force. According to Dangin, "people really are independent now, they are free" in ways that they were not in earlier times, even if rajas did always have to heed the people. But this, he says, is actually "very recent, maybe since around 1990." He explains that "After independence, they were still afraid.... The people did not yet understand," but here he is talking also about the relationship

---

16. Note that Europeans have not always or necessarily been egalitarian or democratic influences. The Dutch, for example, also romanticized and idealized Southeast Asian princes. In Sidemen, too, outsiders are enthusiastic to know Balinese royalty and are taken with its pageant. The prince is becoming modern, but derives glamour also in the eyes of outsiders from not being too modern. This phenomenon obviously is not unique to Bali; cf. for example Barney Cohen on how the British were the fanatics about dressing up the Indian princes in their traditional wear.

between local and state powers: "At independence," he says, "we were still held tightly by the government and the police."[17]

Obviously Dangin has critics aplenty as well, including people outside of his realm, especially people of high caste who were concerned that he would rise to a more regional position of power (cf. his running for *bupati* [head of regency] in the aftermath of the maligya ritual). Nor, of course, are all cokordas like this. More often than not, one now hears of cokordas as having become too materialistic and of princedoms and kingdoms that have lost their connection to people, as reflected in the fact that they now have to pay for everything when they stage a big ritual. It is even considered that Sidemen is getting stronger than Karangasem because, says Dangin, "We have connection to the people. People of this region consider it strong if you want to be close to the people, and Puri Karangasem is less close."

Applying these same criteria, from the perspective of Sidemen, Klungkung is still highly respected and powerful, while Ubud, like Karangasem, is said no longer to be so. Regarding Ubud, MacRae has shown that the palace is "symbolically reclaiming" its former kingdom through a "program of patronage" (1999:128; see also MacRae 1997). But he also describes the successor to the charismatic Cokorda Sukawati of Ubud as someone who lost the connection to the people. The successor was Sukawati's eldest son, Cokorda Raka Sukawati: "Educated in Dutch schools and groomed for the upper echelons of the native civil service, he ultimately became closer to the Dutch than his own family let alone the common people of Ubud" (MacRae 1999:132). MacRae does not indicate that new charismatic leaders have emerged, nor that there has been an emphasis on people connections; the "ideal role of the puri" is focused instead on "a sacred duty to maintain 'tradition'" (1999:139). While this is also a component of the role of the Jero Gede Sidemen, it is not surprising that it would be highlighted in the tourist center of Ubud, where "tradition" is more commoditized perhaps than anywhere else on Bali.[18]

---

17. Elsewhere Dangin says, "Even after independence we were still pressured/oppressed by the government and the police. And the leaders, even Sukarno, were harsh. Because we had only just achieved independence, and they could not yet give…, the people were still ignorant."

18. In addition to defining themselves against Ubud in relation to the foundation of their respective powers, Sidemen defines themselves against Ubud also in relation to tourism: Their vision for the future of tourism in Sidemen is that it be "not like Ubud." Ideas related to this are discussed in village meetings led by Cokorda Mayun (who worked them out with Tjokorda Gede Dangin). Ubud, interestingly, approached its development of tourism with the idea of not wanting to be like Kuta (Picard 1996).

From the Ubud area come also examples of cokordas who disregard their responsibilities in the relationship between rulers and followers. Specifically, there are cases where the cokordas have seized or have attempted to seize the land once conferred upon their followers as pacatu (cf. MacRae 2003b). Where such abuses of power occur, however, there are also likely to be consequences for the cokordas—In the present day they do lose their connections to the people and end up having to pay for services and supplies. This is something that the modern palace of Ubud, which has an unusually high tourism income, may be able to afford, not so the Jero Gede Sidemen. Although Ubud is described as a "negara (state) of hearts and minds," supported not only by material patronage, but also "by reactivation of divine legitimacy" (MacRae 2003b:143), MacRae's article confirms the impression expressed in Sidemen that Ubud has become "materialistic" and that the palace has to pay for everything (cf. the opinions regarding doing ritual service, *ngayah*, expressed in chapter 3). He mentions public contributions of large amounts of money and, overall, emphasizes material exchange as the basis for the ritual network, "essentially money for labor" or "ideological dominance backed by material patronage" paid for largely by tourism and land transactions (2003b:140, 142, 153). In Ubud, in the end, it appears also to come down to financial rewards for either side of the relationship, the rewards in the case of the palace taking the form of tourist revenues (2003b:144–147).

In Sidemen, the Jero Gede certainly also gains "symbolic capital" that in various ways converts into material capital (cf. Bourdieu 1977; see MacRae's analysis for Ubud, 1999:144–147); and, as we have seen, part of the exchange relationship between princes and followers does involve material contributions. However, although no amount of material input is negligible to the village economies of this area, this is far from the main basis on which the Jero Gede Sidemen can attract followers.[19] At this level of the system, coupled with the realities of the contemporary and complex world, the prince and princedom retain relevance in large part through their role as liaison for their people to hierarchies beyond, to governmental and nation-state structures that may be more disempowering than local hierarchies. Other factors that will help ensure the continuity and perhaps some form of revitalization of princedoms include possibly the need to unite with "powers of the people" in the face of the new Western elite, as in the Amankila resort case, or, to put it more

---

19. In the end, there is in both Ubud and Sidemen, as MacRae expresses it, "a skillful blending of material and ideological strategies" (1999:142), working from different historical backgrounds and with different resources.

generally, in the face of globalization; and, as shall be addressed in the next chapter, in the face of the threat presented by Islamic fundamentalism. If people were feeling more empowered by national and global citizenship than is the case, the princedom may not have continued to have the relevance to them that it does. Instead there is an ongoing accommodation between the forces of people and princes as people are becoming more empowered within their princedom, but also through their princedom, precisely because it does have the appeal as well of enhancing their position within the nation and wider world.

Though Dangin finds that "things are changing a bit, materialistic aspects are taking on more importance, and this is dangerous," there is little indication overall in Sidemen other than that its princedom likely will continue into the future in some incarnation. This is not a mere argument of cultural continuity. The role of the modern prince emerges out of modern contexts.[20] When asked whether he is worried that the connections on which the princedom is built might disappear in the times to come, Raka does not hesitate to respond in a way that entirely puts the onus on the members of the Jero Gede Sidemen themselves: "No, not as long as I always do right by them. If I do not do right by them, they will forget also....I have to memasyarakat, I have to reach out to them. This is called "ancient law" [*dresta*]. Balinese always remember the situation of their forefathers....The good from the past is still remembered today."

At the maligya ritual, people certainly remembered. The ancestral ritual drew supporters from near and far; it also drew the imagination of the Bupati and it drew presidential candidate Megawati Sukarnoputri. At this time of historical transition, in an atmosphere that in many places gave expression to powers of the people, the followers of the Jero Gede Sidemen gathered in force around the princes to apply their power to buttressing an essentially hierarchical system. Through the maligya ritual, the Jero Gede Sidemen was able to mobilize a caste- and achievement-based princedom, reinforce its bonds, and take advantage of the opportunity for enhanced political leadership at a time of national upheaval.

---

20. Lutkehaus, too, points to an "ongoing process of reinterpretation and renegotiation of the authority and status of the Manam tanepoa" (1990a:307).

PART THREE

WORLD CHANGE

Chapter Seven

The Keris, The Princedom, and the Nation State

Having looked at what lies behind the participation in the Sidemen Maligya of various groups of people, at the principles of the relationships between followers and princes and how these have been accommodated in interaction with changing historical and political contexts, pursuit of the question as to why and how the princedom persists in a changing world now turns us to the relationship between the ritual and its own role in world change. As emerges from the last two chapters, there appears recently to have been a coterminous rise of powers of the people and of the princedom, and the princedom continues to exist in part also because, through it, followers gain more power in their dealings with government bureaucracies. We shall now revisit Megawati's attendance of the maligya ritual and the significance of the ancestral keris as a starting point for considering how, through the ritual, the Princedom of Sidemen also is positioning itself within and in relation to the nation-state, acting within and upon the world. The legitimating interaction between Megawati and the keris is viewed locally as having influenced the national presidential candidacy, as well as having readdressed historical slights in the relationship between the princedom and the surrounding regional palaces, and empowering the princes to work for the larger good of their people. Through the ritual and the keris, the princedom is positioning itself with niches of power that give at least a sense of some degree of autonomy and of an ability to respond to outside threats. It became particularly obvious at a time of uncertainty and transition, as was the situation in Indonesia in 1998, that the princedom may become a means for a feeling of both individual and Balinese empowerment vis-à-vis the wider world. Yet even as various political developments interfaced with the ritual, nothing that happened was conceived as political activity; rather a negation of politics pervaded the discourse of the Sidemen Maligya.

Megawati in Sidemen:
Not Politics; A Ritual Coup

Ritual participants, members of the noble house and followers alike, emphasized with striking frequency how inappropriate it would be to engage in
political activity while in preparation for so important of a ritual as the maligya, and there was corresponding denial by most that anything pertaining
to the ritual should have anything whatsoever to do with politics. What was
negated included any semblance of feudalism as well as of party politics.
Thus the idea that the ritual should have been performed "so that people will
continue to be on good terms with us; that we summon these people and
that then becomes permanent," was denied; instead, "It is a pledge because
of a moral responsibility. There is no political element at all" (Raka). Politics in the princedom, "that is what happened in former [i.e. feudal] times"
(Raka). The negation of politics included also that the efforts of the ritual
should have anything to do with party politics: "For example people who
formerly were PKI [Communist Party members] now came to the ceremony.
There were many like that. There were Golkar people. Dangin is PDI [De-
mocratic Party]; yet Golkar people [members of the government party of the
Suharto regime] came to the house. There was no political element. There
were only historical connections, moral connections" (Raka). A few participants of the younger generation, meanwhile, emphasized that this was political, but they also pointed out that under no circumstances would their
parents' generation ever say so. On some level, the deliberate efforts to dis-
associate ritual from politics of course also underscores the extent to which
it has occurred to people, in the first place, that it might in fact have a political function. It is worth taking a closer look at what lies behind the distancing from politics.[1]

---

1. It appears that there is the same distancing from "politics" in Ubud, and that it is
contrasted with traditional notions of power. Citing Hilbery (1979) MacRae describes Cokorda Raka Sukawati's younger brother who became leader of the puri in 1931: "Cokorda
Agung, never a creature of politics like his brother, was increasingly alienated by these problems [surrounding the struggle for nationalism and the rise of communism] and withdrew
even further...He was more inclined to see problems in terms of their supernatural
(niskala) causes, and he devoted his energies accordingly to such projects as the restoration of temples and barong" (1999:135). In a footnote to this, MacRae writes, that "this
has been the official position adopted by Puri Ubud toward politics ever since. Indeed, it
has been a factor in a culture of indifference or even antipathy toward any kind of translocal politics — the dominant political orientation today" (1999:152).

First of all, the prohibition in the context of ritual against behavior construed as being negative and the separation of holy work and impure work are not inventions of the twentieth century. Schulte Nordholt mentions that "in 1840 the Dewa Agung managed a postponement [of war between Badung and Mengwi] because of a great maligya....which was in preparation just then [in Klungkung]" (1996a:120). The argument that "war would obstruct its progress" compares to what one hears today about the inappropriateness of engaging in extreme political activity at the time of such a ritual (1996a:120). Stuart-Fox also draws attention to how, reflecting a common Austronesian tradition, "one constant factor in the relationship between Pura Besakih and the succession of political entities in Bali is the separation of religious centre from political centre" (1991:37).[2] He observes that "One would assume that the frequent turmoil [between kingdoms in Bali] would have made travelling difficult and dangerous, and it would seem unlikely that rulers from more distant states attended very often....Yet the rulers often did cooperate, as the many treaties (*paswara*) among states indicate, and Pura Besakih, and religious affairs generally, would have been a sphere where cooperation was thought desirable. Different politics did not necessarily preclude joint ritual enterprise" (1991:30). In other words, there is precedence for the rhetoric of refraining from letting politics—and surely strife—get in the way of important ritual.

Yet the labeling of certain activities as "politics" and of ritual as "culture," and "politics" as separate from "culture," along with the wariness of anything designated as political, trace to colonial days when the Dutch administration, concerned that political activism would spread to Bali, sought to define or isolate and uphold the cultural, but not the political aspects of Balinese society (cf. Schulte Nordholt 1999:258–259, 277; see also Picard's writings about how Balinese identity was 'culturalized' to prevent it from becoming politicized, e.g. 1999). This is a distinction, moreover, that was furthered and disseminated by artistic expatriates in Bali as well as by early both pre- and postwar anthropologists. As a political historian, Robinson understandably expresses astonishment at how "the image of a Bali aloof from politics also survived the fifteen-year period of chronic political conflict from 1950–1965" (1995:7) and at how fieldwork carried out in these periods could produce ethnographies

---

2. As he points out, "Save perhaps for the early Mataram period in Java, in Java and Bali political and religious spheres of life have had distinct centres, which differs from the Indian norm. There was no great temple complex at the Majapahit capital. And although Gelgel...had its Pura Dasar, it never rivalled Pura Besakih as the paramount Temple of the Realm." (1991:20–21).

"remarkable for their lack of attention to time, place, or historical and political context beyond the village level" (1995:8). Conversely, understanding approaches to those larger contexts also requires understanding the local situation, and the anthropological studies in question could give insight, for example, into how "seemingly modern competition is in actuality not one of ideologies, but one of traditional factions, of ancient grudges and time-honored alliances" (H. Geertz 1959:23). Studies with insufficient attention to this dimension are equally incomplete, as indeed is being brought out in some of the newly—post-Suharto's New Order repressive regime—emerging work on the mass killings in 1965. Dwyer and Santikarma thus write that they support the studies that expose the role of elite politics and military intervention, yet in their own ethnographic research on the violence of 1965 in Bali and its lasting repercussions, emphasize "complex weaves of power, culture, emotion, and ritual that cannot be satisfactorily explained by analyses that rely on theories of politically motivated agency" (2003:293). The separation of Balinese culture and politics, meanwhile, also was perpetuated by the Indonesian state in the process of nation building, and it lingers on.

In current Balinese lives, echoing the influence of decades of Suharto's New Order state rhetoric, the denial of politics is linked perhaps most poignantly to the fact that politics came to be almost synonymous with "what the communists did in the sixties." Notwithstanding the centrality of land issues to the conflicts of the time (cf. chapter 4), this is construed most vocally and most often as being about posing a threat to religion, temples, and rituals.[3] In Karangasem, I too heard a couple of examples where people, as Dwyer and Santikarma found, drew "an equivalence between communists and *leak* ['a human who is capable of changing his shape into a fearsome demon, causing madness, illness, or death to his chosen victims'] or between political and supernatural power" (2003:303). Even ordinary citizens, chillingly, all too often still argued that as a result of their political activity the communists "had to be eradicated." Following the bloody events of the 1960s, Suharto's New Order regime, through school curricula, public discourse, and ongoing surveillance, effected a conscious de-politicizing of people as it (politically) manipulated any potential opposition and vilified anyone—and the family and associations

---

3. Note that in the case of opposition to a luxury tourist resort near the regional temple of Tanah Lot, as Picard points out, "ultimately it was religion, not land, that became the primary focus of the controversy," that "religion proved to be the most effective—as well as the most emotionally charged—means of mobilizing public opinion against the project" (1997:205). Picard also notes that "the government ban on political mobilization has strengthened religious loyalties across the country" (1997:199).

of anyone—engaged in anything that could be construed as "politics." Politics, then, has become a way of referring to a turmoil of events that still reverberate through life. For those already in power, denying politics becomes a tool of power. In Indonesia it served to suppress dissent and, in turn, made the government party, Golkar, very politically strong: "Throughout the country, the military and the bureaucracy [were] synonymous with Golkar. They possess[ed] a virtual monopoly on local political power" (Aspinall 1997; see also Pemberton 1994).[4]

While the Dutch administration promoted a policy of maintaining "culture" and "tradition" to prevent oppositional movements from taking hold, the Indonesian nation-state thus has echoed this in the interest of preventing separatism and constructing the nation. Picard characterizes the New Order approach as a "cunning strategy of disempowerment and incorporation" whereby "not only have ethnic identities been domesticated by the state, but they are also being enlisted to contribute to the process of nation-building" (1997:197). In this project, Bali has been a nationally promoted "showcase" of culture, but as has also been pointed out by many, ethnic expression is encouraged only in the capacity of cultural display as defined by the state (Picard, 1997:197; see also Hooker 1993; Kipp 1993; Pemberton 1994). That which is termed "political" has continued to be viewed as contrary to the values of culture and tradition, coming to be synonymous with anything disruptive of peace and with anything unsafe. In this climate, Balinese ritual has long been emphasized as distinctly cultural, traditional, and nonpolitical activity, and in many views, Balinese people, absorbed as they are seen to be with ritual, as distinctly apolitical as well. Highly dependent on the tourist economy, many Balinese have themselves seized upon the image of their island as essentially "cultural," eager to perpetuate their reputation of being apo-

---

4. Golkar was the all-dominant political party of the government, though they insisted that it was not really a political party at all, but as its name indicates merely consisted of "Functional Groups," *Golongan Karya*. All civil servants were required to be members of it. Following Suharto's fall, a reformed Golkar has been resurrected: "In the dying days of the Suharto regime, a dissident group within Golkar stood up against Suharto, and afterwards against Habibie too. They carried on a banner of internal reform unfurled in the late 1980s. Clustering around Harmoko first, then Akbar Tanjung, they faced threats of expulsion. But, in the end, fears that Golkar might lose the election helped them to prevail. They succeeded by turning it into a more conventional political party, cutting formal links with the military and the bureaucracy, building links with business, talking a lot about the rule of law — but all without apologizing for a shady past" (van Klinken 2001). By 2003 many Balinese were expressing increasing disillusionment with Megawati and preference for the reformed Golkar.

litical and above all—safe.[5] It was thus not surprising when the *Bali Post* confirmed traditional Balinese ritual as a recluse from the world of politics by broadcasting the message sent out from Sidemen about Megawati's attendance, that she was in the highland valley to attend an ancestral ritual, concluding: "Bu Mega wants some peace and does not want to talk politics" (August 21, 1998). Rather than discussing Megawati's attendance in terms of politics, then, participants in the maligya ritual forefronted the way in which ritual and ancestral forces are linked to legitimating power.

Followers of the noble house invariably stressed that Megawati "came by invitation; there was no question of politics." Or, as one follower put it, who happened to be wearing a t-shirt declaring support for Megawati's party: "There was not any substance of politics, no. Her *charisma*, that was what people liked. Ibu Mega has many *supporters*; that is the issue. There was *no element of politics*. It was a *normal* invitation" (member of the village of Sanggem, emphases added). There was equally general agreement among all categories of people involved in the maligya ritual that Megawati's role, first of all, was "just to witness" (*menyaksikan*) the ceremony. As Hobart has written, "few important events can take place without a witness. A witness is not a passive spectator but an agent who makes the event part of recorded happening" (1990:329).[6] All eight regency heads (*bupati*) of Bali also were invited and, except for two (from the far west and the far north), all came. In addition, all of the members of the neighborhood organization (*banjar*) to which Cokorda Raka belongs in Amlapura were invited, as were bank colleagues from Denpasar of another family member. Their role, as these participants explained, also was to witness the ceremony, explicitly so that it could be a success. Megawati was arguably one of the highest witnesses possible for Balinese at that time. Habibie was president, but it is doubtful that he would have had the same overall import as Megawati, who—with a Balinese grandmother, as Sukarno's daughter, and as someone who herself had had to fight the injustices of Suharto's New Order—enjoyed massive support locally. In the end, Megawati's participation as witness became a formidable confirmation of Sidemen's position, of how well-connected the noble house is to both visible and invisible sources of power.

---

5. In 2001, the post-reformasi governor of Bali declined to host a meeting in Bali to focus on the current Indonesian political situation. He did not want Bali to become associated with "politics," emphasizing intead the arts and tourism. (See Picard 1996, 1997.) See also MacRae 2003b for a discussion of the "culture of apoliticism" in the tourist area of Ubud.

6. Cf. also how witnesses may serve to validate landownership elsewhere in Indonesia (e.g. Fried 2003:154).

With regard to the extraordinary presence of a rhinoceros at the 1842 maligya ritual in Klungkung, people informed Margaret Wiener that it was because the rulers were so beloved by the gods "that a spirit had provided a rhinoceros, an animal only known through legend, to be sacrificed for the occasion" (1995:70–71). Local informants were not deterred by the information the anthropologist could offer based on historical sources, that in fact "it had been no spirit, merely a Dutchman, who had given it to the court" (1995:70–71). As was explained to her,

> perhaps a Dutchman did deliver the beast, but what could have inspired him to do such a thing but a prompting from the invisible world, a manipulation of his will by the forces that supported the ruler of Klungkung? In short, the rhinoceros was a gift from the spirits, not from the Dutch, even if they had been the vehicle by which the gift had arrived at its destination. [1995:70–71]

Wiener refers to the acquisition of the rhinoceros as "an amazing ritual coup" by the ruler on behalf of his ancestors, a coup which also "probably added immeasurably to his prestige" (1995:70–71), and which, as has also been pointed out, was considered to be much more significant than Dutch attempts to make treaties with the rulers (Vickers 1990:174). Megawati's attendance in Sidemen, too, constituted a form of ritual coup that many thought came about through a prompting indeed from the invisible world, facilitated, as some pointed out, "foremost because of that keris."

The Sidemen Heirloom: A Remarkable Claim

As we have seen, the claim of the Jero Gede Sidemen is that the keris presented to Megawati and of which she had had a vision, is no other than the fourteenth-century Keris Bangawan Canggu or Suda Mala, conferred upon the raja of Bali by the Emperor of Majapahit. The story of the transfer exists not only in oral history, as related by Tjokorda Gede Dangin in chapter 1, but features in the *Babad Dalem*, the written genealogy of Bali's most recognized line of rajas, the Ksatria Dalem or Kapakisan line from which the princes of the Jero Gede Sidemen also trace descent. Keris Bangawan Canggu is one of two keris historically considered most important to the royal power of the Kapakisan rajas of Bali, the other being a keris by the name of Durga Dingkul (cf. Wiener 1995). Whereas a Klungkung perspective highlights the section of the *Babad Dalem* which tells of Durga Dingkul as having established the new raja's authority over Bali (Wiener 1995), a perspective from the Jero Gede Sidemen suggests that this happened only with Bangawan Canggu. As Cokorda Sawitri relates it, "he whom we call Dalem Samprangan [a.k.a. Dalem Kapakisan], his big ship dropped anchor at Gianyar, at Lebih beach. But when Dalem Samprangan got here, Bali still fought." So "Gajah Mada [Bali's conqueror, the Majapahit chief minister] conferred the first keris weapon [upon a Balinese raja], to convince the people of Bali that this is your raja:"

> But it still was not possible to win them over. Not with the second keris either. It did not make Bali peaceful; it did not make Bali harmonious. Finally, the third time, this keris was given [from Majapahit to Dalem Ketut Ngulesir],...this keris Suda Mala [or Bangawan Canggu], and only then did Bali become peaceful.

The interpretation from Sidemen is very much in keeping with the characteristics or nature, if you will, of the keris historically known as Bangawan Canggu, a keris that is conceived as "a force that binds the earth and keeps it steady and that binds hearts to a single center," "bind[s] people to the king, to inspire their devotion" (Wiener 1995:120, 305; *Babad Dalem*).[7] Sawitri goes on explicitly to demonstrate the connection between the keris, ritual, and the political realm when she continues that Dalem Ketut Ngulesir was, in her opinion,

> the first to effect a political strategy with religious ceremony, at Gunung Kawi [and] at Kintamani [Balinese place names]. There he did a kind of reconsolidation, with the groups that formerly were in power here, like the Pasek [one of the "elevated commoner" groups, the title group of village leaders], who were here first, the Pande [a second "elevated commoner" group, the "sub caste" of smiths] and the sages [*bujangga*]. He invited them to perform this ceremony together.

> After this he built the Village Temple, Pura Desa Gelgel, and so in Gelgel it was acknowledged [that he was their raja]. He also built temples to bring into agreement people who had long been in power in Bali. At this point, then, a big palace finally could be built in Gelgel [i.e. by Dalem Ketut Ngulesir after he had gained acceptance].

The part of the *Babad Dalem* wherein Gelgel flourishes and Dalem Ketut Ngulesir along with the heirloom came to exemplify good kingship, is a part

---

7. Recall that all keris are considered as snakes, snakes in motion or snakes in meditation depending on whether they are serpent-bladed or straight-bladed keris. Snakes symbolize connection to the earth, fertility, "the cosmic naga that maintain the stability of the world," and through it all, kingship.

9. Rulers of Gelgel according to Klungkung Babad Dalem

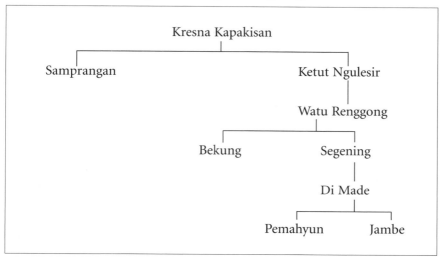

Kresna Kapakisan

Samprangan   Ketut Ngulesir

Watu Renggong

Bekung   Segening

Di Made

Pemahyun   Jambe

the Jero Gede Sidemen shares with all who claim Kapakisan descent. The Jero Gede Sidemen has its own addition to the *Babad Dalem*, moreover, which contextualizes their existence, in fact placing the princes' forefather, Dalem Anom Pemahyun, as the elder and most rightful heir of this kingship.[8] Figures 9 and 10 illustrate genealogically how their tale inserts itself between the brothers Bekung and Segening, known as Gelgel's sterile and fertile raja, respectively.[9] While none of this is mentioned in the *Babad Dalem* recovered

---

8. There are supposedly six *Babad Dalem* from Sidemen, a higher concentration than anywhere else. A comparative study remains to be done of these. The text to which the Jero Gede adheres is the *Babad Dalem Jero Kanginan Sidemen* which, based on the manuscript by Ida I Dewa Made Oka of Jero Kanginan (with a colophon dated 1942), was transcribed to Latin letters in 1982 by Dewa Gde Catra and subsequently has been published locally in Indonesian (Warna et al. 1986, *Babad Dalem* A version; Putra 1993). This *Babad Dalem* is not in the scholarly literature an accepted version of what best approximates historical veracity. Creese footnotes it as an example of how "the invention of illustrious ancestors and family ties is not unknown in the Balinese babad tradition" (1991:243). But her intention is not to dismiss it; she used the Klungkung text mainly because her own work at the time was on Klungkung (personal communication). Many have pointed to the "room for fictional manipulations" in the Balinese sort of genealogical system (Geertz and Geertz 1975:127), but of course it could be the exclusion of the Sidemen link that constituted the manipulation as well.

9. The *Babad Dalem Jero Kanginan Sidemen* holds that Dalem Anom Pemahyun was Dalem di Made's older brother, who supposedly was married to a daughter of Bekung, in

10. Rulers of Gelgel according to Sidemen Babad Dalem

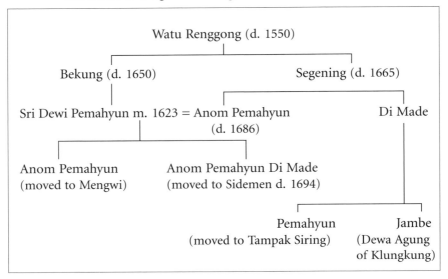

from the priestly house in Klungkung (*Babad Dalem* H2935), the Sidemen *Babad Dalem* chronicles the fate of the princes' forefather in connection with the seventeenth-century strife and split of the dynasty in Gelgel. It separates him and thus the more immediate line of descent of the princes of Sidemen, along with the keris, from the rest of the Kapakisan lineage, for the claim to possession of Keris Bangawan Canggu by the Jero Gede Sidemen is linked to their genealogical claim. The Sidemen *Babad Dalem* also distinguishes itself from the more common version of *Babad Dalem* by relating that the keris left Gelgel before this center fully dissolved and hence well before a court was even reestablished in Klungkung. As the present day heirs at Sidemen see it, their forefather acted in order to save Bali: In the midst of dynastic strife, he had the wisdom to retreat. He seceded from Gelgel, but only after first having taken his rightful place and only after assuming ownership of Keris Bangawan Canggu. When the coup eventually took place in Gelgel, his youngest son was asked by the existing local lord to take hold of Sidemen (a.k.a.Singarsa). It is said they specifically wanted someone from the Dalem line. So in 1676 (as the date is given), Ida I Dewa Anom Pemahyun Di Made estab-

---

a first patri-parallel cousin alliance. One wonders if it might be possible that Bekung was considered sterile merely because he had no sons.

lished a palace and became raja in Sidemen, constituting the beginning of the Jero Gede Sidemen.

In the twentieth century, many important keris and other heirlooms were seized or looted by the Dutch from the larger palaces, especially from those that fell in the court *puputan*, the mass sacrifices or massacres during which the inhabitants of the courts walked or ran into the fire of the Dutch. Members of the Jero Gede Sidemen remark that certainly representatives of the colonizing powers in Bali also came to Sidemen with an interest in such items, but they had had time to take precautions by burying the objects in the high caste family temple: "In one hole they used a kind of tub, they put a lid on it, and they buried it. Then above that they built a structure so that it would not be known....If they had not done so, the objects would have been taken by the Dutch, or if not by the Dutch, by the Japanese" (Cokorda Pemangku). And so it is that, to this day, the raja's keris, Keris Sudamala or Bangawan Canggu, is said to reside with the princes at the noble house, the Jero Gede Sidemen.

Assessing the Claim to Ownership of Keris Bangawan Canggu

It is probably not possible to determine whether or not the keris in the Jero Gede Sidemen's possession really is the original Bangawan Canggu. Pursuit toward authenticating the identity of the keris through physical attributes stumbles across many uncertainties, as hilts are interchangeable and there is not a detailed base line description by which to assess the present object's blade. Swiss Anthropologist Urs Ramseyer does find that "through its construction and, above all, by the style of the illustrations on its blade, Keris Sudamala reveals its origins in the East Javanese Majapahit Empire" (1995:270). He cites expert evidence that even "the grip in the shape of the demon Kalantaka, which is constructed from several parts, originates from Majapahit and presumably always has belonged to the blade" (1995:270–271). But Ramseyer also agrees that there are those who contest these assertions (personal communication). Surrendering the keris to more systematic scrutiny for material dating might achieve a determination whether this keris genuinely is a fourteenth-century heirloom,[10] but even if that were affirmed, in the absence of

---

10. Van Duuren writes that "Age determination is a matter of the painstakingly precise charting of historic dapurs, [striations in the blade] of identifying various pamors and defining styles and regional variations" (1998:91). He points out that "no centuries-old kris

an adequate original description with which to compare it, it would not be possible to establish definitively whether or not the keris at the noble house is (the original) Keris Bangawan Canggu.[11] Either way, these were never the terms through which Balinese observers or participants addressed the matter. Not dismissing importance of the object's physical characteristics, from a Balinese perspective there are additional criteria for assessing it.

For example, the kind of ruler with strong connections to the people that Tjokorda Gede Dangin envisions himself and his forefathers as being, and as they are envisioned at least by their followers, is in keeping with the associations of this particular keris.[12] In other words, they are appropriate for each other. Also, Sidemen is known for the unique nature of its relationship with the invisible realm, the kind of relationship emphasized by Wiener as having constituted Klungkung's power (1995). Sidemen has a reputation as a place of powerful magic, giving rise to individuals with special powers and to remarkable events involving these.[13] And, just as we have seen that it is risky to have a ceremony beyond your standing (cf. chapter 2), so one of the important tests to the claim of the Jero Gede Sidemen is linked to the risk involved in making false claims and in having in your possession a keris that exceeds you. A story is told of a forefather of the Jero Gede Sidemen, who had once been ordered by the Raja of Karangasem to kill the second lord appointed to Sidemen by his predecessor (the appointments of second lords were made following Karangasem's conquest of Sidemen's to keep in check the power of the

---

has ever come to us unaltered. Many krisses were reassembled, their sheaths were replaced, their hilts renovated" (1998:91). "The fact remains that the blade is the heart of the kris.... Therefore the dating of the weapon in its entirety is frequently based on this one particularly hardy component, which has frequently survived its own accessories" (1998:91).

11. Tambiah wonders what happened to Balinese royal sacred objects when dynasties changed, as in Southeast Asian Buddhist realms "travels of Buddha statues...provide a chain or genealogy of kingdoms and polities that these statues have legitimated" (1985:329), as indeed we find in the Jero Gede Sidemen's story too, (cf. also e.g. Wiener 1995, Schulte Nordholt 1996a). Tambiah suggests another interesting possibility: "famous sacra of Southeast Asian Buddhist realms...had a marvelous history of passing from hand to hand between diverse kings and realms, and in this process spawning 'copies' of the 'original' which helped disperse the radiant powers of the sacra to satellite realms and the outer regions" (1985:328).

12. The connection between kingship and events surrounding keris is demonstrated also in *Babad Blabatuh*, of which Schulte Nordholt notes that it "equates a new ruler with each event surrounding the history of the family's sacred keris and hence the number of rulers in this work tends to be somewhat inflated" (Creese 1991:250 n. 22).

13. Some of Klungkung's most powerful priests also came from Sidemen. In fact priests themselves often are viewed as a form of regalia (*pusaka*) of the rajas.

noble house). The keris used for this purpose subsequently was seized by the Raja of Karangasem, only later to be sold on. Tjokorda Gede Dangin explains that he has tried to buy it back, offering up to fifteen million rupiah for it (approximately six thousand U.S. dollars at the time), but to no avail. Meanwhile, he explains, misfortune has fallen upon the illegitimate owners:

> Before their efforts were fruitful, now they have gone bankrupt, because that keris is not appropriate [*cocok*] for them. They are not supposed to be in possession of it, they are ordinary people, low people [referring to caste standing, *orang biasa, orang rendah*]. It must be a raja that keeps that keris. If not, if it is not a raja, [the illegitimate owners] usually will fall.[14]

There is also the aspect of "behavior" that can serve to verify the identity of an object. A powerful object in itself congeals power, but there has also to be a demonstration of it; it has to be made manifest in the world (cf. also Errington 1983). Through the maligya ritual, the Sidemen keris was indeed confirmed to behave as Bangawan Canggu, both by attracting lots of followers and by the mystical events surrounding it. Finally, to most Balinese, the ultimate test to claims of legitimacy, as of those to claims of higher status through ancestry, is often whether others accept the claims, particularly those of equivalent or higher standing. This is how Megawati and the keris entered into a mutual endorsement in the context of the Sidemen Maligya.[15]

Endorsement of President and Princes

At the time, no explicit explanation was made or needed as to the significance of the keris incidence with Megawati, for it is common knowledge, as Wiener has observed, that "what matters most about keris is their effect on

---

14. The gold staff of office conferred upon the (by the Dutch created) Raja of Sumba (Hoskins 1993) apparently also was alienated from its rightful owners, when, after having been pawned, it was purchased by a new owner who took it with him to Jakarta against the protests of the family of the original owner. It is interpreted as divine justice that he subsequently lost the staff when his house was burglarized (Hoskins, personal communication). Similarly, there was divine retribution following the theft of the urn that embodied the traditional office of the priest of the sea worms (Hoskins 1993:135–136).

15. People also sometimes apply a precautionary principle—you never know what power might be behind this and it might be unwise too lightly to dismiss someone's claims. (The SidhaKarya story is one story told to illustrate this point.)

consciousness...keris do not only affect the consciousness of their possessors; powerful ones are said to affect others as well:"

> Powerful keris may work magic, which is a name we give to what surprises us into acknowledging that there is more to the way we act and perceive in the world than we normally agree to agree about. Such surprises are efficacious, for they allow people to step beyond the boundaries of what they normally can accomplish or sense. This may seem a mystification, but then Balinese do not claim to understand how these things work. Primarily they are allowed to operate without interpretation, without the active intervention of authoritative discourses. [1995:70]

At first the keris incident with Megawati was merely reinforced by other stories, including ones about how earlier in the afternoon, women preparing offerings in the inner temple area had seen a strong light emitting from the enclosed shrine within the family temple where the keris was kept, and the story of what had taken place with the keris in anticipation of Megawati's arrival. Two years after the event of the maligya ritual, the presiding priestly prince relates the event behind the latter story:

> What happened was that Ibu Mega [Megawati] was to come here a day before the apex of the ritual. Indeed at that time, in the family temple, I had already requested permission of the keris to bring it out from its storage place. I was going to bathe it, to *wangsuh* it. After I had placed it in the big pavillion [*balai pasamuhan*], my older brother, Cokorda, said to not bathe the keris until later, after Bu Mega's arrival. Ok then, so be it. So I just placed it there for the time being....People were bustling....I left it there for a bit. Now, because it was said that Bu Mega was about to arrive, I climbed up, with the help of [my brother-in-law, and temple assistant]. I was already ready with everything necessary for the bathing. So I took hold of the keris, I was going to bathe it. Then it was as if [my brother-in-law] was startled; he saw the rays, and the rays had smoke above them. And I said, "what's going on?" "It is shaking." I was like this up there [shakes vigorously, holding his hands out in front of himself]. Shaking, shaking. But outside there was no shaking, in fact people were bustling. As you know in the family temple, in the purified area for making offerings [the *suci*], it bustles. The Brahmana were making components of [an offering], to the point of panic. Finally they all saw the rays above. The rays emitted, the shaking

stopped, the shaking of those rays.... They say they were like rays of crystal. Perfectly clean. They were beyond description. [Cokorda Pemangku]

The brother-in-law assisting him remembers that

Mega had already arrived. I went up to bathe the keris, went up [with Cokorda Pemangku]. Cokorda Mangku bathed it.... He asked me to fetch a cloth,...and I did. I returned to that big pavillion. Then, above it, there were rays, beautiful rays. Like rays of the moon, the full moon. Not strong rays, but very beautiful. Cokorda Mangku was like this [he shakes]. It was shaking there, in that one place. I saw it, up above. Cokorda Pemangku with the keris was like this. It was frightening. There once was an ancestor here who was struck only ever so slightly with that keris, and yet she died, right in the family temple.[16] I was afraid of that. I went up there, it was really shaking, I saw the rays. [Dewa Gede Raka]

This was the set up for Megawati's subsequent recognition of the keris. In addition to such stories, in the evening following the interaction between Megawati and the keris, after Megawati had returned to her dwellings and members and friends of the family of the noble house sat around watching play back of video footage from the events involving her, Tjokorda Gede Dangin talked about how strong she is, how she is not afraid of anything. He also talked about how she wanted to go shopping at the market, and about how, on the whole, she wants to be close to the people. In the end, many sources of legitimization of her authority were evoked: descent, qualities of leadership, and connection to the powerful keris—all commentary that was sure to spread in the village and surrounding areas.

Later, upon specific elicitation of interpretations of the keris incident, Cokorda Raka explained that what happened with Megawati "means that she will receive power from that keris." He laughed, "maybe because she was going to become Vice President," for, as we have seen, in the election of the year following the maligya ritual, the vast majority of voting Balinese were to vote for Megawati's party. Although she did not receive enough cabinet votes to become president at the time, she became Vice President to President Gus Dur. In 2001, however, following the impeachment of Gus Dur, she took over the presidency, becoming what some viewed as the first president elected with

---

16. This was a daughter of the house who refused an arranged marriage to Gelgel and committed suicide with the keris in the high caste family temple.

popular support since the inception of the Indonesian nation-state with her father at its head. Raka explained that the keris can give her power even if there is not a historical connection between his ancestors and hers.[17] It also became quite explicit that the incident in part was an issue of verification of the identity of the keris, and with it the genealogical claims of the princes of the Jero Gede Sidemen: Cokorda Pemangku explained that the rays that emitted from the keris were maybe the strength of the soul or spirit of the keris, that came out at that time "because Ibu Mega wished to ask for its holy water, the *wangsupada*, because she is a believer. She believes that this keris constitutes a holy water that can give a certain calm, safety, well-being, and peace." When Megawati saw the keris and said she had come across this keris before, *"after that it was apparent that this was the true keris, this was really it"* (Cokorda Pemangku, emphasis added). And a priest at one of Sidemen's priestly houses emphasized that only something very powerful indeed could have drawn in someone like Megawati. In other words, he said—again according it legitimacy—*"it must have been the keris."* He added that the crafting of this keris had been undertaken according to the most intricate rules, on the right day, at the right hour, and down to the minute. This was done so it would indeed be extraordinary (Pedande Gede Tianyar, emphasis added).

Pak Komang at the village of Kebung, relating with great enthusiasm the occurrences surrounding Megawati's interaction with the keris, elaborated that "Megawati also took a small keris from her bag when she was in the family temple that night. She held the Betara Keris [Betara is a title for a deity] with her right hand, her own keris with her left hand." The smaller keris was one of her father's Balinese keris, from Tampaksiring, where Sukarno who was half Balinese, in 1954 had built a palace above the bathing pools of the temple of a holy spring.[18] The small keris that Megawati pulled on the occasion of the

---

17. Note that the women, too, viewed themselves as suppliers of objects that empowered Megawati. One night at Raka's house, as Sawitri, her mother, and her aunt lay before sleep, the two older women started talking about the maligya ritual. They talked about how Megawati, after having prayed, had asked for two of the gold flowers (*kwangen*) of the kind used on the puspa linggas and which had been provided by the aunt, I Dewa Alit. These they also talked of as having the purpose of concentrating Megawati's power.

18. While it is known that Sukarno had a keris collection, nothing appears to have been written of it and we do not know how it was divided upon his death. There are stories, however, of encounters in Java with the Balinese son of Sukarno's main keris finder, himself now a keris finder whose services are sought by military figures. Kaja McGowan, who had the opportunity to accompany him on a number of his quests describes that he would go into trance to become various animals, running long distances on his knees, while his patrons drove alongside. In certain spots, he would start digging, pulling away at branches and dirt,

maligya ritual, it was said, was the keris that had protected her father during several assassination attempts. Yet the keris of the Jero Gede Sidemen was clearly the more powerful of the two, said Pak Komang of Kebung, who concluded regarding the events of Megawati and the keris of the Jero Gede Sidemen that *"moreover, this is the proof"* of the power and legitimacy of the keris (emphasis added).

Most followers of the Jero Gede Sidemen were not in the high caste family temple that night, but nonetheless heard about the incident. Thus Ngurah Sidemen, a descendant of the lord that brought the heirs of the noble house to Sidemen, though not there in person, had heard about how "Megawati came to the merajaan and saw the keris with its handle of gold," and he, too, continued that *"this incident was the proof of a certain kingdom in Sidemen, brought from Gelgel"* (emphasis added). Ngurah Sidemen tells this story, of the keris and the flight from Gelgel, as completely as do the family members of the Jero Gede Sidemen. When asked whether people in Sidemen in general know about the keris, he reiterated,

> Yes, they know that keris is there, they know it to this day today. *It is proof of the connection to Klungkung, that these are the descendants of Ida Dalem, up until now; it is the proof of that.* If there were no proof, it would not be received [i.e. accepted by the people]. Consequently it is very important for a raja to carry keris, suda mala objects, regalia, large bowls of gold. This is proof of an extraordinarily holy descent (emphasis added).

Tjokorda Gede Dangin, himself, concluded about the significance of what happened with Megawati that:

> *This proves that that keris truly is the raja's*; it really is the gift from the Raja of the Majapahit, from Hayam Wuruk. For there was only one keris given by the Raja Nusantara, the Raja Majapahit, only this one. In the case of the keris at Klungkung, that was given by Gajah Mada, the minister. It is lower....In the case of this one, Bangawan Canggu, it was directly from the raja, from Hayam Wuruk. At that time, when there was a gathering at the Majapahit, there was also a

---

until he unearthed jewels or pulled out a keris. In trance, he would speak a mixture of Balinese and Kawi and he would name the person for whom he was supposed to uncover an item. Bowls of holy water were brought along on these trips, in which he would drop any newly found object prior to presenting it to its new owner. One not infrequently hears of people on quests for powerful objects.

ligya there. This was the first ligya that any Balinese attended (emphasis added).

Following the 1998 maligya ritual, several people mentioned that they would not come to just anyone to work as they had for this ritual, but because they know the history, they come and, some added, "foremost because of that keris." Thus, at the Sidemen Maligya, this keris was central to some of the connections that materialized, through its immaterial powers providing a form of material proof of the legitimacy of the Jero Gede Sidemen, of the respect and service owed to the noble house and its princes, much as in chapter 4 we saw proof of the relationships to the Jero Gede Sidemen to be embedded in the material proof of land. The power of the keris was recreated and reinforced through the maligya ritual, specifically through the incidence with Megawati, breathing new life into the relationships of the princedom. It boosted Megawati's presidency and the position of the princes, with further implications for the connection between the princedom and the world beyond.

Reestablished Connection between Sidemen and Klungkung

Through the ritual, the Jero Gede Sidemen could redress its historical relations to Klungkung and Karangasem. Those who came from the palace of Klungkung to participate in the maligya ritual are referred to as family, because they are Ksatria Dalem. Cokorda Sawitri explains:

> Because of that [the family connection], two days before the apex of the work, the Semarabawa people (that palace is called 'Semarabawa') came here as family. They participated in the construction of the symbolic representations of my ancestors. It was they who did the dressing and decorating. Also at the time of making the porridge, at the ceremony in the middle of the night, there was family from there. Four times, if I am not wrong, they came here. We also, in accordance with adat, notify them, because it was they who became rajas [i.e. of Klungkung]....We actually are older...but it was they that became rajas. That is something that we, on our behalf, must recognize, and they, they come to help our ritual work be complete.

Tjokorda Gede Dangin is quite explicit that only with the maligya ritual was the connection between Sidemen and Klungkung really established again. As he continues, "Now the people of Klungkung are beginning to come here, and that is really terrific." Royalty from Klungkung now attend the *Tumpek Landep* ceremony at Sidemen, a day of ceremony for metal objects, during which they pray to the keris. He and others point out that Klungkung has difficulty now because it does not have its heirloom; and so the royal family from Klungkung come to Sidemen. Says Tjokorda Gede Dangin, "If there is a temple festival here, they also come. Sometimes there is no temple festival or anything, and they still come. This is for the keris, because of the keris, and what it stands for.... It is actually for the ancestors. This keris is definitely symbolic of the ancestors." Because they are considered family, the royal house of Klungkung has access to the keris in ways that others do not. Emphasizing that the keris is not his personal possession, but belongs to the extended family, Dangin explicitly says that they are "included in the ownership:"

> It is just that I actually am the one with responsibility for it. In the future, if Klungkung has a ceremony, and they need that keris, it will be brought to Klungkung. They are welcome to do that. But after being done with the ceremony there, it will be returned here again. They are not allowed to own it directly.

Thus, even as he is stressing Klungkung's inclusion in the ownership, Dangin is also subtly asserting or at least implying Sidemen's superior position in this regard. Their *Babad Dalem* already reveals that they are descendants of the older brother from Gelgel, but the keris, which can be used in public display and interaction, underscores the claim to seniority and legitimacy. The focus now is on reestablishing mutually respectful connections. Dangin explains:

> The connection was already destroyed from before. Now it begins. They come here. They came first. Later if I am notified, maybe I will also go there [i.e. to pray at their palace]. This is good.... I love my family. I honor history. Truly I am a bit fanatic about the family there, in the sense of tradition. Not in a feudal way.

Following the maligya ritual, Dangin started making visits to Klungkung frequently, he says, to talk over their history and clear up what happened to split them. Only then did they jointly start becoming fully aware of how the raja of Karangasem manipulated Sidemen to create a rift between them. As Dangin has said earlier, the domination of Karangasem was the downfall of Sidemen. Thus, the maligya ritual became a vehicle for asserting the Jero Gede Sidemen in relation to the palace in Amlapura also, and the latter's lack of attendance was commented on.[19] Notably, as mentioned above, the entire neighborhood association of the Amlapura palace's neighborhood *was* brought in to witness the noble house's ritual.

The maligya ritual became an opportunity also for the Sidemen noble house to, in the princes terms, effect a counter-government strategy, promoting Megawati as presidential candidate and, in the process, boosting its own position, that it may remain focused on working to benefit Bali.

Counter-Government Strategy: For the Common Good

It may be said that the role of providing political leadership was accepted by Tjokorda Gede Dangin of the noble house at the transitional time surrounding Suharto's fall from power, even when it was used to stress repeatedly that this was not a time to engage in politics, that it would be impure to do so. First the "political" advice was given to await the outcome of the national confusion; later Megawati was brought in to attend the ritual. As we have seen, Tjokorda Gede Dangin withdrew from his official role in national politics after experiencing distaste for what he termed the "arrogance" of government, including conflict with the bupati (head of regency) at the time, an heir of the Amlapura Palace. We have also heard of Dangin's talk of "noncooperation," working outside of government. In this context he does go on to admit a deliberate purpose for inviting Megawati to the maligya ritual:[20]

> That is why I invited Megawati [because of the arrogance of the local government]. Prior to that, I had often encountered Mbak Megawati. OK, I thought, she is better for the people. Westerners also supported Megawati. They supported her because she is for the people. Also she was being pressured by the government [as was he].

Dangin, the Jero Gede Sidemen, and the participants in the princedom are at once resistant and subtly subversive in their allegiance to an order that to them

---

19. In the commemorative note of the 1842 Klungkung Maligya, "the absence of the 'lord' of the western Balinese kingdom of Tabanan is an important issue, and one discussed in another text on the ritual of 1842, since it shows an act of great disloyalty, and implies that the of Tabanan refuses to accept the hegemonic position of Klungkung" (Vickers 1990:174).

20. Bloch comments that historical innovators in the Merina circumcision ritual likely were conscious of the political implications of their actions (1986:1962).

transcends that of the nation-state. Says Dangin, "Our raja is our ancestor. My ancestor is my raja. We have the keris as symbol, that is the raja. Because it belonged to the raja. I consider him to still exist. It is to this that I pay respect, that I *sembah*. I pay homage to the keris as my ancestor, as my raja." The Keris Bangawan Canggu conveys considerable standing to the Jero Gede Sidemen and becomes a powerful symbol of a kind of autonomy from present government structures, however much power these might otherwise have.

The preparations for the maligya ritual were well underway before the political situation developed with which it came into play, so one could not claim that the particular situation and political opportunity resulting from Suharto's downfall motivated it. Yet, some outsiders are convinced that the whole maligya ritual was part of a strategy building up to Dangin's positioning of himself as bupati candidate for the 2000 elections to replace the existing bupati. The latter had been in office for two five-year periods and his administration was called into question upon Suharto's downfall. Dangin, in other words, could have been fulfilling his duty to his ancestors and severing their earthly ties, to pave the way for his own rise to the position in the nation-state governmental structure that is sometimes equated with kingship: the heir to the throne in Karangasem was bupati for many years; in Klungkung the bupati still is drawn from the royal ranks.[21] Dangin had indicated that only if he were to become raja again, would he take on the title of Ida I Dewa Gede, at least implying this possibility. As it turned out he did indeed run for bupati, only later to withdraw his candidacy. A few followers speculated that he had done so because there had been an issue with his polygamy—and indeed it is not atypical in Indonesia for polygamy to be considered inconsistent with government office (cf. e.g. Hoskins 1998:31). Dangin's explanation is somewhat different:

> I am too old....It is better for me to be independent. I have too many traditional ideas. I want to promote full Balinese culture. This certainly would be "dried up" [*di tegal*] by those in Jakarta. If I were bupati, I would be certain to change out those people. Many people

---

21. Dangin also points out that there still are royal family in Jogya and elsewhere, even if they are not in the government: "The important thing to remember is the important connection to the ancestors. Even if we are not in government, we are one, we are harmonious, this is important for the ancestors. There already is no government connection. It so happens that we also often become government officials. It is considered that we work with the government, becoming bupati, becoming governor. It is not because of the power of our titles. It is because we work for the people. But besides this, traditionally, it is family that is still strong."

would be upset, because I would strive for a good government, so that it really and truly would be for the people. I would restore tradition. I would do away with all of the Javanese names for things. I would no longer use the term *dusun*; it has to be *banjar* [neighborhood association]. The word *camat* would not be used, but *punggawa* [lord] would be taken into use again. I would reject a lot of things… That which is liked in Bali, I certainly would implement.

Dangin abdicates as bupati candidate, then, with wording that carries some parallel to the abdication of his forefather, Dalem Pemahyun, from the throne in Gelgel: He has at heart the greater benefit of Bali. His emphasis is much on an agenda to "re-Balinize," by contrast to other movements to "re-Indianize" (or to nationalize). He obviously was not successful on this platform as a bupati candidate, but whether it was Megawati herself who discouraged him is not clear. A few years after the maligya ritual there is a bit of a sense that the potential contained in the interaction with Megawati at the ritual was not fully realized, and, as we have seen, Megawati's "safari of prayer" to Bali proved a bit of a liability to her when she was accused by some political opponents of being more Hindu than Muslim. In Sidemen it is still stressed that ties are close, but that she is "cautious to not exhibit favoritism." As policies of decentralization are underway in Indonesia, meanwhile, Dangin continues to create opportunities for implementing his own visions for his realm (Pedersen 2004).

In the aftermath of the maligya ritual, the Jero Gede Sidemen has again been left with its degree of autonomy from government, claiming its special position in history. This is brought home also in another story, a story of how the new governor of Bali supposedly at one point requested Keris Bangawan Canggu. Says Dangin,

The governor sent somebody here to ask to bring it to him, to the office of the governor….I asked, why take it there? He was out of line….What does that mean? It is base. You cannot do that, have the Betara Keris sought by the governor. I am Ksatria Dalem [a descendant of Bali's foremost line of rajas]. Are you a Ksatria? From where? That is what I asked him. He is not of the "race" of Bali's rajas….

Did you say this to him?

Yes. I had to….This is the governor. As a governor I respect him…. But, if we return to tradition…, my raja is a person from the Majapahit. I am the keeper of the keris. Neither he nor any other person can hold it. If they encounter it outside, that is different, anyone is permitted to see it. But they have to sit at a lower level than it. Only the Klungkung people are allowed to sit high, and only they are allowed to handle the keris.... Not even all [of the family here] may do that, only the most important of them. And be it the governor or be it a general that comes, they are not allowed to.

But Megawati was allowed to? "Yes, she was, because I was aware that she was an important person. I permitted it" (Dangin). Cokorda Pemangku confirmed that the governor "asked to have the keris brought to the governor's seat in Denpasar, Bali's capital. It had to do with the political situation at the time and the peacefulness and safety of Bali. That was the purpose. But I did not agree with it." Why not?

> So that there would not later be politicking,... so that it would not be used to seek a position of power. So that I do not have a keris that is pure and whose value cannot be figured that is used for politicking, used to seek a position for an individual and who knows what.... I consulted with my family, with my older brother for example, I explained the situation to him and we decided that we could not do that. If the governor really wants it, it would be better for him to come here, to request its holy water or to pray here.... If he were to come here there would be no problem. We are open to anyone. If people come, we never turn them away.

In explaining the refusal of the governor's request, it was stressed that, by contrast, if it had been the people of Bali asking for the keris, they would have been welcome to it. When Cokorda Pemangku talked about the holy water of the keris, he pointed out that

> it is not just for the purposes of the family... nor is it just for the benefit of certain individuals. It is for anyone who needs it; they are welcome. The holy water of the keris is not just used for people, but also for the realm, for the rice terraces and the fields, as a magical prevention against pests [penangkal]. It is for the world.[22]

----

22. In Thailand seasonal royal rites of changing the clothes of the Emerald Buddha, also associated with rainmaking and fertility, continue to this day. See Tambiah for a description of this rite, for as he says, "that a 'constitutional monarchy' and a 'modernizing' country of the late twentieth century should continue with a cosmic ritual, to which a fervent efficacy is attributed by many Thai, merits and ethnographic report" (Tambiah 1985:330–331). He describes that the king "sprinkled lustral water on the people, all now

It is perhaps noteworthy that Dangin in his rendition of the story of the gift of the keris from Majapahit, rather than relating, as does Klungkung's version, that Bangawan Canggu was given because of Dalem Ketut Ngulesir's personal bodily blemish (cf. Wiener 1995:118–119), emphasized that it was a gift for a blemish in the realm of Bali. The king's body is equated with the body of the realm (cf. Kantorowicz for an elaboration on this notion in medieval Europe; Lutkehaus, 1995, regarding this notion on an Austronesian island), and the keris is for the good of the realm. In this regard, the governor's request was construed as being for personal gain, whereas ultimately healing of the realm was seen to be behind the significance of Megawati's participation. There was much talk of how important it was that she was there for the maligya ritual, a purification ceremony so big that it maybe could bring a strong balance in her and in the country. In connection with Megawati's attendance of the 1998 ritual, there had also been mention of the fact that Megawati, along with with her father, President Sukarno, had been present at the Eka Dasa Rudra in 1963, the 100 year purification ceremony of extensive sacrifice at Besakih, the central Bali temple located up from Sidemen on the slopes of Mount Agung.

At a time when Balinese were anxious that large, world renewing state rituals be resumed on Bali, to the point of continuing to urge that the nation-state help support rituals at Besakih, President Sukarno had pressed for Eka Dasa Rudra to be held in 1963 (or, according to the Balinese calendar, in the year Saka 1884), rather than at the proper end of the Balinese century in 1979 (Saka 1900). According to the texts that lay out these matters, there is some latitude in the timing of the ceremony, as the overall state of the world may indicate the need for a ceremony other than at the precise turn of centuries. By the 1960s there had been the years of struggle over land reform, with intensifying mass rallies and confrontations between Nationalist Party and Communist Party supporters (cf. chapter 4). Farmers, moreover, had been plagued with pests and crop failures and overall economic conditions had been deteriorating seriously. Presumably Sukarno—as did many Balinese—felt the need for a ritual boost to his own reign amidst the economic and political tur-

---

on their knees, hands joined in respectful worship and receiving the auspicious water of life with an intensity and eagerness that has to be seen to be believed" (1985: 336–338, ethnographic report in appendix). It is interesting that the Jero Gede Sidemen links interest in/requests for the keris to both the level of the nation-state (Megawati) and the level of Bali (the governor). In Thailand it is the monarch who has the Emerald Buddha and is "chief officiant" of its rites, assisted by his main court Brahman as well as officials of the royal household and the government (1985:336).

moil in which it was embroiled. Given the President's request and the ongoing instability, it was rationalized that an earlier ceremony might indeed be in order. It is unclear exactly when Eka Dasa Rudra might have been held in the past, but, points out Stuart-Fox, "the frequency of texts dealing with Eka Dasa Rudra and the detailed instructions about offerings and so on, suggests, that it indeed must once have been held" (1982:28). He assesses that it most likely "was held during the reign of Dalem Baturenggong towards the middle of the sixteenth century when the kingdom of Gelgel was at the height of its power, under the direction of the very influential court priest Danghyang Nirartha" (1982:28). As he continues,

> Eka Dasa Rudra is a "bringer of good fortune to the world" (*pamahayu jagat*). It brings good fortune and harmony to the world in both its aspects: the world of nature (macrocosm) and the world of man (microcosm). For one aim of the festival is to affect and strengthen the spiritual life of those taking part, leading to harmony, justice, and prosperity. [1982:28]

The same might be said for many larger Balinese ceremonies, as it was for the Sidemen Maligya. In retrospect, however, the timing of the encompassing Eka Dasa Rudra, referred to as Indonesia's most important Hindu ceremony,[23] was ill advised. Reflecting the real risk of ritual failure and its broader consequences to Balinese, the effort ended in disaster. The first rituals began October 10 1962 and continued until April 20 1963, with the large sacrifice that is central to this ceremony to fall on March 8. But with preparations already well underway, Mount Agung started showing signs of eruption. When a delegation ascended the mountain for the ceremony to collect holy water, it was met with smoke and rumbling. The ritual continued, but by February the mountain was in full eruption, causing extensive death and destruction. It was two years later that Sukarno was ousted and hundreds of thousands of supposed communists were massacred throughout Java and Bali.[24]

---

23. During Eka Dasa Rudra, no death announcements should be made, no cremations held. Postcremation rites were permitted however, and a very large one took place in Sanur during March 1963.

24. Eka Dasa Rudra was held again in 1979, year 1900 on the Balinese Saka (lunar-solar) calendar. It is not specified that it be held on any particular day during the double zero year. For Saka 1900, the new moon of the ninth month was chosen, March 28, 1979. This time the event was attended by Suharto.

The comparison between Sukarno's relationship to the ritual in 1963 and Megawati's in 1998 was not elaborated, but the connection was made, and it is not insignificant that Megawati now made a point of adhering to ritual time rather than forcing the ritual to adhere to her time. Sukarno had violated the integrity of the ritual; Megawati's may have been a kind of restorative gesture. With display of respect—and willingness to give primacy to ritual over politics—as when she waited for the ancestors to indicate the right time for her to proceed to the Jero Gede Sidemen on August 18, Megawati came to meet the keris; she did not ask for it to come to her. A follower of the noble house, a neighborhood organization leader and a farmer, speculated that Megawati, too, might have wanted to request the keris, yet "She only got to see it. Maybe she would have liked to ask for it, but it was not given to her. It was not given to her, for you cannot do that with the heirloom." Likewise, the governor was welcome to tap some of its power, but the object, the keris, should not unduly be moved from its proper place or from the custodianship of the Jero Gede Sidemen.[25]

While the keris clearly does provide opportunity for asserting a kind of timeless superiority over any power structures that might be, there are also concessions. It is noteworthy, perhaps, that Dangin, rather than talking of Bangawan Canggu as evoking warfare as well as healing (cf Wiener 1995:118–119), emphasizes instead that Bangawan Canggu is not for war: "Suda Mala may not be used for warfare; it is for purification only." He has another keris for war, a keris that is said to have been by his side throughout the upheaval of the 1960s. Thus, he says of Keris Suda Mala, Bangawan Cangguh,

> It is for purifying both individual mental impurities and is for purifying the earth. Therefore it has the highest value. It is the gift of the

---

25. It is indeed usually the case that potent (*pingit*) and sacred objects cannot be too openly circulated but must be wrapped and hidden, often locked in shrines, only to appear for special ceremonial occasions. This is in part to prevent theft, but there is also a prevailing idea that such objects should not be seen or touched unless for an appropriate purpose. An interesting problem arose in the eighties with lontar manuscripts which, too, are believed to retain power by being stored in special boxes. When such manuscripts were brought out for their text to be transcribed, various manuscript versions of similar subjects suddenly became the object of an unprecedented comparative scrutiny. Previously, each could keep intact its differences, conferring a certain power that now was diminished. Similarly with keris and other sacred objects if they are allowed to become too demystified. Dangin offers that in the past he may have been too liberal in allowing the keris to be brought out for visitors to see, sometimes even without ceremony. He realizes now that this was wrong, he says. Cf. also Hoskins regarding the consequences of moving the sacred urn of the priest of the sea worms to be joined to a colonially imposed office (1993:125–131).

raja. If given by an ordinary person, it would just be for war. But this keris is not for war....Because of that, it has a *naga basuki*...its base is a *naga* [serpent]. It is for purification.

Highlighting purification over warfare is fitting with the role that rajas were supposed to have following their "restoration" in the 1930s by the Dutch administration (cf. Schulte Nordholt 1999:258–259) and that traditional leaders are supposed to have now. It also renders the keris itself less threatening to governmental powers. In the aftermath of Dutch conquest of Bali, as Wiener has commented, ironically it was the colonial government that considered the keris to be powerful, while Balinese at that point linked their defeat to the loss of these very powers (1995:345). In 1908, Resident de Bruyn Kops wrote in a report to the Governor General regarding the keris seized by the Dutch that "the people attribute [to these] the possession of supernatural forces," wherefore he recommended that "to bring these again in the possession of Balinese lords would not thus be defensible" (Wiener 1995:345). Van Duuren writes about the personalities of some keris, or what he calls their "genie-in-the-bottle" quality, "tales about unruly weapons seeking adventure independent of their owners, out to drink blood" (1998:61). Other keris "would not be drawn from their sheaths at essential moments, or, on the contrary, would rattle in their sheaths, desiring to be drawn," and so forth (van Duuren 1998:61). One particularly fascinating tale is of an ancient Malaysian keris. This keris, which "had for years been in a glass case in a museum, was claimed to be unable to forget its bloody past; it allegedly left the museum to wander about at night and kill rancorous old enemies. Afterward it cleansed itself meticulously, returning to its usual spot again in the morning" (van Duuren 1998:61). These kinds of stories were well known to the Dutch, as they are to contemporary nation-state officials. To Tjokorda Gede Dangin there is still a strategic value to stressing that this heirloom keris is purificatory only. It is not a blood-seeking object—or princedom—that is emerging at the center of action here. At the same time, neither the princes nor their followers hesitate to point out that they would withstand and resist any outside threats, articulating in particular the need to stand up to globalization, Indianization, and to the threat of Islam.

Tjokorda Gede Dangin expressed a common sentiment against global homogenization when he reminisced that

> Sukarno was for Indonesia. Let Bali be Bali. Let Java be Java. This was the good thing about Sukarno. Do not let Western culture, for example, make too much of an inroad, then we will only end up losing our own culture. This is what Sukarno meant....If we let this happen the world will end up an impoverished place. It will only be Western cul-

> ture that is left....It is the same in Indonesia. Leave Java alone, and
> Bali, Lombok, etc. I agree with that....If there is no tradition, there is
> no culture....This is what Bung Karno advocated. Don't make hotels
> like in Japan. Make them in a Balinese style. A modern Bali, he said.
> Keep it Balinese, but clean it up. That is the better road to take.

There has also been an ongoing move among some Balinese intellectuals toward neo-Indianization, whereby they seek to reinfuse Balinese religious practice in accordance with original Hindu scripts, or outright convert to Indian
sects (see Picard 1997, 1999; Howe 2001, 2004; Ngurah Bagus 2004; Ramstedt 2004). As a result, the priests and princes who mostly resist this have found
renewed common purpose. As an indication of how these matters are talked
about, Dangin mentions a certain leading priest that has "played politics," participating in party politics and taking a prominent role in the Hindu Darma
Council, the regulatory body under the Indonesian state for the Hindu religion, involved also in streamlining Hindu belief and practice on Bali (see Ngurah Bagus 2004; Picard 2004). This man now has become a consecrated priest
who is "for Bali" and "does defend the Balinese ways," as Dangin phrases it; "he
is good. He opposes the Indian way....He defends *agama* [Balinese religion]."

Beyond globalization and neo-Indianization, and even "Indonesianization"
of Balinese religion (cf. Picard 1997:200), a particularly pressing issue for
many Balinese has been a perceived threat of fundamentalist Islam. Although
the notion of the need to protect Bali against the incursion of Islamic influences featured prominently in colonial discourse (see Picard 1999:21–23), Balinese, themselves, who undeniably remain conscious of being a numerical
minority in a nation of mainly Islamic populations, tend to trace this not to
colonial policy, but point out that it has been an issue of varying concern since
the fall of Majapahit.[26] This is an issue, moreover, that people say has taken

---

26. Picard points out that the reinstatement of Balinese rajas in the 1930s in large part
was motivated by the Dutch "effort to contain the spread of Islamic radicalism and various nationalist and communist movements that had arisen in Java and Sumatra. To them
it was becoming apparent that the Balinese nobility, whom they regarded as the vehicle of
the Hinduization of Bali and the pillar of its traditional order, was the strongest barrier
against the spread of Islam and the seepage of subversive ideas into Bali" (1999:21). He
goes on to argue that "by looking for the singularity of Bali in its Hindu heritage while conceiving of Balinese identity as formed through an opposition to Islam, the Dutch established the framework within which the Balinese were going to define themselves" (1999:23).
There is no doubt but that all of this was an important part of Dutch discourse and policy, nor that the Dutch discourse influenced Balinese discourse, yet the Dutch were not the
originators of the Balinese sense of a threat from Islam.

on new dimensions since the terrorist bombing in 2002 of a nightclub in the tourist area of Kuta. But already in the 1998 maligya ritual, there was a strong and expressed consciousness in this large symbolic effort, of Balinese continuing to assert themselves in the face of the possibility that Islam in Indonesia could become more fundamentalist. Dangin explains:

> Indonesia is difficult, because there is a lot of Islam here....There is not fundamentalism yet; right now people want to disintegrate, ethnic conflict is happening....If Islamic fundamentalism were to come to power, it would be very dangerous....This would not be good for Indonesia, nor would it be good internationally....I have heard it a lot that they would want everyone to be Islamic. That is how they talk. It is dangerous that they talk like that. There are many Christians, many Buddhists, and many Hindus in Indonesia. They want to choose their own fate.

Dangin emphasizes that forcing people only leads to trouble:

> People already have a religion. It is already good; in Bali it is already good. Do not seek to exchange it with Islam. Do not try to change it to Christianity. People still want to do this. It is wrong....It causes misery and suffering; it causes natural disasters; it results in war. There is no longer any peace. It is a form of greediness, wanting to force your own ideas. You cannot force humans. Dogs you can force. If you force people they will rise in war. If not now, then later they will fight it. Because here there is wind which will kindle the fire and the water will boil....That is how people are. They will burn; they will fight...

On behalf of the participants, coming together in ritual as a princedom already is a response to external threats and a reminder of the potential to mobilize again to face intensified dangers should the need arise.

Ritual and World Change

The participants in the maligya ritual believed that they were acting in and upon the world. Through the ritual certain forms of power were activated, displayed, and even generated, and they were so in interaction with the world beyond. As the maligya ritual progressed, we saw that large-scale ritual happens in a historical context and, conversely, history happens in the ritual context. The local and the national, ritual and historical time frames, as well as the manifest and the nonmanifest worlds, acted with and upon one another. In response to both ancestral obligations and historical exigency, invoking mandalas of all scales, the ritual participants situated themselves as one version of a Southeast Asian negara, which can influence and ultimately help bring harmony to the state of the world. This is a far cry from those perspectives that saw or continue to see Bali characterized by any kind of steady state of harmony. Rather, it is because everything is inherently fraught also with disharmony that continuous effort must be made to try to at least minimize it. Far from just conceived as static stereotypical reproduction, Balinese ritual such as the maligya can be an act of "spinning" (cf. Vickers 1991) and participants can, when successful, help effect a spinning into new times. Balinese *are* engaged with the present world, and they, in fact, can use the idea of cycles and ritual language as a means for transformation.

For the ancestors, as seen in chapter 2, the ceremony is about doing all within the power of the living to help their souls on their way. Various rituals are performed for the purpose of cleansing any bad karma they might have. Through this, it is hoped that the ancestral souls may even be spun out of the circle of reincarnation, that they may moksa. This is vividly imaged in talk about how the linggas (the Brahmana ancestors who serve as "guides") lead the way, flying in orbit around the universe until they find the path out. This, from the perspective of the noble house, *is* different for "ordinary people," meaning people of low caste, who, it is generally believed, still must reincarnate, but can reincarnate in new ways, not just in ongoing cycles of more of the same. And the ritual is dynamic not only for the dead. As we have seen, this form of ritual may in fact also be viewed as a ritual of kingship, which rajas typically had to perform before they could assume their full titles; they had to clear the way, so to speak, by deifying the previous raja—and there *were* those who argued that the event of the maligya ritual in 1998 was central to the head of the Jero Gede Sidemen's upcoming bid for the position of regional government head (bupati). But the ritual is also dynamic for all who participate and, through doing so, change their karma, their feelings about themselves and their surroundings. There was much talk of the significance of this ceremony on a scale beyond individual souls, for the Balinese, and for Indonesians, in a time with such "crisis of faith" in the government.[27] There was, it was said, a need to generate confidence and for a

---

27. Robinson and Bessell mention the "crisis of trust" in relation the Voice of Concerned Mothers who, in a by now famous "milk demonstration" in Jakarta, protested the impact of the monetary crisis on women. Three of the women were arrested and tried amid much publicity: "During their trial, they drew attention not just to the effects of the economic crisis but also to the 'crisis of trust' in the government" (2002:4).

strong anchor on both the local and national levels. Explicit references were made to the past, expressing concern for the pattern of crises. "We had crisis in the 40s, crisis in the 60s, and now crisis in the 90s. We have an economic crisis and lose our orientations," it was said in dismay. "We don't want such a thing to happen again twenty or thirty years from now. This ceremony will give strength, and can help propel us into a better future." Through their ritual action, moreover, participants were reminding themselves that they could act in ways other than through ritual as well.

In Bali, as elsewhere, there was an immediate reaction following Suharto's fall to the suppression of politics during his New Order regime, an "exuberant eruption of political activity" (Eklof 1999). In the streets of Sidemen just months after the maligya ritual, the recognition of repressed politics was reflected during Megawati's campaign when slogan stickers were pasted all over which read "Do not be afraid of talking politics!" There were also gathering sheds decorated with "pro-Mega" posters and slogans. Eklof wrote in the magazine *Inside Indonesia* that in spots like this throughout Bali,

> In the evenings, the youngsters assembled in the sheds to talk politics and to listen to protest songs and recordings of Megawati's opening speech of the congress [of the Democratic Party held in Bali in October 1998]. Every day, from the early afternoon until late at night, the main roads around Denpasar were crammed with thousands of people.... Sitting on top of their vehicles or hanging out the windows, the celebrators tirelessly waved their red flags and shouted "Mega! Mega!" or "Hidup Mega!" (Long Live Mega) in chorus. [1999]

The release of political discourse did not extend into the discourse of ritual, and by 2003 the exuberance had long since dimmed. Mainly intellectuals remained enthusiastic about new freedoms in post-Suharto Indonesia under the presidency of Megawati, freedoms of expression and political organization. Many others expressed dismay over what they construed more as political confusion. Megawati was not reelected in the presidential election of 2004.

While some kinds of politics certainly are talked about more openly now, in Bali as in Indonesia generally, the dirty connotations of politics have taken on new meaning following what is locally referred to as "Bali's Black October," the 2002 bombing in Kuta. In Bali, the threat of political activity is increasingly identified with Islamic fundamentalism, and, by contrast, the view persists of Balinese people as comparatively apolitical—even if they did show a distinct political voice in their overwhelming support of Megawati, to the point in some cases of rioting when she was not instituted as president in 1999, and even if many do indicate quite forcefully that they will continue to do so against Islamic fundamentalism. Both indigenous and international media, meanwhile, have continued to try to propagate Bali's image as the ever-un-ruffled paradise island. The commercial motives of this are obvious in the case of an island so dependent on its tourist economy, yet it was not uncommon either for outside observers with considerable experience in Bali to note with some exasperation that, rather than getting involved in meaningful politics, Balinese if anything only were busier than ever with what still gets construed as their apolitical rituals.[28] It remains, however, that their rituals, defined as they are as separate and apart from politics, do also to many Balinese play an important role as response to national and international politics, specifically to what many perceive as the homogenizing, and to various degrees threatening, effects of globalization and national Islam. That they see ritual as one appropriate response is not merely because this is what they have learned goes into being "authentically Balinese" (cf. Picard 1999); precolonially, too, ritual was a response to threat (cf. Schulte Nordholt 1996a).

As its participants will stress, the Sidemen Maligya was genuinely focused on the very traditional and very spiritual activity of deifying the ancestors, but it also became a site for meaningful confirmation of the potential for both supernatural and actual action in the world. Tjokorda Gede Dangin, when pointing out that Balinese people too "will burn" and "fight" if pushed, continued with regard to the threat of Islam,

> We should have learned this lesson from history....In Java, in the era of the fall of Majapahit....Hindus were killed; temples were destroyed... all per the recommendation of the Islamic government. That is what we fear now. The recommendation that all Balinese may be killed, that they may destroy the temples. If that were to come, we would wage war.

Already in 1998, many followers of the Jero Gede Sidemen independently echoed this sentiment. If there were to be an attempt by an extremist government in Jakarta to impose on Bali, they said, then everything would shift back to the tradition of princedoms and there would indeed be war. Many followers pointed out that, in the past, the *ketungan*, the wooden trough, was pounded to call people to war; in 1998 it was so to draw people to ritual—But it could be so again for war. At the time of the fall of Suharto and of the rioting in Jakarta, people in eastern Bali expressed that they would descend into the streets (*turun ke jalan*) only if told to do so, as happened in the 1960s, through the "egalitarian" neigh-

---

28. MacRae heard similar remarks (2003:30). MacRae (2003) and Nakatani (2003) also comment on the intensification at this time in Bali of ritual activity in response to the world in disarray.

borhood associations (*banjar*) or through the princedom. Were there ever to be a mobilization of people against "attack by visible enemies" from the outside, it could well, as in ritual, follow once more the old princedom-based principles.[29]

The Sidemen Maligya and Megawati's attendance and interaction with the keris serve most obviously the status elevation of the noble house and especially the prince who is the head of the house; but today, through his empowerment, his people become empowered too. People also derive political benefit from being part of a princedom, which in many cases is the only way for them to gain a sense of agency in an ever-changing, increasingly complex world. This is so with regard to practical everyday concerns on the local and regional level, as emerged in chapter 5, but also with regard to larger national and international forces. People are becoming more empowered not only within their princedom as the princes, in response to changing historical circumstances, must become less and less "feudal," but sometimes also through their princedom, such that all of them, lords and followers, may engage more effectively with these changes. At a historical moment awash with political activity, a small Balinese negara was reborn in Sidemen through the voluntary participation of the descendants of former subjects, not just so that the princes could rise in status and as political leaders, but in part also because by participating in the status elevation of their princes, the followers, in turn, enhance their own sense of empowerment.

---

29. Van der Kraan has noted that also in the colonial era Balinese resistance differed: Balinese resistance did not, as in West Sumatra from 1803–37, take on the form of a so-cial movement led by religious figures (*ulama*). Rather, Balinese resistance derived its strength from the independent attitude of the Balinese princes and, above all, from the willingness of their followers to come to their assistance (1980:ix). As Robinson notes, "al-though Bali's royal families later earned a reputation for collaboration with the Dutch, five of the island's kingdoms…came under Dutch control only after military resistance at var-ious times between 1846 and 1908" (1995:24).

CHAPTER EIGHT

CONCLUSION

Balinese kingship is believed to have all but disappeared with the early twentieth-century "finishings" (*puputan*), mass suicides or massacres, of the independent Balinese courts which completed Dutch colonization of Bali, and in the aftermath with the Dutch administration's targeting of what was construed as feudalism, only to be finally phased out with the incorporation of Bali into the Indonesian nation-state in the course of the century, where the value of not being feudal likewise has figured prominently and bureaucratic structures have been adopted. "In Bali," Hobart says, "apart from transmogrifying intricate networks of ties between princes, overseers and peasants into administrative villages or irrigation complexes, subtle regional differences in understanding of economic and political clientage and ranking became rigidified into monolithic systems of land tenure and caste" (1990:316). Hand in hand, the fluid Balinese negara and their power base, with their land-based pacatu ties, lord-follower relationships, and royal rituals, are said to have vanished (cf e.g. Geertz 1980; Guermonprez 1989; Howe 1995; Wiener 1995; Schulte Nordholt 1996a, 2002).[1] The keris, too, has been declared "part of a practically extinct phase of Indonesian cultural history...an object without especial meaning or power" (van Duuren 1998). Even Wiener, who otherwise recovers appreciation for the role of keris in Balinese history and kingship and for the connection in Bali between power in the invisible and visible realms, concludes that "among the things finished in the *puputan* was the identification of royal power with keris and all that this entailed" (1995:329).

Yet, as has been argued through this book, the noble house, the Jero Gede Sidemen, based on nonrigid "intricate networks" and ongoing accommodations between princes and people, still plays a role in contemporary Bali. How and why, I have asked, does the princedom persist in a small mountain valley, in such a way that a Majapahit keris, the princes, the people of their realm, and

---

1. It is generally agreed that only Brahmana priests have kept their role (cf. e.g. Rubinstein 1991a). The sense of annihilation is also how "fights to the finish" and the demise of kingdoms are talked about in Balinese dynastic chronicles. But even from the *puputan* some royalty escaped and returned to develop their roles in various ways.

a nation-state presidential candidate—in the midst of Indonesia's turmoil in 1998—could enter into the mutually affirming interaction that happened at the maligya ritual? The answer as we have seen is multifaceted and complex.

The argument made here in regard to the princedom is not a mere argument for continuity, an argument that "traditional culture" perseveres no matter what. The small-scale negara is not just a survival, left encapsulated as everything around it changed, preserved as it was in "Bali as museum." There is continuity, but there is also change. The Balinese princedom is transformed, recreated by the princes and followers, sometimes through what historian Nicholas Thomas has described as processes of "oppositional reification and inversion" (1997:208), as the modern negara takes form in response to, or in dialogue with, global, colonialist, nationalist, and touristified discourses pertinent to Balinese kingship—and citizenship. But it continues to do so also in response to local discourses and to its history with surrounding kingdoms. It is based not just on action which "goes without saying" or even which "cannot be said for lack of an available discourse," to take Bourdieu's points between "misrecognition" and "awakening of political consciousness" (1979:170), for it is positioned at a hub of discourses and ongoing responses to both local and external conditions of existence.

Accommodations and Appropriated Discourses

In part the princedom continues to have relevance because it was not made up just of what the Dutch, followed by the national government, saw and targeted as feudalism but was a realm according with negara dynamics, a fluid realm based on means of attracting followers that did not rely on coercion or land ownership, a realm wherein the bases for relationships have been adapted to changing conditions. That the past has sometimes been strategically refashioned toward this end, does not diminish the results, for such creativity is intrinsic to cultural process.

Thus, the explicit material ties of pacatu are no longer; yet amazingly there is still intensive devotion and donation of labor from voluntary subjects to the Jero Gede Sidemen, who appeal to these ties in ways different than previously imagined. As we have seen, this connection is construed in large part as being about reverence for the ancestral gift of land. Balinese may not consider their rajas gods, but since they deify their ancestors, this creates ties between groups that were ancestrally connected, ties that are not easily alienable. Beyond the ongoing appeal to relationships based on evidence embedded in land and ancestral decrees, with the pursuant dangers of violating them, another facet that has come to the fore is an emphasis on mutuality in the system. People are followers also because they get something out of it (cf. also Boon 1977; Reid 1983; Schulte Nordholt 1996a; Wolters 1999). The Jero Gede Sidemen still does have a material base from which the princes can provide some assistance, but above all, they fulfill this part of their role as descendants of rulers through providing various services to their followers, including attention to ritual, and by continuing to adapt to changing circumstances. Through all of the historical contexts involving an empowerment of people and delegitimization of feudal tendencies, the Jero Gede Sidemen concomitantly has tried to situate itself to be well aligned with rising powers and also has worked to remain so with its followers. In this process people and princes of the princedom have appropriated the antifeudal discourse that was forwarded by the colonizers and later nationalists, subsequently to take root in the nation-state.

The members of the noble house define the princedom today as upholding ancestral tradition against both old "feudalism" and contemporary "politicking." They also have come increasingly and consciously to highlight the populist facets of the good raja and to emphasize the strategy of *memasyarakat*, connecting with and working for the people. There is conscious effort and hard work on the part of the Jero Gede Sidemen to establish and maintain connections with its people. Much as do leaders of egalitarian neighborhood and irrigation organizations (cf. Birkelbach 1973; Barth 1993), Tjokorda Gede Dangin expresses the difficulty of a leadership position, in this case specifically the pressure to get out to the people: "There are thousands of people; I do not have enough feet for that." But it is the Jero Gede Sidemen's diligence in this respect that has given the noble house an edge today, by contrast to palaces which are said to have become powerless even if they may have been rich in land and many people once had responsibilities to them. It is true, as has typically been emphasized, that royal houses often have lost power due to internal strife and lack of cohesion toward the outside; but, equally true, many have lost power also because they lost connection to the people. In order to remain influential, in short, the princes of Sidemen have had to become more oriented toward their followers in the context of the historical changes related to Bali's colonization and later independence and the nationalist spirit. Attention to this was part of a deliberate strategy of the Jero Gede Sidemen as the twentieth century progressed. The recognition of powers of the people, along with the emphasis on memasyarakat, have become increasingly important in the postcolonial era, as royal positions became more precarious and imbued with less coercive power than before. Balinese rajas did lose real power during various historical transitions and only some have succeeded in recreating it again.

It has not been external colonial and nation-state policies and global influences exclusively that have pressured rajas toward more populist practices; their powers likely always to some extent have been circumscribed by the powers of their followers. The proliferation of kingdoms and lordships in Bali, even in the preceding centuries, were characterized by a considerable degree of uncertainty that would-be rajas had to contend with, rendering them vulnerable not only to each other but also to the forces of the people. In fact, there are examples of actions in those times, too, where people expelled or even killed unpopular lords or leaders (cf. Robinson 1995). Conversely in the present day, although there is the concession that you have to also earn your caste privilege, the princes are still in the end upholding and continuing to assert the idea of caste; only now there is an emphasis on how it is their deeds that will reveal those who are true and worthy Ksatria of royal heritage. What their combined inherited and achieved privileges brought them, in this case, were the followers and the labor that made it possible to still present themselves as princes—with credibility—as they did through the maligya ritual, even to the future president of Indonesia.

At the same time, the people and princes of the princedom have appropriated the colonial and national discourses of apolitical ritual. Although, again, there is some precolonial precedent to this notion, recent scholars have shown how the image of Balinese cultural elements as apolitical was constructed through colonial, scholarly, and New Order rhetoric and politics, involving also Balinese intellectuals, and as part of a strategy of controlling local identities to prevent dissidence (cf. e.g.Picard 1999, Hough 1999). Entering the twenty-first century and highly dependent on the tourist economy, Balinese, in general, are themselves eager to perpetuate their image as being fundamentally apolitical and, above all, safe. This is to encourage tourism and, on the part of the princes, to avoid coming across as (feudal) power mongers. (Cf. also Picard's analysis of the "touristification" of Balinese culture and how it "proceeds from within by blurring the boundaries between the inside and the outside...between that which belongs to 'culture' and that which pertains to 'tourism'" [1997:182–183].) In the end, a view frequently persists, either explicit or implicit, of Balinese people, in general, as comparatively apolitical. In Bali after all, where, relative to other Indonesian provinces, there is a high standard of living and at least some sense of political representation at the national level, people are not mounting the politically organized and easily recognized forms of resistance that we have seen in Aceh, West Papua, or East Timor.

It remains that "tradition" and "ritual" often continue to be viewed as essentially conservative forces and Bali as a tourist-island-repository of these.[2] Yet their rituals, to many Balinese, do also constitute a form of engagement and even resistance that has precolonial precedent, although it is shaped as well by subsequent developments. In the end, Balinese are not necessarily accepting either in relation to national and/or international politics. The Sidemen Maligya, as its participants will stress, genuinely was focused on the very spiritual activity of honoring the ancestors. At the same time, it came into interaction with national and political events, which in Balinese notions of causality does not merely happen according to what we would call coincidence. Concurrences of cycles of events hold significance. As presidential candidates were invited to the highland valley and people in large numbers joined in the ritual effort, the princes and participants also mediated connections between the ancestral ritual and national politics. Through this, it was evident that the ancestral ritual became as well a site of resistance and an indicator of potential for further resistance, even at a time when both indigenous and international media were busier than ever propagating Bali's image of being largely uninvolved with serious politics.

We have heard that Tjokorda Gede Dangin has said he leaves the outside activism to the younger members of his family, but also urges them in their endeavors, and we have gotten a sense of the range of activities of his niece, Cokorda Sawitri. The year following the maligya ritual, she presented a performance piece, "the Defence of Dirah," an adaptation of the classic *Calon Arang* story of Rangda, the powerful widow-witch, typically depicted as a fierce looking monster with wild hair, pendulous breasts, fangs and long finger nails. Approaching the issue of resistance from this angle, too, with publicly stated messages, Sawitri associates resistance with spiritual and "cultural" activity. The point of departure for her in developing the performance was,

---

2. In the colonial era too, as van der Kraan has noted, Balinese resistance differed from that elsewhere: Balinese resistance did not, as in West Sumatra from 1803–37, take on the form of a social movement led by religious figures (*ulama*). Rather, Balinese resistance had a far more conservative, traditional character. It derived its strength from the fiercely independent attitude of the Balinese princes and, above all, from the willingness of their followers to come to their assistance. Partly due to the effectiveness of this aristocracy-led resistance, the Balinese region was one of the last areas in the Indonesian archipelago where indigenous rulers managed to retain their independence (1980:ix). Robinson notes that "athough Bali's royal families later earned a reputation for collaboration with the Dutch, five of the island's kingdoms...came under Dutch control only after military resistance at various times between 1846 and 1908" (1995:24).

as is often her practice, in "tradition," through a study of *lontar* (palm-leaf manuscripts) as a basis for her interpretation. The understanding she arrived at regarding the *Calon Arang* story has Dirah representing a cult that resisted King Airlangga and his priest on religious grounds. (King Airlangga was the son of a Balinese king and Javanese princess who came to rule Java in 1041AD.) In interviews, Sawitri made explicit an association of Dirah with Megawati and with nonphysical resistance: "When attacked by the king, the Dirah group defended themselves spiritually rather than physically, in similar fashion to Megawati's moral and legal resistance to the Soeharto regime after the routing of her party base" (Hatley 2002:137). In a passage that brings to mind a number of parallels to what has been said surrounding aspects of the Jero Gede Sidemen's position and the role of the Sidemen Maligya, Hatley summarizes one of Sawitri's performances from a *Bali Post* review (Asmaudi and Dwikora 1999):

> Cok Sawitri performed her vision of the story of Calon Arang, a widow of the district of Dirah, as a victim of political violence perpetrated by centralized, male-controlled state power. With her wild bloodied hair and piercing glance, the widow is a fearful figure, capable of breeching into the king's fortress and slaying thousands of his men. But she retreats into the forest to avoid bloodshed, to carry out…moral and cultural resistance. Even when the king's forces pursue her and attack her followers' quarters, she advises her supporters not to resist. But the king's men spread tales of her evil magic and destructive acts, to blacken her image with the people. The power holders of today, the narrator reports, are similarly oppressive and violent. The ordinary people may indeed have turned against the 'king' and forced him to step down, but lies spread by his regime, and those before it, live on. [Hatley 2002:137]

In Sawitri's vision, explains Hatley, "Calon Arang's struggle is not against universal patriarchy but totalitarian state power. The inspiration for this work, the artist reports, was the July 1996 attack by Soeharto regime thugs on the headquarters of Megawati Sukarnoputri's party. For Cok Sawitri, Megawati at this time was a symbol of the nation's suffering—"negeri saya jadi janda" [my country has been made a widow]—abused and marginalized" (Hatley 2002:137). Sawitri is here referring to a line from one of her unpublished poems, entitled "21 May 1998," the date of Suharto's resignation (Sawitri n.d.; see Sawitri 2003 for another of her poems "Aku Pulang Kampung," "I Return to the Village"). In connection with her performance of the "Defence of Dirah," Sawitri made public statements underscoring that hers was a message of resistance to be applied to situations of repression in general: "What I wish is for everyone to carry out resistance in their own space'" (Dian 2000).

The princedom and its ritual may be viewed as such spaces. In fact, in the modern world, the princedom may become a vehicle—for some the only vehicle—for a sense of both individual and Balinese empowerment vis-à-vis the nation-state and the wider world. Both people power, on the one hand, and old forms of "feudalism," on the other, are said to be on the rise in Southeast Asia. The example of the Sidemen princedom shows how and why these two seemingly contradictory trends may go hand in hand. Thus the princedom persists, working the people and the princes, keeping active the memory of land connections, and making its claims to legitimacy on the basis of genealogies that have been contested for centuries. Much of this is manifested in the heirloom keris, the Keris Sudha Mala or Bangawan Canggu, which, half a millennium after the initial gift from the Javanese Emperor at the maligya ritual at Majapahit, appeared again in a great ancestral ritual. To play a central role in the renewed claims to power of the smaller Balinese noble house, the Jero Gede Sidemen.

The claims of the noble house are quite extraordinary. Through their ritual at the time of national upheaval, the princes created an opportunity for appropriating the discourse of kingship at the highest level of legitimacy. Making their claims charismatically (cf. Brenneis 2003:221), they took their audience into account: They did not make direct proclamations, in which form the claims surely would not have been received, but would have appeared presumptuous, "feudal" and "political."

A History Object and Displaced Agency

Throughout this book, many examples of displaced agency have surfaced: Agency has been displaced unto the very ritual itself and to many occurrences associated with it—the dreams, visions, and trances, and the keris. There are dead ancestors acting through living beings and things, people referring to themselves not as individual political strategists but as representatives of the collective of the house or lineage, and there has been a strategy of displacing agency by avoiding the word "politics." As we have seen, participation in the maligya ritual of members of the former government, nationalist, or communist parties, is explained as "having no political element," although an alternative explanation well might be that all of this was very political indeed. The participation of former communist party adherents could in fact be viewed as a kind of purification from subversive leftism, and Megawati's participation cannot help but be in some way political; she was after all running for president. There is a prevailing individual versus collective dynamic, too, in the discourse of these Balinese actors. Political players reject individual power games and manipulative strategies, which are not socially acceptable, stressing instead the gain in prestige of the collective. The advantage of displacing political agency is that the actors do not seem to be seeking personal power; and yet, it is a device that is used again and again. The displacement of agency emerges most evidently in the case of the heirloom keris, where "the actions" of the object take on profound significance.

The keris is a Balinese idiom for talking about power, and the use of the idiom is important to the Jero Gede Sidemen's constitution of its princedom. Janet Hoskins has challenged the presumed supremacy of narrative historical representation over other forms, such as "history objects" which "preserve a sense of past and collective memory" and which, in some traditions, have particularly great import (1993:xiv). In Sidemen, the history object, the keris, features in the *Babad Dalem*, the historical narrative of the dynasty to which it was given and within which it belongs, but it features also in the dynastic chronicle of the noble house that separates it from this mainstream history and takes it on its path to the highland valley. At the maligya ritual, the keris stepped out of the not always reconciled narrative of past history, so to speak, to enter into the present flow of history. For as Hoskins also says, "objects and sequences do not necessarily result in a 'reification' or 'objectification' of the past, but can also be part of a process of creative regeneration" (1993:xiv; see also p. 119).

In Sidemen, the keris both reifies a version of the past, a version of the *Babad Dalem*—by identifying itself, so to speak; by the very claim of its presence[3]—and plays a role in historical process and change, with implications for the future. In Bali dynasties have vied for legitimacy through the writing each of their own histories. Given the contested past and varying versions of the *Babad Dalem*, and the need on behalf of the Jero Gede Sidemen, in a strategy that spans generations, to recover from prior discreditations, the object here speaks louder than the narrative, for it can be entered into and acknowledged in public interaction. But beyond legitimating a version of the past, it becomes a historical agent or facilitator, involving some of the most significant contemporary political agents in Bali and Indonesia. The keris helped give new life to the Sidemen princedom and, as is argued locally, to Megawati's candi-

---

3. Note that in Kodi, too, the history objects can provide evidence "of the veracity of narratives" (Hoskins 1993:120).

dacy. The event of the maligya ritual, meanwhile, also gave new life to the keris, which became more desired, as reflected in stories of attempted theft and of the governor's request, but also, as a result, now must be more restricted.

According to the dynastic chronicle of the *Babad Dalem*, the keris was presented to the Balinese raja by the Javanese emperor in the fourteenth century with the words: "This is a sign of my love for you, a proof that we are one." At the turn to the twenty-first century, as we have seen, Tjokorda Gede Dangin professes loyalty not to rajas but to this keris (chapter 7), which also brings to mind Heine-Geldern's observation that sometimes it is the object that is said to rule and the owner merely to be the controller of its power:

> [The] magical character of the regalia is even more stressed in the Malay Peninsula and in Indonesia [than in the rest of Southeast Asia]. It culminates in the curious conception prevalent among the Bugis and Makassarese of Celebes, according to which it is really the regalia which reign, the prince governing the state only in their name. [1956:9]

Such a conception echoes the argument referred to at different points in this study, that temples not rajas matter most (cf. Guermonprez 1989). Here it is the objects that endure; the people are but the vehicles to carry out the necessary connections between the objects and the world. Similarly, Tambiah, in his model of Southeast Asian states as "galactic polities," emphasizes the special place of sacred objects: Since galactic polities are

> characterized by divine kingship accompanied by perennial rebellions and secessions, sacred objects...had a special place. Recognized as permanent embodiments of virtue and power, they helped provide their temporary possessors with legitimation, and at the same time embodied a genealogy of kingship by serving as the common thread. [1985:329]

Hoskins, too, finds that "the focus on objects as markers of past traditions creates an impression of stability, which seems to represent enduring offices and relationships as less open to variation than a person-centered genealogical model" (1993:138, see also Errington 1983). And yet, as Hoskins also reminds us:

> At the same time, this stability can be illusory, for the offices and relationships do not in fact remain unchanged, even though the objects that represent them maintain a reassuringly ancient appearance. The

traces of the past left in objects can be manipulated, as can other forms of historical evidence. [1993:138]

So it is that the keris, in order to be powerful, must be entered into the kind of event that we have seen here, making its argument on several levels. Thanks to the princes' skillful use of it, it was reinvested with royal power, and the keris became a vehicle also for Megawati to displace her political agency. The historical relations and powers of the people as described in previous chapters set the stage for the princes of the Jero Gede Sidemen to generate for Keris Bangawan Canggu the power that they did during the maligya ritual. As seen in the last chapter, Balinese actors do speak as if objects have agency, but, as this study attests, although the keris helps mobilize popular support for the Jero Gede Sidemen, it does not do so mystically. It would be but an empty symbol without the people behind it. It is by conjoining the object with the practice of working the people that the members of the Jero Gede Sidemen have used the keris carefully to build up its power as well as their own. With the ritual of the maligya, the Jero Gede Sidemen created a grand context wherein this power and the underlying relations could be displayed. The whole event gained further by the national historical circumstances within which it found itself.

Ritual and Status Elevation through a Power Vacuum

At the historical moment surrounding Suharto's fall from power in 1998, the princes situated themselves both in relation to rising powers and to their followers, involving each of these in an enormous event that buttressed their own hierarchical position. The transitional period beginning in 1998 is comparable to earlier social revolutions in Bali associated with regime shifts — from the Colonial Era to Independence and from Sukarno's rule to Suharto's rule. Those, too, were times when people, as now, were feeling more powerful. At the same time they also were times characterized locally by a power vacuum during which many were looking to reestablish hierarchy.

The phrase "power vacuum," coined and discussed by Ben Anderson, refers to the notion that the defeat of existing powers leaves a vacuum which results in struggles to establish or dominate state structures (1972). Robinson follows Anderson when he links the violent political conflict among Balinese in 1945–49 and 1965–66 to the sudden collapse of central state power, and the varying pattern of killings across Bali in the latter period to the strength of the local state in any given area (1995:10). According to Anderson, conflict in this situation is influenced by the strength of the local states, and can be prevented when they use their authority to do so (1972). But, reminds Robinson, "the reason lies not just in the absence or weakness of state authority but in the active participation of elements of the state apparatus in the process of political protest or conflict" (1995:11). We might add that it is not merely a question of state authority and elements of state apparatus versus (nonstate) locals. The local princedom is an authority in a different vein, of quite different position and motivation, but one that also, as we saw in chapter 6, played a leading role within the local community at the collapse of nation state power both in the 1960s and in the 1990s.

James Siegel, too, argued that when there is uncertainty and "perceived weakness of the national hierarchy," "there is an attempt locally to reestablish hierarchy" (1986:89). Thus, after the overthrow of Sukarno in the 1960s, he pointed out, Javanese turned inward and looked for sources of hierarchy in places such as the local community (1986:89). It was a similar process that unfolded in Sidemen after Suharto was brought down in 1998. In Siegel's example, the local attempt to reestablish hierarchy happened through shadow puppet performances, which had become tied to a national hierarchy with Sukarno at the apex. In Sidemen it happened through ritual, when after the fall of Suharto, Sidemen became a locus of local power and hierarchy, as people streamed to the Jero Gede to participate in their ritual of ancestral deification.

Ritual has been compared to warfare in that it can open an arena in which events may go awry and chaos prevail (cf. Schulte Nordholt 1991:10). When you link such risk to this particular ritual happening at a time of upheaval in Indonesia and the dangers associated with a state of power vacuum, it becomes particularly obvious that many unpredictable forces were in motion. The stakes were high, but conversely, there was also much to gain. The arena opened through the combined risks of ritual and power vacuum is also one of potential. Leaders often must gamble to accentuate their power, as did the members of the Jero Gede Sidemen by setting out in the first place to perform such a ritual for which they would depend on so many people, and then by inviting dignitaries such as Habibie and Megawati to their local ritual. People from outside the area reacted to the news that these invitations had been sent with some astonishment, but generally put judgement aside to await the outcome. In the outcome, the Sidemen Maligya reestablished a local hierarchy, tied to a national hierarchy, with Sukarno's daughter, herself a presidential candidate, at the apex.[4] So in Sidemen,

---

4. Cf. the role of claiming connection to Majapahit: Now there is a parallel claim of connection to national leaders; that is, to Sukarno and Megawati, albeit that the direction of connection is inverted. In the past, Bali's leaders came from the Empire (Majapahit),

the maligya ritual launched the princedom into a position of greater renown. More than just a rite for the souls of the ancestors, it became a rite of status elevation. As symbolized in the keris, it was the mobilization of visible and invisible forces in connection with the ritual that ultimately brought into relief the hierarchical system and the power of the Jero Gede Sidemen and its princedom.

Revival and Escalation versus Reformist Trends in Ritual

As a consequence of colonial rule there was, along with a decline in the negara, a decline in the performance of large-scale rituals, such that toward the middle of the twentieth century, Balinese nobles, some of whom were reinstated as rajas, no longer were able to fulfill the responsibilities of staging state rituals on behalf of the realm. As Geertz pointed out, "these newly bureaucratized lords found themselves in the position of continuing to expect (and to be expected by the populace) to hold the theatre-state rituals, but without the political institution by which the task had previously been accomplished" (1980:255). By 1964, Geertz noted a growing sentiment that rituals might be irrelevant to modern life. Boon, too, drew attention to "this budding attitude of reformism—championed by the urban, elite Parisada organization [an organization that establishes doctrine for Indonesian Hindu religious practices], many of whose members are Brahmana" (1977:217). Linda Connor, more recently (1996), has discussed the rationalization and simplification of death rites in particular, and it is a discussion that continues to be heard throughout Bali. In the context of the maligya ritual as well, some reformist minded Balinese did indeed point out that from the perspective of the ancestors' souls the maligya ritual is redundant. Thus one Brahmana (not a consecrated priest and not related to any of the priestly houses in Sidemen) said outright: "maligya rituals are unnecessary. If they already have had the cremation and the souls are purified, and there strictly is not more to be done, why still have the maligya ritual" (Ida Bagus Rai)? Even Tjokorda Gede Dangin agrees that from a technical perspective on the journey of the soul, this is true.

And, yet, many Balinese appear to believe that the ceremonies are about ensuring a better place in heaven for their forefathers. They know that ultimately it is karma that determines this, but, as one woman put it, it is like haggling

---

now the leaders of the Empire (the Nation) come from Bali—and this gives them legitimacy. Bali's new leaders, in turn, of course also derive legitimacy from their connection to these national figures.

with God on their behalf ["tawar menawar dengan tuhan"] in the event that you might be able to secure them a better outcome. This brings to mind again the notion of bartering with the lord and, more apropos, the story of Bima's journey to hell and heaven, which was performed with shadow puppetry at the maligya ritual. Here a living descendant—granted a very powerful semi-divine living descendant—is able to fight first demons to release parental souls from hell, then take on gods to gain them the elixir of life (*amertha*), after which they no longer boil in hell, but, fully purified, can enter heaven. Cokorda Raka has no doubt but that "all people would try to put on a big ceremony for their ancestors if they could," largely to help secure them a better reincarnation; "it is the expense that is difficult." Referring to the *Babad Kayu Manis,* Cokorda Pemangku tells a story from the Majapahit Maligya:

> There was this minister [*patih*] who asked, is it really true that my ancestors will find heaven if I perform this ritual for them? The priest that was present answered, if you need proof in order to believe, please go over there. Sit there and concentrate, like an ascetic. So he sat there, under the fish and the like [*kenara kenari*], like the ones at the [ancestral platform for the Sidemen Maligya]. And then a heavenly voice [*suara akasa*] came to him, a voice from the invisible sphere [*suara gaib*]: "All of your ancestors have made it to heaven." Only then did he believe. And it was not just he that heard it, everyone else present heard it too. That is why people believe. A maligya truly will get the souls of your ancestors to heaven.

Cokorda Pemangku adds that "My ancestor, Dalem Ketut, brought this ceremony to Bali," in other words, as he did the keris, which he was given at precisely such a ceremony.

> In his own case, says Raka, having completed the maligya ritual has made him "feel at peace."

> I have fulfilled my obligations to my ancestors and I can already place my ancestors in heaven. This is a question of religious sentiment. It is very Hindu....Before I still felt burdened, it was something that I always thought about. Now, not so anymore. I feel contented, knowing that my father, my mother, my grandmother, that they all already are there. It is difficult to explain it.

This echoes the emotion attributed to the descendants performing the fourteenth-century maligya ritual at Majapahit, the *Shradda* ceremony, as described in the *Nagarakertagama* manuscript:

"The princes felt relieved and serene when the celebration was over,
nothing disturbed their thoughts —" (Robson 1995:74, canto 67, 3).

It seems to hold that the trends to which Geertz and Boon rightly drew our
attention have not really taken off. Two to three decades later, ceremonies are,
if anything, on the increase. In 1998, there was still considerable controversy,
resulting in newspaper debates, when a member of the Amlapura royal family who had been married to a Dutch woman and had spent much of his working career abroad, gave his deceased wife only a small crematorium cremation. Shortly after this, he (an elderly man) officially joined a neighborhood
organization (*banjar*) in Amlapura, though he has not lived there since he was
very young. Locally, people were convinced at the time that he had found, in
dealing with his wife's death ceremonies, that he needed them after all, that
without that most local support of his people, even he, a person of royal descent and international reputation, was lost.

By contrast to the erosion of ceremony in the colonial and immediate postcolonial eras, the end of the twentieth century found not only modern Balinese, but also more Balinese holding even larger and even more splendid ceremonies than ever before. It used to be said that if one encountered a maligya
ritual eleven times in a lifetime, the karmic benefit gained would be equivalent to having undergone the ceremony oneself. Ramseyer, in 1977, also based
in the Karangasem area, wrote of these "last and most expensive stages of the
purification of the soul" as being "rarely performed, and often only after several decades" (179). At Griya Ulah in Sidemen, in 2000, they still do not think
anyone could ever achieve attending eleven maligya rituals; but to others it is
obvious that inflation has been happening, even just over the past decade, and
that this no longer is necessarily an impossible feat.[5] Not only were many Balinese by the end of the twentieth century, with an overall healthier economy
than ever and an atmosphere of cultural reassertion, staging large-scale rituals again; even during the Asian financial crisis, "the krisis moneter" as it was
referred to locally, it was joked that in Bali, if there is a ceremony, there is no
financial crisis ["Di Bali, kalau ada upacara, tidak ada krisis moneter"]. Picard notes, "One finds allusions in the press accusing the Balinese of holding
ever more spectacular ceremonies with the intention of impressing the tourists

---

5. I Dewa Gede Catra, a *lontar* specialist, who often is called on to read at such ceremonies, suggests that "it is first and foremost because of the economic factor, which is better than in earlier times. Secondly, the openness in the religious sector. People already have
acknowledgement from the government that the Hindu religion is on a par with other religions, and, moreover, the knowledge of the people in the area of religion is heightened.
These are the reasons why" (July 30, 2000).

rather than pleasing the gods..." (1997:195). In Sidemen, however, there was no hint at this ceremony being for the benefit of tourists, who were present only for one major day, the day also of the large sacrifice of animals, an assortment from all of Bali's habitats.

Among many it holds true, as one priest from a priestly house in Sidemen assessed: "If people have money, they will use it for God, for temple preservation and restoration, and, above all, for ceremonies" (Pedanda Tianyar). As it has been phrased by Sahlins, "The first commercial impulse of the people, is not to become just like us but more like themselves" (1993:17). Pedande Tianyar, a priest in Sidemen, pointed out that if the Jero Gede Sidemen were to have opted for a smaller ceremony, it would have been the people who would have judged them. "What can we do?" reflected another priest, "People want the big ceremonies. There is nothing we can do about that." (Of course it bears noting that the priests also depend on such ceremonies for their livelihood [cf. Connor 1996].)

Trends in Bali toward reformism also at the time were taken by Boon as an indication of the "potential rift between religious, economic, and political affairs," whereas in the past, "any bald conflict between sacred ceremonialism and other concerns was unlikely, since ritual provided the backdrop and often the realization of any political, economic, or otherwise pragmatic measure" (1977:216–217). While this kind of tension certainly does exist for Balinese today, the 1998 maligya ritual of the Jero Gede Sidemen testifies that even in contemporary Bali, at least in eastern Bali, there still are rituals in which these spheres come together. Picard has observed that in parts of Bali there has been a "deculturation of religion and erosion of the ritual function of the arts" (1997:197). As he says, the nationally promoted "showcase vision" of culture "does not acknowledge that which forms the core of a culture...and that which sustains the sense of identity of the participants of this culture" (1997:197). But in Bali there can also be something beyond the showcase, something of that which "forms the core" and "sustains the identity" that still exists, and recognizing this does not merely reflect a scholarly proclivity for viewing Bali as a "vaunt of resilience" (cf. Picard 1999:16). The ties of the Sidemen princedom at the foot of Mount Agung, historically and physically situated between Klungkung and Karangasem, may for some lay dormant until needed; and the ancestral ties, which bind it, can be forgotten until economic and political circumstances serve as reminders to potential participants in the princedom to "remember" it again. Then it, too, can be engaged with changing circumstances and discourses and is indeed linked to action in the world. In the end, the example of the traditional princedom and the role that it plays in the postcolonial era and at a time of historical transition addresses a key issue in the theory of globalization, namely how important indigenous political forms may be in the twenty-first century.

Indigenous Political Form in the Twenty-first Century

This study has shown that the changes resulting from colonization and modernization notwithstanding, the dynamics of the negara continue to some extent in contemporary Bali: Connection to invisible powers, the relationship between priests and rajas, the mobilization of people, the assumption of the role of prince in the princedom, the symbolism of royal heirloom keris, and the role of ritual. The extent to which old forms persist is denied by some, or seen merely as feudal remnant and indicative of premodern consciousness, lacking in rational reflection. But as others have argued (contra Max Weber and Anthony Giddens) reflexivity is not solely a characteristic of modernity, or incongruous with tradition and action according to custom. Jack Goody finds that while some things necessarily change slowly, such as language, this "is much less true of ritual and even less true of 'myth' in the sense of long recitations which [may...] vary greatly over time and space (1998:xviii). In his work with a genre of Ghanaian recitation, he documents such variation, "including in highly significant spheres like notions of the High God and of the creation of the world" (1998:xviii). He finds that "culture, precedent or even mental templates may lay down some vague parameters but within these boundaries, individual reciters speculate widely about the nature of super-natural beings and their relation with the universe," without, says Goody, ap-pearing "too constrained by past formulations of the problem" (1998:xviii). In the case of Sidemen, too, we see a creative use of the past in the present.

Voluntary participation as subjects in a hierarchical princedom is easily viewed as a lack of reflexivity and certainly as a lack of class-based conscious-ness on the part of the followers. Human rights activist Mulya Lubis, at a U.S. Indonesia Open Forum in Washington, D.C., expressed the common concern for the "culture of corruption" and "appalling condition" in Indonesia at large, which he fears will only get worse: "The institutional reform that has been at-tempted thus far is only aimed at the center. When decentralization gets un-derway and power shifts to the provinces and the regencies," he expects the "emergence of small kings and small conglomerates" as the corrupt system is disseminated (January 18 2001). Schulte Nordholt suggests a comparison with the Philippines, the political leadership of which has been referred to as "bossism," "characterized by a monopoly of political and economic means by local and regional strongmen, who maintain strategic relationships with the state," predicting that "large parts of decentralized Indonesia [will be...] ruled by political *preman*," a word that has come to designate a "trafficker in political violence" (2002:10). Similarly, many of the contributors to Robinson and Bessel's edited volume on issues of gender, equity, and development in post-Suharto Indonesia express concern that the devolution of power into local institutions will entail an erosion of human rights that have been gained through more centralized efforts (2002). These are all crucial concerns, and they are concerns I share. At the same time it seems important also to understand that there might, as argued here, be ways in which, for example, a modern princedom empowers people, by contrast to often not so empowering centralized institutions.

Through the collective work of the Sidemen Maligya, not only the Jero Gede Sidemen but also its followers acquired creative power, the ability to "spin the world." Transcending in many cases their everyday lives as rice farming peasants or *tuak* tappers, the final step in the ritual process is the apperception also of a more complex and powerful sense of selfhood on the part of the performers of the ritual, also with regard to the world beyond the valley. There is a sense that, with ties established and reinforced within and through the ritual, this has implications also for activities outside of the ritual. Thus, as has been proposed here, although people certainly in the modern era are gaining more power *within* their princedom, as lords cannot rule by force (though they still wield other forms of power), they also do so *through* their princedom. This, again, is how the increase in the powers of the people and the revitalization of princedoms might be coupled.

Once more, this is not a simple argument of cultural continuity. Certainly there is continuity—what is happening now is a variation of a strategy that is not necessarily a total break with precolonial Balinese kingship, as has been outright stated or implied by so many scholars. However devastating, all did not come to an end with *puputan*, the "fights to the finish," court massacres or mass sacrifices. One might speculate whether Sidemen's situation by virtue of being part of Karangasem is influenced by the fact that Karangasem did not confront the Dutch with a puputan. Things were in some ways "finished" less definitively in Karangasem, where a royal line was inserted by and cooperated with the Dutch and, as a result, were less directly ruled by the colonial government (Robinson 1995:25). It is frequently commented that Karangasem remains more conservative than other areas of Bali in terms of language use and other aspects of court culture. On the other hand, there was also heroism in confronting the

Dutch with puputan, which served to empower the kingdoms that chose that route, although those who survived of course were those who escaped the deadly confrontation. Alternatively, perhaps Sidemen gains in part from being situated between these courses of history: The Sidemen Princedom never was a major kingdom and had neither the shattering experience of the puputan as did Klungkung, nor the stigma, as does Karangasem, of having gained its position through the Dutch. Instead, the Jero Gede Sidemen had already been "discredited," as the present heirs put it, and remained an inconspicuous princedom; yet the princes have continued their efforts to, as they see it, fulfill their destiny.

The maligya ritual, the proximate purpose of which was to purify and deify ancestors of the royal house, also in the present gave shape to the princedom. In so doing, it yielded insights from the level of the princedom that apply to our existing understanding of the dynamics of Southeast Asian negara in Bali, while also revealing that these dynamics continue to play a role in twentieth- and twenty-first-century life and politics. In Bali, the ritual sphere has in the past been a site for positioning in relation to competing rajas and princes, to the colonial order, and now is so to the nation-state and globalizing world.[6] Even as scholars have gained recognition of the importance of ritual to nineteenth-century Balinese politics, not much attention has been paid to its significance since the mid-twentieth century. Yet, far from being separate from the world of politics, ritual remains an intrinsically political domain. It is a significant source of royal power and prestige in the community (and sometimes wider society) and a site where the princes and their followers, all nation-state subjects, can withstand state domination. In the modern princedom, furthermore, there is a self-conscious opposition of "tradition"—which is good and involves historical ties to ancestors—to all things "feudal"—which are bad and involve ties to a different kind of authority. In Sidemen, building on a continuation of their (traditional) power, there appears to be an ongoing attempt on behalf of the princes to construct a new vision of the negara for the future, a negara that can work for the people, even as it promotes the hereditary princes.

And so the princedom continues to have relevance. Tjokorda Gede Dangin has on several occasions made the point that it is better for him to operate within his traditional role than in an official one.

---

6. Note that although globalization has dispersed the princedom, it never was a bounded unit to begin with, and global interconnections also enables the princedom's participants to stay in touch and return home from afar—not just from Germany and Jakarta; improved communications locally allow also the people of northern Bali to "remember" Sidemen now.

I am much stronger through this. Because this way I often procure materials, I ask for assistance, I collaborate with friends from overseas. I can ask them to help me, talk about ideas for what I would like to improve....Ok, this cultural practice is supported; go ahead with this temple, etc. With this I have power. I do not need a lot of materials to be of support.

On the basis of a Balinese text (*Kidung Nderet*, a song about a crisis in the kingdom of Mengwi), in his article on "Leadership and the limits of political control: A Balinese 'Response' to Clifford Geertz," Schulte Nordholt—as we have heard participants in the princedom do—emphasizes the important role of "remembering:"

> One of the central themes of the kidung is that the negara rested in the very first place on personal bonds of loyalty between the center and its satellites, and between the leader and his followers. In order to maintain these relationships they had to be remembered, and commemorated, in texts, in temples, on the battlefields, and in rituals. Underlying the ritual enactment of the negara was a complex and hierarchical network of loyalties which had to be preserved and reinforced by visible leaders who were to be trusted. Perhaps the most important political activity of these leaders was to remember. The moral lesson of the kidung is that it shows what happens if a leader starts to forget: the negara simply falls apart. Remembrance formed one of the basis 'institutions' of the nineteenth-century Balinese negara" (1993:305).

Again, it is striking the extent to which the modern princedom resonates with what we have come to understand of the precolonial negara.

Cokorda Raka, toward the end of chapter 6, expressed confidence that the princedom would persist "as long as I always do right by them" (i.e. the followers), and this indeed involves the work of "remembering." Raka's view implies also that only if the Jero Gede Sidemen lets it will the system fall apart. This compares to a prevalent sentiment that it was local disintegration and weakness that allowed the Dutch to take over Klungkung in 1908, or allowed Karangasem to move into Sidemen in the eighteenth century.[7] While West-

---

7. The theme resurfaces again in Dwyer and Santikarma's recent analysis of the 1960s killings, for they state that "many Balinese believe that the strongest sparks of the violence were lit within their communities rather than by the translocal forces of the state or the political parties" (2003:305). As a result, "they believe that healing, if and when it comes, must be locally based" (2003:305).

ern scholars sometimes have the presumption to think that European colonizers were able to wipe out everything or, alternatively, to have been the defining shapers of everything that is now taken to be Balinese culture or tradition, it is remarkable that many Balinese do not see the "Other" as the all-powerful causal force in this history (see also Wiener 1995). It is in fact a theme in many Balinese stories that powerful people become vulnerable only after they, themselves, somehow—deliberately or inadvertently—take action to undo their invulnerabilty. Applying this to the situation of conquest does result in a feeling of being more in control of, or at least integral to, their own destiny than to think they were simply overpowered. Now, in the face of new pressures, Raka, as have others, points out that "the disposition of the Balinese is such that the more they are pressured, the stronger they will get." People frequently draw on the examples of Kuta or Sanur, so filled with tourists, to point out that, yet, their neighborhood association and temple systems only get stronger.

In the village of Sanggem, when asked if the princedom ties would keep going, people laughed that of course they would, for the elders would always pass these on. The young man who lives and works in Kuta explained: "I have a child, later I will tell that child, 'We are followers of the Jero Gede Sidemen.' Then when my child has a child, he will let him know again. That is how it is." And if there is a child that does not heed this? I wondered.

> O, it seems that, with the people of Bali, problems of ritual duty or having to do with family, it is as though this does not exist. It is sure that they will know....It is not possible to disregard your family like that...Take me. I work in Kuta. But every three months, maybe every two months, I definitely go to the Jero. That is how it is....The thing is that the Jero very much helps the people of Sanggem. Both with regard to money, for improvements of one sort or another, for example renovating the *gong* [instruments for the gamelan ensemble], and with everything else. We just have to complain a bit, complain to the Jero, and there will be help from the side of the Jero. And if there is a ceremony at the Jero, people from here will *ngayah* [perform ritual service].

And the ancestral ceremonies? Nobody doubts that they will continue. Again at Sanggem they expressed that "there is a fund of love...and there are always forefathers for whom there will not yet have been the requisite ceremonies."

What we see in Sidemen is partly the powerful position of the lords at the intermediary level. In the past, it was largely here that mobilization of manpower for greater rajas happened. But beyond this, the Jero Gede Sidemen claims the highest royal authority of all—direct descent from the rajas of Gelgel as well as possession of the foremost heirloom, Keris Bangawan Canggu. We have seen that the keris is considered to be an agent and even a ruler; yet that it would be empty symbolism were its powers not built and sustained through the Jero Gede Sidemen's means of working the people. In the great ritual of the maligya, all of the Jero Gede Sidemen's status claims and efforts at creating connections with people were given an arena in which to be played out.

In the past, the participants in a princedom mobilized for war as well as for ritual. In 1998, the participants in the Sidemen princedom mobilized for ritual. Their ritual mobilization helps create, for the participants, a sense of self, a sense of Balineseness and of a place in the larger picture, both vis-a-vis the Indonesian nation and vis-a-vis the rest of the world, representatives from both of which were drawn in to participate as witnesses of the ritual. With the ritual as a facilitator, the Sidemen princedom also mobilized for elections, for Megawati as president and for the local election of a member of the Jero Gede Sidemen as village head. Although rulers in the past sought endorsement as embodiments of communal spirit rather than seeking popular election, the show of supporters for elections is not altogether different from how people sometimes previously were mobilized in the context of warring strife to be presented as a demonstration of human resources (cf. van der Kraan 1995 for examples of this toward the Dutch). And it remains that ritual mobilization of the princedom holds the possibility that the participants equally could do so for more traditionally recognized resistance, should conditions come to construe an unacceptable and otherwise overpowering threat. Indeed, we have already seen the power of the notion of possibility, the possibility that subjects could be sold as slaves or, conversely, that subjects could *matilas* (change lords) or disrupt the soul's journey toward reincarnation.

The Sidemen Maligya is one example of how ritual and agents of traditional power can be involved in times of crisis. This does not mean that this necessarily is how they would be so at any time, nor should we expect the followers at all times to express their roles as subjects. As political options have opened up in Indonesia since Suharto's fall, with a profusion of political parties, there has been conflict within the area of Sidemen, too, surrounding who and what to support, including whether to follow the lead of the Jero Gede Sidemen or not. This is nothing new to the princedom, which has been through many crises, through policies and historical developments that threatened to sever the lord-follower ties. Princes do not just automatically continue to have followers. But, as Indonesia under the presidency of Megawati progressed with decentralization legislation, the Jero Gede Sidemen, in fact continued to take a leadership role locally (Pedersen 2004). At the time of writing, Tjokorda Gede Dangin is, as he puts it, mobilising neighbourhood organizations in the area to work out ways of meeting the new decentralization laws on the local area's own terms, so they already have a plan in place before the regional administration itself gets any further in implementing the law (Pedersen 2004). The people of Sidemen involved in the project even envision themselves as trailblazers for other areas of Bali in this regard. At the same time, Dangin is working with farmers' organizations in attempts to return to more organic farming. And he has other projects going as well, continuing to fulfil his role as leader of his people (Pedersen 2004).

World Renewal

Through these chapters, a combined theme of fertility and power has wound, like the snake of the keris, the cosmic object that embodies both male and female characteristics, the symbol that binds together the realm. The ritual of the maligya is about the recycling of souls and regeneration at all levels of existence. At the inception of the princedom, the Jero Gede Sidemen gave land to the followers, and the followers realized its fertile potential into rice fields and salak plantations. When the village of Kebung was about to die out, it was the Jero Gede Sidemen that provided them a fertile woman. The princes of the Jero Gede Sidemen summon gods to the village temple and pray for fertility on behalf of the realm. And the phallus of their keris, an embodiment of the female symbol of the serpent, conferred legitimacy upon Megawati, Indonesia's female President, who herself, empowered as she is by the ancestral spirit of her father, in a way is double gendered, uniting male and female elements in a productive way.

Through the elucidation of the princedom in the preceding chapters, we have seen that there is an emphasis on the ruler connected to the Keris Bangawan Canggu to be a ruler with powers of attraction and to be a ruler that heals and mediates differences in the realm. There are themes throughout also of mutuality productive of the relationship between the palace and its followers, and we have seen that there have been ongoing accommodations through time between princes and people. The princedom persists in part also because it was and is not an autocracy, but continues to manifest many of the characteristics of early Southeast Asian negara, both symbolically and practically. The belief system is still there, belief in the continued need to maintain relationships with ancestors and in the impact of the invisible on the visible world. There is still faith and the symbolism still appeals. There was and is also a good deal of local autonomy for villagers, who work for their raja when needed, especially for ceremonies, but who also, when called upon, may go to the election booth, and, in the past, would go to war—as, say some, they potentially would again.

In the end, a maligya ritual is said to be fertile for the negara and the world, to bring it prosperity and happiness. Cokorda Sawitri concludes,

> for every yadnya ceremony, the goal is not just for those putting it on, but actually for the whole world, for the harmony of the world. You saw that, earlier [at payadnyan, at the closure of the maligya ritual], we found a sprouting coconut [makes a motion with her hand from her lap up, as the movement of a growth, a sprouting]. What is the story of this? With that coconut, if it is planted, we will have another coconut tree. This is symbolic of the maligya ritual.[8]

---

8. See Strathern and Stewart (1999:9) for analysis of a female spirit cult performance in Papua New Guinea, where special seedlings are planted as a part of the ritual, representing the cult's aim of ensuring health and fertility.

GLOSSARY

Adat	Custom. Also referred to as tradition.
Anak Agung	A ruling class/noble title. Title for kings.
Are	A unit of land. One hundred *are* equal one acre.
Arya	Title for nobles who came to Bali during the Majapahit era. Now a clan prefix used by clans of all varna.
Awig-Awig	Customary law.
Bagawanta	Also purowita. A Brahmana priest in ritual service to a lord, especially a paramount lord.
Babad	Historical narrative.
Bali Aga	Mountain Balinese, considered the "original people of Bali," who resisted Indic court culture.
Balai	Also balé. Open sided pavillion.
Balian	Spirit medium, healer.
Banjar	Neighborhood organization.
Betara/betari	God, deity (masculine/feminine).
Bhuta kala	Demons, chthonic forces.
Brahmana	One of the four varna. Priestly caste.
Bu	See Ibu.
Bupati	Government head of regency.
Cokorda	Also Tjokorda. A ruling class/noble title. Paramount lord, "king."
Corvee	Physical labor duties to the Dutch colonial administration.
Dadia	Kin group.

Dalem	Title of Bali's paramount kings. Believed descended from Kapakisan, the first Javanese king to Bali.
Dangin	Name of the head of the Sidemen Noble House.
Desa	Village.
Dewa	God. High caste title.
Dewa Agung	Kingly title, usually of Klungkung's king.
Gajah Mada	Chief minister of Majapahit who conquered Bali.
Gelgel	Bali's central kingdom, fourteenth to seventeenth centuries.
Golkar	Political party, government party under Suharto.
Griya	Priestly compound.
Gusti	High caste title, lesser ksatria or wesia.
Hayum Wuruk	Emperor of fourteenth century Javanese empire.
Ibu	Mother. Polite address of older or more highly positioned women. Also Bu.
I Dewa Gede	High caste title, ksatria.
Jaba	"Outsiders;" those who "do not have caste" (Sudra, commoners).
Jero Gede	Noble house.
Kaja	Upstream, north.
Kakawin	Sanskrit metered epic poem.
Kapakisan	The first Javanese king to Bali. Dynasty of Bali's foremost rulers.
Kawi	Old Javanese, poetic language.
Kepala Desa	Village head.
Keris	Long dagger, often with an undulating blade. Some are heirlooms; some are considered magical. Also kris.
Kesaktian	Power. The basis of charisma. See also sakti.
Kidung	Uses more complex metres and a different form of kawi than kakawin.
Ksatria	One of the four varna, high caste of rulers.
Ksatria Dalem	Royal Ksatria.
Lingga	Effigy representing ancestor; used for the maligya ritual.

Lontar	Palm whose dried leaves may be incised; manuscripts.
Lurah	Village chief
Majapahit	Fourteenth century Javanese empire, including Java and parts of Sumatra and other Indonesian Islands. A Javanese court poet claimed that his ruler " 'protected' most of mainland Southeast Asia."
Maligya	Postcremation ceremony to purify and deify deceased ancestors.
Mandala	Hindu-Buddhist magical cosmological scheme or geometric composition of satellites surrounding a powerful center; image for the negara as a fluid polity.
Merajaan	High caste family temple.
Memasyarakat	Mingle and connect with people; work for the people.
Naga	Dragon-serpent from Hindu mythology. Also naga pasa.
Negara	Southeast Asian state form, "kingdom."
New Order	Political era under President Suharto. Coined to replace the old "chaotic" order of President Sukarno.
Ngayah	Perform ritual labor/service. Connotes making an effort, doing one's best. Must involve no cash transactions/ remunerations.
Ngayahan ke dalem	Palace service. In the past included war.
Niskala	Invisible, immaterial world.
Odalan	Celebration of the founding of a temple (every Balinese year; i.e. six months).
Pacatu	Land given by lord for followers to farm in return for palace service.
Padmasana	Lotus seat, shrine.
Pande	Title name for subcaste of smiths. Elevated sudra.
Parisada	Administrative council of Bali-Hindu religion.
Pasek	Title name for an elevated sudra subcaste, village leaders.
Patih	Chief minister.
Payadnyan	Ritual site for the maligya, located away from the noble house.

PDI	Indonesian Democratic Party.
PDI-P	Indonesian Democratic Party of Struggle.
Pedande	Consecrated Brahmana priest.
Pemangku	Non-Brahmana priest.
Perbekel	District head. Usually below punggawa.
PKI	Indonesian Communist Party.
Punggawa	Lord of the realm.
Puri	Palace.
Pusaka	Heirloom regalia.
Puputan	"The finish," "the ending." Mass court sacrifice in the face of imminent defeat. Most notorious are the early twentieth-century puputan of two southern Balinese courts in preference to being seized by the Dutch, but puputan occurred in the face of non-European enemies as well.
Pura	Temple.
Pura Dalem	Village temple dedicated to chthonic forces.
Pura Desa	Village temple.
Pura Puseh	Main village temple.
Purowita	Also bagawanta. A Brahmana priest in ritual service to a lord, especially a paramount lord.
Raja	"King."
Rangda	Fierce female aspect of Siwa, Siwa's consort, "Queen of Witches."
Saka	Balinese year, i.e., Indic solar/lunar year, 78 years behind the Gregorian calendar. Also Caka.
Sakti	Powerful; associated with good relationships to the supernatural realm and with the possession of powerful objects/heirloom regalia. See also kesaktian.
Sang Hyang	Also Dang Hyang. Title of deity.
Sawah	Irrigated rice.
Sekala	Visible, material world.
Shradda	Death rite in the ancient Majapahit empire, like the maligya.

Siwa	One of the three primary manifestations of the supreme god; the destroyer (the other two are Brahma, the creator, and Wisnu, the preserver).
Subak	Association of irrigation farmers.
Suci	Pure, section of the family temple purified for ritual preparations.
Suda mala	Lit. good-bad, or cleansed from stain and impurity, purifying and healing. Another name for the Sidemen keris, a.k.a. Bangawan Cangguh.
Sudra	One of the four varna, commoners.
Surya/sisya	Teacher/pupil. Surya = sun.
Tjokorda	See Cokorda.
Triwangsa	the "twice born;" those "who have caste" (Brahmana, Ksatria, or Wesia).
Varna	Four major caste groups, Sudra, Wesia, Ksatria, Brahmana.
Wesia	One of the four varna, merchants and lesser nobility, i.e. gustis.

REFERENCES

Adas, Michael. 1981. "From Avoidance to Confrontation: Peasant Protest in Precolonial and Colonial Southeast Asia." *Comparative Studies in Society and History* 23: 217–47.

Adelaar, K. Alexander. 1997. "An Exploration of Directional Systems in West Indonesia and Madagascar." In Gunther Senft (ed), *Referring to Space: Studies in Austronesian and Papuan Languages*. Oxford: Oxford University Press.

Agung, Anak Agung Gde. 1991. *Bali in the 19th Century*. Jakarta: Yayasan Obor Indonesia.

Agung, Anak Agung Ketut. 1991. *Kupu Kupu Kuning Yang Terbang di Selat Lombok*. Bali: Upada Sastra.

Alexander, Bobby C. 1991. *Victor Turner Revisited: Ritual as Social Change*. Oxford: Oxford University Press.

Ananta Toer, Pramoedya. 1999. "He Gave Unity to Indonesia, Dignity to the Downtrodden and Anxiety to the Powerful, Who Finally Brought Him Down." *Time Asia* 100: August 23–30, Vol. 154 No. 7/8.

Anderson, Benedict. 1972. "The Idea of Power in Javanese Culture." In C. Holt, ed. *Culture and Politics in Indonesia*. Ithaca: Cornell University Press.

Appadurai, Arjun. (ed), 1986. "Is Homo Hierarchicus?" *American Ethnologist* 13(4) 745–761.

Ardika, I. W., and Peter Bellwood. 1991. "1991 Sembiran: The Beginnings of Indian Contact with Bali." *Antiquity* 65: 221–232.

———. 1997. "Sembiran and the First Indian Contacts with Bali: an update." *Antiquity* 71:193–195.

Asmaudi, Nuryana, and Putu Wirata Dwikora. 1999. "'Parade Monolog 1999' Rangda Ini Dirah Itu Kambing Hitam Politik? *Bali Post* 5 September.

Aspinall, Ed. 1996. "What Happened Before the Riots?" *Inside Indonesia* no. 48 October–December.

———. 1997. "What Price Victory? The 1997 Elections. *Inside Indonesia* no. 51 July–September.

Aung Thwin, Michael. 1983. "Athi, Kyun-Taw, Hpayà-Kyun: Varieties of Commendation and Dependence in Pre-Colonial Burma." In A. J. S. Reid (ed), 1983. *Slavery, Bondage and Dependency in Southeast Asia*. New York: St. Martin's Press.

Barth, Fredrik. 1993. *Balinese Worlds*. Chicago: University of Chicago Press.

Baso, Zohra, and Nurul Ilmi Idrus 2002. "Women's Activism against Violence in South Sulawesi." In Kathryn Robinson and Sharon Bessel (eds), *Women in Indonesia: Gender, Equity and Development*. Singapore: Institute of Southeast Asian Studies.

Bateson, Gregory. 1970a [1937]. "An Old Temple and a New Myth." In Jane Belo (ed), *Traditional Balinese Culture*. New York: Columbia University Press.

———. 1970b [1963]. "Bali: The Value System of a Steady State." In Jane Belo (ed), *Traditional Balinese Culture*. New York: Columbia University Press.

Bateson, Gregory, and Margaret Mead. 1972 [1942]. *Balinese Character: A Photographic Analysis*. New York: New York Academy of Sciences.

Belo, Jane. 1953. *Bali: Temple Festival*. American Ethnological Society Monographs, 22. New York: J.J. Augustin.

———. 1970 [1937]. *Traditional Balinese Culture*. New York: Columbia University Press.

Birkelbach, A. W., Jr. 1973. "The Subak Association." *Indonesia* 16:154–169.

Bloch, Maurice. 1986. *From Blessing to Violence: History and Ideology in the Circumcision Ritual of the Merina of Madagascar*. Cambridge: Cambridge University Press.

———. 1989. *Ritual, History and Power: Selected Papers in Anthropology*. London: Athlone Press.

Boon, James. 1977. *The Anthropological Romance of Bali: Dynamic Perspectives in Marriage & Caste, Politics and Religion*. Cambridge: Cambridge University Press.

Bourdieu, Pierre. [1977] 1979. *Outline of a Theory of Practice*. Cambridge: Cambridge University Press.

———. 1991. *Language and Symbolic Power*. Cambridge: Harvard University Press.

Bowen, John R. 1986. "On the Political Construction of Tradition: Gotong Royong in Indonesia." *Journal of Asian Studies*. 45 (May): 545–561.

Brenneis, Donald. 2003. "Reflections: Toward New Conceptions of Rights." In C. Zerner, (ed), *Culture and the Question of Rights*. Durham: Duke University Press.

Brenner, Suzanne A. 1998. *The Domestication of Desire: Women, Wealth, and Modernity in Java*. Princeton: Princeton University Press.

Brinkgreve, Francine. 1981. "Maligia: Zuiveringsceremonie op Bali." *Veere Naasten Naderbij*. Leiden, Rijksmuseum voor Volkenkunde, 15, 2: 29–41.

———. 1996 [1992]. *Offerings: The Ritual Art of Bali*. Sanur: Image Network Indonesia.

Christie, Jan Wisseman. 1986. "Negara, Mandala, and Despotic State: Images of Early Java," in David G. Marr and A.C. Milner (eds.), *Southeast Asia in the 9th to 14th Centuries*. Singapore: Institute of Southeast Asian Studies Singapore.

Claessen, H.J.M. 2000. "Ideology, Leadership and Fertility: Evaluating a Model of Polynesian Chiefship." *Bijdragen tot de Taal-, Land, en Volkenkunde* 156–4: 707–735.

Coedès, G. 1937–1966. *Les Inscriptions du Cambodge*, 8 vols. Paris: Editions de Boccard.

———. 1968 [1965]. *The Indianized States of Southeast Asia*. In Walter F. Vella, (ed.), Honolulu: East-West Center Press.

Colombijn, Freek. 2002. "Maling, Maling! The Lynching of Petty Criminals." In Colombijn, Freek. and J. T. Lindblad (eds.), *Roots of Violence in Indonesia*. Leiden: KITLV Press.

Colombijn, Freek, and J. Thomas Lindblad (eds.), 2002. *Roots of Violence in Indonesia*. Leiden: KITLV Press.

Comaroff, Jean. 1985. *Body of Power; Spirit of Resistance*. Chicago: Chicago University Press.

Connor, Linda. 1979. "Corpse Abuse and Trance in Bali: The Cultural Mediation of Aggression," *Mankind* 12: 104–18.

———. 1996. "Contesting and Transforming the Work for the Dead in Bali: The Case of Ngaben Ngirit." In Adrian Vickers, (ed), *Being Modern In Bali: Image and Change*. Monograph 43. Yale Southeast Asia Studies.

Covarrubias, Miguel. 1972 [1946, 1937]. *Bali*. Kuala Lumpur: Oxford University Press.

Creese, Helen. 1991. "Balinese Babad as Historical Sources: A Reinterpretation of the Fall of Gelgel." *Bijdragen tot de Taal-, Land, en Volkenkunde* 147: 236–60.

———. 1995 "Chronologies and Chronograms: An Interim Response to Hägerdal." *Bijdragen tot de Taal-, Land, en Volkenkunde* 151: 125–131.

———. 1997. "New Kingdoms, Old Concerns: Balinese Identities in the Eighteenth and Nineteenth Centuries" in Anthony Reid, (ed), *The Last Stand of Autonomous States, 1750–1870. Responses to Modernity in the Diverse Worlds of Southeast Asia and Korea*. Basingstoke: McMillan

———. 2000. "In Search of Majapahit: The Transformation of Balinese Identities." In Adrian Vickers and I Nyoman Darma Putra (eds.), with Michele Ford, *To Change Bali*. Denpasar: Bali Post.

Cribb, Robert (ed.). 1990. *The Indonesian Killings. Studies from Java and Bali*. Clayton: Monash Southeast Asia Program.

Dalton, Bill. 1997. *Bali Handbook*. Second Edition. Chico, California: Moon Publications.

Dian, Intan Ungaling. 2000. "Kala 'Calon Arang' Gugat Pembelokan Sejarah," *Kompas*, 28 November.

van Dijk, Kees. 2002. "The Good, the Bad and the Ugly." In Freek Colombijn and J. Thomas Lindblad (eds.), *Roots of Violence in Indonesia*. Leiden: KITLV Press.

Dirks, Nicholas B. 1987. *The Hollow Crown: Ethnohistory of an Indian Kingdom*. Cambridge: Cambridge University Press.

———. 1994. "Ritual and Resistance: Subversion as Social Fact." In Nicholas Dirks, Geoff Eley, and Sherry B. Ortner (eds.), *Culture/ Power/ History*. NJ: Princeton University Press.

———. 1995. "The Conversion of Caste: Location, Translation, and Appropriation." In Peter van der Veer (ed), *Conversion to Modernities*. N.Y.: Routledge.

———. 1993. *Castes of Mind: Colonialism and the Making of Modern India*. Princeton: Princeton University Press.

Djelantik, Anak Agung M. 1997. *The Birthmark: Memoirs of a Balinese Prince*. Singapore: Periplus Editions.

Douaire-Marsaudon, Françoise. 1998. *Les Premier Fruits; Parenté, Identité Sexuelle et Pouvoirs en Polynésie Occidentale (Tonga, Wallis et Furuna)*. Paris: Editions de la Maison Sciences de L'Homme.

Dubois, Pierre. 1837. *Rapport aan den Heere Directeur van's—Lands Producten en Civiele Magazijnen, Besoeki, 9 Maart 1837. Kol. 4247*. The Hague: Algemeen Rijksarchief.

Dumont, Louis. 1980 [1972]. *Homo Hierarchicus*. London: Paladin.

Durkheim, Emile. [1893, 1912]. 1954. *Elementary Forms of Religious Life*. Illinois: Free Press.

van Duuren, David. 1998 [1996]. *The Kris: An Earthly Approach to a Cosmic Symbol*. Wijk en Aalburg, the Netherlands: Pictures Publishers.

Dwyer, Leslie, and Degung Santikarma. 2003. "'When the World Turned to Chaos:' 1965 and Its Aftermath in Bali, Indonesia." In Robert Gellaty and Ben Kiernan (eds.), *The Specter of Genocide: Mass Murder in Historical Perspective*. Cambridge: Cambridge University Press.

Eiseman, Fred B., Jr. 1990. *Bali: Sekala and Niskala Vol 1: Essays on Religion, Ritual, and Art*. Singapore: Periplus Editions.

Eklof, Stefan. 1999. "Megamania!" *Inside Indonesia*. No. 57. January–March.

Errington, Shelly. 1983. "The Place of Regalia in Luwu." In L. Gesick, (ed.), *Centers, Symbols, and Hierarchies: Essays on the Classical states of Southeast Asia*. New Haven: Yale University, Southeast Asia Studies. Monograph Series 26.

Foucault, Michel. 1979. *Discipline and Punish: The Birth of the Prison*. New York: Vintage Books.

———. 1980. *Knowledge/Power: Selected Interviews and Other Writings*. New York: Pantheon.

Fox, James (ed.). 1980. *The Flow of Life*. Harvard: Harvard University Press.

———. 1997. *The Poetic Power of Place: Comparative Perspectives on Austronesian Ideas of Locality*. Canberra: The Australian National University.

Francillon, Gérard. 1980. "Incursions upon Wehali: A Modern History of an Ancient Empire." In James Fox (ed), *The Flow of Life*. Harvard: Harvard University Press.

Fried, Stephanie. 2003. "Writing for Their Lives: Bentian Dayak Authors and Indonesian Development Discourse." In C. Zerner, (ed), *Culture and the Question of Rights*. Durham: Duke University Press.

Geertz, Clifford. 1973a [1966]. "Person, Time, and Conduct in Bali." In *The Interpretation of Cultures*. New York: Basic Books.

———. 1973b. "Notes on the Balinese Cockfight." In *The Interpretation of Cultures*. New York: Basic Books.

———. 1976. *The Religion of Java*. Chicago: Chicago University Press.

———. 1980. *Negara: The Theatre State in Nineteenth Century Bali*. Princeton: Princeton University Press.

———. 2003. Comment to "The Precolonial Balinese State Reconsidered," by Hauser-Schäublin 2003. *Current Anthropology* Volume 44, Number 2, April.

Geertz, Clifford, and Hildred Geertz 1975. *Kinship in Bali*. Chicago: The University of Chicago Press.

Geertz, Hildred. 1959. "The Balinese Village." In G.W. Skinner (ed.), *Local, Ethnic, and National Loyalties in Village Indonesia*. New Haven: Yale University Southeast Asia Studies.

van Gennep, Arnold. 1960 [1908]. *The Rites of Passage*. Chicago: Chicago University Press.

Gesick, Lorraine (ed.). 1983. *Centers, Symbols and Hierarchies; Essays on the Classical States of Southeast Asia*. New Haven: Yale University, Southeast Asia Studies. Monograph Series 26.

Gluckman, Max. 1954. *Rituals of Rebellion in South-East Africa*. Manchester: Manchester University Press.

———. 1955. *Custom and Conflict in Africa*. Oxford: Blackwell Press.

———. 1965. *Politics, Law and Ritual in Tribal Society*. Chicago: Aldine Publishing Company.

Godelier, Maurice, and Marilyn Strathern. 1995. *Big Men and Great Men: Personification of Power in Melanesia*. Cambridge: Cambridge University Press.

Goody, Jack. 2002. *The Third Bagre*. Durham: Carolina Academic Press.

Goris, Roelof. 1954. *Prasasti Bali*. 2 vols. Bandung.

———. 1960. "The Religious Character of the Village Community." In J. L. Swellengrebel (ed.), *Bali: Studies in Life, Thought and Ritual*. The Hague: W. van Hoeve.

————. 1969 [1939]. "The Decennial Festival in theVillage of Selat." In J. L. Swellengrebel, (ed.), *Bali: Studies in Life, Thought, and Ritual,* pp. 113–130. The Hague: W. van Hoeve.

Gramsci, Antonio. 1971. *Selections from the Prison Notebooks.* New York: International Publishers.

Grimes, Barbara D. 1997 "Knowing Your Place: Representing Relations of Precedence and Origin on the Buru Landscape." In James Fox (ed.), *The Poetic Power of Place: Comparative Perspectives on Austronesian Ideas of Locality.* Canberra: The Australian National University.

Guermonprez, Jean-François. 1989. "Dual Sovereignty in Nineteenth-Century Bali." *History and Anthropology* Vol. 4: 189–207.

1990. "On the Elusive Balinese Village: Hierarchy and Values Versus Political Models." *Review of Indonesian and Malaysian Affairs* 24:55–89.

Gullick, J. M. 1958. *Indigenous Political Systems of Western Malaya.* London: Athlone Press.

Hagesteijn, Renee. 1989. *Circle of Kings: Political Dynamics in Early Continental Southeast Asia.* Dordrecht and Providence: Foris Publications.

Hall, D. G. E. 1984. *A History of Southeast Asia.* New York: St. Martin's Press.

Hara, Minoru. 1973. "The King as a Husband of the Earth (mahi-pati)." *Asiatische Studien* 27: 2.

Hatley, Barbara. 2002. "Literature, Mythology and Regime Change: Some Observations on Recent Indonesian Women's Writing." In Kathryn Robinson and Sharon Bessel (eds.), *Women in Indonesia: Gender, Equity and Development.* Singapore: Institute of Southeast Asian Studies.

Hauser-Schäublin, Brigitta. 1997. *Traces of Gods and Men: Temples and Rituals as Landmarks of Social Events and Processes in a South Bali Village.* Berlin: Dietrich Reimer.

————. 2003. "The Precolonial Balinese State Reconsidered: A Critical Evaluation of Theory Construction on the Relationship between Irrigation, the State, and Ritual." *Current Anthropology* Vol. 44, Nr. 2, April.

Heine-Geldern, Robert. 1956 [1942]. *Conceptions of State and Kingship in Southeast Asia.* Data Paper: Number 18. Ithaca, New York: Southeast Asia Program, Cornell University.

Hicks, David. 1984. *A Maternal Religion: The Role of Women in Tetum Myth and Ritual.* Illinois: Center for Southeast Asian Studies.

Hobart, Angela, Urs Ramseyer and Albert Leemann. 1996. *The Peoples of Bali.* UK/USA: Blackwell Publishers.

Hobart, Mark. 1978. "The Path of the Soul: The Legitimacy of Nature in Balinese Conceptions of Space." In G. B. Milner (ed.), *Natural Symbols in Southeast Asia.* London: School of Oriental and African Studies.

————. 1979. *A Balinese Village and Its Field of Social Relations.* Ph.D. Diss., University of London: School of Oriental and African Studies.

————. 1990. "Who Do You Think You Are? The Authorized Balinese." In Fardon, (ed), *Localizing Strategies: Regional Traditions of Ethnographic Writing.* Edinburgh: Scottish Academic Press.

Holmberg, David. 2000 "Derision, Exorcism, and the Ritual Production of power." *American Ethnologist* Vol. 27, nr. 4.

Hooker, Virginia (ed.). 1993. *Culture and Society in New Order Indonesia.* Kuala Lumpur: Oxford University Press.

Hooykaas, C. 1973. *Kama and Kala: Materials for the Study of the Shadow Theatre in Bali.* Amsterdam.

————. 1977. *A Balinese Temple Festival.* The Hague: Nijhoff.

Hoskins, Janet. 1993. *The Play of Time: Kodi Perspectives on Calendars, History and Exchange.* Berkeley: University of California Press.

————. 1998. *Biographical Objects: How Things Tell the Stories of People's Lives.* New York: Routledge.

Hough, Brett. 1999. "Education for the Performing Arts: Contesting and Mediating Identity in Contemporary Bali." In Raechelle Rubenstein and Linda Connor (eds.), *Staying Local in the Global Village.* Hawai'i: Hawai'i University Press.

Howe, Leo. 1987. "Caste in Bali and India: Levels of Comparison." In L. Holy (ed.), *Comparative Anthropology.* Oxford: Basil Blackwell.

————. 1991. "Rice, Ideology, and the Legitimation of Hierarchy in Bali." *Man* (N.S.) 26, 445–467.

————. 1995. *Status Mobility in Contemporary Bali: Continuities and Change.* University of Hull. Centre for South-East Asian Studies.

————. 2000. "Risk, Ritual, and Performance." *Journal of the Royal Anthropological Institute.* (N.S.) 6: 63–79.

————. 2001. *Hinduism & Hierarchy in Bali.* New Mexico: School of American Research Press.

————. 2004. "Hinduism, Identity, and Social Conflict." In Martin Ramstedt (ed.), *Hinduism in Modern Indonesia: A Minority Religion Between Local, National, and Global Interests.* New York: Routledge Curzon.

Hägerdal, Hans. 1995a. "Bali in the Sixteenth and Seventeenth Centuries: Suggestions for a Chronology of the Gelgel Period." *Bijdragen tot de Taal-, Land, en Volkenkunde* 151: 101–124.

————. 1995b. Reply to Dr. Helen Creese. *Bijdragen tot de Taal-, Land, en Volkenkunde* 151: 292–93.

Jenkins, Ronald. 1994. *Subversive Laughter: The Liberating Power of Laughter.* New York: The Free Press.

Jessup, Helen I. 1990. *Court Arts of Indonesia*. New York: The Asia Society Galleries.

Kachru, Braj B. 1983. *The Indianization of English*. Oxford: Oxford University Press.

Kachru, Braj B. (ed.). 1982. The *Other Tongue*. Chicago: University of Illinois Press.

Kantorowicz, Ernst H. 1957. *The King's Two Bodies: A Study in Mediaeval Political Theology*. Princeton: Princeton University Press.

Karafet, Tatiana M., J.S. Lansing, Alan J. Redd, Joseph Watkins, I. W. Ardika, S.P.K. Surata, Laura Mayer, Michael Bamshad, Lynn Jorde, and Michael Hammer. In press. "A Balinese Y Chromosome Perspective on the Peopling of Indonesia: Genetic constributions from pre-Neolithic hunter-gatherers, Austronesian farmers, and Indian traders." *Human Biology*.

Keane, Webb. 1997. *Signs of Recognition: Powers and Hazards of Representation in an Indonesian Society*. Berkeley: University of California Press.

Kipp, Rita Smith. 1993. *Dissociated Identities: Ethnicity, Religion, and Class in an Indonesian Society*. Ann Arbor: University of Michigan Press.

van Klinken, Gerry. 1996a. "Megawati for President Move." *Inside Indonesia* Digest No. 04.

———. 1996b. "Megawati Out?" *Inside Indonesia* Digest No. 14.

———. 1998. "From Go-Go to Yo-Yo." *Inside Indonesia* No. 54 April–June.

———. 2001. "The New Conservatives: Golkar and PDIP Parliamentarians Join Forces to Pull Down Gus Dur." *Inside Indonesia* April–June.

Korn, V. E. 1932 [1924]. *Het Adatrecht van Bali*. Second Edition. The Hague.

van der Kraan, Alfons. 1980. *Lombok: Conquest, Colonization and Underdevelopment, 1870–1940*. Singapore, Kuala Lumpur, Hong Kong: Heinemann Educational Books (Asia) Ltd.

———. 1983. "Bali: Slavery and Slave Trade." In Anthony Reid (ed.), *Slavery, Bondage and Dependency in Southeast Asia*. New York: St. Martin's Press.

———. 1995. *Bali At War: A History of the Dutch-Balinese Conflict of 1846–49*. Monash Paper No. 34. Victoria, Australia: Amazon Press.

Kulke, Hermann. 1986. The Early and the Imperial Kingdom in Southeast Asian History. In David Marr and A. C. Milner (eds.), *Southeast Asia in the 9th to 14th Centuries*. Singapore: Institute of Southeast Asian Studies.

van Langenberg, Michael. 1996. "How Might the Suharto Era Conclude?" *Inside Indonesia* No. 48.

Lansing, J. Stephen. 1983a. *The Three Worlds of Bali*. Praeger Publishers.

———. 1983b. "The Indianization of Bali." *Journal of South and Southeast Asian Studies* 14(2): 409–421.

———. 1991. *Priests and Programmers: Technologies of Power in the Engineered Landscape of Bali*. Princeton, New Jersey: Princeton University Press.

————. 1995. *The Balinese.* Harcourt Brace College Publishers.

————. 2003. Comment to "The Precolonial Balinese State Reconsidered," by Hauser-Schäublin 2003. *Current Anthropology,* Volume 44, Number 2, April.

————. In press. *Perfect Order: Recognizing Complexity in Bali.* Princeton University Press.

Lansing, J. Stephen, and James Kremer. 1993 "Emergent Properties of Balinese Water Temple Networks: Coadaptation on a Rugged Fitness Landscape." *American Anthropologist* 95(1): 97–114.

Lansing, J. Stephen, A.J. Redd, T.M. Karafet, J. Watkins, I.W. Ardika, S.P.K. Surata, J.S. Schoenfelder, M. Campbell, A.M. Merriwether, and M. F. Hammer. 2004. "An Indian Trader in Ancient Bali?" *Antiquity* Vol 78#300 June, pp. 289–203.

van Leur, J.C. 1955. *Indonesian Trade and Society; Essays in Asian Social and Economic History.* The Hague: W. van Hoeve.

Lewis, Douglas. 1988. *People of the Source: The Social and Ceremonial Order of Tana Wai Brama on Flores.* Holland: Foris Publications.

Lutkehaus, Nancy. 1990a. "The Tambaran of the Tanepoa: Traditional and Modern Forms of Leadership on Manam Island." In Nancy Lutkehaus et al. (eds.), *Sepik Heritage.* Durham: Carolina Academic Press.

————. 1990b. "Hierarchy and 'Heroic Society.' Manam Variations in Sepik Social Structure." *Oceania,* 60.

————. 1995. *Zaria's Fire.* Durham: Carolina Academic Press.

MacRae, Graeme. 1997. *Economy, Ritual and History in a Balinese Tourist Town.* Ph.D. Diss., University of Auckland.

————. 1999 "Acting Global, Thinking Local in a Balinese Tourist Town." In Raechelle Rubenstein and Linda Connor (eds.), *Staying Local in the Global Village.* Hawaii: University of Hawaii Press.

————. 2003a. "Art and Peace in the Safest Place in the World: a Culture of Apoliticism in Bali." In Thomas Reuter (ed.), *Inequality, Crisis and Social Change in Indonesia: The Muted Worlds of Bali.* Routledge.

————. 2003b. "The Value of Land in Bali: Land Tenure, Landreform and Commodification." In T. Reuter, (ed), *Inequality, Crisis and Social Change in Indonesia: The Muted Worlds of Bali.* Routledge.

Marr, David, and A.C. Milner (eds.). 1986. *Southeast Asia in the 9th to 14th Centuries.* Singapore: Institute of Southeast Asian Studies Singapore.

Marriott, McKim. 1968. "The Feast of Love." In Milton Singer (ed.), *Krishna: Myths, Rites, Attitudes.* Chicago: Chicago University Press.

Mauss, Marcel. 1967. *The Gift: Forms and Functions of Exchange in Archaic Societies.* London: W. W. Norton & Company.

McGowan, Kaja Maria. 1995. "Balancing on Bamboo: Women in Balinese Art." *Southeast Asia Today.* Issue on Asian Art & Culture. Volume VIII, Number I: 75–95. Oxford University Press.

———. 1996. *Jewels in a Cup: The Role of Containers in Balinese Landscape and Art.* Ph.D. Diss., Cornell University.

McWilliam, Andrew. 1999. "From Lord of the earth to village-head: Adapting to the nation-state in West Timor." *Bijdragen tot de Taal-, Land-, en Volkenkunde* 155: 121–144.

———. 2002. *Paths of Origin, Gates of Life: A Study of Place and Precedence in Southwest Timor.* Leiden: KITLV Press.

Merson, Katharane. 1971. *Seven Plus Seven: Mysterious Life-Rituals in Bali.* New York: Vantage Press.

Moertono, Soemarsaid. 1968. *State and Statecraft in Old Java.* Cornell Modern Indonesia Project Monograph Series. Ithaca: Cornell University.

Monnerie, Denis. 1998. "Oceanian Comparison Reconsidered. The Mono-Alu Problem." *Social Anthropology* 6, 1, 91–107.

Mosko, Mark. 1992a. "Motherless Sons: Divine Kings and Partible Persons in Melanesia and Polynesia." *Man* (n.s.) 27: 697–717.

———. 1992b. "Other Message, Other Missions; or, Sahlins Among the Melanesians." *Oceania* 63 (2): 97–112.

———. 1995. "Rethinking Trobriand chieftainship." *Journal of Royal Anthropological Institute* 1, 762–85.

Muller, Jean-Claude. 1981. "'Divine Kingship' in Chiefdoms and States: A Single Ideological Model." In H.J.M. Claessen and P. Skalnik (eds.), *The Study of the State.* The Hague: Mouton.

Nakatani, Ayami. 1999. "'Eating Threads': Brocades as Cash Crop for Weaving Mothers and Daughters in Bali." In Raechelle Rubinstein and Linda Connor (eds.), *Staying Local in the Global Village.* Hawaii: Hawaii University Press.

———. 2003. "Ritual as 'Work:' the Invisibility of Women's Socio-Economic and Religious Roles in a Changing Balinese Society." In Thomas Reuter (ed.), *Inequality, Crisis and Social Change in Indonesia: The Muted Worlds of Bali.* Routledge.

Ngurah Bagus, I Gusti. 2004. "Parisada Hindu Dharma Indonesia in a Society in Transformation." In Martin Ramstedt (ed.), *Hinduism in Modern Indonesia.* New York: Routledge Curzon.

Obeyesekere, Gananath. 1997 [1992]. *The Apotheosis of Captain Cook: European Mythmaking in the Pacific.* Princeton: Princeton University Press.

O'Connor, Stanley. 1985. "Metallurgy and Immortality at Candi Sukuh, Central Java." *Indonesia* 39 (April).

Onghokham. 1978. "The Inscrutable and the Paranoid: An Investigation into the Sources of the Brotodiningrat Affair." In *Southeast Asian Transitions: Approaches Through Social History*. New Haven: Yale University Press.

Ortner, Sherry B. 1994 [1984]. "Theory in Anthropology since the Sixties." In Nicholas Dirks, Geoff Eley, and Sherry B. Ortner (eds.), *Culture/ Power/History*. NJ: Princeton University Press.

Ottino, Arlette. 2001. *The Universe Within: A Balinese Village through Ritual Practice*. Paris: Kathala.

Pannell, Sandra. 1997. "From the Poetics of Place to the Politics of Space: Redefining Cultural Landscapes on Damer, Maluku Tenggara." In James Fox (ed.), *The Poetic Power of Place*. Canberra: The Australian National University.

Pedersen, Lene. 2002. "Ambiguous Bleeding: Purity and Sacrifice in Bali." *Ethnology*, vol. 41 no. 4, Fall, pp. 303–15.

———. 2004. "Responding to Decentralization In the Aftermath of the Bali Bombing." Paper presented at Central Washington University Anthropology Brown Bag Lecture.

Pels, Pels et al. (eds.). 1999. *Colonial Subjects*. Michigan: University of Michigan.

Pemberton, John. 1994. *On The Subject of Java*. Ithaca: Cornell University Press.

Picard, Michel. 1996 [1992]. *Bali: Cultural Tourism and Touristic Culture*. Singapore: Archipelago Press.

———. 1997. "Cultural Tourism, Nation-Building, and Regional Culture: The Making of a Balinese Identity." In Michel Picard and Robert E. Wood (eds.), *Tourism, Ethnicity, and the State in Asian and Pacific Societies*. Honolulu: University of Hawaii Press.

———. 1999. "The Discourse of Kebalian: Transcultural Constructions of Balinese Identity." In Raechelle Rubinstein and Linda Connor (eds.), *Staying Local in the Global Village*. Hawaii: University of Hawai'i Press.

———. 2004. "What's in a Name? Agama Hindu Bali in the Making." In Martin Ramstedt, (ed), *Hinduism in Modern Indonesia*. New York: Routledge Curzon.

Pigeaud, Theodore. 1960. *Java in the 14th Century: A Study in Cultural History. The Nagara-Kertagama by Rakawi Prapanca of Majapahit, 1365 A.D.* 5 vols. The Hague: Martinus Nijhoff.

Pijar. 1998. "We Want a New Government!" *Inside Indonesia* No. 54 April–June.

Pitana, Gede. 1997. *In Search of Difference: Origin Groups, Status and Identity in Contemporary Bali*. Ph.D. Diss. Australian National University.

———. 1999. "Status Struggles and the Priesthood in Contemporary Bali." In Raechelle Rubinstein and Linda Connor (eds.), *Staying Local in the Global Village*. Hawaii: University of Hawaii Press.

Pucci, Idana. 1985. *The Epic of Life: A Balinese Journey of the Soul.* New York: Alfred van der Marck Editions.

Putra, Ida Bagus Gde. 1985. "Pelaksanaan Landreform dan Keresahan Masyarakat di Kabupaten Karangasem (1960–1965)." Thesis, Udayana University, Denpasar.

Putra, Ida Bagus Rai. 1993. *Babad Dalem.* Bali: Upada Sastra.

Quigley, Declan. 2000. "Scapegoats: The Killing of Kings and Ordinary People." *Journal of Royal Anthropological Institute* 6: 237–254.

Ramseyer, Urs. 1977. *The Art and Culture of Bali.* New York: Oxford University Press.

———. 1995. "Wie Ki Sudamala nach Sidemen Kam: Geschichte und Endogener Wandel in einem Balinesischen Dorf." *Kulturen und Raum.* Zürich: Verlag Rüegger.

Ramstedt, Martin, (ed), 2004. *Hinduism in Modern Indonesia: A Minority Religion Between Local, National, and Global Interests.* New York: Routledge Curzon.

Reid, Anthony J.S. (ed), 1983. *Slavery, Bondage and Dependency in Southeast Asia.* New York: St. Martin's Press.

———. 1988 *Southeast Asia in the Age of Commerce 1450–1680, Vol 1: The Lands Below the Winds.* New Haven: Yale University Press.

Reuter, Thomas. 1999. "People of the Mountains, People of the Sea: Negotiating the Local and the Foreign in Bali." In Raechelle Rubinstein and Linda Connor (eds.), *Staying Local in the Global Village.* Hawaii: University of Hawaii Press.

———. 2001. "Review of: Visible and invisible realms," by Margaret Wiener. Chicago: Chicago University Press. *Journal of Southeast Asian Studies* 32(2).

———. 2002a. *Custodians of the Sacred Mountains: Culture and Society in the Highlands of Bali.* Hawaii: University of Hawaii Press.

———. 2002b. *The House of Our Ancestors: Precedence and Dualism in Highland Balinese Society.* Leiden: KITLV Press.

Robinson, Geoffrey. 1995. *The Dark Side of Paradise: Political Violence in Bali.* Ithaca: Cornell University Press.

Robinson, Kathryn, and Sharon Bessel (eds.). 2002. *Women in Indonesia: Gender, Equity and Development.* Singapore: Institute of Southeast Asian Studies.

Robertson Smith, W. 1972. *The Religion of the Semites.* New York: Shocken Books.

Robson, Stuart O. 1995. *Desawarnana (Negarakertagama) by Mpu Prapanca.* Leiden: KITLV Press.

Rubinstein, Raechelle. 1991a. "The Brahmana According to Their Babad. In Hildred Geertz (ed.), *State and Society in Bali.* Leiden: KITLV Press.

————. 1991b. "Alliance and Allegiance: the Case of the Banjar War." Paper Presented at the Artistic Representation in Social Action conference, Princeton University. Published 1996 in Vickers (ed.), *Being Modern in Bali: Image and Change*. Monograph 43. New Haven: Yale University Southeast Asia Studies.

Sahlins, Marshall. 1963. "Poor Man, Rich Man, Big Man, Chief. Political Types in Melanesia and Polynesia." *Comparative Studies in Society and History* 5: 285–303.

————. 1968 *Tribesmen*. New Jersey: Prentice Hall Inc.

————. 1985. *Islands of History*. Chicago: Chicago University Press.

————. 1993. "Goodbye to Tristes Tropes: Ethnography in the Context of Modern World History." *Journal of Modern History* 56 (March) 1–25.

————. 1995. *How Natives Think: About Captain Cook, For Example*. Chicago: University of Chicago Press.

Sailendra (pseudonym of an Asian academic teaching at an Australian university). 1996. "Megawati: 'Why Not a Woman President?" Interview with Megawati Sukarnoputri, August 1996. *Inside Indonesia* October–December.

Sangren, P. Steven. 1991. "Dialectics of Alienation. Individuals and Collectives in Chinese Religion. *Man: The Journal of the Royal Anthropological Institute* 26(1): 67–86.

Sawitri, Cok. 2000. "Mengapa PDI-Perjuangan Menang Mutlak di Bali(?)." Paper presented at meetings for the Society of Balinese Scholars, Denpasar, Bali.

————. 2001a. "The Night Owl and the Red Moon." *Latitudes Magazine* February.

————. 2001b. "Women in Indonesia Military." *Latitudes Magazine* November 2001.

————. 2003 [2001]. "Aku Pulang Kampung." In Ramseyer, Urs and I Gusti Raka Panji Tisna. 2003 [2001]. *Bali-Dalem Dua Dunia: Portret Diri Yang Kritis*. Bali: Matamera Book. Also available in English: *Bali-Living in Two Worlds*. Basel: Verlag Schwabe & Co. AG.

————. n.d. "21 Mei 1998." Unpublished poem.

Scarborough, Vernon L., J. W. Schoenfelder, and J. Stephen Lansing. 2000. "Early Statecraft on Bali: The Water Temple Complex and the Decentralization of the Political Economy." *Research in Economic Anthropology* 20: 299–330.

Schaareman, Danker. 1986. *Tatulingga: Tradition and Continuity*. Basel: Museum fur Volkerkunde.

Schulte Nordholt, Henk. 1980. *Macht, Mensen en Middelen: Patronen en Dynamiek in de Balische-politiek* ca. 1700–1840. Ph.D. Diss. Free University of Amsterdam.

————. 1981. "Negara: A theatre state?" *Bijdragen tot de Taal-, Land, en Volkenkunde* 137:470–6.

————. 1986. *Bali: Colonial Conceptions and Political Change 1700–1940: From Shifting Hierarchies to 'Fixed Order.'* Rotterdam.

————. 1991 *State, Village, and Ritual in Bali*. Amsterdam: Free University Press.

————. 1993. "Leadership and the Limits of Political control: A Balinese 'Response' to Clifford Geertz." *Social Anthropology* Vol. 1, part 3, p. 291–307

————. 1996a [1988]. *The Spell of Power: A History of Balinese Politics. 1650–1940*. Leiden: KITLV Press.

————. 1996b. "Review of Visible and Invisible Realms: Power, Magic, and Colonial Conquest in Bali, by Margaret Wiener." *Journal of the Royal Anthropological Institute*. September: 580–581.

————. 1999. The Making of Traditional Bali: Colonial Ethnography and Bureaucratic Reproductions. In Pels Pels et al. (eds.), *Colonial Subjects*. Ann Arbor: University of Michigan Press.

————. 2002. "A Genealogy of Violence." In Freek Colombijn. and Thomas Lindblad (eds.), *Roots of Violence in Indonesia*. Leiden: KITLV Press.

Sharma, U. and M. Searle-Chatterjee (eds.). 1995. *Contextualizing Caste*. Oxford: Blackwell.

Siegel, James. 1986. *Solo In The New Order: Language and Hierarchy in an Indonesian City*. Princeton: Princeton University Press.

Skinner, Quentin. 1981. "Review of Clifford Geertz, *Negara*." *New York Review of Books*, 28, 6; 16 April: 35–37.

Smith, Larry (ed). 1987. *Discourse Across Cultures*. New York: Prentice Hall.

Soedjatmoko. 1967. "Indonesia: Problems and Opportunities." *Australian Outlook* 21, December.

Solyom, Garrett. 1978. *The World of the Javanese Keris*. Hawaii: East-West Center.

van Stein Callenfels, P.V. 1947. "De Rechten der Vorsten op Bali." *Indonesia* 193–208.

Stewart, Pamela J., and Andrew Strathern. 2001. "Origins versus Creative Powers: The Interplay of Movement and Fixity." In *Emplaced Myth: space, narrative, and knowledge in Aboriginal Australia and Papua New Guinea*, Rumsey, Alan and J. Weiner (eds.). University of Hawai'i Press.

————. 2002a. *Remaking the World: Myth, Mining, and Ritual Change among the Duna of Papua New Guinea*. Washington, D.C.: Smithsonian Institution Press.

————. 2002b. Water in Place: The Hagen and Duna People of Papua New Guinea. *Journal of Ritual Studies* 16(1): 108–119.

————. 2002c. Foreword to *The Third Bagre*, by Jack Goody. Durham: Carolina Academic Press.

Strathern, Andrew, and Pamela J. Stewart. 1999. *The Spirit is Coming!: A Photographic-Textual Exposition of the Female Spirit Cult Performance in*

Mount Hagen, Papua New Guinea. Pittsburgh: The Deixis Publishing Foundation, Inc.

———. 2002. *The Python's Back: Pathways of Comparison between Indonesia and Melanesia*. Bergin and Garvey, Greenwood Publishing.

Stuart-Fox, David J. 1982. *Once A Century: Pura Besakih and the Eka Dasa Rudra Festival*. Jakarta: Penerbit Citra Indonesia and Penerbit Sinar Harapan.

———. 1987 Pura Besakih: A Study of Balinese Religion and Society. Ph.D. Diss., Australian National University.

———. 1991. "Pura Besakih: Temple-State Relations from Precolonial to Modern Times." In Hildred Geertz (ed.), *State and Society in Bali*. Netherlands: Koninklijk Instituut voor Taal-, Land-, en Volkenkunde.

———. 2002. *Pura Besakih: Temple, Religion and Society in Bali*. Leiden: KITLV Press.

van Swieten, J. 1849. *Krijgsverrichtingen tegen het Eiland Bali in 1848*. Den Haag: Erven Doorman.

Tambiah, Stanley J. 1985. *Culture, Thought, and Social Action: An Anthropological Perspective*. Cambridge: Harvard University Press.

Thomas, Nicholas. 1990. *Marquesan Societies: Inequality and Political Transformation in Eastern Polynesia*. Oxford: Clarendon.

———. 1997. *In Oceania. Visions, Artifacts, Histories*. Durham and London: Duke University Press.

Turner, Victor. 1969. *The Ritual Process: Structure and Anti-Structure*. Chicago: Aldine.

Valeri, Valerio. 1985. *Kingship and Sacrifice: Ritual and Society in Ancient Hawaii*. Chicago: University of Chicago Press.

———. 2001. *Fragments from Forests and Libraries. Essays by Valerio Valeri*. Janet Hoskins, (ed). Durham: Carolina Academic Press.

Vickers, Adrian. 1982a. "A Balinese Illustrated Manuscript of the Siwaratrikalpa." *Bijdragen tot de Taal-, Land, en Volkenkunde* 138: 443–469.

———. 1982b. "The Writing of Kakawin and Kidung on Bali." *Bijdragen tot de Taal-, Land-, en Volkenkunde I* 138: 492–493.

———. 1984. "Ritual and Representation in Nineteenth-Century Bali." *Review of Indonesian and Malaysian Affairs* 18: 1–35.

———. 1989. *Bali: A Paradise Created. Ringwood*. Victoria: Penguin.

———. 1991. "Ritual Written: The Song of the Ligya or the Killing of the Rhinoceros." In Hildred Geertz (ed.), *State and Society in Bali*. Leiden: KITLV.

———. 1990. "Balinese Texts and Historiography." *History and Theory* 29 (2): 158–78.

Vickers, Adrian (ed.). 1996. *Being Modern In Bali: Image and Change*. Monograph 43. Yale Southeast Asia Studies.

Vickers, Adrian, and I Nyoman Darma Putra, with Michele Ford (eds.). 2000. *To Change Bali: Essays in Honor of I Gusti Ngurah Bagus.* Denpasar: Bali Post.

Walters, R. 1980. "Signs of the Times: Clifford Geertz and Historians." *Social Research*, 47: 537–56.

Warna, I Wayan, et al. 1986. *Babad Dalem: Teks dan Terjemahan.* Denpasar: Dinas Pendidikan dan Kebudayaan Propinsi Daerah Tingkat I Bali.

Warren, Carol. 1993a. *Adat and Dinas: Balinese Communities in the Indonesian State.* Singapore: Oxford University Press.

———. 1993b. "Disrupted Death Ceremonies: Popular Culture and the Ethnography of Bali." *Oceania* 64.

Waterson, Roxana 1997. "The Contested Landscapes of Myth and History in Tana Toraja." In James Fox (ed.), *The Poetic Power of Place: Comparative Perspectives on Austronesian Ideas of Locality.* Canberra: The Australian National University.

Weiner, Anette. 1976. *Women of Value, Men of Renown.* Austin: University of Texas.

———. 1988. *The Trobriand Islanders of Papua New Guinea.* New York: Holt, Rinehart, and Winston.

———. 1992. *Inalienable Possessions: The Paradox of Keeping-While-Giving.* Berkeley: University of California Press.

White, Geoffrey M., and Lamont Lindstrom (eds.), 1997. *Chiefs Today: Traditional Pacific Leadership and the Postcolonial State (Contemporary Issues in Asia and the Pacific).* Stanford: Stanford University Press.

Wiener, Margaret. 1994. "Object Lessons: Dutch Colonialism and the Looting of Bali." *History and Anthropology* 6 (4): 347–70.

———. 1995. *Visible and Invisible Realms: Power, Magic, and Colonial Conquest in Bali.* Chicago: The University of Chicago Press.

Wolters, Oliver W. 1999 [1982]. *History, Culture, and Region in Southeast Asian Perspectives.* Ithaca: Southeast Asia Program Publications.

Worsley, Peter J. 1972. *Babad Buleleng.* The Hague: Martinus Nijhoff.

Zoetmulder, P. J. 1982. *Old Javanese English Dictionary.* (2 vols. with S. Robson) The Hague: Nijhoff.

INDEX

Adas Michael, 22, 22n.26, 27

agency, displacement of 21, 42, 120, 301–304; direct, 21, 26, 42, 46, 120; local efficacy, 39, 46, 261, 293

Agung, Mount, 12, 15, 55, 62, 69, 70, 72n.15, 120, 124, 124n.7, 125, 126, 127, 128, 154, 172, 178, 194, 225, 284, 285, 309; *photo*: 95

Amlapura. *See* Karangasem

Anak Agung Gde Agung, 236–237

Ananta Toer, Pramoedya, 247

ancestors: abodes of, 120, 124, 125, 307; approval of, 76, 77, 190, 192, 199; as rajas, 281; awakening of, 80, 89; bisama (ancestral agreements) and oaths of; 182, 186–192, 193, 236, 296–297; deification of, 3, 26, 40, 57–60, 69, 70, 90, 94, 290, 292, 296; displaced agency and, 42, 301; effigies of, 26, 61–62, 66, 70, 81–82, 83, 86, 89, 92, 132, 278 (*see also* priests, effigies of souls as guides); enjoyment of offerings of, 61n.5, 68, 75–76, 87; food cravings and, 89, 92; hierarchy and, 191, 226n.32, 231n.38, 252n.13, 290; invention of, 269n.8; keris and, 5, 279; love for, 66; obligations to, 21, 28, 46, 49, 61, 66, 72, 137, 281, 290, 307, 314–315; as part of the community of the living, 60–61, 187n.25, 188, 195, 316; presence of, 5, 29, 84, 86, 87, 88, 92, 124, 150, 225; reverence of, 185, 191, 193; universalist religion vs, 60, 60n.3, 76n.16, 195. *See also* ancestral connections; maligya; Megawati; remembering; Shradda ceremony; *photos* of effigies: 105, 108–111, 116–117

ancestral connections, 32, 36, 137, 296; as binding princedom, 309;

Anderson, Benedict, 199, 200, 200n.8, 304–305

Aquino, Corazon, 244, 244n.9

Aspinall, Ed, 245, 246, 265

Aung Thwin, Michael, 143

Austronesian, 40n.40, 59, 60n.3, 72, 120, 122, 130, 263, 284. *See also* eastern Indonesian.

Babad Dalem, 8n.8, 25, 194, 194n.2, 267, 268–270; of Klungkung, 8n.8, 269–270, 269n.8; of Sidemen, 8n.8, 9, 268–270; 269n.8, 302. *See also* dynastic chronicles.

Badung, 20, 243, 263

Bangawan Cangguh (aka *Suda Mala*). *See* keris: Bangawan Cangguh (heirloom of the Jero Gede Sidemen)

bartering (negotiating): with lords or chiefs, 183–184, 231, 307; with gods, 306–307

Bateson, Gregory, 55n.1, 56, 75, 238

belief, 38, 135, 137, 185, 316; as mystification, 29, 274; mystical, 10–11n13, 10–11, 21, 242; seeking proof for, 307. *See also* keris: mystical events; keris: as proof; land: as proof

beraya, 139–142, 143–145, 152, 153. *See also* followers; subjects

Berg, Richard, 210–215, 255

Besakih, 15–16, 16n19, 123, 124, 125, 126, 127, 187, 187n.26, 194n.2, 220, 225n31, 234, 263; Eka Dasa Rudra ritual at, 284–286

big-men, 206, 229–230, 229n.35, 231n.38. *See also* chieftainship; prowess: men of

Bloch, Maurice, 21, 30, 30n.33, 31n.35, 35, 42, 60n.3, 61, 68, 135–136, 185n.24, 280n.20

Bloemen Wanders, van. 236

Boon, James, 149n.33, 166n.3, 171, 184n.22, 227, 297, 306, 308

Bourdieu, Pierre, 21, 29, 42, 90–91, 257, 296

Brahmana, 40, 68, 126, 132, 142, 152, 196, 223, 274, 306; Brahmana Buda, 130; compounds in Sidemen, 130, 131, 133, 138, 210, 226, 309; multifaceted role of, 130; as rulers, 130. *See also* caste, Griya Ulah, priests, war

Buleleng, 22, 189, 236, 237

caste, 30n.33, 34, 35, 37, 46–48, 60, 61, 62–63, 62n.6, 81, 132n.13, 133, 141 158, 170, 175, 188n.27, 191n.30, 193, 196, 197–198n.5, 206, 209, 209n.21, 210, 221n.27, 221, 224, 226n.32, 282–283, 290, 295, 298; challenge to, 142, 174, 196–197, 219, 242; Indian, 129. *See also* hierarchy; ritual: hierarchy and status

causation: Balinese process of, 33, 299; concurrences of events and timeframes, 33, 91, 299; in ritual, 29

change and continuity. *See* culture, globalization, Indonesia, Jero Gede Sidemen, Kingship, Princedom.

charisma, 20, 40, 199, 225, 247, 256, 266

chieftainship, 229–231, 231n.38; Fijian, 201n.11; Papua New Guinean, 231–232. *See also* bigmen; prowess: men of

circumambulations, 80, 83, 122, 124, 125

Claessen, H.J.M., 231, 241n.7

claims of hierarchy and status: charismatic vs direct claims, 301; posthumous furthering of, 59; risks of false claims, 272–273, 273n.14; risks of not living up to expected behavior in relation to, 206, 239; tests of claims to, 273; ways of making, 42, 64, 70, 119, 133, 159, 238, 268–270, 293,

301, 302, 133. *See also:* Majapahit: claims to descent from
Cokorda (also Tjokorda), defined 7n.7, 217.
Cokorda Mayun, 152, 155, 221–222, 256n.18
Cokorda Pemangku (non-Brahmana priest of Jero Gede Side men), 5, 44, 84, 156, 157, 179, 188, 191, 205, 220–221, 271, 274–275, 276, 307
Cokorda Raka, 44, 47n.42, 58, 60, 61, 62, 63n.8, 65, 66, 72, 82, 85, 88, 90, 92, 132–133, 137, 138, 139, 140, 140n.21, 155, 156, 177–180, 190, 202–206, 209, 211, 213, 218–220, 241, 243, 248, 252, 262, 266, 275, 307, 314; on future of princedom and importance of remembering, 258, 313–314
Cokorda Sawitri, 13, 44, 47n.42, 59, 65–66, 80, 86, 88, 89, 90, 187, 210, 218, 223–225, 222n.28, 225n.30, 248, 268, 278, 299–300, 317
Colombijn, F., 175, 249n.11; and Thomas Lindblad, 249
colonialism in Bali. *See* Dutch
Comaroff, Jean, 35
commensality, 48, 73, 226
conflict resolution: compared to mediation in the US, 213–214; role of oaths in, 215. *See also* Tjokorda Gede Dangin: conflict resolution
Connor, Linda, 241n.7, 306
contest state, 22, 22n.26, 28n.31, 29n.32. *See also* galactic polity;

kingship; negara; princedom; theatre state
cooperation, 36–38, 48, 130, 257–258, 311; between rulers, 263; between rulers and priests, 18, 24, 66, 119, 128–133, 159, 194–195, 272n.13, 285, 288, 310; *go tong royong*, 134, 134n.16.
corpse abuse. *See ngarap-ngarapan*
cosmology, Balinese universe, 17, 26, 43, 49, 58, 70, 193–194; imbalance of, 174–175; order of, 175, 290
Creese, Helen, 8n.8, 13, 14, 14n.17, 14n.18, 17n.22, 129n.11, 144, 144n.27, 198n.6, 269n8
Cribb, Robert, 55, 175
crisis, 158, 315; economic, 77, 173, 284, 290n.27, 308; of mind and faith, 88, 290, 290n.27; pattern of, 291; political, 174, 175, 244–248, 253, 284, 292
culture, 13, 313–314; Balinese culture as apolitical, 298–299; Bali as showcase of, 38, 309; Balinese obsessions of, 18; beyond coherence of, 34; change and continuity of, 296, 298–299, 311, 312; fear of loss of, 287–288; foreign admiration of, 38; Dangin's promotion of, 281–282, 287–288; of corruption, 310; reassertion of 308; touristification of, 298

Dalem Ketut Ngulesir, 8, 8n.9, 13, 14, 122n.6, 126, 268, 284, 307; as god of love, 194
decentralization of post-Suharto Indonesia, 310–311; corruption

and, 310; emergence of small kings and, 310; Jero Gede Sidemen/Tjokorda Gede Dangin and, 315–316; local empowerment and, 311, 315–316; erosion of human rights and, 311; gender and, 311; political violence and, 311

deification, 26, 59–60, 195, 233; ancestor worship versus universalist religion and, 60, 60n.3, 195. *See also* ancestors

deities, 68, 70, 86, 87, 91, 92, 195, 242, 244, 307; visiting, 225. *See also* ancestors: abodes of; ancestors: deification of

demokrasi, 77, 78; influences re: democracy, 231, 255, 255n.16

demons (and chthonic forces) 68, 70, 79, 194n.2, 220, 226, 242, 264, 307; abodes of, 120; Illusion Demon (Mayadanawa), 234–235, 242

descent groups, 82, 83, 138–139, 139n.20, 141, 145, 151, 169, 171, 197–198n.5, 211, 217; displaced agency and, 301; 302

Dewa Agung (Great Lord), 154, 206, 206n.17, 235, 243, 263

Déwa Anom Pemahyun Di Madé. *See* Jero Gede Sidemen: forefather of

Dewa Ayu Alit, 44, 58–59, 65–66, 69, 69n.12, 87, 90, 204, 222–223, 243

Dewa Gede Catra, 157, 182, 269n.8, 308n.5

Dirks, Nicholas, 11, 35, 40n.40, 48, 234, 238–239

domination, 20, 35, 36, 37, 38, 77, 257, 300–301, 312

dreams, 64, 66, 75, 80, 81, 84, 218, 267, 301. *See also* trance

Dumont, Louis, 47–48, 80n.18, 129, 129n.12, 130, 159, 194

Durga Dingkul. *See* keris: Durga Dingkul

Durkheim, Emile, 28, 34

Dutch in Bali: Balinese kingdoms and, 23–24, 42, 43, 134n.15, 135n.17, 252, 253, 293n.29, 306, 311–312; Balinese lords and, 23, 136, 239n.4, 252, 253, 254, 256; bureaucracy of, 23, 43; caste and, 63, 170, 252; colonial discourse of, 39, 231, 288, 288n.26, 296, 297, 298; conquest of Bali, 22, 24, 148, 148n.32, 171, 172n.10, 189, 237, 271, 287, 295, 313–314; corvée labor and, 135, 135n.18; corvée labor vs palace service, 135; effort to contain radicalism, 288n.26; "ethical" colonial project of, 16; mystical events and, 10–11n.13, 287; post WWII attempted return of, 253; rajas and, 20, 43, 93, 170, 171, 252, 253, 253n.14, 267, 287, 288n.26, 306, 311–312, 315; reforms and policies of, 23, 43, 155–156, 156n.37, 166, 170–171, 172n.9, 184, 207, 207n.18, 252, 255n.16, 295, 296, 298; separation of ritual/culture from politics, 263, 265; treaties and, 22; violence and, 249

van Duuren, David, 5.n.3, 6, 287

dynastic chronicles, 14, 24, 126,
130, 230, 307; competition and,
15, 147n.28, 252, 252n.13, 301.
See also Babad Dalem; Majapahit: claims to descent from
Dwyer, Leslie and Degung Santikarma, 55, 176, 240

Eastern Indonesian, 31n.34, 129,
149, 185, 198n.6. *See also* Austronesian.
egalitarian, 28, 48, 149, 159, 191,
191n.30, 193, 193n.1, 222n.28,
229, 255n.16; associations, 34,
134, 198n.7, 203, 254, 297
Eklof, Stefan, 245, 248, 291
Errington, Shelly, 273, 303
expatriates, 254–255, 263. *See also*
tourism
exploitation, 38, 136, 183, 184,
236–237

feeding, 26, 69, 78, 87, 89, 136,
140, 140n.21, 141, 168, 180,
183–184, 195, 219, 221n.28, 230
fertility, 316; followers and lords
contribute to, 27–28, 150, 154,
229, 316; keris and, 5–6,
268n.7, 316; lembu and, 80n.18;
ritual and, 27, 27n.30, 317,
317n.8; rulers and, 28n.31, 50,
200, 200n.8, 205n.16, 226–229,
269, 269n.9, 283n.22; serpent
and, 5–6, 268n.7, 316; women
and, 222n.28
feudalism and anti-feudalism,
16n.20, 62, 138, 139, 170–171,
171n.8, 179, 186, 203, 206, 253,

262, 279, 293, 295, 296, 297,
298, 301, 310, 312
flexibility: of subject categories,
143–145; in Burma, 143; of
landownership, 167. *See also*
kingship: fluidity of; negara: fluidity of
followers, 3, 26, 44, 91, 141,
229n.35; asking forgiveness, 178;
attraction of, 21, 194n.2, 257,
273, 277, 296, 316; autonomy
of, 316; benefits of lords to, 21,
22, 27–28, 184n.22, 192, 193,
200, 207–231, 293, 297, 314; be-
stowal of title by, 41, 50, 202,
206, 206n.17, 220; change in relationship with lords, 178– 179,
182, 186, 252n.13, 255; competi-
tion/work for, 15, 315; critical
reflection and, 38, 50, 299, 310;
false consciousness and, 38, 310;
financial need of, 182–183; historical relationships to lords, 32,
167; importance to lords, 42, 50,
82, 119, 158, 169, 184, 243, 258,
293n.29, 297, 298, 304; loss of
connection to, 256–257, 297;
mutuality with lords, 27–28, 41,
136, 138, 145, 147n.28, 150,
159, 183, 191, 193, 204, 230,
231, 231n.37, 233, 255, 297,
316; ongoing accommodations
between lords and, 261, 295,
297, 316; palace service to lords,
135, 143, 165, 185, 296; *pengiring* 142–143, 143–145, 153, 154,
167, 171, 204; powers of,
233–244, 251, 252, 252n.13,

253, 258, 309; princes as followers of Brahmana, 132; risks to,
209, 217, 233, 236, 251, 297; rituals as, 61n.5; show of, 78, 85,
134, 315; souls as, 62, 70, 81,
142n.24; ties and obligations to
lords of, 3, 11–12, 17, 21, 28,
32, 42–43, 49, 135, 137–138,
153, 157, 186, 191, 192; ties hin-
dering land reform, 173, 177,
179; *photos*: 102. *See also* ritual:
duty; historical connection; land;
rulers; slaves; subjects forgetting,
38, 186–192, 217–218, 309. *See
also* remembering
Fox, James, 120, 129, 185n.23,
196n.3

galactic polity, 17n.23, 121n.4, 163,
303. *See also* contest state; kingship; negara; princedom; theatre
state
gamble, 34, 91, 305; by engaging
unruly forces, 241, 305
Gde Pitana, 37, 47, 188n.27,
193n.1
Geertz, Clifford, 11n.14, 12,
12n.15, 17n.23, 18–22, 24, 25,
39–40, 41, 41n.40, 42, 46, 48,
49, 56, 91, 134, 139, 140n.21,
143, 144, 158, 163–164n.1, 166,
166n.3, 169, 170, 171, 195–196;
197– 198n.5, 206n.17, 217, 237,
238, 242n.8, 243, 269n.8, 295,
306, 308, 313
Geertz, Hildred, 46, 48, 264,
269n.8
Gelgel: as seat of Bali's Golden Age,
14, 14n.17, 25, 125, 129, 268,

285; chronology of, 14n.18; dynasty of, 15, 24, 206n.17, 315;
fractioning of, 9–10, 14, 15, 25,
130–131, 147, 151, 154, 190,
236, 252, 270; sterile vs fertile
rajas of, 269, 269n.9; temples of,
127, 263n.2, 268. *See also* Jero
Gede Sidemen: Gelgel and; Ksatria Dalem; priests: Nirartha; Sri
Kresna Kapakisan
gender: abstinence and, 200,
200–201n.10; charismatic leadership and, 199; corvée labor
and, 135n.18; deities and, 70,
124, 126–127; division of ritual
labor, 5, 67–68, 68n.11, 73, 81,
87–88, 89, 132, 132n.14, 134,
274; duality and complemen-
taity, 5–6, 7n.6, 198n.6; effigies
and, 81n19; Indonesian presidency and, 247; landrights and,
223, 223n.29; raja's pick of
women, 200–201, 233; sexual
prowess and, 200–201; titles
and, 47; union of male and female, 72, 81n.19, 316; violence
and, 38n.37, 247, 249, 249n.10,
300; women as leaders, 65–66,
198, 198n.6, 199, 224–225;
photo from ritual site: 100. *See
also* Keris; marriage; menstruation; offerings; power: gender
and; trance
van Gennep, Arnold, 238–239
globalization, 12, 24, 121n.4,
257n.19, 309–310, 310–316,
315; as context for local change
and continuity, 12, 24, 26, 27,
159, 257–258, 287, 299; as

threat, 287, 288, 292, 296, 298; role of traditional political forms in era of, 12, 26, 27, 309, 310

Goody, Jack, 310

Goris, Roelof, 163–164n.1, 185n.24

governance, 21, 32, 41, 49, 159, 184, 205n.15, 229, 230, 236. See also Tjokorda Gede Dangin

Griya Ulah of Sidemen, 67, 70, 83, 131, 132, 139, 308

Guermonprez, Jean-François, 129n.12, 130, 187, 187n.26, 194–195, 295, 303

Gusti Ngurah Bagus, 288

Gusti Ngurah Sidemen. See Sidemen, lord of

Habibie, 3, 77, 83, 158, 265n.4, 266, 305

Hatley, Barbara, 224, 300

Hauser-Schäublin, Brigitta, 16n.20, 17n21, 19, 25–26, 29n.32, 56, 126, 128n.10, 139n.20, 187, 228–229

Hayam Wuruk, Emperor, 8, 8n.9, 194, 277, 301

Heine-Geldern, Robert, 6, 122, 194, 197–198n.5, 234, 303

hierarchy: ambivalence and challenge to, 34, 62, 142, 174, 241, 242, 254; asymmetries and reciprocities of, 36; Dumontian, 159, impermanence of, 36, 158; in built environment, 26; incorporation of egalitarian elements, 48, 159, 193; of local vs wider world, 27, 28, 29, 33, 36, 37, 38, 48–51, 257, 258, 305; markers of, 46–48, 70, 81, 86, 87, 149, 149n.33, 230, 238, 242; reconstitution of, 11, 36, 37, 48–51, 57, 64, 94, 158, 258, 304–305; remembering the ancestors and, 191; stories to maintain, 64, 192; voluntary, 192; work for privilege of, 11, 32, 50, 193–232, 297, 298, 315. See also caste; ritual: hierarchy and status and

Historical connection, 137–138, 138–145, 159, 185, 191, 191n.28, 219, 262, 312; villages with, 145–157. See also land: pacatu; forgetting; remembering;

historical moments and transitions, 29, 32, 41, 50, 57, 158, 261, 293, 297–298, 304–305

Hobart, Angela, et al, 8n.11, 141n.22

Hobart, Mark, 70n.13, 87, 121n3, 130, 134, 139, 187n.25, 295

holy water, 9, 78, 79, 122; from keris, 276; trip for, 125–128, 128n.10, 129, 190, 283, 283n.22; photo: 103

Holmberg, David, 35, 40n.40, 120n.1

Hoskins, Janet, 5, 6, 5, 76n.16, 121n.2, 129, 205n.16, 222n.28, 254n.15, 273n.14, 281, 286, 302, 302n.3, 303

Howe, Leo, 19, 30n.33, 36, 46, 48, 64, 91n20, 130, 188n. 29, 288, 295

Ida Bagus Gde Putra, 176, 177, 179

identity: local, 26, 28, 315; as Balinese, 7n5, 38, 39, 76, 263, 288n.26, 292, 309, 315; as authentic Balinese, 39, 292; Balinese identity as apolitical, 263, 291–292; coproduction of, 39; empowered, 311; defense of "Balinese way," 288; "primordial essence" of, 39; transcending, 311. *See also* Majapahit: claims to descent from

ignorance, 253, 253n.14, 255–256, 256n.17

indianization, 13, 47–48, 288n.26; neo-indianization as threat, 287, 288

Indonesia: administrative structures of, 207, 207n.18, 223, 265, 281; "arrogance" of local representatives of, 208, 280; as context for local change and continuity, 42, 50, 159, 252, 261, 295, 298–299; as ritual sponsor, 30n.33, 187, 284–286; dignitaries of, 3, 38, 41, 298, 299, 305, 315; discourse of, 38, 39, 231, 264–265, 296, 297, 298; elections of, 40, 244–245, 247–248, 275–276, 291–292, 315; elections at local level, 221–222, 315, 316–317; events of the Sidemen Maligya and, 76–88, 91, 158; gender and, 300; independence of, 24, 172, 172n.10, 182, 187, 253; in flux, 37, 77, 119; laws and policies of, 207, 208n20, 288, 296, 298, 306, laws and policies of decentralization of, 310–311, 315–316; nationalist struggle for, 23, 24, 172, 172n.10, 177, 239n.4, 253, 262n.1; New Order of (Suharto), 32, 77, 79, 176, 202n.14, 241, 245, 264–265, 266, 291, 298; representation in, 298; repression of political activity, 239, 258, 264–266; ritual as response to, 38, 39n.39, 77, 79, 292, 292n.28, 312; ritual as purifying for, 85; state vs local hierarchy and, 38, 158, 255–256, 256n.17; suffering of, 300; traditional elites and, 281, 281n.21, 282–283, 287, 305–306n.4, 309–310, 310–316; unification of (Sukarno), 248. *See also* reform era of post-Suharto Indonesia.

inequality, 21, 25, 36, 136

invitations, 3, 26, 34, 38, 73, 83, 155, 191n.28, 266, 280, 299, 305

irrigation, 12, 12n.15, 13, 16, 18n.25, 69, 124, 126, 127, 145, 148, 149, 164; associations of, 17, 17n.21, 43, 76, 83, 157, 166, 198n.7, 203, 227–228, 297, 316; conflict over, 154–157, 228; ritual and, 225–229. *See also* kingship: irrigation and

Islam: Dutch efforts to contain spread of radical, 288; fear of, 258; in Sidemen, 141n.23, 182; on Bali, 153; on Java, 14, 129; radical Islam as threat, 287, 288, 291–292

Jero Gede Sidemen, 3, 12, 12n.15, 44, 147n.29, 251, 255; agriculture/irrigation and, 225–229, 283; lords of as Dalem or rajas, 24, 138, 139, 143, 148, 157–158, 277; as palace, 143, 154, 168,

169; as source of land, 151, 185, 191; benefits of followers to, 169, 297; claims of, 24–25, 41, 41n.41, 268–270, 276, 301, 315; claims of assessed, 271–273, 275–278, 295–296; conferral and journey of heirloom keris to, 7–10, 24–25, 130–131, 270–271, 277–278, 284, 302, 307; conquest of, 24, 131, 313–314; transformation and continuity of, 42, 171, 295–296, 296–301, 312–313; descent of, 24–25; defined in contrast to Ubud, 256n18; diminished status of, 23, 43, 138n.19, 253, 302, 312; during crisis of 1980s, 177–181; edge of, 297; establishment of, 10, 15, 147, 151n.34, 270–271; family system of, 217–225; financial need of, 156–157, 253; forefather of, 10, 15, 24, 128, 130, 147, 149, 151, 155, 190, 210, 269, 282; Gelgel and, 10, 15, 82, 151, 153, 190, 277, 279, 315; intermarriage with Karangasem of, 23, 82–83, 221, 243; Karangasem and, 132, 148, 217, 243, 253, 272–273, 278, 279–280, 296, 309; Klungkung and, 24–25, 81, 132, 217, 253, 254, 277, 278–280, 296, 309; leadership of, 23, 77, 151, 152, 197–218, 224, 280, 315–317; material assistance from, 136–137, 152, 154, 257, 297, 314; men of, 218–222; non-cooperation of, 254, 280–281; opposition to, 62–63, 138, 145, 256, 315; reassertion and reconstitution of, 24, 25, 40, 46, 48–51, 93–94, 119, 147n.28, 158, 169, 206, 232, 261, 269, 296, 301–304, 306, 312; reconceptualization of: crafting modern roles, 193, 232, 253–254, 257, 257n19, 258, 297, 312–313; recent predecessors of, 199, 202, 205, 213, 252–254; resources of, 73, 76, 119, 133, 136, 180, 212, 215, 216, 217–218, 297; role of, 40, 151, 152, 154, 169–170, 183; schooling and, 201–202, 216, 218–219; 222, 253; strategies of, 297, 302, 312; Temege and, 127, 147, 190, 218; village temples and, 225–227; women of, 67–68, 69, 76, 82, 88, 134, 156, 199, 222–225, 221, 276n.17; photos: 96, 116. See also, Babad Dalem; dynastic chronicles; priests; memasyarakat; succession; Tjokorda Gede Dangin (head of Jero Gede Sidemen)

Kapakisan. See Sri Kresna Kapakisan
Karangasem: assignations by, 189; conquest of Sidemen, 12, 16, 155, 272–273; conservatism of, 311–312; during Dutch rule, 23, 253, 311–312; farmers in, 174; during crisis of 1960s, 175–177, 264; intermarriage with Jero Gede Sidemen, 23, 82–83, 204, 243; holdings and seizures of land, 176–177, 180n.17. 180n.18; kingdom of, 12, 41,

119; maligya in, 55, 75, 93; palace of, 34, 44, 93, 176–177, 190, 221, 280; priests of, 131; raja of, 155, 189, 204, 237; regional head of, 79, 200n.8

kavla, 139–143, 143–145, 152. *See also* followers: subjects

Keane, Webb, 29n.34, 33, 38

keris: as agents, 84, 158, 302–304; as biographical objects, 6, 7n.5; as history objects, 7, 302–304; as biographical and history objects, 7n.5, as proof, 147n.28, 277–278; authentication of, 271, 271n.10, 272–278, 295–296; Bangawan Cangguh (heirloom of the Jero Gede Sidemen), 3, 5, 7–11, 13–14, 15, 24–25, 40, 84–85, 87, 158, 267–289, 293, 301, 316; Bangawan Cangguh as raja, 280–281, 303; Bangawan Cangguh compared to Sukarno's keris, 276–277; Bangawan Cangguh requested by governor, 282–283, 283–284n.22, 284, 286, 303; displaced agency and, 42; Durga Dingkul, 267, 277; end of significance and power of, 295; gender and, 5, 7, 275n.16; gifts of, 7–10, 24–25, 178, 267–268, 286, 301; identity and, 6, 7; kingship and, 6–11, 10n13, 13–14, 20, 22, 50, 84–85, 119, 158, 267–268, 272, 316; loss of, 84–85, 178, 271, 273, 287; loss of prevented, 271; Majapahit and, 24, 84–85, 194, 268, 295–296, 301; Megawati and, 3, 5, 7, 10–11, 33, 50, 84, 91, 150,

261–267, 273–278, 286, 293, 295–296, 303; mystical events and, 5, 8–9n.12, 10, 33, 274–275, 286, 287, 303; new life of, 303; power to attract, 273; 276, 316; ranking of, 10, 277; receiving power from, 275–276, 283, 286; regeneration of powers of, 302–304, 315; restricted circulation of, 286, 303; suicide with, 275n.16; Sukarno and, 10, 276, 276n.18; symbolism of, 5–7, 279, 281, 304, 306, 310, 315, 316; the past and, 302–304; unruly, 287; *photo:* 108. *See also* fertility; power; serpent

Ketut Ngulesir. *See* Dalem Ketut Ngulesir

kingship, Balinese, 13, 14, 15, 16–25, 40, 43, 49–50, 159, 196, 251, 252, 295, 298; contemporary, 3, 24, 26, 40–43, 49–51, 143, 158–159, 171, 186–187, 193, 196, 197, 218, 219, 257–258, 278, 292, 295–296, 296–301, 309–310, 312, 313; continuity of, 24, 158–159, 171, 186–187, 193, 310, 311, 313; divine, 13, 17, 20, 42, 159, 193–197, 229, 233–234, 257, 296, 297, 303; fluidity and shifting alliances of, 16, 17, 48, 121, 121n.4, 184, 236, 251, 252, 295, 312n.6; fluidity and shifting alliances of rigidified and territorialized, 172n.9, 295; good/just/unjust, 194, 200n.8, 235n.2, 242, 268; heirlooms or sacra and, 10n.13, 13, 18, 20, 21, 24, 234,

267–268, 268n.7, 272n.11, 272n.12, 272n.13, 277, 303, 310; heirloom keris' role in as over, 295; irrigation and, 17, 154–157, 205, 226–229; land and 16–17, 49–50, 163–192, 163–192 (*see also* land: *pacatu*); people as resource base of, 17, 133–134, 136, 163–165, 171n.8, 182, 310; people's loyalty as main resource of, 184; priest and raja in dual relationship and, 18, 24, 66, 119, 128–133, 159, 194–195, 285, 288, 310; regicide and, 233n.1; rites of, 122; scales of, 17, 25, 41, 42, 159, 195–196, 251; Southeast Asian, 10n13, 17, 17n.23, 21, 5, 11, 121n.4, 122, 136, 163–164, 171n.8, 184, 193–197, 199, 203, 204, 233–234, 290; uncertainty and, 298; varying strategies of, 251, 297; "*See also* contest state; galactic polity; Jero Gede Sidemen; keris; land; mandala; *memasyarakat*; mobilization; negara; princedom; ritual; rulers; supernatural; theatre state

van Klinken, Gerry, 245, 247, 265n.4

Klungkung 8n.8, 10, 12, 15, 20, 21, 22, 24–25, 36, 41, 73–75, 81, 89, 128, 131, 134, 139, 172n.9, 190, 204, 226, 253, 256, 272, 277, 281, 312; establishment of, 206n.17; last raja of, 203, 239; holdings and seizures of land by, 176–177; maligya of, 36, 55n.1, 64n9, 73–75, 91, 204, 263, 267,

280n.19; resistance to, 235, 243–244. *See also* Jero Gede Sidemen: Klungkung and

Korn, V.E. 16, 166n.3, 184n.22, 236

van der Kraan, Alfons, 14n.17, 134n.15, 140n.21, 144, 148n.32, 164, 223, 236, 237, 237n.3, 253n.14, 293n.29, 315

Ksatria Dalem (royal Ksatria), 12, 15, 23, 143, 147, 176–177, 188, 197, 267, 277, 278, 282, 298

land: as proof, 149, 159, 169, 185–186, 191, 296–297; as remembrance, 186; conflict over, 152, 154–157, 211–212, 264, 284; gifts of, 32, 36, 149, 151, 153, 167–169, 180, 181, 185, 191n.29, 191n.30, 193, 296, 316; increased pressure on, 172, 172n.10, 173, 181, 212; landlessness and land reform, 171–181, 181n.20, 181n.21, 183; mixed rights to, 167; pacatu, 49, 135, 165–170, 180, 181–182, 183–185, 185–192, 193, 219; pacatu dismantled, 170–171, 295, 296; pauman, 168–169, 169n.7, 181n.21; seizure of, 176–178, 257; temple and, 156, 164, 181; to eat, 168, 168n.6; usufruct rights to, 15, 230. *See also* ownership

landscape, 120–122, 122–125; social memory and, 185n.23

van Langenberg, Michael, 245, 246

Lansing, Steve, 12n15, 13, 18, 25, 33, 91, 124n.7, 127, 154, 158,

163–164n.1, 164, 187, 193n.1,
228–229
lembu (white bull or cow), 70, 80,
80n.18, 86
Lewis, Douglas, 185
lineages: heads of, 45, 77; keris and,
7n5; of Kapakisan, 25, 130, 142;
ritual work and, 68, 76
local positioning: at a hub of discourses, 296, 309–310; through
keris, 280–281, 286; through
princedom, 32, 36, 38, 293, 301,
304, 309, 311; through ritual,
38, 57, 261, 289, 298, 305, 312,
315
lontar (palm leaf manuscripts), 34,
75, 86, 131, 207, 216, 286,
299–300, 308n.5
lords, 23, 169, 189, 237n.3; as chosen by followers, 236; at intermediary level, 15, 17, 41, 42,
155, 159, 166, 195–196,
314–315; autocracy of, 233, 251,
316; historical relationships to
followers, 32; loss of connection
to followers, 256–257; mutuality
with followers, 27–28, 41, 136,
138, 145, 147n.28, 150, 159,
183, 191, 193, 204, 230, 231,
231n.37, 233, 236, 251, 255,
297, 316; ongoing accommodations of, 295, 297, 316; rights of
followers to desert, *see matilas*;
ties and obligations of followers
to, 3, 11–12, 17, 134–138,
182–183, 230, 309. *See also* Jero
Gede Sidemen; keris; kingship;
perbekel; priests: of the court;

rajas; ritual; rulers; Tjokorda
Gede Dangin.
loyalty and devotion: absence of,
243, 280n.19; as main resource
of lords, 184, 243; between center and satellite, 313; between
ruler and followers, 313; competition for, 236; keris as inspiring
of, 268; of followers to lords, 28,
33, 135, 141, 143, 150, 165, 167,
176–177, 179, 183–184, 210,
240, 254, 296; of lords to keris as
raja, 303
Lubis, Mulya, 310
Lutkehaus, Nancy, 230–231,
231–232, 258n.20, 284

MacRae, Graeme, 26, 40, 147n.28,
180n.19, 190, 214, 239n.4, 256,
257, 257n.19, 262n.1, 266n.5,
292n.28
Majapahit, 8, 8n.9, 8n.12, 12, 13,
17, 32, 263n2; fall of, 129, 159,
187, 194, 235n.2, 288, 292;
flight of, 14, 129n.11; claims to
descent from, 15, 46, 129n.11,
252n.13, 188n.27, 197–198n.5,
305–306n.4; keris from, 24,
84–85, 158, 271, 277, 284; minister from (Gajah Mada), 10, 13;
ritual at, 10, 25, 307
maligya (high level postcremation
ceremony), 3, 8, 10, 11, 25–40,
43, 46, 48–51, 55–94, 119,
132–133, 151, 155, 167, 171,
184, 186, 195, 206, 242, 258,
261, 278, 285, 289–293, 299,
317; as debt, 132; as giving
strength, 290–291, 317; as his-

torical marker, 55; as mortuary ceremony, 40n.40, 59, 229; as kingship/state ritual, 93–94, 133, 281, 290–291, 295–296, 305–306, 315; attendance at, 64–65, 64n.9, 84, 279–280, 280n.19; Balinese life cycle and, 57–60, 61n.5, 290, 312; bringing together religious, economic and political affairs, 309; bureaucratization and, 85; commemorative text of, 55n.1; cosmic order and, 175, 290; emotion and, 82, 83, 92, 307–308; excursions in connection with, 78, 79, 122–125; 125–128, 150; explanation of term, 61, 61n.4; giving shape to princedom, 51, 56, 119, 157–159, 258, 289, 312, 313, 315; in interaction with national events, 32, 73–90, 158, 223, 289–290, 299; in Karangasem, 55, 55n.1; 64n.9, 75, 93, 191n.28; in Klungkung, 36, 55n.1, 64n9, 73–75, 91, 204, 263, 267; in Ubud, 55n.1; karmic merit and, 136, 308; lesser ceremonies as followers, 61n.5; performances at, 64, 86; processions of, 79–80, 82, 83, 86, 128, 154; redundancy of, 306; ritual leftovers of, 89, 92; ritual spaces of, 65–73, 79, 83, 85–90, 122, 307, 317; status and 40, 60–65, 90, 93, 304–306, 315, video and, 86, 124; *photos* from Sidemen Maligya: 98–105, 108–117. *See also* mandala; *mukur*; *ngeluwer*; *ngeroras*; ritual:

climax and; ritual: politics and; ritual: reflection and; ritual: risk and unpredictability of

mandala, 17n.23, 41, 121–128, 290; radial, 128; negara as, 41, 121, 121n.4, 205n.15

marriage, 48, 58, 82–83, 141, 149, 149n.33, 151, 153, 191n.30, 197–198n.5, 199, 200–201, 209–210, 210–211, 219, 220, 222, 224, 241, 243, 269n.9, 275n.16, 281, 316

mass action, 174, 175, 176–177, 244, 248–251; class and, 250–251

Marx, Karl. 16, 16n.20

matilas (right to desert a lord), 235–238, 250n12. *See also* followers: powers of

McGowan, Kaja, 58, 81n.19, 87, 88, 90, 121n3, 122, 124n.7

McWilliam, Andrew, 76n.16, 120–121, 85, 231

Mead, Margaret, 55n.1, 75, 238

Megawati, 3, 3n.2, 4, 7, 29, 32, 34, 37, 40, 50, 83, 85, 87, 91, 141, 150, 158, 202n.13, 258, 261–267, 275, 282, 291–293, 298, 302, 305, 315; ancestors and, 84, 286, as housewife, 244n.9; as Sukarno's "triumphant political comeback," 248, 316; disillusionment with, 217n.24, 248, 265n.4, 282, 291; displaced agency of, 304; legitimization of, 275, 278, 295–296, 305–306n.4, 316; prayer safari of, 248, 282; restorative gesture of, 286; rise of, 244–248,

302–303; the widow-witch and, 300; *photos*: 107, 108, 113, 117. See also Keris

memasyarakat, 82, 197, 202–207, 207n.18; of earlier rulers, 152, 202, 203–204; of Jero Gede Sidemen, 50, 152, 154, 159, 202–207, 218–225, 234–244, 254, 255, 258, 297, 312

memory, 32, 40, 171, 205; embodied in land, 185, 185n.23, 185n.24, 196, 301; of the princedom manifested in ritual, 158; of idea for and beginning of Sidemen Maligya, 65–68, 125; kept active, 301

Mengwi, 21, 22, 39, 63n.8, 93, 165, 166, 170, 172n.9, 183, 196n.3, 197–198n.5, 200n.8, 227n.33, 228, 263, 313

menstruation, 6, 6n.4, 7, 68, 76

Mershon, Katharane, 55n.1, 191n.28

mobilization, 17, 26, 49–50, 73, 76, 134, 138–139, 139n.20, 148n.31, 151, 152, 158, 239, 258, 264n3, 289, 292–293, 304, 310, 314, 315, 316–317; categories of, 139–157, 306; *photos*: 102

Monnerie, Denis, 59, 231n.38

mukur (medium level postcremation ceremony), 61. *See also* maligya

Nakatani, Ayami, 215n.23, 292n.28

natural disasters, 55, 172, 178, 194, 243–244, 289

negara, 11, 11n.14, 13, 23, 24, 25, 41, 42, 290; as multicentric, 41, 159; at small-scale, 13, 17, 36, 40, 41, 195–197, 251; decline of, 306; disappearance of, 23–24, 42–43, 227n.33, 295; fluidity of, 43, 50–51, 94, 121, 121n.4, 167, 184, 234, 251, 295; impermanence of, 158; issues debated and, 11, 49; negara dynamics of, 11, 11n.14, 17, 42, 43, 49, 158, 296, 310, 312; new vision for, 312; rise of, 13; ritual enactment of, 18, 313; rebirth of, 293, 295–296; transformation and continuity of, 42, 50, 310. *See also* contest state; galactic polity; kingship; mandala; princedom; theatre state

neighborhood association, 58, 67, 76, 83, 134, 138, 140, 141, 198n.7, 203, 211n.22, 219, 221n.26, 239, 266, 280, 292, 297, 308, 314, 316; Jero Gede Sidemen and, 254

ngarap-ngarapan (disrupting cremations ceremonies), 238–243. *See also* followers: powers of

ngayah. See ritual duty/labor/service; followers: palace service to lords

ngeluwer, 63, 63n.8

ngeroras, (low level postcremation ceremony), 60, 61, 81, 189–190. *See also* maligya

Nyoman Maue (former village leader, Sanggem), 152–154

Obeyesekere, Gananath, 59

objects: ancestral, 5–7; 50; as permanent embodiments/proof, 20, 28, 302n3, 303; as possibly illusory/manipulated, 303–304; biographical 6, 7n.5; biographical and history, 7n.5; history, 7, 301–304; of court, 14; power and, 5–7; 20, 21, 24, 276n.18, 286n25; rulers as, 22; vs narrative representation, 302. *See also* keris: kingship

O'Connor, Stanley, 5

offerings, 3, 5, 26, 61, 61n.5, 63, 67–68, 68n.11, 72, 72n.15, 73–76, 82, 121, 134, 141n.23, 154, 163–164n.1, 242, 274, 285; distribution of leftovers from, 89, 92, 209, 210, 211n.22, 242; role in land dispute, 212; *photos* from ritual site: 100, 114

Ortner, Sherry, 36, 37, 40n.40, 68

ownership: by deity, 155–157, 163n.1, 181, 185n.24, 187; of everything, 163–164, 163n.1, 230; of irrigation source, 154–157; of keris Bangawan Cangguh, 279; of land, 144, 154–157, 163n.1, 164–165, 167, 170, 172, 180, 181, 182, 191, 230, 266n.6; of land disputed, 211–212; of people, 141n.22, 144, 169, 190, 203, 221; of uncultivated land, 168

pacatu. *See* land: pacatu

Pak Komang (former village head, Kebung), 145–150, 234–235, 251, 276–277

parkan, 139–143, 143–145, 168, 210, 219. *See also* followers: subjects

Pasek, 142, 145, 148, 150, 151, 154, 168, 188n.27, 189, 193n.1, 268

past, creative use of, 32, 38, 147n.28, 191, 232, 255, 296, 310

Pedande Gede Tianyar, 276, 309

Pemberton, John, 38, 241, 242, 242n.8, 265

pengiring. *See* followers

people power, 244–251. *See also* followers: powers of

perbekel, 18, 23, 166, 169, 208, 209, 252

performances, artistic, 26, 86, 130, 141n.23, 191n.28, 200n.8, 208, 220, 223–224, 237, 299–300, 305; erosion of ritual function of, 309; *photo*: 112. *See also* shadow puppetry

Picard, Michel, 37, 38, 39, 134n.16, 196n.3, 197, 263, 264n3, 265, 266n.5, 288, 292, 298, 308, 309

Pigeaud, Theodore, 8n9, 194

politics, 180n.17, 195–196, 207, 216, 292, 305; consciousness and, 296; displaced agency and, 301; exuberant eruption of, 291; identified with Islamic radicalism, 291; lack of ethnographic attention to, 263–264; negation and suppression of, 261; 262–267, 291, 297, 298, 301–302; political division, 217n.24; 236, 253, 315; political movements, 288n.26; proliferation of, 315; playing politics, 288; *photo*: 117

political parties: Communist, 173, 174, 174n.14, 175–181, 216, 239, 240, 262, 284; Golkar, 77, 78, 262, 265, 265n.4; Indonesian Democratic Party, 85, 87, 244–246, 262; Indonesian Democratic Party of Struggle, 3, 3n.2, 85, 218n.25, 246, 248, 300. Nationalist Party, 173, 174, 175, 177, 240, 244, 284;

population expansion, 139n.20, 140, 154, 156, 157, 172, 181–182

populism. See memasyarakat

possibility: notion of, 144–145, 208–209, 215, 233, 237, 238, 241–242, 315, 317

postcremation ceremony. See ngeroras, mukur, maligya, ngeluwer

power, 49, 234, 235, 302, 316; abuse of, 50, 298; activation of, 122, 124, 125, 158, 200, 243, 289; ancestral, 6, 40, 266; chiefly on Fiji, 201n.11; coercive, 297, 311; coterminous rise of people's and princedom's, 261, 293, 301, 311; decentralization and shift of, 310–311; empowerment, 290, 293, 297, 301, 311, 312, 313–314; Foucault and, 20–21, 129–130; gender and, 44, 200, 223n.29, 224–225, 276n.17, 299–300; Gramsci and, 20–21; idioms of, 11, 42, 119, 302; keris and 6, 7, 10, 40, 42, 84, 150, 273, 275, 287, 302; keris' power ended, 295; Klungkung and, 15, 164–165n.2; landscape and, 120–125; Majapahit and, 15; manifest, 21, 120, 157, 273; new spheres of, 254, 297–298; notions of, 120, 120n.1; people/followers and, 50, 122n.6, 128–129, 183, 233–258, 255, 301, 304; personal vs collective, 301–302; priests and, 128–133, 285; priests, as rajas regalia and, 18, 272n.13; purity and, 129n.12, 130; ritual and, 21, 29, 36, 69, 195, 266, 289, 312; rulers and, 20–21, 40, 49, 119, 122, 130, 187, 195–197, 199, 233, 238, 241, 253, 312; secular and spiritual commingled, 18–130, 196n3; secular and spiritual separated, 129, 129n.12, 196n.3; struggles of, 130, 233, 236, 252, 253, 263, 303, 312; supernatural and, 21, 120, 130, 199, 264, 266, 287; surrender of, 313–314; symbolic, 21, 122; traditional, 40, 208, 312, 315; vacuum of, 37, 158, 304–306. See also prowess

practice theory, 36, 42, 68, 90–91. See also ritual: as practice

priests, 26, 89, 152, 152n.35; as slaveholders, 182; effigies of souls as guides, 62, 70, 81, 83, 86, 132–133, 150, 290; livelihood from ceremonies, 309; Nirartha, 126, 126n.9, 129, 132–133, 285; of the court, 18, 24, 66, 119, 128–133, 159, 272n.13, 285, 288, 310; of the court as rajas regalia, 18, 272n.13; politics and, 130–131,

288; powers of, 128–129; presiding at maligya, 66, 72, 76, 81, 87–88, 90, 132–133; priestess, 76, 81n.19, 132, 132n.14, 224; ranked with rajas, 194–195; *photos* from ritual site: 101, 105, 108, 115

princedom, 15, 17, 19, 28, 40, 41, 41n.41, 42, 49–51, 157–159, 171, 187, 192, 261, 278, 287, 305, 309; as materialistic now, 256, 257; as pure now, 251; come together in ritual, 51, 56, 119, 157–159, 258, 289, 312, 313, 315; transformation and continuity of, 24, 42, 159, 171, 257–258, 261, 293, 296–301, 310, 312, 313, 315; history object and, 302–304; perspective of, 40, 41, 44, 159, 159n.38, 166, 184, 185, 191, 193, 196, 206n.17, 215, 224, 238, 241, 251, 253, 312; return to, 292–293; role in era of globalization, 309–310, 310–316. *See also* Jero Gede Sidemen; kingship; local positioning: through princedom; negara: small-scale

prowess, men of, 199, 205n.15, 229–230, 229n.35; sexual, 200–201, 201n.11; Sukarno and, 201n.11. *See also*, charisma; rulers: qualities of

punggawa. See lords

puputan (mass sacrifices or massacres), 22, 23n.27, 24, 43, 81, 271, 295, 311–312; loss of keris and, 84–85, 271

purification, 8n.11; life-cycle rites and, 26, 57–61, 63; of ancestors, 86, 94, 306, 307; of Megawati, 85; of sacrificial animals, 83; of people, 76, 80, 89, 154, 286, 301–302; of realm, 9, 85, 224, 227n.33, 283, 284, 286–287; of ritual space 68–69, 80, 84; *suda mala* and, 8, 8n.11

purowita (also *bagawanta*). *See* priests of the court

Quigley, Declan, 233n.1, 241n.7

rajas: as coordinators of irrigation, 228–229; as forgettable, 187; as householders, 195; as owners of everything, 163–164; as owners of the uncultivated, 168; as passive objects, 195; as representatives of the collective, 187; conferral of keris upon, 7–10, 277–278, Geertz's view of, 18, 41; lords and princes as, 15, 24–25, 41, 119, 138, 139, 143, 148, 157–158, 277; loss of power and, 297–298; most notorious of, 14; priests and, 18, 24, 66, 119, 128–133, 159, 194–195, 272n.13, 285, 288, 310; reinstatement as "self-rulers," 23, 253, 287, 288n.26; reinstated rajas unable to perform rituals of the realm, 306; temples and, 195, 303. *See also* Jero Gede Sidemen; keris; kingship; lords; ritual; rulers; Tjokorda Gede Dangin

Ramseyer, Urs, 30n.33, 62n.6, 271, 308

Ramstedt, Martin, 60n.3, 288

reform era of post-Suharto Indonesia, 77, 79, 218n.25, 221, 224, 249n.11, 265n.4, 266n.5, 291

regional heads (bupati), 37, 208, 218, 225, 258, 266, 280; Dangin as candidate for, 256, 281–282, 290

Reid, Anthony, 22, 144, 144n.26, 163, 170, 171n.8, 297

reincarnation, 57, 58, 59, 80, 89, 126, 187, 290, 307, 315

religion (Balinese): "Balineseness" and, 39; Bali's hypnotic mix of, 250; Brahmana as teachers of, 130; conflict resolution and, 214; deculturation of, 309; "caste" and, 63; defense of, 288; equality and heightened knowledge of, 308n.5, mobilization and, 264n3; ritual vs text-focused, 67; rationalization of, 67; streamlining of, 288, 306; threats to, 174, 264, 288, 289; universalist religion vs ancestral, 60, 60n.3, 76n.16, 195.

remembering, 38, 138, 140, 141, 149, 169, 178–179, 186–192, 203, 209, 217–218, 258, 312n.6, 313, 314; economic and political circumstances as reminders, 309. See also forgetting

resistance: Balinese vs elsewhere in Indonesia, 298–299, 299n.2; cockfighting and, 237; in own space, 301; masked dance and, 237; to autocratic rule, 234–235, 239; to Dutch, 237, 293n.29; to equality, 242; to hierarchy, 242; to Klungkung, 235; to Majapahit rule 13; to national and international politics, 298–299, 312; spiritual and cultural, 299–300; spiritual and cultural resistance indicating potential for physical, 315; to court culture, 15, 47. See also ritual: resistance and conflict and

Reuter, Thomas, 18n.25, 21, 47, 235n.2

ritual: as action in the world, 27, 29, 30–31, 39, 49–50, 56–57, 68, 73–94, 158, 261, 268, 281, 285, 289–293, 295–296, 312, 315; as culture/cultural arts, 39, 263, 298–299; as holy work, 28, 32, 68, 75, 203, 220–221, 263; as lens for analysis, 11, 12, 42, 43; as multi-centered, 29; as operating on different levels, 27, 37–38; as practice, 33, 34, 42, 56–57, 119, 158; as response to nation-state, 38, 39n.39, 77, 79, 292, 292n.28, 312; as response to threat, 22, 39, 40, 289, 292, 315; Bali and, 38–39; climax and, 3, 39, 56, 57, 80, 81, 82, 85, 90–94; climax/anti-climax and, 89, 92; cokorda or raja presence at village rituals, 207, 221, 223, 225–229; competition and, 15, 19, 25, 35; consequences of errors in, 60–61, 63–64, 241, 243; cremation, 35, 58, 61, 64, 69–70, 137, 195, 211n.22, 220, 239n.4, 240, 242n.8, 306; cremation tower, 70, 72, 86, 89, 141, 238, 239, 242 (see also ngarap-ngarapan); displaced agency and, 42, 301; duty of (*ngayah*, ritual labor/service), 3, 11–12, 28, 49, 51, 56, 134–138, 140n.21, 143, 149, 150, 151, 153–154, 155, 157, 165, 166, 168, 169–171, 185, 251, 314; duty of vs payment for, 136, 256, 257; duty of vs corvée labor, 135; elaboration of, 39, 61; emotion and, 28–29, 82, 92, 290, 307–308; experience of, 56, 57; hierarchy and status and, 25, 29, 29n.32, 30n.33, 31, 33, 34–35, 37, 49, 57, 61–65, 70, 133, 158, 313; Huaulu boys' initiation and, 28–29; Indian, 35; kingship and, 21, 26, 25–40, 41, 93, 194, 194n.2, 297, 310, 313; kinship rites of ridicule (Africa and Polynesia), 241n.7; life and death cycle and, 26, 57–60, 61, 69, 72n.14, 90, 195, 231n.38, 308; Merina of Madagascar and, 30–31, 135; mystification and, 31, 31n.35, 34–35, 42, 49, 136; of realm, 93–94, 133, 227n.33. 230, 283, 306; pageant of, 24, 50, 91; politics and, 19, 30, 30n.33, 31, 32, 40, 40n.40, 42, 49, 56, 76–88, 90, 158–159, 262–267, 280, 280n.20, 281, 291–292, 298, 309, 312; postcremation (*see maligya, mukur, ngeroras, ngeluwer*); pressure of, 61, 66; proliferation of, 30n.33, 39, 62n.6, 63, 292n.28; 306–310; proliferation of due to economy, 308n.5, 309; for tourists vs for deities 308–309; reflection and, 29, 30, 31, 32, 33, 36, 42, 49, 57, 85, 88, 90–91, 134 290; reformist trends and, 306–310; resistance and conflict and, 27, 34–38, 62, 91, 238–239, 301; restrictions and, 68–69, 75; risk and unpredictability and, 33–38, 56, 63, 91, 91n20, 119, 158, 238–239, 242, 285, 305, rites of rebellion, 238–239, 241, 242; role of, 19, 19n.25, 21–22, 24, 25–40; sociogenesis and, 25–26, 29n.32, 31, 36, 37, 158; symbolic and functional aspects of , 27–28, 30–31, 40, 43, 49, 61, 91, 289; Thai Emerald Buddha and, 10n.13; time and, 56–57, 68, 75, 76, 81, 83, 90, 286; West African fertility and, 27n.30; witnesses and, 34, 73, 124, 243, 266, 266n.5, 280, 315. *See also* Bloch; Comaroff; cooperation; Dirks; Durkheim; fertility; maligya; offerings; Ortner; theatre state; Turner; Valeri; war; world renewal.

Robinson, Geoff, 55, 164–165n.2, 171–181, 184, 239n.4, 253, 263–264, 293n.29, 298, 304–305, 311

Robinson, Kathryn and Sharon Bessel, 224, 290n.27, 311

Rubinstein, Raechelle, 126, 130, 152n.35

rulers (and leaders): achieved position of, 32, 50, 51, 196–197,

229, 229n.35; ascription and achievement combined, 196–197, 206, 229, 231n.38, 298, 312; Brahmana as, 130; circumscribed powers of, 32, 122n.6, 159, 231, 233–258, 298; exercise vs control of violence by, 184, 233, 241; identity with realm, 122n.6, 284; legitimacy gain or loss of, 20, 24, 25, 31, 42, 119, 122n.6, 195, 206, 233–234, 243–244, 257, 266 267, 273, 295–296, 298, 301, 303 (*see also* Demon, Illusion story; *matilas*); material resources of, 26, 49, 66, 133, 152, 154, 172, 257, 297; overthrow or murder of, 122n.6, 233–234, 243–244, 298; power and, 20–21, 40, 49, 119, 122, 130, 187, 195–197, 199, 233, 238, 241, 253, 312; priests and, 18, 24, 66, 119, 128–133, 159, 285, 310; priests as regalia of, 18, 272n.13; priests ranked with, 194–195; protection and, 22, 28n.31, 40; qualities of, 20, 22, 42, 50, 77, 193, 195–196, 199, 203, 229–232, 272, 315, 316 (*see also* memasyarakat); roles of, 41, 77, 152, 152n.35, 225–229; sacra and, 18, 20, 24, 25, 272n.13; seeking popular election, 315, 316–317; treaties with Dutch, 22; women as, 198n.6, 199, 200–201n.10. *See also* fertility: rulers and; keris; kingship; lords; rajas; ritual; Tjokorda Gede Dangin

Sahlins, Marshall, 59–60, 201n.11, 229n.35, 230–231, 309
Schaareman, Danker, 93, 174n15, 191n.28, 227
Schulte Nordholt, Henk, 7, 12n.15, 19, 21–22, 23, 30, 36, 39, 40, 63n.8, 91, 93–94, 134, 135n.18, 136, 140n.21, 144, 158, 165, 166, 167, 170, 171, 172n.9, 183, 184, 196n.3, 197–198n.5, 198n.6, 200n.9, 204, 209n.21, 227n.33, 228, 236, 243–244, 249, 253, 263, 272n.11, 272n.12, 287, 292, 295, 297, 305, 310–311, 313
serpent: keris and, 5–6, 268n.7, 287, 316; kingship and, 6, 6n4; symbolism of, 5n.3, 5–6, 6n.4, 72, 126, 316; *photos* from ritual site: 98, 99. *See also* fertility
shadow puppetry, 8n.11, 64, 86, 208, 305, 307
sharecropping, 166, 170, 171, 173, 173n.12, 174n15, 180n.17, 181–182, 183. *See also* land: land reform
Shradda ceremony, 10, 307–308. *See also* Majapahit: ritual at
shrines, 26, 58, 68, 90, 151n.34, 225n.31
Sidemen, 3, 12, 15, 16, 36, 39, 42, 43, 44, 123, 124, 125, 128, 139, 142, 144, 150, 153n.36, 154, 165, 168, 180n.17, 184, 203, 255, 291, 302, 305, 309; as source of powerful priests, 272n.13; during crisis of 1960s, 174, 176; early lord of, 15,

16n19, 41, 119, 139, 147, 219, 270, 277; *Pura Puseh* (village origin temple of) 15–16, 225–227; situation of, 41, 119, 154, 309, 312; thriving realm of, 16, 252; *photos* of area: 95, 97, 118. *See also* Jero Gede Sidemen; princedom.

Siegel, James, 305

Siwa, 70, 80, 86, 126

slavery, 32, 82, 137, 140, 140n.21, 141, 141n.22, 143–145, 167, 182, 219, 237n.3

Solyom, Garrett, 5, 6

spirit mediums, 76, 188, 188n.27, 189–190

Sri Kresna Kapakisan, 12, 13, 15, 25, 130, 142, 194, 194n.2, 206n.17, 267, 268, 270

state: concept of, 18, 18n.24, 19; issue concerning, 49; weakness of, 249n11. *See also* negara; theatre state

Stewart, Pamela and Andrew Strathern, xix–xxiii, 30, 191

Strathern, Andrew and Pamela Stewart, 6, 6.n4, 65n.10, 121n.2, 317n.8

Stuart-Fox, David, 16n.19, 77, 85, 125, 127, 138n.19, 151n.34, 194, 263, 263n.2, 285

subjects, 32, 33, 34, 36, 38, 40, 49, 50, 51, 64, 72, 82, 143–145, 168, 171, 192, 194, 219, 293, 296, 315; of Brahmana, 130, 219; of nation-state, 312; voluntary, 49, 51, 190, 192, 293, 296, 310. *See also beraya*; followers; ritual: duty of.

succession, 14, 196, 197–198n.5, 199; absence of successor, 15; dispute and, 14; Jero Gede Sidemen and, 199, 224–225; primogeniture and, 197–198; sacra and, 20; "telescoping" of generations and, 14

Suharto, 3, 32, 37, 55, 56, 77, 158, 174, 174n.14, 176, 240, 244–246, 249, 253, 253n.14, 264, 265n.4, 266, 280, 281, 291, 300, 304, 305, 315; *photos*: 106

Sukarno, 3, 10, 55, 83, 85, 172n.10, 174, 177, 201n.11, 216, 240, 244–248, 253, 256n17, 266, 276, 284, 285n.24, 286, 287, 304, 305, 305–306n.4; *photo*: 107. *See also* keris: Sukarno and

Sukayasa (village leader south of Sidemen), 137–138, 142–143, 188, 209–210

supernatural (invisible realm), 91, 262n.1, 292, 306; relationships to, 20, 21, 24, 34, 119, 120–125, 128–130, 158, 199, 267, 272, 285, 310, 316. *See also* power

symbolism, polyvalency of, 31, 31n.34. See also, keris: symbolism of; serpent: symbolism of.

Tabanan, 22, 164–165n.2, 166n.3, 227, 280n.19

Tambiah, Stanley, 10n13, 17, 17n.23, 19, 20, 22, 41, 121n.4, 148n.31, 163, 165, 187, 196, 197–198n.5, 199, 203, 272n.11, 303

tax, 72, 155, 157, 165, 170, 171, 180–181n.19; first fruits and, 72

Telaga Waja River, 12, 123

temples, 25–26, 207, 226n.32, 314; as locus of Balinese culture, 187, 194, 303; at Gelgel, 127, 263n.2, 268; connection to lords and, 149, 152, 195, 218, 225–229; destruction of, 292; Jero Gede Sidemen and, 220, 225–229 (*see also* temple: family and); island-wide, 78, 79, 125–128, 128n.10, 149; family and, 5, 58, 66, 67, 68, 75, 76, 83, 84, 90, 121, 123, 138, 149, 151, 154, 155, 186, 189, 190, 277; on Sidemen Maligya prayer trip, 123–124; reconstruction of, 152, 163–164n.1, 212, 262n.1; regional and, 29n.32, 128n.10, 139n.20; social networks and, 25–26, 78n.17. *See also* land

terrorism, 172n.11, 224, 289, 291

thanks-giving, 32, 87–88, 133; *photos*: 115

theatre state, 18, 19, 21, 22, 25, 166, 306. *See also* contest state; galactic polity; kingship; negara; princedom; ritual

Thomas, Nicholas, 230–231, 296

threat. *See* globalization: as threat; Indianization: neo-Indianization as threat; Islam: radical Islam as threat; negation and suppression of ; religion: threats to; ritual: as response to threat; Tjokorda Gede Dangin: on religion and threat to religion

title groups, 46–48; tracing of, 206n.17. *See also* caste

Tjokorda, defined 7n.7. *See also* Cokorda

Tjokorda Gede Dangin (head of the Jero Gede Sidemen), 5, 7–10, 13, 15, 23, 37, 43, 44, 63, 65, 77–78, 79, 82, 84, 85, 87, 119, 124, 131, 137, 138, 151, 153, 167–169, 178, 180, 180n.17, 182, 184, 196–202, 202–206, 224, 251, 252, 253, 255, 256n18, 267, 274, 286, 297, 299, 303, 316; as advocate, 207; as liaison to government, 77, 208, 256, 297; as liaison to foreign sponsorship, 216, 313; as village head, 207, 208, 209; critics of, 256; during national political shifts, 77–94; 217, 258, 280, 281, 297, 316; expatriate influence on, 254–255, 255n.16 (*see also* Berg, Richard); fear of, 255; on becoming head of noble house, 198–199; children of, 66, 79, 82, 199, 216, 218n.25, 226; conflict resolution and, 183, 207–215; material assistance from, 207, 212, 215, 313; on changes in princedom, 258; on own power, 208, 312–313; on connection with Klungkung, 278–279; on keeping Bali Balinese, 287–288, 313; on Megawati, 275, 280–281; on redundancy of maligya, 306; on religion and threat to religion, 288–289, 292; wives of, 64, 65, 68, 88, 151, 153, 181, 200, 215, 223, 225, 233, 235, 243; *photos*: 114, 115